MW00443022

WE DID EVERYTHING BUT WIN

Former New York Rangers Remember the Emile Francis Era (1964–1976)

GEORGE GRIMM

Foreword by
Emile Francis

SPORTS PUBLISHING

Copyright © 2017 by George Grimm

All rights reserved. No part of this book may be reproduced in any manner without the express written consent of the publisher, except in the case of brief excerpts in critical reviews or articles. All inquiries should be addressed to Sports Publishing, 307 West 36th Street, 11th Floor, New York, NY 10018.

Sports Publishing books may be purchased in bulk at special discounts for sales promotion, corporate gifts, fund-raising, or educational purposes. Special editions can also be created to specifications. For details, contact the Special Sales Department, Sports Publishing, 307 West 36th Street, 11th Floor, New York, NY 10018 or sportspubbooks@skyhorsepublishing.com.

Sports Publishing® is a registered trademark of Skyhorse Publishing, Inc.®, a Delaware corporation.

Visit our website at www.sportspubbooks.com.

10 9 8 7 6 5 4 3 2

Library of Congress Cataloging-in-Publication Data is available on file.

Cover design by Tom Lau
Cover photo: From the Lens of George Kalinsky

All photos in insert courtesy of Jay Moran, unless otherwise noted.

ISBN: 978-1-5107-2230-9
Ebook ISBN: 978-1-5107-2231-6

Printed in the United States of America

This book is dedicated to my father George Grimm,
who introduced me to the Rangers so many years ago,
and to John Halligan who encouraged me to write about them.

CONTENTS

FOREWORD

THE NEW YORK Rangers have a long, rich, and colorful history and I was very proud to be part of it as a player, general manager, and coach.

When I took over as general manager in 1964 the Rangers had not made the playoffs in three years and only once in the previous six seasons. The farm system wasn't producing, players from other teams didn't want to be traded here, and the players we had were small. One year I sent our uniforms from the previous season to one of our junior clubs so they could use them and a week later I got a call from their general manager saying that the uniforms were too small.

It took some time but we were able to reorganize the minor league system, increase the number of our junior clubs, add more scouts, and start to bring in players that had the skill and size to bring the team back to respectability.

I was lucky enough to coach some of the greatest players in Ranger history: Jean Ratelle, Rod Gilbert, Harry Howell, Brad Park, Ed Giacomin, Walt Tkaczuk, and many others. And within a couple of years we were able to turn the organization around and make the playoffs for nine consecutive seasons.

We had some very good teams. We did everything but win. We were good enough to win two or three Stanley Cups but in order to win you've got to be good and you've got to be lucky. You've gotta be healthy. You've got to stay away from injuries.

But I was always very proud of my players, they worked hard, never quit, and they always gave it everything they had. They knew the systems that I put in place and didn't stray from those systems. We always competed. And they were a great group to coach. They were like a family and stuck up for one another.

I had to make some tough decisions along the way but that's what general managers are paid to do. Some of those decisions worked out and some didn't but I've never had any regrets. The years I spent in New York were the best years of my life.

—Emile Francis
West Palm Beach, Florida

INTRODUCTION

THEIR JOURNEY BEGAN almost sixty years ago when a young father took his very small son by the hand and led him to New York City and to a dark, smoky place with a lot of steps and a bright white sheet of ice at the center.

Little did the young boy know that what he was about to experience at the "old" Madison Square Garden that night would stay with him for the rest of his life.

Down on the ice, players dressed in brightly colored uniforms skated effortlessly as heavily padded goaltenders kicked and swatted at pucks fired with crooked sticks. The rest of the people in the arena seemed to react in unison to the action on the ice as their gasps, groans, and cheers came as one. The little boy instantly began to love this game and this place, for its speed and color and the excitement it brought into his young life.

The boy began reading everything he could get his hands on about this Canadian sport. He learned about its history and heroes, players like Maurice and Henri Richard and Jean Beliveau, Eddie Shore and Howie Morenz, Gordie Howe, Terry Sawchuk, and Johnny Bower. He also read about Lord Stanley of Preston and his fabled Cup and men like Frank Boucher, Davey Kerr, the Cook brothers and Lester Patrick who had won it for the Rangers not all that long ago in the '30s and '40s.

He memorized the words to "O Canada" and "The Rangers Victory Song" and asked his mother for a Rangers jersey for Christmas. The request prompted the usual "We'll see" response, but a few weeks later the boy unwrapped one of the greatest presents he had ever received—a blue Rangers jersey with a big number 1 on the back! The youngster sat glued to the television on Saturday nights while Win Elliot and Bob Wolff brought the heroics of "Gump" Worsley, Andy Bathgate, and Harry Howell into his living room. He played table hockey with his dad in the kitchen, always having to be the Bruins to his father's Rangers. He soon became the only kid on his block who owned a hockey stick as he shot a ball against the factory wall across the street. His neighbors must have thought the kid was nuts!

At the time, the Rangers and Bruins battled for fifth place instead of first and the Stanley Cup was something that Toronto, Montreal, and Detroit played for. But it wasn't about winning and losing back then, just about watching the game and marveling at the artistry of the players. But as the boy grew into a teenager the Rangers signed "Boom Boom" Geoffrion and made the playoffs for the first time since he began watching them. His father stood on a pre-dawn line for playoff tickets. But that spring, the Blueshirts brought tears to the young man's eyes for the first time as they lost four straight to the mighty Canadiens. The father knew those tears would not be the last.

The years went by. The boy used his high school ID card to buy side balcony seats at the old Garden for $1.25 and later shared season tickets in the blue seats with his father when the new Garden opened. They also shared the joys and disappointments of being a Rangers fan while the likes of Ed Giacomin, Brad Park, Jean Ratelle, Rod Gilbert, Walter Tkaczuk, Ted Irvine, and Pete "Stemmer" Stemkowski performed before them. But as each era came and went, the results were the same. With each passing year, the tears became fewer as the expectations dimmed. Both wanted to believe, but neither actually thought they'd ever see a Rangers Stanley Cup victory together.

But then something truly amazing happened. Somehow the sun, the moon, and the stars aligned perfectly and at about eleven o'clock on the evening of June 14, 1994, the son telephoned his father and they watched the spectacle together, speechless. The tears once again flowed from their eyes, for the journey had finally led to the Promised Land. Although in different cities, they were sharing their first Stanley Cup together. Words failed them. A huge weight had been removed from their shoulders. Their lives had changed forever. They would never again have to hear chants of "1940" or feel embarrassed when asked the eternal question, "What's the matter with your Rangers?"

As you've probably guessed by now, I am the young boy in this story. Pop is gone now but I'm forever grateful to him for introducing me to the game of hockey and the New York Rangers, and taking me on the longest, most frustrating, and yet most rewarding journey of my life.

This book is a tribute to the Rangers of my youth, Plante and Paille, Giacomin and Villemure. Harry Howell and Jim "The Chief" Neilson, "The Old Smoothies," The "G-A-G Line," and The "Bulldog Line." "Boomer," "Stemmer," "Sarge," Park, and Tkaczuk and, of course, "The Cat." It's the story of Emile Francis and his players and those seasons. The highs and the lows. The inspiring victories, the devastating losses, and the funny moments along the way. I hope you enjoy it.

—George Grimm
April 2017

1

Muzz Must Go!

BY THE FALL of 1964, it was clear that the New York Rangers were in need of a change. They had not qualified for the Stanley Cup playoffs in three years and Madison Square Garden management, as well as the fans, was losing patience with general manager Muzz Patrick. In his nine years at the helm, the Blueshirts had made it to the postseason just four times, were ousted in the first round each time, and had gone through five coaches. Attendance was down, especially on weeknights, and towards the end of the 1963–64 season with the Blueshirts firmly ensconced in fifth place, the fans began serenading Patrick with rhythmic chants of "Muzz Must Go!" One night the ever-creative fans brought balloons imprinted with "Muzz Must Go!" on one side and the French translation, "Muzz Allez Doit" on the other. Patrick was understandably upset and embarrassed by the fans' actions. And it didn't help that when he joined his family following the game he noticed that his young daughter Lori was holding one of the balloons. "I knew she didn't understand the significance of it," Patrick said later. "But you can't take a balloon away from your little girl."

Patrick's job was in jeopardy for a number of reasons. In 1960, one of his biggest supporters, team president John Reed Kilpatrick, died and the Graham Paige Investment Corporation gained control of the Garden, naming Irving Mitchell Felt as CEO. Admiral John J. Bergen became the team president but was later replaced by a smart New York lawyer named William Jennings who was not fond of Patrick nor his love for New York City's nightlife.

Patrick also made two moves that did not sit well with the fans or immediately change the Rangers' fortunes. In June of 1963 he sent fan favorite, goalie Lorne "Gump" Worsley, along with Dave Balon, Leon Rochefort, and Len Ronson to Montreal for netminder Jacques Plante, Donnie Marshall, and Phil Goyette. Marshall and Goyette played very well and were major contributors to the rebuilding of the franchise that was to come, but Plante, the centerpiece of the deal who was supposed to be the next Rangers savior, was a bust and eventually wound up in the minors.

Then in February of 1964, he sent team captain Andy Bathgate, another fan favorite, and Don McKenney to Toronto for Bob Nevin, Dick Duff, Rod Seiling, Arnie Brown, and Billy Collins. The deal eventually paid off as Nevin, Seiling, and Brown became key players in the rebuilding process, but Patrick would unfortunately not be around to reap those rewards.

The end of the Muzz Patrick era came early in the 1964–65 season when Plante was sent down to the Rangers' Baltimore farm team. Plante blasted the Rangers management, coaches, and training conditions in a wire service story that was buried in the back of the *New York Herald-Tribune.* However, Stan Fischler, then a reporter for the *New York Journal-American,* contacted Plante in Baltimore to validate the story. When Plante continued to ridicule Patrick, coach Red Sullivan, and everything else associated with the Blueshirts, Fischler wrote his own story which subsequently made headlines, attracting the attention of the Rangers.

An incensed Patrick called Plante back to New York for an explanation and later at the ensuing news conference got into an argument with Fischler, twice calling him a "prick." The episode greatly embarrassed new team president William Jennings and Muzz resigned as general manager the next day, October 30, 1964, and was bumped upstairs and put in charge of the upcoming move to the new Madison Square Garden.

Patrick was replaced by Emile "The Cat" Francis, who had been his assistant general manager since 1962. Francis, a former goaltender, played professional hockey for 15 years, mostly in the minor leagues. He made it to the NHL with Chicago in 1946 and was traded to the Rangers along with Alex Kaleta for fellow netminder "Sugar" Jim Henry in 1948. In New York he was primarily a backup for Chuck Rayner, seeing action in only 22 games over four seasons and posting a 3.19 goals against average. In total, Francis played in 95 NHL games, registering one shutout and a 3.76 GAA.

The Cat

Emile Percy Francis was born on September 13, 1926, in North Battleford, Saskatchewan, and learned early on that he would have to work hard if he wanted to survive.

EMILE FRANCIS: "I came from nothing. My dad died when I was seven years old, it was during the depression. He was thirty-seven and had leukemia. My mother had to go back to work as a nurse for seventy-five dollars a month working from seven in the morning to seven at night. No vacation, no time off. I was selling newspapers on the street when I was eight years old. The paper was five cents and I'd get half a penny for every paper I sold. I had to hustle all my life."

Young Emile snuck into his first hockey game by hiding under the coat of one of the visiting Flin Flon Bombers who were in town to play the North Battleford Beavers. It cost a quarter to get into the game but Emile didn't have a quarter. Noticing that the visiting players changed at a hotel about a block away from the arena and wore their coats over their uniforms, Emile asked the biggest player, Butch Stahan, if he could hide under his coat to get into the game. Stahan said "Come on, kid" and Emile was in. "I was mesmerized," he recalls, and thus a hockey lifer was born.

As a child, Emile started out as a center but played all of the other positions as well. Advised by his uncle to pick a position and stick with it, Emile decided to be a goaltender because they played the entire game. He played a handful of games for the local Battleford Beavers of the

Saskatchewan Junior League in 1941–42 when he was only fifteen years old. When he was seventeen, he moved away from home to play in the Eastern Amateur Hockey League with the Philadelphia Falcons in 1943–44 and the Washington Lions in 1944–45.

After a year in the Canadian Armed Forces, Emile returned to Saskatchewan to play for the Moose Jaw Canucks and it was then that he earned the nickname that he would be known by the rest of his career. The Canucks were in the midst of an eighteen-game undefeated streak and Emile's play so impressed Scotty Melville, a local sportswriter, that he wrote "The Moose Jaw Canucks unveiled a new goalkeeper named Emile Francis and he's quick as a cat."

From there Emile bounced around hockey's professional leagues, making stops in Chicago and New York (NHL), New Haven, Cincinnati, Cleveland, Vancouver, Saskatoon, Seattle, Victoria, and Spokane before retiring in 1960.

EMILE FRANCIS: "I broke into the NHL in 1946–47 with the Chicago Black Hawks. Chicago was in last place and you know when you're in last place in January you either get another goalkeeper or you fire the coach. In that case they had a guy named Paul Bibeault playing goal and they brought me in and the first game was against Boston. And it was as funny as hell, before Jacques Plante, I used to come out of the net to handle the puck. So the puck comes in about fifteen feet inside our blue line. I was just about to clear the puck and who the hell do I run into but Milt Schmidt. He was one of the best centers in the National Hockey League. He hit me so hard for crissakes I think he knocked me right out of my jockstrap. My gloves went one way, my stick went another way. Chicago always used to announce the attendance. And it's still in their record book, they had 22,000 people in the building one night but they only had 16,600 seats! So the next day at practice there were twenty fire marshals there. From then on Chicago always announced 16,600 as their attendance, but you can be sure they had 20,000 in there. They were paying somebody off I'm sure.

"So after a while the coach, Charlie Conacher, said to me 'As long as I'm the coach of this team you'll always be the goalkeeper, so don't worry about anything.' So I'm feeling pretty safe and I can send out my laundry and dry cleaning. No sooner had I done that but I got a call from Bill Tobin, the owner, he says 'I just wanted to let you know that you've been traded to the New York Rangers.' I said you can't trade me. He said 'What do you mean I can't trade you?' I said, I just sent out my laundry. He said, 'You can pick that up on your next trip into Chicago.'

"After they traded me to New York they brought in two veteran goalkeepers. The first guy was Sugar Jim Henry, because that was the deal, I went to New York and Henry went to Chicago. After that they brought in Frankie Brimsek. He was a great goaltender, but he was thirty-seven, thirty-eight years old. And all those guys they brought in, their goals against average was always higher than mine and I was only twenty-one years old.

"So the Rangers made a change, Frank Boucher stepped down as coach and brought in Lynn Patrick who was coaching in New Haven. And I was playing for Patrick in New Haven. So Chuck Rayner got hurt and the next game was in Chicago and they called me up to play. So it was Lynn Patrick's first game coaching the Rangers and we beat them, 3–2. Now Bill Tobin always sat in the corner to the right of the visiting net. So when the game ended I took my thumb and I went 'up your ass' towards Tobin. So the next day I got a call from the president of the league, 'We got a complaint, did you do this, did you do that?' I said yes I did. So he says 'Well, it's gonna cost you $500.' God, I think I was only making about $5,000 back then so it was a lot of money.

"But this guy Tobin was really something. First of all they tried to sign me in training camp but I wouldn't sign for what they were offering. I went and played in the Western League and eventually they came back with a better offer. I didn't get what I wanted but I got a hell of a lot more than their first offer. So now the season ends and I go into his office. He's sitting with the PR director and says 'what are you doing here?'

"I said 'I came here to talk to you.'

"'Talk to me about what?'

"'Well, talk to you about my transportation going home.'

"He says, 'We brought you here, you can take yourself home.'

"I said, 'I don't think that's fair, I live further away than anybody else on this team. Most of the guys here are from Eastern Canada. I come from Western Canada.'

"He said, 'I didn't tell you where to live!'

"But that's the way they operated. He and I never got along from the beginning, starting with the negotiations so when we beat them I wanted to give him the finger."

Francis was small (5 foot 7, 150 pounds), but he was quick and had a good glove hand. He also gained a reputation as a tough, feisty competitor who had the mental and physical toughness needed to play hockey's most demanding position.

In his book *When the Rangers were Young,* Frank Boucher related a couple of stories which demonstrated Emile's courage. Boucher was the Rangers GM and he was in New Haven watching his top farm club play Providence when Emile was hit in the face with a shot from the point.

"He was a little fellow, five-seven or so and weighing 155 pounds and his view was blocked by a big defenseman named Jerry Claude, six-two and burly. He didn't see the shot from the point which Claude could have blocked but ducked at the last instant. The puck hit Cat in the mouth and nose. It loosened six teeth and cut his nose badly. I went down to the dressing room to see how he was. He was the only New Haven goaltender so he knew he would have to go back into the net when the doctor was finished patching him up. 'Has anyone got any brandy?' I asked. Someone produced a bottle and I poured a stiff slug for Emile. He downed it, shook his head, climbed to his feet, and went back into the padded cell.

There was another night in New York when the puck tore his lip so badly that it curled around his nose. Our club doctor Vincent Nardiello did the stitching with Emile sprawled on his back in the dressing room. I knew from experience that the most painful part of the body stitching was around the nose and lips and eyes. Emile kept saying 'Doc, doc for the love of Mike, hurry up!' He was really suffering, but he just laid there telling the doctor to get the damned job done. Emile had more guts than most. He lost eighteen teeth during his career, had his nose broken five times and needed something like 250 stitches to close up the cuts. He had ligaments torn in both knees and required surgery on his right ankle. Dr. Kazuo Yanagisawa, another Ranger doctor, operated on his shoulder in 1951 because of chronic pain following a shoulder separation."

Even though Francis had a less than spectacular playing career, he nevertheless changed the way goaltenders played their position by developing the forerunner of the modern day goaltender's gloves. Unhappy with the catching gloves that netminders used at the time, he decided to try to improve them while he was with the Black Hawks. Since he played a lot of baseball during the off season, he asked his trainer to take a first baseman's mitt to the shoemaker and have him sew the cuff of a regular hockey glove onto it. And the rest, as they say, is history.

EMILE FRANCIS: "I used that glove for about a year and a half and nobody said anything. But we were playing in Detroit and King Clancy was the referee. In those days the game was at eight o'clock and we were on the ice at 7:45 and you'd warm up for fifteen minutes and then they'd start the game. So Jack Adams, the Detroit coach and general manager, and Clancy are pointing down at me. I'm thinking maybe there's no goal judge. But I look behind me and there's a goal judge and I wonder what the hell are they pointing at.

"So Clancy comes over and says, 'Let me see that glove you're wearing. What is this?' So I said, what do you mean what is this—it's a glove.

"Clancy says, 'You can't use that.'

"'What do you mean I can't use it?'

"'He says it's too big.'

"I say 'it's a trapper mitt, George McQuinn model, he played for the Yankees. I put a cuff on it.'

"He says, 'Well you can't use it.'

"I said, 'King, if I can't use it, you don't have a game.'

"He says, 'What are you talking about?'

"I said 'that's the only glove I've got. I'm not gonna use a players glove to play goal with. If I can't use that I don't play.' So he asks me, 'Where are you going next?' I said Montreal.

"He says, 'Good. I'm gonna call [league president] Clarence Campbell. He can decide what you're gonna do with that glove.'

"So I had to go see Campbell, and he had been a colonel in the army and he was questioning me like I was on trial for killing people. 'Where did you get that glove, how much did you pay for it, who put that cuff on?' He questioned me for an hour. He asked me, 'Why did you want this kind of glove?' I told him look at the goalkeepers gloves, they're stupid. They've got this little web between your thumb and fore-finger so you're catching everything in the palm of your hand, I won't last two seasons playing goal with that kind of glove. I need something to protect my hand.

"But what I didn't tell him was that when I got that puck in that trapper mitt, it didn't get out. I played baseball as a shortstop, but I knew that the trapper would hold the puck. Goalkeepers used to knock the puck down. Not me. With that first baseman's mitt it stayed in there. The mistake I made was that two days after my meeting with Campbell, word got out and within thirty days CCM and Rawlings came out with trapper mitts designed after what I had done. I should have put a patent on it, but I never thought about it. I was just trying to prove my point because I was small and my glove hand was the biggest part of my game. I probably didn't know what a patent was in those days."

But Emile didn't stop there. His next innovation was an early prototype of the blocker glove.

EMILE FRANCIS: "In Chicago we had a trainer by the name of Eddie Froelich and he'd been the trainer for the New York Yankees for twenty years all through the days of Joe McCarthy. When baseball season was over he'd come and work for the Black Hawks. So I got hit on my right wrist, which was the blocker side and they thought it was broken, but it wasn't. I said to Eddie, we have to get some protection on that right side. And so he came up with these pads that were like a sponge, three-quarters of an inch thick and he'd tape it on my glove. But I got hit a couple of more times and I told Eddie that the sponge won't work. So we sat down and talked about it to see what we could come up with. We started with a half inch thick piece of felt the width of the glove and made inserts in it so we could strap it to the glove. So Eddie says that the best protection you could have would be to get the knee cap off a shin guard. So we got a knee cap off and he got a guy to sew it on the back of that felt. That's what we came up with and I used that all the years that I played. Now it wasn't nearly as good as what they have now but it was still better than what we had before. And the league didn't give me any problems. I guess they figured after the first go around they better leave me alone."

Francis acquired his managerial skills early in life. When he was twelve years old, the nuns at his school put him in charge of the hockey and baseball teams. The school won its first hockey championship with Emile in charge.

During his playing days, Emile had put together and managed baseball teams in Western Canada during the off season, winning seven championships in ten years. Francis was the shortstop and playing manager, recruiting players from the United States and Cuba, and gaining valuable experience in handling people. So when he retired, it was natural for him to move right into coaching.

EMILE FRANCIS: "When I retired in 1960 there were only six teams in the NHL and Chicago, Detroit, and New York offered me jobs to coach in their organizations. Chicago wanted me to coach in Moose Jaw but they had to make a deal to get my rights away from Spokane and they were asking for players or money and [Chicago GM] Tommy Ivan wouldn't do that. This went on for two months and I finally said to their chief scout, Tiny Thompson, 'This has gone too far, forget it. He's had two months to make a deal. If I have to go back to playing I'll do that. Meantime I've been scouting for you, I've been signing players to go to Moose Jaw and I don't even know if I even have to go back there myself.' So he says, 'Well, I'm sorry to hear that. So in other words you don't want to be considered.' I said, 'No, I'm not and that's it.' So in the meantime it came out about two or three days later that they had signed Metro Prystai who had played with me in Moose Jaw, to be their coach and general manager.

"So right away who calls but Muzz Patrick. He says, 'We talked about a month ago. I thought you were going to Moose Jaw.'

"I said 'that's right.'

"He said, 'I just heard they hired Metro Prystai, what the hell happened?'

"'Well, Tommy Ivan screwed around for two months and couldn't make a deal with Spokane.'

"So he said, 'If I can make a deal with them would you come and work for us?'

"I said sure.

"So he calls back an hour later and said 'Okay you're all set.' He already had a deal made. He said, 'You have two choices, we've got a farm club in Trois Rivieres that we're moving to Kitchener and we just bought a junior team in Guelph. Where do you want to start?'

"Well I tell you, I've been in pro hockey for fifteen years and I'd just as soon work with the junior team. I'll go the bottom and work my way up. I'd rather go there and work with the kids and that's what I did.

"I went to Guelph and inherited Jean Ratelle and Rod Gilbert. The first day I started training camp, I stepped on the ice and I had two different shifts of thirty-five players apiece and these two guys, I watched them and thought *Holy Christ, who are they?* They played together on the same line and they went together like ham and eggs. I mean they were like eighteen and nineteen, but they were far beyond their age. You could tell right off the bat that these guys were gonna be great players. And I'm coming off fifteen years of playing professional hockey and thought these were the two best players I've ever seen. And I had played with some good guys when I was a Junior, Metro Prystai and Bert Olmstead, guys that went on to have great NHL careers. But these two guys I could tell the first day in training camp. I thought what the hell are these guys doing here? I knew that they were the future of the New York Rangers."

Led by Ratelle and Gilbert, who won the league's scoring title, the Guelph Royals finished first in the OHA but lost to St. Michael's Majors in the finals. The next season, with both Gilbert and Ratelle called up to the Rangers, the Royals fell to fifth place. But Francis had made an impression on his bosses and was brought to New York and named assistant general manager.

When Patrick was let go, Francis was offered the GM job, but Emile didn't exactly jump at the opportunity.

EMILE FRANCIS: "Muzz was the man who brought me there and I was gonna quit and I told him so. He said, 'You little son of a bitch, I brought you here to eventually run the Rangers. You better not quit.' That's the kind of guy Muzz was.

"So I had to sit down and meet with Bill Jennings, the president of the New York Rangers. He said 'we're gonna offer you the job as general manager of the Rangers.' I said 'well, I'll tell you what, I'll only take the job under one condition.' He said 'what's that?' I said 'If we make the playoffs, and we're gonna make them, we have to be able to play here in Madison Square Garden. It's not fair, number one to the players and number two to the fans. For all these years when the playoffs came the circus took precedent over the Rangers. I was here in 1950; I was the backup goalkeeper to Charlie Rayner. We had the first two games at home against the Montreal Canadiens, went to Montreal for the next four and won that series. Now we're in the finals against the Detroit Red Wings, five of the seven games were played in Detroit including the seventh game that went into double overtime and two games were played in Toronto, which was the Rangers' home ice. I'll come on one condition, that we have home ice in the playoffs' and they've had every home game since then that they were entitled to.

"I mean we put people on the moon and we couldn't find something to put between the boards and the ice so the basketball fans weren't cold. That was always the argument there, number one they didn't want ice below the basketball fans and then in the spring the circus would come in and in April they always had three performances a day. So they still had three performances a day and we still played at night. But they had to come up with a rubber surface that they put over the ice so then they just had to pull that up and away we'd go at night."

The Bathgate Trade

For many years Andy Bathgate was the Rangers' lone superstar. A product of the same Guelph Biltmore pipeline that brought players like Harry Howell and Lou Fontinato to New York, Bathgate played 719 games over 12 seasons for the Rangers, scoring 272 goals and adding 457 assists. The 6 foot, 180 pound right winger won the Hart Trophy as the league's Most Valuable Player in 1958–59 and made eight All-Star appearances for the Rangers. He was also indirectly responsible for the introduction of the goaltender's mask when his backhand shot ripped into the face of Montreal's Jacques Plante on November 1, 1959, at Madison Square Garden. Montreal coach Toe Blake had a choice of allowing Plante to wear the mask or let one of the Rangers house netminders, Joe Schaefer or Arnie Nocks, tend goal for the Canadiens. He chose Plante and the mask and history was made.

But in a rebuilding move, Muzz Patrick sent the thirty-one-year-old Bathgate and forward Don McKenney to Toronto for wingers Dick Duff, Bob Nevin, and Billy Collins as well as young defensemen Arnie Brown and Rod Seiling on February 22, 1964. Bathgate went on to win the only Stanley Cup of his career that spring with Toronto, while Nevin, Brown, and Seiling became mainstays in New York.

Bathgate always claimed that he was traded because he tried to talk Patrick out of trading young Jean Ratelle. "Look what happened to me when the Rangers wanted to trade Jean Ratelle," Bathgate told reporters. "I was captain at the time and I felt that I had something to say. I really put forth a case for keeping Ratelle and Muzz Patrick told me right then and there, 'You're getting too big for your britches.' Right after that I was history. I was traded because I spoke up for a guy who they didn't think was tough enough."

EMILE FRANCIS: "I was involved in the Bathgate trade because I had been coaching for Guelph. The key for us dealing with Toronto was the future. I had been coaching in that league for two years. In those days the NHL teams owned sponsor clubs. Toronto had two sponsor clubs, the Toronto Marlboros and the Toronto St. Mike's. And I knew those two organizations like the back of my hand. So since we were going to deal with Toronto, we were going to dip into their farm system. By then I was the assistant general manager and we kept going back and forth and back and forth talking about Rod Seiling and Arnie Brown, Bob Nevin, Dickie Duff. Shit, I knew those guys because I had seen them all the time. We played them a lot and I had a book on all those guys, believe me."

Ironically, on the night of the trade, the Rangers were scheduled to play the Maple Leafs in Toronto. So the players involved joined their new teams simply by switching locker rooms.

BOB NEVIN, *Right Wing, 1964–71*: "I got the phone call about five o'clock from King Clancy, the assistant GM of the Leafs, He said, 'Bob, when you come down to the Gardens for the game tonight go to the other dressing room. We just traded you to the Rangers. Good Luck. Bye.'

"I thought, *Holy Cow, what does a guy have to do?* I was twenty-five-years old and we had won the Stanley Cup two years in a row and I thought I was a pretty solid player for the team. I was on the ice in Chicago when we won the first Cup. We got a penalty and they put Davey Keon and myself out there and we were both pretty young guys so I thought that I was going to be there for quite a while.

"I knew it was part of the game but it was bit of a shocker for me. They didn't have the draft back then. I signed what they called a "C" form when I was fourteen, fifteen years old and that meant that I was sort of owned by the Maple Leafs, which was fine with me because I grew up in Toronto. So it was a pretty big shock. After winning two Stanley Cups you figure the team's pretty solid and they weren't going to be making any changes at that point.

"It was tough that first game playing against the Leafs. I think half of my passes were going to Frank Mahovlich because we had played on the same line before I realized I better not do that, he's not my line mate anymore."

SAL MESSINA, *Emergency Goaltender, 1962–64*: "I was traveling with the team at the time and we were in the hotel room in Toronto and the two dressing rooms are literally fifteen feet apart. And there was a lot of noise out in the hall and we go out and they're saying, 'Andy got traded, Andy got traded.' It was shocking. And they just switched rooms. But it was good for Andy, he won a Cup.

ROD SEILING, *Defenseman, 1964–74*: "It was a shock. I was only eighteen years old and you don't expect to be traded when you're eighteen playing junior hockey. It was more of a shock because I heard about it on the radio, not from the Leafs. I think I was well received by the veterans; there was no animosity. I worked very hard because I wanted to make the Rangers. I came to that first training camp with the objective of making the team, which I did."

The Patrick Brothers

Lynn and Murray "Muzz" Patrick were the sons of Ranger patriarch Lester Patrick, the Rangers' fabled first coach and general manager. Both sons excelled in any sport they tried their hand at. In their teenaged years, they were teammates on the Victoria Blue Ribbons team that won the Canadian amateur basketball championship in 1933. Both also played rugby, football, and competed in track and field while in high school. Lynn played professional football with the Montreal Winged Wheelers and Winnipeg Blue Bombers of the Canadian Football League. While with Winnipeg, he caught a sixty-eight-yard touchdown pass setting a record for the longest completion in league history. Muzz took up boxing and became the Canadian amateur heavyweight champion at age nineteen. In fact, Muzz became the only athlete in history to compete in four sports at the Montreal Forum: hockey, basketball, boxing, and bike racing. Later in his career, he would become the only man ever to play three different sports at Madison Square Garden: hockey, boxing, and bike racing.

But it was hockey that was in their blood and hockey in which they excelled.

Lynn, the older of the brothers, made an impression when he tried out for the Rangers prior to the 1934–35 season. However, his father Lester, fearing accusations of nepotism, was hesitant about signing his son to a contract. But when veterans Frank Boucher and Bill Cook told Lester that they thought his son could help the Rangers, Lester signed him to a $3,500 contract with a $300 bonus. Lynn got off to a rough start and the press had a field day. The Garden crowd started calling the smooth skating forward "Sonja," in reference to skating star Sonja Henie and taunting him with "We want Somers" chants, referring to Art Somers, the popular winger that he replaced. Lynn persevered however, and his play soon improved and he finished the season with nine goals and 13 assists. Over the next few seasons Patrick established himself as an offensive threat, scoring 32 goals in 1941–42 to lead the NHL.

His brother Muzz played one game for the Rangers during the 1937–38 season and became a regular the following year. As a player, Muzz was the direct opposite of his brother and quickly became a fan favorite. At 6-foot-2, 200 pounds, he was an imposing figure on defense, gaining fame and respect around the league with a one-punch knockout of Boston's Eddie Shore in 1939. He also scored the double-overtime winner against Toronto in Game Five of the 1940 Stanley Cup Finals that kept the Rangers' hopes alive. Two nights later, the Patrick brothers and the rest of their Blueshirts teammates won the Stanley Cup on an overtime goal by Bryan Hextall.

When World War II broke out Muzz became the first NHL player to enlist in the armed forces. Lynn soon followed. When the war ended, both returned for brief stints with the Rangers in 1945–46 and retired at the end of the season.

Lynn spent a few seasons coaching the Rangers' farm team in New Haven until his father brought him back to the Rangers in December of 1948 to replace Frank Boucher as coach. The Patricks became the first father and son duo to coach the same team. Years later, Lynn's son Craig also coached the team in the early 1980s, making the Rangers the only team in the NHL that has been coached by three generations of the same family.

In 1950, Lynn led the Rangers to the Stanley Cup finals against the Detroit Red Wings. The series went seven games and ended when Detroit's Pete Babando beat Chuck Rayner at 8:31 of the second overtime. Although it appeared that the Rangers had found themselves a coach, Lynn suddenly resigned after the series. Saying that he didn't want to raise his family in New York, he accepted an offer to coach for a team in Victoria that was owned by his father. Before the next season started however, Lynn got a call and a tremendous offer from Art Ross to be coach of the Boston Bruins. It proved to be an offer he couldn't refuse.

In Boston, Patrick took the Bruins to the Stanley Cup playoffs in each of his first four seasons behind the bench, making it to the finals once. He took on the added duties of general manager in 1953 and turned the coaching reins over to Milt Schmidt on Christmas Day, 1954. He remained the Bruins' GM until the end of the 1964–65 season when after missing the playoffs for six consecutive years, he was replaced by Leighton "Hap" Emms.

When Muzz Patrick retired in 1946 he went out west to manage minor league teams in Tacoma and Seattle. He returned to the Rangers and replaced Frank Boucher as coach midway through the 1953–54 season, finishing in fifth place. He remained behind the bench for the entire 1954–55 season, once again finishing in fifth place. Despite his lack of coaching success, he was named general manager in 1955, once again replacing Boucher. He hired the fiery Phil Watson as coach and the Rangers made the playoffs each of the next three seasons. Unfortunately, they never got past the first round. Watson was fired during the 1959–60 season and replaced by Alf Pike. But the Rangers did not make the playoffs again until 1961–62 when they acquired Doug Harvey from Montreal and installed him as player-coach. Harvey led them to a fourth place finish, but once again they lost in the opening round. They then missed the playoffs again in each of the next two seasons. Ironically, the Rangers' playoff dry spell coincided with that of the Bruins as both teams battled for fifth and sixth place year after year. Their combined futility inspired reporters in both cities to make up a fictitious trophy, the Patrick Cup, which would be awarded to the team that finished with the better record.

2

1964–65

Reorganizing and Rebuilding

THE TEAM EMILE Francis inherited from Muzz Patrick was skilled but small and not getting any younger. The 1963–64 Rangers had finished in fifth place, seventeen points behind the fourth place Detroit Red Wings and only six points ahead of the Boston Bruins. The Blueshirts had problems both offensively and defensively, scoring only 186 goals, the fewest by any Ranger team since the 1956–57 season and surrendering a whopping 242 goals, the most in the league and the most they had given up since the 1960–61 season. Even the last-place Bruins gave up 30 fewer goals than the Blueshirts.

Clearly, there was a lot of work to be done.

Francis knew first hand that his team had to get bigger. When he was the assistant GM, he got a call one day from the general manager of the Rangers' developmental team in Kitchener, Ontario. The team's uniforms were old and threadbare and they needed new ones. Francis told him that he'd send them the Rangers uniforms from the previous season, a common practice in those days. They were used, but still in good shape. A few days later Francis got another call from Kitchener—they received the uniforms but they were too small.

Most of the Rangers forwards were small by league standards at the time. According to the Society for International Hockey Research, the average height and weight for NHL forwards and defensemen in 1964 was 5-foot-9 and 181 pounds. Goaltenders are compared separately. As a team the Rangers averaged 5 foot 9 inches and 180 pounds, close to the league standard. However, their forwards weighed in at an average of 175 pounds. They also had two of the smallest forwards in the league, Val Fonteyne (5-foot-9, 150 pounds) and Camille "The Eel" Henry (generously listed as 5-foot-10, 150 pounds).

Francis also had to change the way the Rangers were viewed by the rest of the NHL. For many years it seemed that there was no real commitment to winning or to acquiring the kind of players that could take the team to the next level; that of being competitive every year instead of just once or twice every decade. For many years the philosophy seemed to be make a trade, change a few faces, and hope for the best.

The perception of the Rangers around the NHL was so bad that many of the better players in the league didn't want to come to New York. In 1960 Muzz Patrick made a deal with Detroit that would have brought Leonard "Red" Kelly and Billy McNeill to the Rangers in exchange for Bill Gadsby and Eddie Shack. Kelly, thirty-three, an eight-time All-Star who had already won four Stanley Cups and the Norris Trophy as well as multiple Lady Byng Trophies as the league's most gentlemanly player with the Red Wings, refused to report to the Rangers and retired, McNeill also refused to report and was suspended for the remainder of the season by the Wings and the deal was voided. Then Maple Leafs coach George "Punch" Imlach stepped in and sent Marc Reaume to the Red Wings for Kelly, who gladly unretired and won another four Stanley Cups with Toronto. McNeill was claimed by the Rangers in the Intra-League draft that June but later sold back to Detroit for cash in January of 1961 without ever playing a game for the Blueshirts.

Eventually Shack was traded to Toronto for Pat Hannigan and Johnny Wilson in November 1960 and won four Stanley Cups while with the Leafs. Gadsby was subsequently dealt to Detroit for minor leaguer Les Hunt in June of 1961. Hunt never played a game for the Rangers, or in the NHL for that matter. Of the three principals in the original deal, Gadsby was the only one who played his entire career without being on a Stanley Cup-winning team.

EDDIE SHACK, *Left Wing, 1958–60:* "I would have been happy to go to Detroit. With Gordie [Howe] and all the guys there it was a good deal for me and then when Red wouldn't go, I was sort of pissed off at him. But it turned out for the best because I wound up with the Maple Leafs and I met my wife in Toronto and we had kids and we've been married for fifty-two years. But if I had gone to Detroit I would have probably married someone from Detroit and I would be living there now. But it was a great thing for me because I played my juniors in Guelph, I'm from Sudbury, and I'm still living in Toronto."

Under Patrick, Rangers management wouldn't even consider a minor change that could have helped them win a few more games at home. During his first season in New York, Jacques Plante pointed out that the Rangers were defending the goal furthest from their bench for two periods. The distance made it difficult to make forward line or defensive changes on the fly and it was almost impossible for the netminder to dash to the bench on a delayed penalty. Patrick thanked Plante for his concern, but refused to make the change, explaining that season ticket holders had selected their seats based on being closest to the Ranger goal for two periods. In Patrick's mind, keeping the paying customers happy was more important than a few more points in the standings.

All of that changed when Francis took over and established a "new look" for the Rangers that was designed to add youth, size, and depth to the Blueshirts roster.

"Our problem was many faceted," Francis said at the time. "It involved more than just the Rangers. It involved our whole farm system, the lifeblood of any hockey club. The Rangers' farm system was simply not producing top-caliber hockey players. This had to be corrected immediately."

With the support of Garden chairman Irving Mitchell Felt and team president William Jennings, Francis reorganized the franchise from top to bottom. The farm system underwent a much-needed overhaul and expansion to bring the organization up to the level of the rest of the league. For example, successful teams like Toronto and Montreal had as many as sixteen development teams while the Rangers only had four. Within a year, the scouting staff was doubled and many of Patrick's old cronies were let go.

Even though the Rangers' affiliated clubs in the AHL, WHL, and CHL were each doing well in the standings, their rosters were loaded with players that were not going to make it to the NHL as Rangers. Yet these players were taking up valuable roster spots that could have been used for prospects with greater potential. Each player in the organziation was reevaluated and those who were deemed expendable were either let go or thrown into trades for skaters with more potential. Francis also strove to have enough depth to create a competition for each position, believing that a team has to be competitive among its own players before it can be competitive in the league.

Francis had coach Red Sullivan install systems of play, outlining the way he wanted them to bring the puck up ice and where each player should be positioned. There would be a set way of killing penalties and forechecking. He then had the coaches on each of the Rangers affiliated teams use the same system, making the transition easier as players moved up through the ranks.

"What we needed was a completely new method of operation throughout our amateur system," Francis said. "We had to have one set pattern of play, the same pattern to be used all the way through our organization."

DONNIE MARSHALL, *Left Wing, 1963–70*: "When Emile took over it started to feel like management was interested in the players, interested in getting better. Emile started to put in a system of things we should be doing on the ice when we got out of our end zone with the forechecking and all. It became more of a system and you could play within that system. It wasn't much different than what they did in Montreal. When you got the puck you usually had an idea of where everybody was supposed to be. You didn't have to start looking for them. You could play your particular style, as long as you stayed within the system. Emile also thought highly of his players and he wanted them to be comfortable playing in New York. It's a big city and a lot of players came from small towns in Canada."

"You really can't appreciate what Emile's done unless you were here before he came," left wing Vic Hadfield told Gary Ronberg of *Sports Illustrated* in a March 1970 article entitled "Flashing Blades for a Mini-Mastermind." "You have no idea how hard it is to play night after night just knowing that you're going to lose. Oh maybe once in a while we'd play great for a period or two, or we might even be leading going into the third period. But then the other team would come out and play well for ten or twelve minutes and cancel out everything good we'd done in forty minutes. Lose a few like that and you really get discouraged."

Orland Kurtenbach who had played briefly as a rookie for the Rangers in 1961 under Patrick and coach Alf Pike also saw the difference in management's approach to the game when he was reacquired prior to the 1966–67 season.

ORLAND KURTENBACH, *Center, 1961, 1966–70*: "There didn't seem to be much scouting going on in New York when I first got there. But Emile was the start of the farm system. He was progressive. He had a very good idea of what a farm system should be and he brought that to New York. Because I think at that time Toronto and Montreal dominated in that area. But he came in and initiated a new system from what we were used to and I thought as a future coach here's something I can use and emulate.

"He did a great job. He was good for hockey. But then in 1967 Emile had made some trades and different things to bring the club up to snuff as far as being competitive with the rest of the league. He brought [Bernie] Geoffrion in and there were a bunch of us fighting for a center spot. He had some young defensemen, Arnie Brown, Jimmy Neilson to go with Harry Howell. In my recollection Emile had come up from juniors and so farm clubs were very important to him. But in the meantime I think by Christmas we were around first place and in the old six-team league that was something because there were a lot of strong clubs as far as Montreal, Toronto, Detroit, and Chicago was on their way up too.

Emile brought a business format to it and started bringing up a lot of young kids like Brad Park and Walt Tkaczuk as time went on."

Even the younger players could see how the Blueshirts were responding to Emile's leadership. Arnie Brown, who was only twenty-two years old when he was acquired in the Bathgate trade, could also see how the character of the team began to change under Francis.

ARNIE BROWN, *Defenseman, 1964–71:* "The trade to the Rangers created a whole new atmosphere for the guys who were there and really having a bad time. And Francis developed a system, coming out of your end, turning in the corner and the winger on the outside coming across and stuff and so we got pretty confident that we could move the puck. And then Vic [Hadfield] was always a tough guy and a good fighter, so we had some toughness and we had some people who, if you had to get into a fight, win or lose, would back you up. But before when I was there, no one would take that position. Standing up for the other players and stuff like that."

EMILE FRANCIS: "I always insisted that there be one defenseman in front of the net, rather than leaving nobody there. There were a lot of goals being scored. Our goals against was horrendous so I wanted to cut back on the goals against because defense to me was the number one priority. So we set up a system that if one defenseman had to go into one corner, the other defensemen had stay in front of the net and the center would come back and go into the open corner.

"Then from there we started to move out, let's say the center was coming up the left side and if he got cut off by the opposing winger, the pass would go to the winger who would cut across the blue line. And forechecking was the same. We would get to the puck as quickly as we could and if the center would go to the puck, the winger would come in behind him so that we would always have two guys. If they moved the puck to behind the net or to the winger the second guy coming in would go cover that. It would put some pressure on them in their end. We had a system for the power play, a system for every part of the game. But it all started back in our own end because we had a cut down on the goals against and within five years we won the Vezina Trophy."

Francis also added to the Rangers front office staff by bringing in Jackie Gordon as his assistant general manager. The pair had been teammates in New York in 1950 as well as in New Haven, Cleveland, and Cincinnati of the AHL. Gordon had been named the Executive of the Year by *The Hockey News* in 1963 for his work in building the Cleveland Barons into one of the most successful franchises in the AHL. "You better get a couple of new suitcases," Francis told Gordon when he introduced him to the press, "because you'll be using them from now on," alluding to Gordon's job of keeping tabs on Rangers prospects in the minor and junior leagues.

Player development would be another of Gordon's responsibilities, a job that, as Francis put it, required "diplomacy, salesmanship and speed. A scout who is interested in a youngster must sell himself first and then the organization. If the scout makes a bad impression, the boy isn't likely to sign. We have a standing set of rules for scouts approaching young players. If the boy is under eighteen, we talk to his coach first and then to his parents. Then if he's interested in signing, he is not allowed to do so until his parents approve the agreement." Francis then described the traits that scouts looked for in young players. "We like three tangible items in the boys we scout. First, they must be able to skate well, second, we look for size, and third, their shooting ability. Most important, though, is his desire. A boy must want to succeed. A scout can tell by talking to a youngster if he has that quality."

Yet another obstacle to be dealt with was the team's inadequate practice rink, Iceland, which was on the top floor of the Garden. The rink was small, dark, oddly shaped, and for some strange reason, had aluminum boards. Built for figure skating and used for public sessions, it was approximately 140 feet long and 75 feet wide and one end was cut off at an angle, so there wasn't a full corner. Former Ranger Eddie Shack said it was like playing in a garbage can. Shack would fire shots at the boards whenever he saw coach Phil Watson, whom he was not fond of, trying to speak to the team or give one-on-one instructions to an individual player. Watson had to yell at him to cut it out.

DONNIE MARSHALL: "It was different playing in that little rink upstairs (laughs). It wasn't the best for the team but that's what you had and that's what you had to do. But it was small and it wasn't good for the hockey team."

DICK DUFF, *Left Wing, 1964*: "I can still hear the shots coming off of those aluminum boards! And it was about half the size of the rink at the Garden. It was like a figure skating rink. But in Toronto or Montreal if a guy had a slight injury, they'd say nobody's going on the ice. This guy's going on the ice for the next half hour. That was the priority. And they'd clean the ice, get it ready and he'd go out there. There was nothing else going on out there because they'd say [Frank] Mahovlich has to skate today or [Yvan] Cournoyer's gotta skate today. These guys were coming off injuries and they had to skate. It was different.

"Ratelle, Gilbert, Hadfield, they had some damn good players there over the years. I think if they had the same kind of set up we had in Toronto and Montreal they would have won more often. But they couldn't always practice in their own rink. In Toronto and Montreal we played in the same rink as juniors as we did as pros. So it was a built in advantage."

EMILE FRANCIS: "There was a rink up on the fifth floor, Sonia Heine used to train there. It was about 140 feet long and 75 feet wide and one end was all glass, the sun would come in there, they didn't even have blinds. Well if you were the goalkeeper at the other end of the ice you'd never see the puck coming. The most important things when you're putting a hockey team together are your power play, penalty killing and your forechecking and backchecking. But we couldn't practice any of them because the rink had tin boards. You couldn't have body contact because if a player touched his skate on the boards the equipment guy had to take the guy's skate, go down five floors, run over to the dressing room and sharpen the skate. It took forty minutes for the guy to come back up. So we couldn't practice properly. I said to myself, I don't know how the hell they got by with this. To think that they had done this since 1926, and won three Stanley Cups. That's the rink that they practiced in. I don't know why whoever was running that club would have put up with that or why they never went out and built a rink on their own. Teams used to come in to play us, like Detroit or Toronto and they'd look at it and couldn't believe it. That's where you practice?

"The first thing I did was to move the practice out of there to Long Island. That was the only place I could find. Commack, Long Island, where the Long Island Ducks played. It was about an hour's drive out of Manhattan. Then about a year after that I found a rink in New Hyde Park called Skateland. But that rink was the same as the Garden, 185 by 85 feet, but I wanted a 200 by 85 foot rink. So I worked out of New Hyde Park for about five years or so. And then I had lived in Long Beach and I worked with the City of Long Beach to build us a rink right there."

Francis also had concerns about where his players were living. For many years the players were scattered around Manhattan and parts of New Jersey. For example, when first traded to the Rangers, Donnie Marshall and Phil Goyette rented an apartment with Rod Gilbert in Weehawken, New Jersey, and would take a bus from there to the Port Authority building in midtown Manhattan and walk up Eighth Avenue to the Garden.

EMILE FRANCIS: "I didn't want the players living in Manhattan. In the summertime there would be 100,000 people in Long Beach but in the winter there were these nice homes out there completely furnished that you could rent. Well, shit, I got working on that. I got a real estate guy and I had all the homes lined up where the players could move their families for the winter and the people were only too glad to rent them. Rod Gilbert was the only guy I think that was living in the city. They all lived out there. Plus the fact that I knew where everyone was. You know in Manhattan they could get lost. And I'd call a practice for ten o'clock in the morning and if a guy was living in Manhattan he had to get up pretty early to get out there. We had an ideal set up. It was a small area and all the players lived within four to six blocks of one another. And their wives got to know one another and that built up a kind of camaraderie not only with the players but with their wives. It was a really tight-knit group and that's what you wanted; one big happy family.

"And then I treated New York like being on the road. In other words if we had a home game during the week, I'd bring the players into the city, I'd have my skate, my team meeting and then there was a hotel right across the street. We'd all eat together and then I'd have rooms for them where they'd go up and rest for two, three hours. Then if we came in off the road on a Saturday night and we had a home game on Sunday I'd put them right into the hotel. We'd get up in the morning, have a little skate, have a meal and some rest and then be ready to play that night. So that way they were getting their rest. Because if you had to travel into the city on the day of the game you'd get caught in the traffic. And I'll tell you our home record immediately got better because they were getting their rest and not fighting traffic."

The 1964–65 Season

Emile Francis was at a disadvantage on several fronts right from the start of the 1964–65 season. First, the Rangers already had a 2–3–3 record by the time he was named general manager on October 30 and therefore he didn't get the opportunity to shape the team as he may have wanted in training camp. Secondly, Jean Ratelle, who was one of the Rangers' budding stars, was not with the team, having walked out of camp over a contract dispute with Muzz Patrick.

Patrick was notoriously tightfisted when dealing with younger players. For example, when Rod Gilbert was set to sign his first contract with the Rangers, he brought his father along to help him negotiate. Patrick offered Gilbert a two-year contract at $7,000 for the first year and $9,000 for the second year. Both Gilbert and his father thought he was worth more but Patrick stuck to his offer. However, Gilbert wanted to play in the NHL so he signed the deal.

Then, after two solid seasons, Gilbert thought he was due for a raise but Patrick offered the same $9,000 he made the previous season. Gilbert mentioned Patrick's offer to coach Doug Harvey who told the young winger not to accept anything less than $16,000. Gilbert went to Patrick, asking for $16,000 but the GM barely budged, raising his offer just $500 to $9,500. Gilbert then took his case to league president Clarence Campbell, who agreed that he was indeed worth $16,000. Campbell even called Patrick to tell him that Gilbert should get the money. Patrick reluctantly agreed but when it came time to sign the new contract, it was for $14,500 instead of $16,000. When Gilbert questioned the amount, Patrick told him that it was Campbell who promised him $16,000, not him. He then sent Gilbert out to practice and told everyone within earshot how overpaid Gilbert was. Embarrassed, Gilbert soon signed the $14,500 contract.

Francis had coached Ratelle in Guelph and knew that he could be a major contributor for years to come. He made the re-signing of Ratelle a priority and reached an agreement on a contract with the center just four days after he was named GM. Ratelle was then sent to Baltimore for a brief conditioning stint.

EMILE FRANCIS: "Jean Ratelle had trouble in training camp, he couldn't get what he wanted and he went home. When I took over the first thing I did, the first call I made, I don't even think I told them I'd take the job, the first call I made was to Ratelle in Montreal. I said, 'Jean get your ass down here, you're back in the lineup and you're not going anywhere.' So I brought him right back because I knew that he would be a key to what we were trying to do."

Patrick had also questioned Ratelle's toughness and at one point, team captain Andy Bathgate got into a heated argument with the GM over Ratelle and Patrick's desire to trade him.

EMILE FRANCIS: "Ratelle was tough. Fighting no, but he didn't have to fight because nobody ever bothered him, but toughness comes in many different ways. I'll give you an example. I got a call from his mother at two o'clock in the morning. We had just gotten into the hotel and she tells me that his father had died. He was a dentist. She said, 'I didn't want to shock Jean and I was wondering if you would be good enough to tell him for me and have him call me.' So after I told him, I said that we'd arrange transportation back to Montreal. Now we were playing that night. So he goes 'No, no Emile, don't do that. There's nothing I can do right now. I want to play tonight then I can go home on Monday.' And then he said, 'I'll be back to play on Wednesday.' Now to me that shows what you're made of. That's toughness."

Emile's biggest, problem, however, was in goal where Jacques Plante was proving to be more trouble than he was worth.

Plante was one of the greatest goaltenders to ever strap on a pair of pads. But when he came to the Rangers in a blockbuster trade it became all too apparent that on most nights, like any other goaltender, he was only as good as the team in front of him.

Plante became a Ranger on June 4, 1963, when he was traded along with Donnie Marshall and Phil Goyette for Gump Worsley, Dave Balon, Leon Rochefort, and Len Ronson. Jacques was shocked by the deal; after all he had won six Vezina trophies and six Stanley Cups in his 10 years in Montreal. But over time, he had worn out his welcome with coach Toe Blake as well as his teammates. Blake thought he was a hypochondriac and could no longer depend on him due to his many illnesses and allergies, either real or imagined. Plante's teammates were not sad to see him go either. "It might have been a surprise when he was traded," said Henri Richard, "but nobody complained."

But the Rangers had high hopes for Plante and gave him a contract for $24,000 a year that ranked near the top of the NHL pay scale in those days. It was certainly much more than he made in Montreal. Plante was also given special privileges like staying at a different hotel if one of his many allergies kicked up. The Rangers also said that if necessary they would book flights that would get him to road games two hours before the opening faceoff and allow him to skip practices when he felt he needed a rest.

At his first press conference as a Ranger, Plante claimed that he still "had it" and blamed much of his problems on the pressure of playing in Montreal, where he was expected to "win every game." He also blamed his many health problems on the harsh Montreal winters, saying that the milder New York climate would be good for him. Unfortunately his bitterness began to show as he took the opportunity to take digs at the Canadiens. "The Rangers are on their way up and the Canadiens are on their way down," Plante proclaimed. "Geoffrion doesn't have as hard a shot as he used to, [Jean] Beliveau has been sick, Henri Richard loses too many scoring chances trying to pull the goalie out of position and [Gilles] Tremblay shoots off the wrong foot."

EMILE FRANCIS: "I was at that press conference as the assistant general manager at the time and I couldn't believe what Plante was saying. The Canadiens never forgot that, it was like committing suicide."

Plante made his Ranger debut on October 9, 1963, in Chicago, making 40 saves but losing 3–1. Two nights later, the Rangers traveled to Montreal to face Plante's former teammates, who were looking forward to the game to say the least. The Canadiens fired 59 shots at Plante and won 6–2. Geoffrion scored on a slap shot and skated by the crease to ask Plante, "Hey Jacques, if my shot is so slow, how come you can't see it anymore?"

In the home opener, Jacques posted a 34-save 3–0 shutout over Detroit in front of 15,240 fans, the largest opening night crowd in sixteen years. It was his 59th career shutout. He also shut out the Bruins eight days later.

From there on, the 1963–64 season became a series of winless streaks interrupted here and there by a few victories. And as the losses mounted, the bloom soon began to fall off Plante's rose.

The highlight of Plante's season was the night of March 8, when he made 33 saves against the Canadiens in a scoreless tie at Madison Square Garden.

It should come as no surprise that Plante faced more shots as a Ranger then he did in Montreal. In 1963–64 he saw an average of 38 shots a game, the most in the league and a full 10 shots more per game than the year before. Extrapolated over the 70-game season, that's 700 more shots than he was used to seeing as a member of the Canadiens.

Jacques played in 65 games for the Rangers in 1963–64, posting a 22–36–7 record with a 3.38 GAA and three shutouts. He made 2,222 saves but gave up 220 goals; both totals were the highest of his NHL career to date. Gilles Villemure made his Rangers debut that season as well, playing five games and going 0-2-3 with a 3.60 GAA. The Rangers finished in fifth place with a 22–38–10 record, 17 points behind fourth-place Detroit but only six points ahead of the Bruins. More telling was that they allowed 242 goals, the most in the league and nine more than the previous season with a combination of Gump Worsley, Marcel Paille, and Marcel Pelletier in goal.

But now Francis was in charge and he had seen and heard enough of Plante to know that he was not the kind of goaltender that he wanted to build a team around.

EMILE FRANCIS: "Plante drove the poor trainers crazy. He had about forty-eight different pieces of equipment. Nothing was ever right with him. He was a loner to begin with. He just didn't fit in with the team the way a goalkeeper should fit in. He was never going to be the kind of goalkeeper that the players would work their butts off for. I mean when you're playing goal, you've gotta be a team player because, shit, you've gotta depend on those guys in front of you. But if you're a selfish guy of any kind or if you're a loner or you don't mix with the rest of the players including your defensemen and the guys playing up front, they may just say 'Screw you.' It would be like if you were a quarterback and your line didn't like you, you could get killed."

DONNIE MARSHALL: "I played a lot of years with Jacques Plante. I played with him in Buffalo in the American League, I played nine years with him in Montreal, and then when we came to the Rangers. And then the last year I was in the league we were both playing for Toronto. I thought he was an excellent goalkeeper. He was very innovative. He was one of the first to go behind the net to stop the puck and the first goalkeeper to wear a mask. I remember the night he put the mask on, we were playing in New York and he really got hit. He was really cut open and he put the mask on and went back out there. He was a good goalkeeper but just a different personality. He was a bit of a loner. But all goalies are a little different, but maybe they have to be to play that position."

SAL MESSINA: "Jacques was a loner. He used to knit toques [knitted hats]. He was an interesting guy, though, a different kind of a guy. But he was really interested in goaltending, really serious about it. Interested in teaching it. He worked with Gilles Villemure in training camp a lot and I'm sure he helped him a lot."

When Plante started complaining of knee pain early in training camp, he was quickly sent to Baltimore of the AHL to play himself into shape. He was replaced by journeyman Marcel Paille. (Ironically both Plante and Paille were from Shawinigan Falls, Quebec.) This gave Francis a chance to look at Paille since he didn't want to rush twenty-four-year-old prospect Gilles Villemure into the NHL. The thirty-two-year-old Paille had been in the Rangers organization since the 1957–58 season when he played 33 games stepping in for Gump Worsley, who had been sent to the minors. Overall, Paille came into the season with 68 NHL games under his belt, a 3.34 goals against average, and two shutouts.

The Blueshirts defense was anchored by thirty-two-year-old Harry Howell, who was in his 13th season with the Rangers. Joining Harry on the blueline were Jim "The Chief" Neilson, who was twenty-three and entering his third NHL season, and Arnie Brown and Rod Seiling, who were acquired from Toronto in the Andy Bathgate trade.

Up front, the forwards included veterans Bob Nevin, Dick Duff, Donnie Marshall, Phil Goyette, Camille Henry, Val Fonteyne, Earl Ingarfield, as well as younger players such as Rod Gilbert, Jean Ratelle, Vic Hadfield, and Lou Angotti.

Marcel Paille played the first eleven games of the season, posting a 3–5–3 record. But he twisted a knee in practice on November 7 in Toronto and Plante was recalled on an emergency basis and shut out the Maple Leafs 1–0, earning first star of the game honors. From that point on, he and Paille shared the netminding duties for the rest of the season.

Two months into the season the Rangers were in third place with an 8–8–4 record but then Bob Nevin suffered a separated shoulder in early

December. Nevin missed only six games but was bothered by the injury the rest of the season. Other injuries hampered the Rangers' progress that season and they soon fell out of contention. Arnie Brown suffered cracked ribs which kept him out of the lineup for twelve games and a severe virus forced Phil Goyette to miss eighteen games.

Francis started moving players in December, sending disgruntled winger Dick Duff and minor league center Dave McComb to Montreal for speedy winger Billy Hicke and the loan of minor league goaltender Jean Guy Morissette. Duff had been acquired in the Andy Bathgate trade but was never happy in New York. He didn't like losing or the fact that it didn't seem to bother some of his teammates.

Then in February of 1965, Francis traded fan favorite and team captain Camille Henry along with Wally Chevrier, Don Johns, and Billy Taylor to the Chicago Black Hawks for defenseman Wayne Hillman and wingers Doug Robinson and John Brenneman. Hillman (6–1, 205 lbs.) and Robinson (6–2, 195 lbs.) brought size and toughness to the Rangers lineup. Robinson was teamed with Rod Gilbert and Jean Ratelle and recorded 22 points in 21 games with the Rangers that season.

Bob Nevin was named team captain following the Henry trade.

BOB NEVIN: "That was unbelievable to be named captain of an original six team. I had only been with the team for about a year when they made the announcement. So I was quite proud of the fact that I was being made the captain."

Francis also put Val Fonteyne, a 5-foot-9, 150 pound, thirty-one-year-old forward on waivers, where he was claimed by Detroit.

In all, Francis shuffled thirty-six players in and out of the lineup during the season. Among them was a Swedish player named Ulf Sterner, the first European to play in the NHL.

The season ended with the Rangers in fifth place with a 20–38–12 record, 22 points behind the fourth-place Toronto Maple Leafs. Only an 8–5–1 record against the Boston Bruins kept them out of the NHL's cellar.

Rod Gilbert, the flashy twenty-four-year-old right winger, led the team in goals (25), assists (36), and points (61) and finished seventh among the league's top scorers. Indicative of the Rangers' offensive woes, despite being traded with more than a month left in the season, Camille Henry still led the Rangers in power play goals (13) and game-winners (5).

Jean Ratelle, who had been recalled from Baltimore after recording nine goals and four assists in his first eight games with the Clippers, got off to a slow start in New York. But after being reunited with Gilbert, his boyhood buddy, Ratelle finished strong with 14 goals and 21 assists, scoring 11 of those goals in the final month of the season when Phil Goyette was out with a severe virus.

The Rangers scored 179 goals but surrendered 246, the most since the 1960–61 season when they gave up 248 goals. Jacques Plante played in only 33 games (10–17–5, 3.37 GAA) while Marcel Paille carried the rest of the load (10–21–7, 3.58 GAA).

Ulf Sterner, the NHL's First European Player

From its inception, the National Hockey League had been populated by mostly Canadian players, with a few Americans sprinkled in here and there for good measure. But that all changed on January 27, 1965, when Ulf Sterner became the first European-trained player to take the ice for an NHL team.

Sterner was born on February 11, 1941, in Deje, Varmland, Sweden. He joined that country's national team when he was seventeen years old and made his Olympic debut in 1960 in Squaw Valley. Sweden failed to earn a medal but Sterner won the Golden Puck Award as Sweden's Player of the Year. He scored a goal in a 5–3 gold medal win over Canada in the 1962 Ice Hockey World Championships. The next year he scored a hat trick in a 4–1 win over Canada.

The Rangers became interested in the 6-foot-2, 187-pound center in 1963 and invited him to training camp. Sterner came to camp and signed a five-game tryout contract but declined to play that season to preserve his amateur status for the 1964 Olympics where he led Sweden with six goals and five assists as they ultimately earned a silver medal.

Sterner reported to the Rangers training camp in 1964 and was assigned to St. Paul of the CHL to become acclimated to the North

American game. Ulf did very well in St. Paul, scoring 12 goals and adding nine assists in only 16 games before being promoted first to Baltimore of the AHL and then to the Rangers.

He made his NHL debut in a 5–2 win over the Boston Bruins. Sterner played well and had a goal disallowed due to an offside call. But he was the target of physical abuse by opposing players who tried to intimidate him. After four games Sterner was sent back to Baltimore where he recorded 18 goals and 26 assists in 52 games and helped the Clippers make the AHL playoffs. He returned to Sweden after the season, where he continued to star in international competition as well as Swedish leagues until his retirement following the 1977–78 season.

It was clear that Sterner had better than average skills. But being raised in Sweden, where offensive zone checking was prohibited, he just wasn't used to the North American style game.

Former Ranger Ulf Nilsson played on a line with Sterner in the 1973 World Championships in Moscow.

ULF NILSSON: "Sterner was one of the best forwards that ever came out of Sweden. I talked to Fred Shero about him and he said that Ulf was one of the most talented players that he had ever seen. He was sort of unusual because he was a big guy for those days and pretty good on his skates for a player of that size. In those days the big guys didn't really move that fast. As most Swedish hockey players, he grew up playing soccer in the summertime so he was actually pretty good handling the puck with his skates too. He had what he called a 'stick, skate, stick' move where he would pretend to pass the puck back but pass it to his skate and kick it up again.

"It must have been really hard to be on your own in a new country with a new style of play. I think it was easier for Anders [Hedberg] and me coming to Winnipeg as teammates."

Although he only had a brief four-game stint with the Rangers, Sterner was a trail blazer and today the NHL is a veritable League of Nations with players from practically every hockey-playing country. And each one of those players owes a debt of gratitude to Ulf Sterner.

John Halligan

In the fall of 1963, a bright young man fresh out of Fordham University got a job as an assistant to Herb Goren, the Rangers public relations director. A year later, Goren moved on to the NHL as a consultant and John Halligan, at the age of twenty-three, took over the top spot and began a long, illustrious career as a publicist, author, historian, raconteur, and friend to all.

A native of Bergen County, New Jersey, Halligan played pond hockey as a youngster and took a liking to the sport. But his affection for the Rangers came when his older brother took him to his first game at the old Madison Square Garden.

"I was a nut. I tried to go to every game at the Garden," Halligan once told an interviewer. "I knew from the time I was thirteen or fourteen that I loved hockey.

"I graduated from Fordham in June 1963, I sent in a resume, and two months after graduation, I got a job with the Rangers—a seasonal job as assistant publicity director. A year later, the guy who was my boss, Herb Goren, went to work for the NHL as a consultant. I was just in the right place at the right time."

At the time, the Rangers were still losing more games than they were winning and attendance was down, especially on weeknights. So Halligan and his small staff, which included a statistician and an assistant named Janet Fischetti who later became his wife, worked long days and nights promoting the Rangers and trying to get them onto the sports pages as much as possible. They also overhauled the Rangers "Blue Book" and it soon became the model for the media guides published by every team in the NHL.

STU HACKEL, *hockey writer:* "He was a terrific guy who built a really great PR organization for the Rangers. He had Janet who was terrific, working and making sure whatever policies were put in place were implemented because John would always say yes and sometimes you can't say yes. So Janet kept it honest. And Artie Friedman did the stats. He was terrific at that and the three of them were a great little PR group for the team."

Then as the Rangers improved under Emile Francis in the late 1960s and early 1970s, attendance was no longer a problem and Halligan's role grew to include vice president of communications and team business manager responsible for, among other things, the team's travel arrangements. He also ran the projector when Emile wanted to show the team game films after practice.

Halligan became a familiar face through his frequent intermission appearances on the few Rangers games that were televised in those days. He also kept stats for the broadcasters which led to an embarrassing moment for him.

"It was the last game of the season, mid-1960s when the team's telecasts were mostly limited to Saturday night road games," Halligan once recalled. "And I had traveled with Win Elliott [the Rangers' TV voice] the entire season doing the statistics in the booth. I was traveling with the Rangers as the PR guy, but to fill my time during the game, I would work for Win in the booth. We had done this for the entire year, and it was the final game of the season, we didn't make the playoffs and Win was saying that it had been a good rebuilding year, and that the team was going to be better next year—and that he would be remiss if he didn't thank his good friend, John Lannigan. I never corrected him on that. That was Win—he'd just make it up as he went along."

But Rangers fans knew his name and his face and he always had a smile and a kind word for everyone. If you told him your name, he'd probably remember it the next time you met. To many fans this energetic leprechaun of a man, with a shock of reddish blond hair that turned white in later years, and impeccably tailored plaid sports jackets, was the face of the New York Rangers.

John had a way about him that made you feel special, like you were part of the inner circle. Of course, being the consummate professional that he was, Halligan never let the cat out of the bag when it came to possible trades or other team business. But he made you feel like you had a friend inside an often not-too-friendly Rangers/MSG organization.

He was a mentor and friend to players, newspapermen, and aspiring writers alike. He helped steer the younger Rangers around the pitfalls of New York and took many young reporters and writers under his wing and gave them encouragement and advice.

STU HACKEL: "He gave me my first job in the National Hockey League. He helped get me there and I saw time and time again with younger people who would come into the office, interns and people like that, he would try to find ways to involve them in the business in one way or another.

"He would go out of his way to make sure that the people who were covering the team got what they needed. Back then of course the players were more accessible but even then John would help out.

"There was the famous story that John told over and over again about one of the New York writers. It was well known that the guy was a drunk. A lot of press rooms at that time had a lot of free beer and some guys took advantage of it and the guy just couldn't even finish his copy and call it in to the desk in New York from the road. So John would write the story and call it in so the Rangers would have a game story in the paper the next day. That was something that he didn't have to do but he did it. That's the extent he would go to help people out.

"Some of the writers told me how important he was in helping them establish themselves as journalists in the hockey world because he would help them out. He had answers to questions, he was forthcoming, and he did it with such great humor.

"John was working for the Rangers for a long time and back then people didn't come and go as quickly as they do now. Some of the guys had been PR directors for a long time and they were more about saying no and not helping you, protecting the players, not wanting to do their job or getting someone else to do the job. But that wasn't John's way. John wanted to help and he was happy to help and there was practically no one in the game that he didn't like.

"He liked people that a lot of other people didn't like. Some of the writers were pretty unlikable and some of the people in hockey didn't like some guys and there was resentment because a guy had written something critical about a team or the league. John's attitude was it doesn't matter, these guys have a job to do and I'm there to help them. He was pretty unique in that way. I got to know all the PR directors in the league and there weren't too many people who operated the way he did."

After leaving the Rangers to work for the NHL in 1983, John returned to the Blueshirts from 1986 to 1990. He returned to the NHL to oversee the league's 75th anniversary in 1991 and the Stanley Cup's 100th anniversary in 1993. He then became the league's director of communications for special projects.

STU HACKEL: "The league wanted badly to heighten its public relations profile and had some people doing that job who weren't great at it. John was obviously the best at what he did, anybody who was in hockey knew that and I think the people in the league office thought well let's get the best guy. Part of it was that [NHL president] John Ziegler did not have the best relationship with the media. He had thought that he had been misunderstood earlier in his tenure. He was criticized and he thought the criticisms were way off base. So I think they thought, well let's get the best PR person. So John got an offer from the league. I don't think he wanted to leave the Rangers but I think the money was a little better. At the time Craig Patrick was the GM and I don't think he wanted John to leave either, but I think that he was busy with other things and didn't really focus on the fact that he was going to lose him. So John went and worked for the league for a couple of years and then Craig was fired and Phil Esposito took over the Rangers and he remembered John from when he played and how good he was. So he wanted John to come back and he did. A lot of it was that John just loved the Rangers. He had pretty much grown up with the team. They were a big part of him and frankly, I think there were some things going on at the league that maybe John thought he wouldn't have made as much of an impact as he did before.

"And then John was hired back by the league. We were doing the 75th anniversary of the league and the 100th anniversary of the Stanley Cup and because of John's knowledge of the game's history and connections he was the perfect person to head that up."

Halligan helped create the Rangers Alumni Association along with Bill Chadwick and Steve Vickers and authored a score of articles and books about the Rangers including *100 Ranger Greats: Superstars, Unsung Heroes and Colorful Characters* and *New York Rangers: Seventy-Five Years.*

Halligan received the Lester Patrick Trophy in 2007 for his long-standing service to hockey in the United States. It was an award that was close to Halligan's heart since he was present at its creation in 1966. "Bill Jennings got Emile Francis and me together and said he wanted to create a trophy to honor Lester Patrick," Halligan recalled at the time. "He said; 'Emile, you take care of the general managers, John, you take care of the press, and I'll take care of the governors.' It was about ten minutes and we were done."

Sadly, John Halligan passed away in January of 2010 of an arrhythmia. He was sixty-eight years old.

NHL commissioner Gary Bettman was among the many who spoke fondly of John at the time of his passing. "John Halligan cherished the character of the game as much as the characters of the game," said Bettman. "He loved the stories of the game and, over his decades in hockey, told those stories with an abiding respect for the history—and humor—so that future generations of fans could enjoy them as much as he did."

Perhaps former Rangers general manager Glen Sather summed up Halligan's legacy best when he said: "John Halligan was an institution with the Rangers, and is as much a part of the tradition and history as any player who has worn the sweater. His tremendous loyalty and love for the organization and the game of hockey will be greatly missed."

EMILE FRANCIS: "John Halligan was one of the most competent people you would ever want to meet. Herb Goren was the PR director when I first came to the Rangers and when I took over John took his place and then he brought in a secretary by the name of Janet who he married. And between the two of them they were a great team. I really miss John. After I came here and he retired we would talk two to three times a week and with all the books he'd write he'd call here to verify everything. He'd send me pictures, 'Who's this guy, who's that guy?' And of course I knew them all because I ran the team for so long. So one day he sends me this picture of me behind the bench and there are four guys with helmets on. And he tells me he can't remember that many Rangers wearing helmets at the same time in those days. I told him, 'John, that was at West Point. We used to go there to scrimmage and we'd take their defensemen and goalie and they'd take ours just to make the game competitive. Those three guys were Army players. I said look at their helmets and their sticks. They've got Army printed on the sticks.' He said 'I'll be darned.'

"But he was a great guy. He was so dedicated to the Rangers. I talked to him the day before he died. I couldn't believe it, that he went like he did. He was a terrific guy."

Author's note: I realized at an early age that I was never going to be a Ranger or a Yankee or any kind of professional athlete. So although I greatly admired many of the Rangers, my real idol growing up was John Halligan. He seemed to have the perfect job. I knew of John from his many appearances on the rare Rangers broadcasts on TV in the 1960s. He was very recognizable so I went up to him, shook his hand and introduced myself a few times when I saw him at the Garden. Then in the late 1980s I began publishing a Ranger newsletter called SportStat . . . The Rangers Report and I sent him copies. He would write back to me and was very supportive of my project. After he retired we began corresponding quite regularly. He told me about a project that he was working on which was going to be a compilation of essays about the Rangers that were written by fans and he asked me to write something for him. I was thrilled! The thought of John Halligan asking me to write something for one of his books was amazing to me. So I sent him a story about how my father had introduced me to the game when I was a youngster and he liked it and said he would use it. Of course it made my day. Unfortunately, John passed away before the book could be completed. But John was always very supportive of my work and I'll always be grateful to him for that.

Marcel Paille

Like many netminders of the pre-expansion era, Marcel Paille had the great misfortune of trying to break into the NHL during what many consider to be the golden age of goaltending. Those were the days of the Original Six, when each team carried only one goalkeeper and five of the incumbents—Johnny Bower, Glenn Hall, Jacques Plante, Terry Sawchuk, and Gump Worsley—were eventually inducted into the Hockey Hall of Fame.

Joseph Marcel Rejean Paille was born on December 8, 1932, in Shawinigan Falls, Quebec, the same small Canadian town that produced the legendary Jacques Plante. He began his junior hockey career at the age of seventeen with the Quebec Citadelles of the QJHL in 1949. When his junior career ended he moved to the Matane Red Rockets (LSLHL) and then the North Bay Trappers (NOHA). It was while he was with North Bay that he was scouted and later signed by the Chicoutimi Saguenéens (QHL) where he earned Rookie of the Year honors in 1956.

Paille was selected by the Rangers from Chicoutimi in the 1956 Inter-League Draft and sent to the Cleveland Barons of the AHL. Marcel played very well that season, posting a 34–25–3 record with seven shutouts and a 3.20 GAA. He also earned a spot on the league's second All-Star team and led the Barons to the Calder Cup championship that spring. At that point, the Rangers considered Marcel to be their "goalie of the future" and moved him to their Providence Reds farm club while trading the rights to thirty-two-year-old Johnny Bower to the Barons.

Paille made his NHL debut on the night of November 2, 1957, shutting out the Bruins 5–0 in Boston. He played a total of 33 games for the Blueshirts that year, posting an 11–15–7 record with a 3.09 GAA while sharing the Rangers netminding duties with Gump Worsley.

While with the Rangers that season, Marcel experimented with an odd-looking white fiberglass mask that has become very familiar to hockey historians over the years. The mask was manufactured by the Brunswick-Balke Collender Company in Toronto and featured a wide Plexiglass eye shield. The contraption was heavy, however, and offered little ventilation. Perspiration from Marcel's forehead ran down into his eyes and the Plexiglass shield became foggy. The experiment ended after a single practice but Marcel donned a more traditional mask while with Providence in the early 1970s.

Over the next seven seasons Marcel bounced between the Rangers and their various farm clubs in Providence, Springfield, Buffalo, Baltimore, and Vancouver, being recalled when Worsley was injured or needed a rest. Paille made a place for himself in AHL history when he joined the Springfield Indians in 1959 and backstopped the team to three consecutive Calder Cup titles. Paille's 47 victories in 1960–61 set an AHL record and he won the Harry "Hap" Holmes Award in 1961 and 1962 for leading the league in goals against average. Overall Paille went 107–54–8 with 12 shutouts in 169 games with Springfield.

Then in 1964–65 as Emile Francis was growing tired of Jacques Plante's diva-like behavior, Marcel was brought up to New York and played in 39 games, posting a 10–21–7 record with a 3.58 GAA.

Former Ranger Dick Duff got to know Marcel during his time in New York and remembered him fondly.

DICK DUFF: "I had a lot of fun with Marcel Paille in the short time I was with the Rangers. We lived in the same place on Eighth Avenue and 45th Street in an apartment building. It was four blocks from the old Madison Square Garden. So one night I said, 'Marcel, where are you going?'

"He said, 'I'm going to have a beer.'

"And I said, 'What kind of beer do you drink, Marcel?'

"He said, 'I like Schaefer beer.'

"I said, 'Why Schaefer?'

"'Because it's the one beer to have when you're having more than one.'"

EMILE FRANCIS: "Paille was a standup goalkeeper. He played his angles very well and gave up very few rebounds. Because of being a standup goalkeeper and playing his angles everything went off into the corner. That was the difference between the old goalkeepers and these young guys now. They go down the way they do and the rebound comes straight out. But if you were a standup goalkeeper playing your angles you'd steer everything off into the corner.

"He was a very calm guy with a lot of poise. He never got excited.

"We were playing against the Chicago Black Hawks and Paille had a pompadour haircut. Bobby Hull came down outside the blue line and he took a slap shot and the puck split his hair! I damn near passed out on the bench. I could see the puck go right through his hair. If it hit him it would've killed him."

Paille played well considering the team that he had in front of him, but the Rangers were in a rebuilding mode and he was traded to Providence that spring as part of the deal that brought Ed Giacomin to the Rangers. Overall, in parts of seven seasons with the Rangers, Marcel saw action in 107 games, going 32–52–22 with two shutouts and a 3.42 GAA. Marcel then spent the next seven seasons in Providence where he became a fan favorite both on and off the ice.

Providence native Michael Venticinque grew up watching Marcel tending goal for the Reds.

MICHAEL VENTICINQUE: "He was quite a goaltender. I was invited to a hockey game one night and I was just fixated on Marcel. I was fascinated by the way he would stand up, come out, cut down on the angles, and occasionally go down . . . but then he was right back up on his feet again. He had an excellent glove hand, he would've made a great first baseman. Believe it or not, I used to go to the games just to watch him play. He was quick and agile and great on the angles.

"He was a great skater too. I used to love going down by the goal judge's booth just to watch his footwork. He was very good one-on-one. I saw him take out two guys on a breakaway, he made the save and took them both out of the play.

"At the time he didn't wear a mask and I remember he got hit in the face and they took him on the bench and stitched him up and he was back on the ice within ten minutes. It was amazing!"

In 1972, at the age of forty, Marcel signed with the Philadelphia Blazers of the WHA who had acquired his rights from the Chicago Cougars. The Blazers doubled the salary that the Reds were paying him, but it was not a good experience for Marcel. He was backing up Bernie Parent, which meant he didn't play that often, sometimes going more than a month between starts. And there were also times, on the road, that he didn't even get a chance to practice. His coach, Phil Watson, treated him with disdain and when he was given a chance to play, of course he was rusty. He finished the season with a 2–8–0 record with a 4.81 GAA. Then after the season when Marcel tried to hook up with another club, he found that Watson had black-balled him, telling everyone that his reflexes were gone and that he was washed up.

MICHAEL VENTICINQUE: "Marcel was a very soft-spoken man, very shy and he kept to himself but he was highly respected. The fans loved him here. He was loved by everybody. I think in all the time I've been interested in hockey I never heard anyone say anything bad about him. In fact when he jumped from the American Hockey League to the World Hockey Association everyone was disappointed but I can understand why he was going because he figured he was going to make more money. But that short stay with the WHA didn't help him any. He tried to come back to Providence but by then the Reds were tied in with the Rangers and they had an abundance of goaltenders. So he hooked up with his old friend Larry Wilson who was coaching the Richmond Robins at the time and Larry took him on and he played one more season and then he retired in 1974."

Marcel played for 15 seasons in the American Hockey League and set many records that still stand today including most games played by a goaltender (765), most minutes played (45,300), most Calder Cup games (87), most playoff minutes played (5,368), most Calder Cup games won (49) and longest playoff shutout streak (207:27). He also placed second in career victories (349) behind Johnny Bower (359). He also posted 36 career AHL shutouts, placing him fifth on the all-time list.

Marcel was inducted into the Springfield Hockey Hall of Fame in 1997. He passed away in 2002 and was inducted posthumously into the American Hockey League Hall of Fame in 2010.

3

1965–66

The Cornerstone
of the Franchise

IT WAS CLEAR that the first order of business for Emile Francis during the summer of 1965 would be to upgrade the Rangers' goaltending situation. Not only was it obvious that Jacques Plante was not the solution, the NHL had made it mandatory that each team now dress two goaltenders for each game. Previously teams were required to dress only one netminder and if he was injured and could not continue an emergency goaltender, sometimes called the "house goalie," could be summoned from the stands.

Francis had his eye on a young netminder named Ed Giacomin who was playing for the Providence Reds of the American Hockey League. Giacomin was a native of Sudbury, Ontario, which in those days was deemed to be the territory of the Detroit Red Wings. Eddie attended a tryout camp for the Red Wings' junior club in Hamilton but was beaten out by Carl Wetzel, a netminder who would go on to have a brief NHL career, playing only two games for Detroit and five games for Minnesota. Giacomin returned to Sudbury and got a job as a mechanic's assistant in a chemical plant and played for commercial leagues.

Since Eddie had never signed a "C" form with Detroit he was basically a free agent and could play for any team that would sign him. He finally caught on with the Washington Presidents of the old Eastern Hockey League in 1959. The Presidents were in last place and needed a netminder for the final weeks of the season, so they called Eddie's older brother Rollie, who had more experience. Rollie couldn't take the time off from work, however, and convinced Eddie to go in his place. Giacomin played the last four games of the season, won them all, and seemed to have a pretty good chance of earning a spot next season.

Unfortunately, during the summer, Eddie suffered severe burns on his legs in a kitchen fire and spent a month in the hospital. He later underwent therapy while doctors were telling him to forget about playing hockey. But Eddie wasn't willing to give up so easily. He reported to training camp in September, arriving at the rink early every morning to wrap his still-healing legs in bandages before anyone could notice. Eddie wound up playing for both the New York Rovers and Clinton Comets that season facing 60 to 70 shots a night while learning his craft. Giacomin then joined the Providence Reds of the AHL in 1960 where he steadily improved each season and began drawing the attention of NHL scouts.

EMILE FRANCIS: "When I took over the Rangers I knew I had to get a goalkeeper. I wore out two suitcases in two years, I went to so many games. I went to see every guy that played professional hockey.

"But I kept going back to Providence. I kept looking at this guy Giacomin. His record didn't tell you much but I liked the way he competed. So I told our scout Johnny Gagnon, 'Johnny, I want you to find out everything you can about this guy. Go to every practice, follow him around after practice, see where he goes, find out how he lives, what kind of family he's got because I got a feeling that this could be a very important move for us. Another thing, you go to every game in Providence and tell me every scout that's coming in there.' So it turns out that Montreal and Detroit were sending in scouts and I had Johnny there all the time.

"I had met half a dozen times with Lou Pieri, the owner of the Providence Reds. Now in those days there were a lot of independent teams like Springfield with Eddie Shore and Hershey with the chocolate factory, but you couldn't get anyone from any of those teams because there was no draft in those days. The only way you could get a player that you wanted was to deal with the minor league club. So Johnny Gagnon tells me that the Red Wings have been here and are sending Johnny Mitchell, their chief scout, in here for Friday's game. And he suggested that I get up there as fast as I could. So I call Lou Pieri and tell him I'm coming to watch the game and I was wondering if there was a possibility that we could sit down and talk after the game, because I think we're getting to the point where we have to make a move. So he tells me, 'Here's what I want you to do, I want to build up a whole new crowd of bobby-soxers to come to the games. These guys that you want to trade to me, I want you to bring their pictures, so I can look at them and I'd prefer to have single guys if at all possible. But I can't meet with you on Friday night but I can see you on Saturday morning at nine o'clock.'

"So I go to the game and I'm nervous as a goddamned cat because I knew this other guy was coming in and he was meeting with Pieri on Friday night. So after the game I go back to the Biltmore Hotel right by the railway station. I didn't want to go through the lobby because when hockey people came to Providence they hung out in the lobby and I didn't want to attract any attention. So I went to the basement and took the elevator and the doors opened on the main floor and in steps Johnny Mitchell, the chief scout of the Detroit Red Wings! So we get to our floor and he says, 'I want to ask you a very confidential question.' So I said, 'Shoot!' 'Do you think that Eddie Giacomin is capable of playing in the National Hockey League?' So I said, 'Johnny, you're asking the wrong guy that question' and I left him and went to bed.

"So I met Pieri the next morning and he asks, 'Who are these guys you're bringing me?' Well, I had a guy who had played for the Cleveland Barons of the AHL named Jim Mikol. He was single, tall, and a professional golfer. Plus the guy's a hell of a hockey player, you know him, he's been in Cleveland. He says, 'OK I'll take him.' Then he says 'If I trade you Giacomin, I'm gonna need a goalkeeper.' OK, I said, Marcel Paille. Turns out I gave him four guys, Aldo Guidolin and a guy named Sandy McGregor. But that was the key deal because for the next ten years Giacomin was the cornerstone of our franchise.

"Giacomin was a competitor. He played with a bad team in Providence but that's how you produce goalkeepers. If I had a goalkeeper and I thought he was going to be a good one I'd put him with the worst team in our system so he'd get a lot of shots. Eddie was the key component and that's where you start. You start in goal, defense and down the middle. Same like in baseball, you start with a catcher, pitcher, second baseman, shortstop and center fielder. And I built ball clubs so I knew all about building teams. That's why I knew that I had to get a goalkeeper and he was the guy I picked."

The deal for the twenty-five-year-old Giacomin was announced on May 17, 1965. At that point the plan was to keep Plante and gradually work Giacomin into the number one spot. Plante, however, perhaps reading the handwriting on the wall, had other plans. He telephoned Francis in early June, telling him that he was going to retire, citing health issues and his desire to spend more time with his family. Plante then said that he planned to make the announcement to the press in two days, giving Francis just forty-eight hours to swing a deal for an experienced netminder before the rest of the GMs in the league knew that he was dealing from a disadvantage.

Francis first tried to get veterans Johnny Bower or Terry Sawchuk from Toronto but was rebuffed by Maple Leaf GM Punch Imlach. He then turned to Montreal where he struck a deal with Canadiens GM Sam Pollock, acquiring goaltender Cesare Maniago along with forward Garry Peters for Noel Price, Earl Ingarfield, Gordon Labossiere, Dave McComb, and cash on June 8, 1965 (Ingarfield was reacquired by the Rangers the following day when Montreal left him unprotected in the intra-league draft).

Maniago, twenty-six, had seen action in 21 NHL games with Toronto and Montreal and came into the season with a 2.90 goals against average. At 6-foot-2, 175 pounds, the lanky native of Trail, British Columbia, was the tallest goaltender in the league at that time. Maniago had spent the previous season with Minneapolis of the Central Hockey League, where he was named to the All-Star team with an impressive 2.75 GAA and a league-leading six shutouts.

That same day, Francis also claimed thirty-four-year-old netminder Don Simmons from Toronto in the intra-league draft. Nicknamed "Dippy Don" for his habit of dropping low to block shots, Simmons was the first NHL netminder to start wearing a mask after it was introduced by Jacques Plante in 1959. Simmons had appeared in 225 NHL games with Boston and Toronto (2.88 GAA with 21 shutouts) and was expected to fill the backup role as well as provide mentoring for the Rangers' younger goaltenders.

Francis also hoped to add a little feistiness to the Rangers lineup by acquiring John McKenzie along with Ray Cullen from the Black Hawks in exchange for Tracy Pratt, Dick Meissner, Dave Richardson, and Mel Pearson on June 4, 1965.

At this point, it may seem that Francis was overpaying in a few of these early deals, sending a lot of players out of the organization, but getting few players in return. This was by design. He had a lot of players that he did not think had a chance of playing for the Rangers taking up roster spots that could be used for real prospects. In short, he didn't have quality to trade but he had quantity and he took advantage of it.

The season began with Giacomin and Simmons in New York and Maniago in Baltimore as the Rangers got off to a 5–5–4 start through their first fourteen games.

But Giacomin was inconsistent through the first few months of the season. He handled the puck very well and liked to wander out of his net and clear it up to his defensemen, earning the nickname "Goalie A-Go-Go" from the press. In effect, he was like a third defenseman. In the beginning the fans loved it, but on too many occasions he was caught out of position, giving the opposition an empty net and easy scoring opportunity.

Giacomin sometimes wandered as far as 15 to 20 feet away from his net and this often caused confusion with his defensemen as well as missed assignments. "His wandering gave us heart failure. We just weren't used to it," Vic Hadfield told reporters at the time.

As the losses piled up, the fans turned on Giacomin, loudly booing each opposition goal and cheering derisively when he made an easy save. When the Rangers went into a deep slump right after Thanksgiving, Francis knew it was time for a change, both behind the bench and in the crease. Francis replaced Red Sullivan as coach on December 6 and Giacomin was sent to Baltimore on January 4, 1966, and replaced by Cesare Maniago.

The Rangers had won only one of their last ten games and had a 5–10–5 record when Francis replaced Sullivan, who had coached the team since December of 1962. It would be the first of three times that Francis would take over as coach of the Blueshirts. When asked if there were any other candidates to replace Sullivan, Francis replied, "You have to have a man who knows our material. Another man outside of our organization would have to take time to learn the material and time is important right now. That's why I named myself as coach." Sullivan stayed with the club as coordinator of player personnel and scouting.

As Giacomin left for Baltimore, at least one of his teammates was not sorry to see him go. "We were losing games we should have won because the other team had better goaltending," one unnamed Ranger told Stan Fischler of the *New York Journal-American*. "There was a game in Toronto where we were tied and should have come out with a point but a little dribbler got by Eddie at the end of the game. That stuff happened too often." The player was never identified, but three days after Eddie was sent to Baltimore, center Lou Angotti was sold to Chicago, where he told reporters, "You work like hell and the guy in the net gives it away."

Giacomin was subsequently recalled two weeks later when Maniago suffered bruised ribs. He remained with the Rangers for the rest of the season but played very little. Giacomin worked diligently in practice and was instructed by Francis to watch the more experienced goaltenders in the league to see how they played the angles and the shooters.

Goaltending was not the only problem the Rangers had that season. Their skilled players were getting pushed around and they really had no one to stand up to the opposition's tough guys. Phil Goyette suffered a very serious injury the day after Christmas when he was speared by Boston defenseman Ted Green, damaging his spleen. He developed pleurisy and missed about a month of the season. Rangers president William Jennings was said to have put a bounty on Green's head and Ranger fans chanted "Get Green" whenever he and the Bruins came to town.

PHIL GOYETTE, *Center, 1963–69, 1972*: "I don't think he did it intentionally. It was a reflex and sometimes when you have a reflex action you don't think whether or not, well I'll do it or I won't do it. Green just turned around and didn't know who it really was. He thought it was someone who was going to ram him into the boards. So that's when he turned around with the stick and I was coming a little too fast I guess and that's when I got it in the stomach. Fortunately for me it wasn't as serious as it could have been. So I ended up out for a few games and that was about it. He hit a part where the previous year I had pleurisy and it caused some bleeding in one of my lungs so I ended up in a hospital in Montreal and they had to drain it but so far it turned out pretty good, I'm still here."

In an effort to beef up the Rangers forwards, Francis sent winger Johnny McKenzie to the Boston Bruins for Reggie Fleming on January 10, 1966. "Reggie the Ruffian," a thirty-year-old 5-foot-10, 195-pound forward was a seven-year NHL veteran who had seen action with Montreal, Chicago (where he had been part of the 1960–61 Stanley Cup-winning Black Hawks), and Boston. During those seven seasons he saw duty as a forward and defenseman and accumulated 43 goals, 55 assists, and 647 penalty minutes.

As a Ranger, he stepped right in and added muscle to the lineup as well as recording 10 goals, 14 assists, and 124 penalty minutes in 35 games (overall his total of 166 penalty minutes was the most in the NHL that season.) Fleming's role was that of a "policeman," a guy who kept the opposition from taking advantage of the smaller players. He was also an agitator. If the Rangers needed a spark, he would get a tap on the shoulder and he would go out and start something. But Fleming was not just a fighter; he was a pretty good hockey player who could score goals and was also good defensively.

The Rangers suffered another setback when Rod Gilbert was forced to undergo season-ending spinal fusion surgery in December. Gilbert originally underwent spinal fusion surgery in 1960 when as a junior he slipped on a lid from an ice cream container that had been thrown onto the ice. But the graft didn't heal properly and his back began acting up again at the beginning of the season. Gilbert wore a truss with steel bars through the first half of the year, but the contraption restricted his movements and he decided to have the second operation, this time in the Mayo Clinic where the surgery was performed by the Rangers' team physician Dr. Kazuo Yanagisawa.

The operation was a success, but during his recovery, Gilbert choked on some of his medications and nearly died in his hospital bed while being visited by Francis and Rangers President Bill Jennings. Gilbert, who claimed to have had an out of body experience, could hear the doctor say 'We can't get a pulse, he's dead.' "There's two doctors and some nurses in there," said Francis, "and I'm looking in and around them, and I said bring him back, damn it he's my best player!" Gilbert has often said that hearing Emile call him his best player is what brought him back.

The Rangers finished the season in last place, one point behind the fifth-place Bruins but 27 points behind the fourth-place Detroit Red Wings. It was the first time they finished in last place since the 1959–60 season. They set a team record for most losses with 41 and gave up 261 goals, the most since the 1943–44 season when the World War II–ravaged Blueshirts surrendered 310 goals.

Bob Nevin led the team with 29 goals, 33 assists, and 62 points. Donnie Marshall had 10 power play goals, and the Blueshirts scored two shorthanded goals. Nevin had one and Lou Angotti had the other. Rod Gilbert played in only 34 games, scoring 10 goals and 15 assists but Jean Ratelle finished third on the team in scoring (21-30-51). Unfortunately like Gilbert, Ratelle also needed back surgery following the season and would miss part of the 1966–67 campaign.

As for the goaltending situation, neither Giacomin nor Maniago had the type of season that would make them the clear-cut starter going into the following season. Giacomin played 35 games and gave up 125 goals, for a 3.68 GAA. Maniago saw action in 28 games, surrendering 94 goals and recording a pair of shutouts for a 3.50 GAA. Don Simmons saw action in 12 games, surrendering 40 goals and posting a 4.36 GAA.

The Old Smoothies

One of the few bright spots of the Rangers 1965–66 season was the formation of a line consisting of Phil Goyette centering Bob Nevin and

Donnie Marshall. Nicknamed "The Old Smoothies," they weren't really that old, but they were experienced and they played like they had been linemates for decades. Together they formed one of the Rangers most famous and effective lines of the 1960s.

EMILE FRANCIS: "I put Goyette, Marshall, and Bob Nevin together and for two years, while Gilbert and Ratelle were getting adjusted to playing in the NHL, that line carried our club and got us into the play-offs. They killed penalties, they were on the power play, they really contributed to our club."

The line's "Old Smoothies" nickname came from the way they passed the puck and worked so smoothly together. It was like each of them knew exactly where the others would be on the ice at any given moment. Actually it was Goyette's great peripheral vision and passing skills that made it look so easy. And all three were experienced forwards that came up through the Montreal or Toronto systems and were well-schooled at playing their positions at both ends of the ice. So in most cases, Goyette knew exactly where to look for either winger and was able to get them the puck.

Goyette (5-foot-10, 170 pounds) won four Stanley Cups with Montreal while being used as a defensive forward. But upon arriving in New York, Phil took the opportunity to display his offensive skills, scoring 98 goals and adding 231 assists in 397 games as a Ranger.

PHIL GOYETTE: "Well, naturally in Montreal there were the two top lines which were pretty hard to put aside because they were such great hockey players. So guys like me and Marshall were basically handling the other teams' big lines defensively and killing off penalties. So we weren't on the ice as often as the other lines. That made the big difference when we went to New York. I ended up on the power play, killing penalties, getting more ice time. You get more ice time, you get more points, you get more points you end up in the top ten scorers in the league. And Emile had a lot of confidence in us and we had experience with Donnie Marshall and Bob Nevin and we knew what we had to do to produce and we did. Even when I played with Camille Henry and Rod Gilbert, Rod was just coming out of junior but he was a top-notch hockey player, so I played with two straight lines pretty much all the time. I even played a little with Andy Bathgate but then he was traded to Toronto, so that broke up that line.

"But Marshall and Nevin and I played quite a few years together. We had the experience of knowing each other's style and when you have that you know when the player has the puck, where he is going or where he's going to be. They would maneuver themselves into a position where I knew that they would be there for passes and so on and they'd likewise do it with me. We already had six years of experience under our belts which is a big difference from someone coming up from juniors who doesn't know how the league works."

Goyette was also one of the best centermen in the league at the time, and Boom Boom Geoffrion once called him "the best faceoff man in the business."

PHIL GOYETTE: "I was pretty good at getting possession of the puck. Fortunately it just happened that I was used to take the majority of the faceoffs with the Canadiens. If there was a crucial faceoff in our zone, Toe Blake would put me out there because I just had that knack of winning the faceoff. So it continued on through the end of my career."

Left winger Donnie Marshall (5-foot-10, 160 pounds) was acquired for his versatility and experience. He could play all three forward positions and also won five consecutive Stanley Cups with Montreal from 1956 to 1960. Francis, who needed experienced leadership to help him rebuild the Rangers, named Marshall and veteran defenseman Harry Howell assistant coaches while both were still playing, a first in the NHL.

Used mostly as a defensive forward and penalty killer in Montreal, Donnie, a great stickhandler and faceoff man, became a two-way threat as a Ranger. His best season was in 1965–66 when he scored 26 goals with 28 assists. In 479 games with the Rangers, Marshall scored a total of 129 goals and added 141 assists while accumulating only 40 penalty minutes.

DONNIE MARSHALL: "In Montreal I was used defensively much more than in New York. They had so many high scoring forwards in Montreal. I had a problem starting out in Montreal, my first year after playing in the American League I broke a bone in my leg in training camp and it put me back. I started late in the season and the lines were fixed so I ended up being a defensive forward, killing penalties and those things and it just seemed to carry on and in New York they needed offense and in the minors, I was always a good offensive player and so I picked it up in New York better than I did in Montreal.

"It was pretty easy to play with them. Phil Goyette was excellent with the puck and if you could get into position he could get the puck to you. Nevin was just a good up and down player, good offensively and good defensively. They both were smart hockey players and it was easy to play with them."

Bob Nevin (6-feet, 190 pounds) was a hard-checking right winger who won two Stanley Cups with Toronto in 1962 and 1963 where he was used mostly as a defensive forward and penalty killer. Francis once called him the best two-way player he ever coached, but it took a while for Bob to win over the Garden fans. After all he was part of the trade that sent away longtime fan favorite Andy Bathgate and Nevin's long skating stride didn't help either. It made it look like he was coasting, but in reality, he was an exceptionally strong skater who was hard to knock off his skates or the puck.

Nevin finally gained the fan's admiration when he scored 29 goals in 1965–66, his second full season in New York. He also became the Rangers captain that season after Camille Henry was traded to Chicago. Bob would go on to top the 20-goal mark five times in his seven-plus-year Ranger career. Nevin scored 168 goals with 174 assists and 105 penalty minutes in 505 games as a Ranger. One of his biggest goals was the sudden death winner that gave the Blueshirts a 4–2 series victory over Toronto in the first round of the 1971 playoffs.

BOB NEVIN: "Phil was one of the best centers that ever played the game so he was great at giving you a chance to score. It was like he had eyes in the back of his head. I think the first year I played with Phil I scored thirty goals and Donnie was a very underrated player, good defensively, a real good positional player and he could score goals too. We just sort of hit it off. We all played in the league a little bit so we all knew what we were doing. And Donnie and I both killed penalties so were getting a lot of ice time."

Throwing three seasoned veterans together doesn't always result in the kind of chemistry that existed between Goyette, Nevin, and Marshall. But with the right kind of players at the right time in their careers a little bit of magic can happen, and the rebuilding Rangers of the mid 1960s needed all the magic they could get.

Emile Francis and the Goal Judge

Goal judges are a part of hockey's proud and sometimes innocent past. They have been replaced in the current NHL by cameras and video reviews in the war room in Toronto and perhaps it's safer that way.

Arthur Reichert was a well-respected fixture at both the old and new Madison Square Gardens, serving in a variety of capacities, but primarily as a goal judge. By his own estimate, he turned on the red light for "somewhere in the neighborhood of 12,000 goals" during a career that spanned from 1932 until his retirement in 1991. However, it was one goal (or non-goal) on the night of November 21, 1965, that caused all hell to break loose and became an unforgettable moment in Rangers lore.

EMILE FRANCIS: "When I took over the Rangers they had made the playoffs only once in ten years. So I knew it was gonna take me a while to turn this thing around. I figured I could get it done in two years and I did. But you had to fight for every inch along the way. So we're playing Detroit and they had Gordie Howe, Alex Delvecchio, Terry Sawchuk, they were a great team. We're leading 2–1 with about four minutes to go in the game, and the play comes down to our end. The puck comes out in front and Normie Ullman takes a quick wrist shot, and then everybody turned and went the other way, back up ice.

"All of a sudden the referee blows the whistle so I'm wondering what the hell is going on here. So the ref goes and talks to the goal judge and then goes to the scorer's bench and they put up a 2 on the scoreboard for Detroit. They scored! So I take off. I gotta squeeze in front of the first row of seats to get to the goal judge, Arthur Reichert. Now in those days the goal judge wasn't in a booth, he just sat on a stool. So I said to Reichert, 'What the hell are you doing putting that light on, that puck wasn't in. The guy who knew better than you whether the puck went in, Ullman, turned and left right away and you put the light on.' So there's a guy sitting there and he says, 'Why don't you screw off?' I said, 'I'm not talking to you.' Well, I turned back to Reichert and this guy stands up and he had two buddies on the other side of Reichert and there were beer cups all over the floor. We found out later when we went to court that they were three firemen on a night out, drinking beer. So, when this guy stands up I figure I'm gonna get one punch in real quick and I nailed him and knocked him right over the seats.

"So then his two friends jumped in. With that Vic Hadfield, who was back at center ice, sees all this commotion and he and the rest of the players come over that glass like commandos. Zing, zing, zing. Meanwhile, my wife's wondering who the kook is that started the riot."

ARNIE BROWN: "I heard Hadfield say, 'Hey that's Emile in there, let's go!' So we put our foot up on the edge of the top of the boards because at that time they had the glass behind the boards a little bit, you could get the side of your skate on that little ledge there, not the blade but the side of the skate and we went up and over the glass. So, it was a real mess. People were shoving and pushing. We were trying to get at this guy because he had Emile and he was hitting him pretty good. And when I came down from the top of the glass, they had portable chairs back there then and my foot went right through the back of the chair. So here we are, people pushing and swinging and I've got my damn foot caught in the chair."

EMILE FRANCIS: "So now here we are, I had a new suit on that's torn in half, I had cuts under both eyes, but we cleared out that whole end. It took about half an hour to straighten things out. They had to take those three guys to one room to stitch them up and took me to another room to stitch me up and Garden security comes in and says, 'Those guys didn't know who you were and they're sorry. You won't bring any charges against them, will you?' I said, 'No, no, forget it. It's all part of the game.'

"So the next day, Bill Jennings comes in with a copy of the *New York Post*. He says, 'How are you doing?' I said 'not very good. About two hours ago a guy came in here and handed me this. I'm being sued for a million dollars!' He said, 'Let me see that.' Then he shows me page three of the *Post* where there's a story that Bruce Norris, owner of the Red Wings, is being sued because he stole some guy's wife. Jennings says, 'Well, you're in the big leagues now; you're in the same league as Bruce Norris.' I said, 'yeah but at least Norris had a nice time. Look at me for crissakes, I've got two black eyes and I ruined a suit.'

"Well, we got to court seven years later and we were there for a month. We were in the Supreme Court building in Brooklyn and towards the end of the trial they started renovating the building. They always brought the jury in behind the judge. But now because of the renovations they had to bring them out in front of me. The last guy on the jury put his hand out and said good luck. Well, they said 'What did you say to him?' He said, 'I'm a Ranger fan. I said good luck.' 'Mistrial!' They declared a mistrial. But we were back two years later and this time there was a different judge and jury and they were awarded $100,000.

"Arthur Reichert was a real competent guy but I was fighting for the life of my hockey club. So not only did I invent the goal glove, but because of that incident they started to put the goal judge in a booth so nobody could get to them."

Joe Schaefer—The House Goalie

Pop Quiz time: Quick, who was the Rangers' first American-born goaltender?

Fans of a certain age might guess 1960 Olympian Jack McCartan. That would be a good guess but it would also be wrong. McCartan played his first game as a Ranger on March 6, 1960, but Joe Schaefer made his Ranger debut on February 17, 1960.

Joe who? Exactly!

Schaefer, a Long Island native, managed an office supply company and worked part-time at Madison Square Garden as the Rangers' practice goalie, statistician, penalty-clock timekeeper, and goal judge. It seemed that whatever the Rangers needed, Schaefer was willing to do it. If they had asked him to clean the ice and play the organ he probably would have given it a try.

Schaefer also became the Garden's emergency goaltender. In the years before the NHL ruled that teams had to dress two goaltenders (1965) for a game, each home team was required to have an emergency goaltender in the stands to be used if either teams' netminder was hurt and could not continue to play in the game. The Canadian teams usually had a promising junior netminder sitting in the stands as their "house goalie," but in the states the teams had to do the best they could with who was available.

Detroit's trainer, Lefty Wilson, saw action in three games, but only once with the Red Wings when he replaced Terry Sawchuk. In the other two appearances, he had to face his own team when he took over for Harry Lumley of Toronto and Don Simmons of Boston. Yes, the NHL was a much different world back then.

Schaefer was first called to duty on the night of February 17, 1960, when Bobby Hull of the Chicago Black Hawks accidentally skated over Gump Worsley's stick hand in the first minute of the second period. Hull's skates ripped through Gump's glove and tore tendons in his hand

The game was delayed for twenty-three minutes as the thirty-five-year-old Schaefer, whose experience was limited to playing goal for the Sands Point Tigers of the amateur Metropolitan Hockey League and a few games in the minors, raced down to the Rangers dressing room to get ready to take Worsley's place. The Rangers held a 1–0 lead when Schaefer, 5-foot-8, 165 pounds, entered the game. Facing Hull and the rest of the hard shooting Hawks, Joe made 17 saves but ended up losing the game 5–1. The *New York Times* reported that "Schaefer had little to offer except courage."

Schaefer made his second emergency appearance on March 8, 1961. Once again, Worsley was the injured netminder and Hull was the culprit. With the score tied at 1–1 midway through the first period, Worsley tore a thigh muscle while attempting to stop Hull's wrist shot. As Schaefer made his way to the dressing room, the Gumper was being carried off the ice on a stretcher. Schaefer made 27 saves, but the Rangers lost, 4–3. However, one Hawk goal deflected off a Ranger defenseman and another came on a two-on-one breakaway.

Each game appearance put Schaefer in a rather unique situation. From a performance standpoint he was severely overmatched and could only perform to the best of his abilities. Basically he was there so that the game could continue; no one really expected game-saving stops from him. It was also a bit of a financial windfall for Schaefer, who earned $100 for each game he played, a hefty raise over the $10 a game he made as an off-ice official. He also had quite a story to tell the next day at the office.

Schaefer also played a small part in NHL history on the night of November 1, 1959, when Andy Bathgate's well-placed backhand shot caught Montreal's Jacques Plante in the face and forced him to leave the game for repairs. Plante told coach Toe Blake that he would not return to the game unless he was allowed to wear his mask. No other netminder had ever worn a mask in an NHL game and Blake was against it.

But faced with the choice of using Schaefer or a thirty-three-year-old usher named Arnie Nocks (who also served as a Ranger practice goalie and later went on to direct *The Soupy Sales Show*) or letting Plante wear the mask, Blake wisely chose Plante and the mask.

After his second Ranger appearance, Schaefer was never again called upon to suit up for a game. He continued as a statistician until 1986 when he retired and moved to South Carolina. His final Rangers stats were two games played (86 minutes), six goals against with a 5.58 goals against average, and an 0–2–0 record. Schaefer passed away in December of 2000 at the age of seventy-six.

Jacques Plante's Continuing Role in Ranger History

Jacques Plante's sudden retirement was not the end of his connection to the Rangers.

In 1967, Bert Olmstead, the coach of the expansion Oakland Seals, hired Plante to be his goaltending consultant. Plante took it a step further, however, signing a tryout contract and appearing in an exhibition game in Port Huron. Since Plante's NHL rights still belonged to the Rangers, Francis tried to make a deal with the Seals for Plante. But when an agreement could not be reached, Jacques left the Seals training camp and returned home. The next season Plante made it known to Francis that he wanted to come out of retirement. But since the Rangers could only protect two netminders (Giacomin and Villemure) Jacques was left exposed in the intra-league draft and selected by the St. Louis Blues where he shared the 1969 Vezina Trophy with teammate Glenn Hall.

But Plante's role in Ranger history didn't end there either. When the Blueshirts acquired Tim Horton from Toronto for Denis Dupere in March of 1970, the Rangers were still owed an unnamed player from St. Louis to complete an earlier trade. Francis had that player to be named later transferred to the Leafs as part of the deal. That player was Plante, who was going to be left unprotected by the Blues anyway.

Plante went on to play for Toronto and Boston in the NHL before moving on to the WHA with Quebec and Edmonton. He retired in 1975 and was elected into the Hockey Hall of Fame in 1978. He died of stomach cancer in February of 1986 at the age of fifty-seven.

Jacques Plante may not have had his best years on Broadway, but he was a character; colorful and controversial and proof that although they might "steal" a game once in a while, a goaltender is really only as good as the team in front of him. Overall, Jacques Plante played in 98 games spanning two seasons as a Ranger, posting a 32–53–12 record with five shutouts and a 3.38 GAA.

4

1966–67

The Boomer and the Playoffs

EMILE FRANCIS CONTINUED to add toughness, depth and veteran leadership to the lineup with the offseason acquisitions of Orland Kurtenbach, Red Berenson, Al MacNeil, and Bernie Geoffrion.

Kurtenbach, a thirty-year-old, 6-foot-2, 190-pound center from Cudworth, Saskatchewan, was claimed from Toronto in the intra-league draft. He was the Western Hockey League's Rookie of the Year in 1957–58 and played 10 games for the Rangers in 1960–61 during Alf Pike's brief stint as coach, recording six assists. He then saw action with Boston and Toronto before being claimed by Francis in June of 1966. Coming into the season, Big Kurt had registered 27 goals, 57 assists, and 239 penalty minutes in 222 NHL games. He was a well-respected enforcer, known for having the fastest fists in the NHL and gave the Rangers some much-needed size up the middle.

ORLAND KURTENBACH: "I didn't look for fights. I think the word *enforcer* denigrated my game. That was designated by the press and the media. I came out as a top scoring junior. When I got to Boston, I eventually played with Dean Prentice and Andy Hebenton and I got lots of ice time. When I got to New York, Jean Ratelle was hurt and I played with Rod Gilbert and Vic Hadfield and I was up in the scoring. But in the old six team league if we played a game in Montreal on Saturday we'd come home and play them again on Sunday so if there were any beefs the night before it would continue. But that wasn't my designation, I didn't like it."

Indeed, Orland's highest penalty minute total was 91 in 1963–64, his first full season in the NHL with Boston. And as his reputation grew, fewer opponents were lining up to take him on. When he did fight, however, the speed and power of his fists became even more apparent due to the white cotton gloves he wore under his hockey gloves because of an allergy.

ORLAND KURTENBACH: "When I was wearing the CCM gloves I got a rash from the dye and it got worse and worse. Dave Balon had the same thing. So in order to try to confine it I talked to the trainers and I wore white gloves in order to keep it from spreading. But I was allergic to the dye in the leather."

Gordon "Red" Berenson was a twenty-six-year-old, six-foot, 190-pound center / left wing who spent the previous five seasons in Montreal trying to crack the powerful Canadiens lineup. In 136 NHL games, Red, one of the few players to wear a helmet in those days, scored 14 goals with 23 assists and 43 penalty minutes. Berenson was acquired from Montreal in exchange for Garry Peters and Ted Taylor in June of 1966 and was expected to help fill the gap at center while Jean Ratelle was recuperating from back surgery.

Francis also claimed Al MacNeil from Montreal in the intra-league draft. MacNeil was a thirty-one-year-old, 5-foot-10, 175-pound defenseman. The seven-year NHL veteran played for Toronto, Montreal, and Chicago and was Wayne Hillman's defensive partner while both were with the Black Hawks. In 392 NHL games, MacNeil recorded 15 goals and 61 assists and racked up 515 penalty minutes. He was expected to add depth and brawn to the Rangers blueline.

And then there was the Boomer.

Bernie "Boom Boom" Geoffrion had a legendary 14-year career with the Montreal Canadiens during which he scored 371 goals and added 388 assists. He broke into the league with style, earning the Calder Trophy as the NHL's Rookie of the Year in 1952 and went on to win six Stanley Cups, the Hart Trophy as the league's MVP, as well as two Art Ross Trophies for winning the scoring title.

Following the 1963–64 season, Montreal owner David Molson gave Geoffrion the opportunity to coach the Canadiens' top farm club, the Quebec Aces of the AHL. Molson also promised him that if he did well in Quebec, he had a shot at coaching the Canadiens in two years. It was a way of easing the thirty-three-year-old Boomer into retirement so that they could bring in the younger, speedier Yvan Cournoyer. But to do that they first had to remove Geoffrion from their reserved list and they needed the cooperation of the rest of the general managers of the then six-team league.

EMILE FRANCIS: "We were at a Board of Governors meeting at the draft in June and Frank Selke, the GM of the Montreal Canadiens, said, 'I would like to have a courtesy waiver from all of you because Boomer is going to retire and we're going to make him the coach of Quebec.' By getting the courtesy waiver they could take him off their reserved list, put him on the retired list and add someone else to the reserved list.

"So I'm sitting there, I'd inherited a bad team, a team that made the playoffs once in ten years. So, I put my hand up and said, 'Well, I'll tell you what. We'll give you a courtesy waiver under one condition. If and when he ever wants to come back and play, then he has to be put on waivers,' never ever thinking that it would happen. But it did happen."

It happened because after two first place finishes but two playoff losses to the Rochester Americans, the Boomer was fired by the Quebec Aces. He then met with Molson to ask about his promise of the Canadiens' head coaching job. Molson told him that Toe Blake was still the coach and the best he could do was offer him a job coaching the Junior Canadiens at a significant cut in salary. Geoffrion felt betrayed and decided to make a comeback to show the Canadiens and their fans that he could still play.

EMILE FRANCIS: "All of a sudden this notice comes in from the Montreal Canadiens that they want to reinstate Boomer and he's on waivers. So, I said to myself, something's funny here. Montreal had a great team, they're not going to reinstate him and risk losing someone else. Some team in this league is screwing around and they think Boomer can help them. So, I said he's not gonna get by us. So, I put a claim in and within twenty-four hours Boomer calls me. He says, 'Emile you don't want me, I haven't played for two years, I'm all finished, I can't skate anymore, I can't do this, I can't do that.' I said, 'Boomer, don't give me any of your bullshit. You wouldn't be talking to me like this unless you had something else in your pocket. Someone else among the other five teams is screwing around and I'll tell you if you ever play in the NHL again it will be with the New York Rangers or you're not gonna play period.'

"So he says, let me think about it and I'll get back to you in a couple of days. So a few days later he calls back and says maybe you and I should talk. I flew up to Montreal and met him at the airport. We talked for two hours and by the time I left I had him under contract. I found out later on it was Punch Imlach of the Toronto Maple Leafs who wanted him. I knew he could help us because he was a great competitor. He had a terrific shot. I could use him on the point of the power play which we needed a point man and he'd play on our second or third line. Plus he had a lot of pride. He had won the Stanley Cup and I knew we needed his leadership on our team. And that's exactly what he gave us. It was the best thing I could have done. He came in there and all the players looked up to him. Boomer knew what it took to win and he set the pattern for the rest of the team. He had the team following his example. He was a tremendous leader not only on the ice, but in the locker room as well."

BOB NEVIN: "Boomer played the point on the power play and he could still shoot it pretty good. He was great. I loved playing with him. He was a lot of fun to be with. He was a very positive guy."

ARNIE BROWN: "Boomer was a really talkative, loud guy and of course the guys were always kidding with him and we had a lot of laughs with him. He really gave us a lot of spirit. And we needed that. We needed somebody who was kind of cocky. And Boomer was cocky as hell and he scored some big goals. He helped us a lot."

EMILE FRANCIS: "That fall we trained in Kingston, Ontario. It was the biggest sheet of ice I could find. It was gonna be the toughest camp they'd ever seen. So, the day before we were gonna start I went out to see how the ice was coming and who's there but Boomer. He turns and sees me and says, 'Emile you're crazy, I'll never make it out of training camp.' I'll tell you that first training camp he wanted to quit on me three times. He said 'I'm gonna die here.' But he helped us, he had great desire, and I knew that would rub off on the other players."

GERALD ESKENAZI, *former sportswriter, New York Times*: "Boom Boom Geoffrion was a great character. His first training camp was a memorable one for me because he was this older and out-of-shape future Hall of Famer and I remember how hard he worked to get into shape. To Boomer hockey was like a war. He was also very different from the other players. He would wear well-tailored suits, his wife was pretty well-dressed and she had a mink coat which also put them separate from these guys that were making $10,000 to $15,000 a year. Boomer had a real sense of himself. He used to speak like the King of England, in the third person. Like the King would say 'The King is happy' but Boomer would say 'Boomer is unhappy.' He was a real character and the players used to make fun of his accent but I'll tell you he was all business on the ice. His first shift on the ice in training camp, I don't remember who it was but they were going along the boards and he gave them an elbow and later he said he just wanted to show him that this is what hockey was all about.

"He had a great sense of himself and a great sense of the Canadiens. He used to refer to the Canadiens all the time which probably annoyed some of the players. But I think that he also felt that he had to give them a taste of class and a taste of winning that they had not had. He was one of the more unforgettable characters I met in hockey."

As the 1966–67 season began, Francis knew that sooner or later he would have to pick a number one netminder and stick with him. His plan was to alternate between Giacomin and Maniago until one of them played himself either in or out of the job. It was going to be a tough decision, but it was made a lot easier on the night of November 9, 1966.

The Rangers were playing Boston that night at Madison Square Garden. Maniago had to leave the game in the second period when he stopped a Johnny McKenzie shot with his chin. As Maniago skated off for stitches, Francis was forced to send Giacomin out to protect the Rangers' 3–1 lead.

The problem started after Maniago was stitched up and returned to the Rangers bench. Francis expected him to return to the net, but Cesare refused, saying that his chin was still sore. Francis, the former netminder who had suffered multiple broken noses, torn ligaments in both knees, separated shoulders, and needed over 250 stitches to close various wounds, was not sympathetic.

On the ice, Giacomin, who had blown third period leads in his last two outings, was hearing it from the crowd and being pressured by the Bruins. First Boston's Ron Murphy was left unprotected in front of the net and scored with 1:29 remaining in the game to bring the Bruins within a goal. Then goaltender Gerry Cheevers was pulled for an extra skater and Wayne Connelly scored to tie the game. Boston had scored twice in 89 seconds and the fans were not happy. They booed and jeered and threw all sorts of garbage towards Giacomin.

"My God, what a terrible thing for people to do to another human being," Boston's Eddie Westfall told reporters following the debacle. "Poor Eddie, he just had to stand there and take it."

EMILE FRANCIS: "We'd played in Toronto on a Saturday night and you know Eddie used to like to get out of the net and handle the puck. So we had a 2–1 lead with about two minutes to go in the game. Toronto threw the puck in the corner, and Eddie came out to play the puck and he missed it and it came right out in front and they put it in the net. That tied the game and in the last minute they scored again to beat us 3–2. I had been alternating at that time, Giacomin one night and Maniago the other because I was trying to decide who I was really gonna select to be the goalkeeper.

"So now the next game we're back in Madison Square Garden and I knew the Toronto game was on TV and I didn't want to put Eddie on the spot because I knew the crowd would get down on him. So I put Maniago in and we're playing the Boston Bruins. Well, we're leading 3–1 early in the second period and there's a scramble in front of our net and down goes Maniago. So [trainer] Frank Paice runs out there and comes back holding a towel to Maniago's chin. I told Frank and Dr. Nardiello to get him back as fast as you can because I didn't want to put Eddie in and have something happen like it did in the game before in Toronto. That Nardiello was fast. He was the Garden's boxing doctor and he could stitch guys up in a minute.

"After a little while Frank comes over and says, 'Okay, he's all fixed up.' So I go over to Cesare and say, 'Okay Cesare, let's go.'

"He says, 'I can't go back out there.'

"I say, 'What do you mean?'

"He says, 'I'm still pretty sore. I don't think I can play anymore tonight.'

"So I say go and sit down and I put Eddie in. Sure as hell the same thing happened as the game before. The Bruins threw the puck in the corner, Eddie misplayed it and they get a goal. They come down again, shoot it in the corner, he misses clearing it and bang, it's in the net. I'll tell you, the Garden erupted. They threw programs, cushions, everything they could get their hands on they threw at Eddie. I felt so bad for him.

"So after the game I was pissed. I got a hold of John Halligan. I was the first guy back then to start filming the games and John was in charge of the films. I said, 'John I'm having a meeting tomorrow at ten o'clock, you get that film ready and I'm going to go over with these guys every goddamn thing that happened.'

"Okay, so next morning, John puts the film on and guess what? It caught fire! Blew up! It caught fire, I had no film left! Things weren't going bad enough for us and now the projector blows up!

"So I bring them all back into the dressing room and I walked around. Okay. I'm gonna tell you verbally exactly what happened. So I go over to Maniago. I said, 'We're in this game as teammates to protect one another. I don't see how you could have been hurt so badly that you couldn't go back into the game. Shit, I've gone back with eight broken noses and over two hundred stitches and I didn't back down, not one minute.' So I said up until now I really didn't know who the hell was going to be the next goalkeeper of the New York Rangers, but now my mind's made up. Eddie Giacomin's gonna be the goalkeeper. And that was in front of the whole team. Then I told Giacomin, 'Eddie, I've never seen anything as embarrassing as what happened last night. Now when those people throw that shit at you, you throw it right back at them and I'll be right beside you.' Well guess what? The next game in Montreal, Giacomin was sensational. His whole career started from that moment on. That's what Eddie needed, as a confidence builder.

"So then I didn't protect Cesare in the expansion draft. I knew I had Villemure in the minors. Maniago went to Minnesota where he had a good career and he had good years later on in Vancouver. It wasn't that I didn't like him or anything, but I had to make a decision, that's what general managers are paid to do."

Maniago was interviewed by author Jay Moran in *The Rangers, The Bruins, and the End of an Era: A Tribute to a Great Rivalry* a few years ago and had this to say about the incident:

"That's where I guess I had a cut and chipped a tooth at the same time. They stitched me up and he (Emile Francis) says well, what do you think? And I said well, I just don't feel right and I believe he got ticked off with that because everything was kind of a macho situation in those days. In other words, you go in, if you're banged up you get stitched up and if you're still a little woozy you go back out. I can remember even earlier in my career, I got into a fight with a fellow by the name of Terry Gray and toppled on the ice and I hit my head and I had a concussion. I spent overnight in the hospital, I was out for a good half hour and Sammy Pollock was our coach and GM in Hull-Ottawa, the farm club of the Montreal Canadiens. I stayed overnight in the hospital in Kingston, went back up to Hull-Ottawa, we had an afternoon game and I was there and he says I want you to play. Okay, fine. Nowadays they wouldn't even take a chance. As I say, there are some injuries along the way, yeah, I mean, there are a lot of times I did play hurt but in this particular instance in New York I just felt that I wasn't right. And he did get ticked off. He did."

Emile's decision really helped turn the season around for the Rangers. At that point the Blueshirts were in last place with a 2–5–3 record, but they then went on a 15–4–3 streak that had them sitting atop the NHL standings at the end of December.

The streak began with an impressive 6–3 victory over the Canadiens at the Forum on November 12. Rod Gilbert scored a pair of goals but Geoffrion stole the spotlight when he scored on a breakaway to give the Rangers the lead. Boomer also had three assists including a pass that led to Harry Howell's clincher. It was only the Rangers' third victory of the season but in true Geoffrion fashion he told the team, "We're as good as any club in the league, we just have to believe!"

Prior to the season the Rangers had been picked to finish at the bottom of the NHL standings, but they spent most of the second half of the season in or near first place. A late season slump dropped them to fourth place but they still made the playoffs for the first time in five years and enjoyed their first winning season since 1957–58. Their 30–28–12, 72-point record represented a 25-point improvement from the previous season. They scored seven less goals (188), but also surrendered 72 fewer goals than in 1965–66.

Ed Giacomin started thirty-six consecutive games from the middle of November through early February and was in goal for every one of the Blueshirts' 30 victories. He earned a spot on the First All-Star team, posting a 2.54 GAA with a league-leading nine shutouts and led the league in games played (68), minutes played by a netminder (3,981), and wins (30). He was selected as the Rangers' MVP and finished second to Chicago's Stan Mikita in the voting for the Hart Trophy, which is given to the league's Most Valuable Player.

And the Garden crowd never threw garbage at Eddie again. In fact he became a fan favorite. Giacomin played a total of 11 seasons with the Blueshirts, posting a 266–172–89 record with a 2.73 GAA and 49 career regular-season shutouts. He shared the Vezina Trophy with Gilles Villemure in 1971, made numerous All-Star appearances, was elected to the Hockey Hall of Fame in 1987 and had his number 1 jersey retired in 1989.

Rod Gilbert led the team in goals with 28 and Phil Goyette led with 49 assists and 61 points. Donnie Marshall scored eight power-play goals and Ken Schinkel recorded two shorthanded goals. Jean Ratelle, who missed the first two months of the season following back surgery, didn't start to return to form until February and scored only six goals with five assists but made steady progress as his ice time increased.

Vic Hadfield, who had scored 18 and 16 goals the two previous seasons, had an off year, entering the last month of the season with only eight goals. But after switching to a Bobby Hull-type curved stick, Vic notched five goals in the Blueshirts' last six games and finished the season with 13. In addition to Giacomin, Harry Howell earned First All-Star honors and Donnie Marshall made the second team. Giacomin, Howell, Neilson, Gilbert, and Nevin also played in the midseason All-Star game.

Bernie Geoffrion played in 58 games in his comeback season, notching 17 goals and adding 25 assists as well as providing much-needed leadership. Not surprisingly, Boomer also led all Rangers scorers against Montreal, recording 3 goals and 11 assists while playing in twelve of the fourteen games between the clubs that season.

The Playoffs

The Rangers' first-round opponent was the defending Stanley Cup champion Montreal Canadiens who finished in second place, only five points ahead of the Blueshirts. The Canadiens had won the season series between the two clubs, 7–5–2, and entered the playoffs riding an 11-game unbeaten streak. They also had a hot goaltender, twenty-one-year-old rookie Rogie Vachon, who was recalled from Houston of the Central League when Gump Worsley suffered a freak injury. The Gumper had been out of action since the middle of March due to a concussion he suffered when hit in the temple by an egg thrown from the balcony in Madison Square Garden. As reported in the *Montreal Gazette*, "The Gumper was hit flush on the right temple by the egg which was thrown from about 100 feet away. The egg-tosser, a 25 year-old fan who had a bag of them when caught by Garden police, got off lucky when Worsley refused to press charges."

The series opened in Montreal with the Rangers getting off to a great start, taking a 4–1 lead on goals by Geoffrion, Hadfield, and a pair by Gilbert. The Blueshirts held that lead until midway through the third period when Montreal scored five unanswered goals in less than nine minutes to take the opener by a 6–4 score.

The Blueshirts fell behind in the second game when Dick Duff scored midway through the opening period. However, Geoffrion was able to tie the score in the second period when he launched a 30-foot slap shot past Vachon. It was Boomer's second goal of the series and the 58th playoff goal of his illustrious career. The teams entered the third period tied, 1–1. The turning point came when Harry Howell was serving a penalty. Yvan Cournoyer was able to deflect Arnie Brown's clearing attempt and the puck went to John Ferguson, who lifted it past Giacomin into the far corner of the net. Ralph Backstrom later added an insurance goal as Montreal won, 3–1.

A standing-room-only crowd of 15,925 greeted the Blueshirts as they took the ice for their first home playoff game since 1962. But the Canadiens came out flying. Claude Larose scored on a rebound of a Ralph Backstrom shot from the corner just 13 seconds into the opening period. Jean Beliveau rifled a 40-foot shot past Giacomin less than three minutes later and the Rangers were on their heels and forced to play catch-up yet again. Jim Neilson cut the lead in half with a 50-foot slapper through a screen and past Vachon later in the first period.

In the second period Montreal regained their two-goal lead when Bobby Rousseau deflected a Henri Richard shot past Giacomin. However, two minutes later Earl Ingarfield brought the Blueshirts back within a goal with a backhander past Vachon. But the Rangers could not get the puck past Vachon in the final period and lost, 3–2, and faced elimination two nights later at the Garden.

The fourth game was played on April 13, 1966, which was the 26th anniversary of the Rangers' last Stanley Cup victory in 1940. Another SRO crowd witnessed a goaltenders' duel that was tied 1–1 at the end of regulation. About five minutes into overtime, Rangers center Red Berenson snared a loose puck and burst over the Montreal blue line where he unleashed a 50-foot shot towards the Canadiens net. Vachon was slow to react and kicked at the puck at the last second and missed! Berenson began to raise his stick in celebration, but it was not to be. The shot hit the post and bounced harmlessly away.

Less than two minutes later Giacomin gloved a shot by Claude Larose, but dropped the puck in the crease to his left. John Ferguson swooped in and swiped at the puck and missed. Giacomin lunged for the puck but as Fergie was sliding towards the end boards he swung his stick at the loose disk again, this time knocking it into the net at 6:28 of overtime. The Garden crowd was stunned. For a few seconds the building became so quiet that the Canadiens could be heard celebrating on the ice. But then the crowd rose and gave the Blueshirts a well-deserved standing ovation. Yes, the overmatched Rangers had lost the series, but they still put up a good fight. Bernie Geoffrion was unbowed following the defeat. "The Canadiens thought it was going to be a cinch," said the Boomer. "Even though it was four straight, it was no cinch."

DONNIE MARSHALL: "The first game we played pretty well but we just didn't have enough going for us in the third period. It would have been nice if the team would have been able to gear itself down a little bit before the playoffs, but when you're struggling to get those points you can't do that."

EMILE FRANCIS: "The reason we lost in four games was that I had to use Harry Howell, Donnie Marshall, Phil Goyette, and Bob Nevin to do everything—power play, kill penalties. We just didn't have the depth to compete with Montreal. But the only way we could get into the playoffs, I had to play the shit out of those guys and we just ran out of gas. And Montreal had a powerhouse, they were loaded. But after the overtime loss the fans gave the players a standing ovation. They lost four straight games but still got a standing ovation."

BOB NEVIN: "Even though we didn't win a game we were pretty competitive against them. So we thought we were getting better, that's for sure. We didn't have a lot of depth at that point in time. Those first couple of years, it took a while to get a couple of the younger guys into the lineup and that helped a lot."

Author's note: I was fifteen years old in the spring of 1967 when the Rangers made the playoffs for the first time since I began following them about three or four years earlier.

In those days, the only way you could get playoff tickets was to be at the box office when they went on sale because they wouldn't last long. So my father stood on a pre-dawn line on a Sunday morning at the Garden waiting for the box office to open and got two tickets to each of the three possible home games. But due to a prior commitment, Pop couldn't go to the first home game, so I went with my grandmother, who was a big Toronto Maple Leafs fan. We had pretty good seats in the end balcony. It turned out that my grandmother didn't like Jean Beliveau and wasn't shy about letting him know about it, yelling "Beliveau, you're a bum!" Grandma was probably in her mid 60s then and being the fine German woman that she was, enjoyed a beer between periods and didn't see anything wrong with sharing it with me and neither did I.

Pop and I watched the fourth game from the Standing Room Only section behind the mezzanine. We had a great spot, right near center ice, so it actually wasn't that bad, except for the standing part. But we had a bar in front of us to lean on. What I remember most about John Ferguson's overtime winner was that it seemed that the entire Garden was holding its breath as the puck was sitting loose in the crease. And when Fergie knocked it past Giacomin on his second try, the place became eerily quiet. You could hear the Canadiens celebrating their victory. And finally a few seconds later the crowd rose to give the Blueshirts a standing ovation.

Rod Gilbert led the Rangers in playoff scoring with two goals and two assists. Bernie Geoffrion also scored a pair of goals for the Blueshirts. Giacomin played in all four games and gave up 14 goals, posting a 3.41 GAA.

But Francis had delivered on his two promises, that the Rangers would make the playoffs and that their postseason home games would indeed be played at Madison Square Garden. For the first time in many years it appeared that the Blueshirts were headed in the right direction.

Harry Howell Night

Harry Howell played in 1,160 games for the Rangers, a team record that, considering the current state of free agency and salary caps, will never be broken.

Howell was a product of the Rangers' Guelph Junior A team that also produced Andy Bathgate, Dean Prentice, Lou Fontinato, and Ron Murphy (who later became Harry's brother-in-law). Following two seasons in Guelph, the 6-foot-1, 195-pound native of Hamilton, Ontario, was promoted to Cincinnati of the AHL, but his stay in the minor leagues was brief. After just one game, Howell made his Ranger debut on the night of October 18, 1952, in Toronto as an emergency call-up to replace an injured defenseman. Howell scored on his first shift, lifting a long shot over the shoulder of Leafs netminder Harry Lumley. Although he was supposed to be with the Rangers for just that one game, Coach Bill Cook asked Harry to come back to New York and practice with the team. As it turned out Harry never returned to the minors and in the next sixteen seasons missed only forty games.

Howell was a steady defenseman but was not a fan favorite at first because of his style. He wasn't a physical player and didn't go out of his way to bash opponents against the boards. But fans soon came to appreciate his smart, steady, efficient play.

In 1955, Harry was named captain of the Rangers at the age of twenty-three, becoming the youngest player to wear the "C" in team history. But he gave up the captaincy to Red Sullivan two seasons later, claiming that he was just too young and citing two bad seasons while serving as captain.

When Emile Francis took over the Rangers, Howell and Donnie Marshall were both named assistant coaches. Harry was responsible for teaching the young defensemen like Arnie Brown and Rod Seiling, while Marshall mentored the younger forwards.

Two nights after he played his 1,000th game as a Ranger, Harry was honored with a night at Madison Square Garden on January 25, 1967. It was the first time the Rangers had honored an active player in that manner. Harry's family was flown in from Hamilton but an even larger contingent of family and friends missed the ceremony due to heavy fog at Kennedy Airport. He was presented with more than $10,000 worth of gifts ranging from cheeses to three different vacations to golf clubs to a Mercury Cougar which was driven onto the ice by former teammates Lou Fontinato and Red Sullivan. It was later said that Howell needed three trips in a station wagon to bring all the gifts home. He was also given a special medal by New York City mayor John V. Lindsay. And as a bonus, the Rangers beat the Bruins, 2–1, that night as well.

Harry enjoyed his best offensive season in 1966–67, scoring 12 goals and adding 28 assists for 40 points and the rest of the league took notice. Often overshadowed by defensemen like Doug Harvey, Pierre Pilote, and Tim Horton, Harry finally was given the recognition he deserved, becoming the first Ranger to receive the Norris Trophy as the league's best defenseman. Upon receiving the award Harry told reporters, "I'm glad I won it this year, because there's a guy in Boston who is going to win it for the next decade—Bobby Orr."

Johnny Bucyk for Earl Ingarfield? It Almost Happened.

Johnny Bucyk was a highly skilled left winger and at 6-feet, 215 pounds was one of the biggest forwards in the NHL at that time. He began his NHL career with Detroit but was traded to Boston after two seasons for Terry Sawchuk in 1957. Bucyk would go on to score 556 goals and 813 assists for 1,369 points in 1,540 NHL games. He also won the Lady Byng Trophy in 1971 and 1974, was a perennial All-Star, and was elected to the Hockey Hall of Fame in 1981.

Earl Ingarfield was a 5-foot-11, 180-pound center who began his Ranger career in 1958–59 and became a mainstay in 1960–61 when he centered a line with Andy Bathgate and Dean Prentice. In 527 games with the Rangers, Earl scored 122 goals with 142 assists for 264 points.

Early in the 1966–67 season the Bruins GM Hap Emms needed a center and Emile Francis was looking for a left winger to play with Jean Ratelle and Rod Gilbert, and a trade was *almost* made.

EMILE FRANCIS: "It was my second full year with the Rangers and they always used to kid that the Rangers and Boston were playing for the Patrick Trophy, who would end up in fifth place. The Bruins hired a general manager by the name of Hap Emms. So the first trip into New York I grabbed him and spent four hours with him before the game. And when I was finished with him I had made a deal. At that time I was looking for a guy to put with Ratelle and Gilbert. I made a deal for John Bucyk. And I was gonna trade him Earl Ingarfield. They needed a center and I needed a left winger.

"So, we shook hands on it, but he said, 'As far as I'm concerned I made a deal with you to trade John Bucyk for Earl Ingarfield. I'll call you tomorrow at noon. I'm new here, I've only been here a month but if [Bruins owner] Weston Adams turns this deal down I promise you that I'll quit at the end of the year.' In other words he was saying that his word was no good. I went home that night and couldn't sleep. I kept thinking if I could put Bucyk on the line with Ratelle and Gilbert would I have a powerhouse or what? But he called me the next day at noon and told me the owner turned the deal down and he quit at the end of the year. Now if I ever got Bucyk to play with Ratelle and Gilbert, Boston never would have won a Stanley Cup I'll tell you that."

Gilbert's Impressive Playoff Debut

Rod Gilbert made his Ranger debut during the 1960–61 season when he was recalled for one game and recorded an assist before being sent back to Guelph. The next season he was brought up for another game, saw little action and once again returned to juniors. But in the spring of 1962, the Rangers were making a rare playoff appearance, facing the Toronto Maple Leafs in the opening round when Gilbert was called up again to replace winger Ken Schinkel, who had suffered a broken toe in the second game of the series.

The Blueshirts had lost the first two games in Toronto and had returned home for Games Three and Four. When the 20-year old Gilbert reported to the Garden before Game Three he didn't expect to see much action. But player-coach Doug Harvey called him into his office and told him he would be playing a regular shift on a line with Dave Balon and Johnny Wilson. Gilbert, wearing number 16 on his back, had a quiet first two periods, but in the third Gilbert passed to an open Dave Balon, who slipped the puck past Johnny Bower for the eventual winning goal in the Rangers' 5–3 victory.

The newly formed Wilson-Balon-Gilbert line started the next game and Rod scored 41 seconds into the contest. Gilbert scored again near the end of the first period to give the Rangers a 2–0 lead. Toronto eventually tied the score, but late in the third period, Gilbert once again got the puck to Balon who put what proved to be the game-winner past Bower as the Rangers won, 4–2.

Unfortunately, the Rangers lost the next two games, both of which were played in Toronto because by then the circus had moved into the Garden, depriving the Blueshirts of their home ice for Game Six. But Gilbert finished the playoffs tied with Earl Ingarfield and Balon for the team lead in scoring with two goals and three assists in four games. It was the first of many impressive performances for the Blueshirts' young, flashy right-winger.

The Metropolitan Hockey League

On December 17, 2015, Emile Francis was presented with the Wayne Gretzky International Award at the US Hockey Hall of Fame induction ceremony in Boston. The award, which was established by the US Hockey Hall of Fame in 1999, is given to international individuals who have made major contributions to the growth and advancement of hockey in the United States. Francis was the ninth recipient.

"Here's a Canadian who comes to New York City in 1964 and he's concerned about helping the local kids," said US Hockey Hall of Fame member Lou Vairo. "What Emile Francis did is an unbelievable achievement that people all over hockey, and that includes America and elsewhere, should respect. What he helped do for hockey at the grassroots level, in my opinion, was worth more than twenty Stanley Cup titles."

In 1966 Emile Francis formed the Metropolitan Junior Hockey League, which is now the longest-operating junior hockey league in the United States. Emile's inspiration for the league was seeing kids playing roller hockey on the streets of the Hell's Kitchen section of Manhattan.

EMILE FRANCIS: "It was within a year of when I took over as general manager and coach. I went for a walk. I walked out of the employee's entrance of the old Garden and made a right when I got to Ninth Avenue and then I made another right and I just started to walk all by myself, thinking about what I had to do to rebuild the Rangers. And I ended up in Hell's Kitchen and I saw these kids playing hockey on roller skates. Now I'd never seen anyone play hockey on roller skates and here they were playing just as naturally as you would play on ice. So I turned around and went back to the Garden but that stayed in my mind and I kept thinking about those kids on roller skates.

"The main thing I had to do was build a hockey team but I also had to build a fan base. So I sold it to the Garden as once they've played the game of hockey they'll be hockey fans for the rest of their lives. It took me a while to research it but I found out there were about five thousand kids in New York alone on roller skates. So I thought that's a whole area that we haven't looked into. I'm gonna start a junior league like we had up in Canada. You could play up until you were twenty years old but I had to find ice for them to play on.

"So the first thing I had to do was get Madison Square Garden in the fold. I arranged a meeting with Bill Jennings and Irving Felt, I explained what had happened and I said I'd like to start with a six team junior league, all kids up to twenty years old. But I need the Garden. I need a place where I can start. Like on Wednesdays and Sundays if I can have the building from one to five and run a doubleheader. They did this all the time at Maple Leaf Gardens, they'd run two junior games with the clock running and they'd run it off in about four hours and then we'd have a couple hours to get the ice clean and get the place ready for our game at night. And we'd let them all in for nothing because we're gonna key in on the people who are coming to see their kids play. By coming to see the games they'll see Madison Square Garden and furthermore once a kid plays hockey he'll always be a fan, even when he's finished playing. And I told them that after a while we can develop players to play in the National Hockey League. So right away Irving Felt jumped in and asked, 'How long do you think it would take to develop a New York kid to play for the Rangers?' I pulled a number out of left field. I told him I think we could develop some kids within ten years. I think that sold the idea when I said ten years. He said let me think about that and a couple of days later they agreed to do it.

"So then I had to find teams and places to play. We got a team from Hell's Kitchen right off the bat, Joey Mullen came from there and his brother Brian. I hired John Muckler to run the league because I knew I didn't have time because I was GM and coach at the time. Muckler was coach of the Long Island Ducks and I made him the president of the league and he could also do a lot of scouting for me. And the first guy to come out of the league was Nicky Fotiu nine years later."

The Met League began with six teams: The West New York (NJ) Raiders, Riverdale Rams, White Plains Plainsmen, New York Green Leafs, New Hyde Park Arrows, and Commack Jets. Two more teams were added the following season and the league was split into two divisions. The league is currently comprised of fifteen teams along the Eastern seaboard from Connecticut through New York, New Jersey, and Pennsylvania. They play a twenty-four-week season culminating with the playoffs for the Foster Cup, named after league commissioner Richard Foster. Among the former Met League players who have gone on to the NHL are: Brian and Joey Mullen, Nick Fotiu, Mike Richter, Jim Dowd, Mark Eaton, and Mike Komisarek.

Emile's dedication to youth hockey didn't end when he left the Rangers. During the time he was executive vice president, general manager, and coach of the St. Louis Blues, he formed the St. Louis Metro Junior B League. In addition, he was awarded the Lester Patrick Trophy in 1982 for his contributions to hockey in the United States, and that same year was inducted into the Hockey Hall of Fame in the Builders category.

EMILE FRANCIS: "The best thing was in 1989 we had an All-Star game in Edmonton and I remember I was there with my wife and that's one of the proudest moments of my life. On one blue line for the Western team was Joe Mullen and on the Eastern team was his brother Brian. I'm telling you I was actually crying. These two guys came out of Hell's Kitchen in New York where I'd first seen hockey played on roller skates, both playing in an All-Star game in the National Hockey League. That was one of the proudest moments I've had in hockey. To see these two guys given the opportunity. My own kids played in that league and they ended up with college scholarships."

5

1967–68

Six New Teams and a New Garden

MAJOR CHANGES WERE on the horizon for both the NHL and the Rangers as the 1967–68 season began. The league doubled in size, expanding from six to twelve teams, adding franchises in Philadelphia, Pittsburgh, Minnesota, St. Louis, Los Angeles, and Oakland. The Rangers also experienced a major change themselves, moving from the old Madison Square Garden on Eighth Avenue and 49th Street, which had been their home since their inception in 1926 to a new building located on Seventh Avenue and 33rd Street.

The expansion draft to stock the new teams was held on June 6, 1967, with each existing team being allowed to protect eleven skaters and one goaltender. The Rangers lost twenty players in the draft including goaltender Cesare Maniago, who was selected by Minnesota. Other players drafted were Wayne Rutledge (Los Angeles), Larry Cahan (Oakland), Ron Boehm (Oakland), Bryan Hextall (Oakland), Bryan Campbell (Los Angeles), Doug Robinson (Los Angeles), Ken Block (Los Angeles), Marc DuFour (Los Angeles), Bill Collins (Minnesota),

Sandy Fitzpatrick (Minnesota), Jim Johnson (Philadelphia), Terry Ball (Philadelphia), Earl Ingarfield (Pittsburgh), Al MacNeil (Pittsburgh), Ken Schinkel (Pittsburgh), Les Hunt (Pittsburgh), Billy Hicke (Oakland), Rod Seiling (St. Louis), and Max Mestinsek (St. Louis).

Later that same day, Seiling was reacquired from St. Louis in exchange for Gary Sabourin, Bob Plager, Gord Kannegiesser, and Tim Ecclestone. "Emile told me that he was getting me back," Seiling later commented. "I was surprised but not disappointed when he brought me back, because he wouldn't have done it if he didn't believe in me."

The Rangers weren't hurt too badly by the draft. Of the players selected only Ingarfield, Schinkel, and MacNeil saw significant ice time during the previous season and each was getting on in years. However, there were still some gaps in the lineup so Francis made three deals to acquire veterans Larry Jeffrey, Camille Henry, and Ron Stewart.

Larry Jeffrey was a twenty-seven-year-old checking forward who was acquired from the Pittsburgh Penguins in exchange for George Konik, Paul Andrea, Dunc McCallum, and Frank Francis following the expansion draft. Jeffrey had previously played for Detroit and Toronto and was a member of the Stanley Cup-winning Leafs squad in 1967.

Camille Henry was reacquired from the Chicago Black Hawks for Paul Shmyr in August of 1967. "The Eel" was one of the Rangers' most popular players before he was dealt to the Black Hawks in 1965. The thirty-four-year-old left winger was expected to add offense to the Rangers' power play.

Ron Stewart, a fifteen-year veteran, was acquired from the St. Louis Blues in exchange for Red Berenson in November 1967. The thirty-five-year-old winger won three Stanley Cups as a member of the Toronto Maple Leafs and was expected to play a defensive role as well as provide veteran leadership with the Rangers. Berenson had been a disappointment, recording only two goals and six assists in 49 games with New York. Ironically his final game with the Rangers was against St. Louis and he must have made a positive impression because the Blues traded for him the next day. Berenson blossomed in the Gateway City, scoring 22 goals during the remainder of the 1967–68 season and adding 84 tallies over the next three years. He helped the Blues get to the Stanley Cup finals three straight times and became the first NHL player to score six goals in a game on the road when the Blues beat the Flyers 8–0 at the Spectrum in November 1968.

As the season began the Rangers jumped off to a 6–1–3 start, but cooled off and fell into a 10–12–3 streak through the end of 1967. They caught fire again in early February and finished the season on a high note, going 17–5–4 in their last twenty-six games. Ed Giacomin registered four shutouts during the streak, including back-to-back whitewashings of Philadelphia and Chicago. When Giacomin finally did surrender a goal against Detroit on March 6, the Garden crowd gave him a standing ovation in appreciation of his efforts. "It was the first time I ever got cheered for allowing a goal," Giacomin later told reporters. "It was quite a thrill."

The highlight of the season came on Saturday night, February 24, when Rod Gilbert scored four goals and added an assist in the Rangers' 6–1 victory over the Canadiens at the Forum. Gilbert also set a team record with 16 shots on goal that night. Their victory snapped the Canadiens' 20-game unbeaten streak, but Gilbert's five-point night earned him cheers from the Forum crowd.

Author's note: I remember that night. My father and I were sitting in the living room watching the game on TV and when Gilbert scored his fourth goal, Pop got up, went in the kitchen and got us both a beer. It was the first time he ever did that so he must have been impressed by Gilbert's performance.

At the other end of the spectrum was the evening of December 23, when the Rangers launched 41 shots at theBruins third-string net-minder Andre Gill, who was a rookie playing in his first NHL game and couldn't beat him. Gill was playing because both Gerry Cheevers and Ed Johnston were out with injuries. The Bruins' backup goaltender that night was a guy named Wayne Doll who was called up from the Long Island Ducks of the Eastern League for the game. It was the only shutout of Gill's short five-game NHL career.

The Blueshirts finished the season in second place with a 39–23–12 record for 90 points, setting team records for victories and points. Their 39 victories represented nine more wins than the previous season and they also improved their goals for and goals against totals, scoring 38 more goals and surrendering six fewer than in 1966–67. Like most of the Original Six teams, the Rangers cleaned up against the new expansion clubs, posting a combined 17–4–3 record for 37 points out of a possible 48. They also outscored the new clubs by an 83–45 margin.

The newly formed Goal-A-Game (G-A-G) line set the pace for the rest of the Blueshirts with Jean Ratelle, Rod Gilbert, and Vic Hadfield each having their best season to date.

Ratelle (32-46-78), who was fully recovered from back surgery, led the team in goals, points, and power-play goals (10) and finished fourth in the NHL scoring race. Gilbert (29-48-77) led the team in assists, and Hadfield (20-19-39) reached the 20-goal plateau for the first time in his career.

The G-A-G line became one of the most famous trios in Ranger history. They played together from the 1967–68 season until 1974 when Hadfield was traded to Pittsburgh and averaged at least a goal a game throughout their time together. The line was formed by Emile Francis out of necessity when it became obvious that he needed to protect two of his best players.

EMILE FRANCIS: "One night we were playing in Toronto and by this time Gilbert and Ratelle were on a line and I had Camille Henry playing with them and Camille Henry weighed 138 pounds. So midway through the second period we're leading 1–0 and I put out Ratelle, Gilbert, and Henry and Punch Imlach, manager and coach of Toronto, puts out his goons, including Eddie Shack. Well I'll tell you, fifteen seconds after the puck was dropped, three guys were lying on the ice, Gilbert, Ratelle, and Henry. So our trainer, Frank Paice, says to me 'Where should I go first?' I said, go to Ratelle.

"So now we're on a little Air Canada charter flight going back to New York after the game and I'm sitting up front and I was so pissed off. I said this will never happen again, not as long as I'm around here. So the next day I had a meeting before the game and I told Hadfield, 'From now on I'm putting you on the line with Ratelle and Gilbert. And if anyone touches any one of those two guys, you kick the shit out of them.' So that was the start of the GAG line and guys would come up to me and say, 'Geez, what a brilliant move putting Hadfield on that line, how did you know he'd end up being a goalscorer?' It was brilliant, all right. I put him there to protect those two guys as a matter of necessity. But he wound up being a fifty-goal scorer."

The line got their nickname when *New York Post* sports columnist Milton Gross was writing a column about them and needed a catchy moniker. He asked Ranger statistician Art "The Dart" Friedman for a suggestion. Friedman, who had a knack for nicknames, came up with G-A-G line for goal-a-game line. The name stuck and was occasionally changed to the T-A-G line (two-a-game) depending on the trio's production.

Phil Goyette scored 25 goals for the first time in his career and Arnie Brown (1-25-26) more than doubled his best overall NHL single season totals to date. Ed Giacomin finished with a 2.44 GAA, the lowest of his career to that point and led the league in games played (66), victories (36), and shutouts (8). Don Simmons appeared in five games, going 2–1–2 with a 2.60 GAA, and Gilles Villemure saw action in four games, posting a 2.40 GAA with one shutout. Giacomin, Gilbert, and Jim Neilson were named to the league's second All-Star squad. Donnie Marshall, Harry Howell, and Giacomin also played in the midseason All-Star game.

The Playoffs

The Rangers' first-round opponents in the playoffs were the fourth-place Chicago Black Hawks. The Blueshirts had barely won the season series, 4–3–3, from the Hawks, who were a strong offensive club with Bobby Hull and Stan Mikita, but weaker defensively. Their 222 goals against were the second most in the East Division behind last place Detroit's 257.

Surprisingly, the main question surrounding the Rangers was Ed Giacomin's ability to stop the potent Black Hawk attack. Giacomin had posted a 3–1–1 regular-season record including a shutout against Chicago, but his 3.35 GAA was higher than against any other team and Francis sat him out for four games against Chicago in January, preferring to start Don Simmons instead.

Oddly enough, the Rangers had never scored a playoff goal against Chicago, having met them in the postseason only once, in 1931, and being shut out twice in a two-game series.

The series began at Madison Square Garden on Thursday, April 4 with a dominating 3–1 Rangers victory on goals by Rod Gilbert, Orland Kurtenbach, and Harry Howell. Unfortunately that same evening, Dr. Martin Luther King Jr. was assassinated in Memphis, Tennessee, by James Earl Ray.

Game Two, which was originally scheduled for Sunday, April 7, was postponed when President Lyndon B. Johnson declared a national day of mourning. The game was rescheduled for April 9, but the delay may have worked in Chicago's favor. Not only did it stall the Rangers' momentum, it also gave several of the Black Hawks' injured players time to rest and recuperate as well as allowing coach Billy Reay to try out different line combinations in an effort to get Bobby Hull on the ice without being shadowed by Ron Stewart.

EMILE FRANCIS: "We beat Chicago in New York the night Martin Luther King was assassinated. So then we got a call from Clarence Campbell because we were supposed to play two nights later. So, he says, 'We'll have to postpone the game because they've already got riots in Chicago and you'll probably have them in New York, too.' So as a result instead of playing on Sunday we didn't play until Tuesday."

The Rangers also learned that they would be without one of their emotional leaders, Boom Boom Geoffrion, for the remainder of the playoffs due to a bleeding ulcer. But the Rangers won the second game, 2–1, on goals by Gilbert and Marshall and went into Chicago with a commanding two games to none lead.

EMILE FRANCIS: "When we got to Chicago you could hear bang, bang, bang. There were fires all over the place. The firemen were trying to put fires out and they were shooting at them. And the only reason that Chicago Stadium didn't get damaged was that they put the Nation Guard in there and that saved the stadium. So I'm thinking to myself,

What the hell are they doing playing here? Christ, there'll be nobody at the game. But the place was sold out. The place was packed."

In the third game, the Rangers led, 3–2, going into the third period, but then the roof caved in as Pit Martin, Stan Mikita, and Dennis Hull scored three unanswered goals in the first nine minutes of the period to pull the Black Hawks ahead, 5–3. Rod Seiling scored late in the period to bring the Blueshirts within a goal but Doug Mohns then scored to restore Chicago's two-goal lead. Gilles Marotte's empty-netter clinched the 7–4 victory. The game was not without its high point for the Rangers, however, as Rod Gilbert set a team record by scoring two goals in 16 seconds in the second period.

Chicago then evened the series by winning the fourth game, 3–1. Despite the loss, Ed Giacomin stood tall in the Rangers crease, facing a total of 44 shots from the Black Hawks, including 23 in the first period alone and 10 within a five minute span in the period. Defenseman Gilles Marotte scored the game-winner on a shot that deflected off Orland Kurtenbach.

The series returned to Madison Square Garden for the fifth game. The contest was tied, 1–1, with 3:14 left in the third period when Chicago's twenty-three-year-old rookie winger Bobby Schmautz, who had scored only three goals all season, was at center ice trying to get off for a line change. He slapped the puck towards the Rangers net, turned and skated off the ice. But what seemed to be a perfectly harmless play turned into a disaster for the Rangers. The shot deflected off defenseman Jim Neilson's stick and flew over Ed Giacomin's left shoulder and into the Rangers' net. The crowd was stunned and so were the Rangers. Final score, Chicago 2, Rangers 1, and for the second game in a row, the game-winning goal went in off a Rangers stick.

The goal by Schmautz was the turning point in the game as well as the series. It seemed to take the life out of the Rangers and two days later the Black Hawks went on to take the sixth game in Chicago, 4–1, and oust the Blueshirts four games to two.

Rod Gilbert led the Rangers in playoff scoring with five goals while Jean Ratelle registered four assists. Donnie Marshall (2-1-3) and Vic

Hadfield (1-2-3) also performed well offensively for the Rangers. Stan Mikita led the Black Hawks with three goals and six assists. Ron Stewart, who registered a goal and an assist, was assigned the task of shadowing Bobby Hull and held the Golden Jet to two goals and three assists. Ed Giacomin surrendered 17 goals (Chicago also scored an empty-netter) in the six-game series for a 2.83 GAA. But Chicago's Denis DeJordy was just a little bit better, allowing only 12 goals for a 2.00 GAA.

ROD SEILING: "We won the first two games hands down and if the series had not been delayed I would bet anything that we would have won four straight. But the series turned around. We lost a bit of our edge, we lost our momentum and Chicago was able to gain some stability back. I don't think they would've won a game if it hadn't been for the delay. But it was very unfortunate, but also very important time in American history. It is what it is."

The 1967 Expansion

In 1967 the National Hockey League doubled in size, expanding from six to twelve teams. It was the most ambitious single-season expansion of any professional sport.

Rangers president Bill Jennings planted the seeds for expansion with a 1963 memo to his fellow NHL governors pushing for two new teams on the West Coast. At the time there was a fear that the Western Hockey League planned to expand and compete with the NHL as a major league. In fact, the next season the WHL refused to sign their minor-league agreement that they would be a feeder league for the NHL. It was thought that placing expansion teams on the West Coast would deter the WHL's plans. Jennings also wanted to expand the NHL's footprint in order to get a national television contract. He originally wanted the two new teams in place by the beginning of the 1964–65 season.

The NHL announced their expansion plans in March of 1965 and began accepting bids from interested cities. The cost of a franchise was $2 million, a figure that one NHL governor later admitted was "pulled out of the air." In addition to the entrance fee, the teams needed to show that they had adequate funding and access to an arena in good repair with seating for at least 12,500. At first there was a fear that not enough cities would be interested, but fourteen bids were submitted including four from Los Angeles and two from Pittsburgh. At the NHL governors meeting on February 8, 1966, the league announced the six new franchises: Los Angeles, Oakland, Pittsburgh, Philadelphia, St. Louis, and Minnesota.

Bids from Baltimore, Buffalo, and Vancouver were rejected. The league awarded a franchise to St. Louis even though they had not submitted an acceptable bid. This was because the St. Louis arena was owned by the Wirtz (Chicago) and Norris (Detroit) families. St. Louis had until April to submit an acceptable bid, or else the franchise would be awarded to Baltimore.

The method of stocking the new clubs with players was also a matter of contention within the NHL's boardroom. League president Clarence Campbell wanted a plan that would allow the existing teams to protect only nine players, thus making the new teams more competitive from the start. The governors of the existing teams wanted to be able to protect fourteen players. A compromise was reached that would allow the teams to protect one goaltender and eleven skaters. Montreal GM Sam Pollock also devised a way for the existing teams to lose even fewer quality players by using a "claim-and-fill" method whereby once a player has been drafted from a team, that team could then add another player to their protected list.

The draft was held on June 6, 1967. In typical NHL fashion, the draft order was picked out of a hat. Terry Sawchuk was the first goaltender chosen, going from Toronto to Los Angeles. The first skater selected was Dave Balon, being picked by Minnesota from the Montreal unprotected list. Other notable players selected were Glenn Hall, Andy Bathgate, and Bobby Baun.

The Rangers' original protected list included: Ed Giacomin, Arnie Brown, Rod Gilbert, Phil Goyette, Vic Hadfield, Wayne Hillman, Harry Howell, Orland Kurtenbach, Donnie Marshall, Bob Nevin, Jim Neilson, and Jean Ratelle. Players added to the list included: Gilles Villemure, Reg Fleming, Red Berenson, Larry Mickey, Bob Plager, Paul Andrea, George Konik, Gary Sabourin, Dunc McCallum, Bob Jones, Bob Blackburn, Bob Ash, Billy Knibbs, Ron Ingram, Gord Vesprava, and Wayne Hall.

To accommodate the six new teams, the season started earlier, ended later, and now included coast-to-coast air travel. The league was restructured into two divisions. The established teams were in the Eastern Division and the expansion teams in the Western Division. The season was expanded to seventy-four games featuring ten games against each conference rival and four games against teams from the other conference.

The New Garden

On November 3, 1960, Garden chairman and president Irving Mitchell Felt announced that plans were being made to build a new Madison Square Garden at an undetermined site. A few days later Felt received a letter from J. W. Ewalt, VP of Real Estate for the Pennsylvania Railroad, offering the air rights to the two-block area occupied by Penn Station in midtown Manhattan. The parties came to terms and in 1963 the process of razing the Pennsylvania Station structure began. The project was not without problems as public outcry over the demolition of the building, which was considered by many as an outstanding example of Beaux-Arts architecture, led to the creation of the New York City Landmarks Preservation Commission.

Ground was broken for the Garden complex in October of 1964. The new arena would be the fourth building to bear the Madison Square Garden name.

The first "Garden" was an old railroad shed in Madison Square Park that P. T. Barnum had previously leased as a hippodrome in 1874. The building changed hands a number of times until it was taken over in 1879 by William K. Vanderbilt and officially named Madison Square Garden. That building was replaced by a new, more elaborate structure at the same location which opened on June 16, 1890, with an Eduard Strauss concert and ballet.

The third Madison Square Garden was a barn of a building, built on Eighth Avenue between 49th and 50th Streets in a remarkable 249 days at a cost of $5,600,000. It was primarily built for boxing but opened on November 28, 1925, with a six-day bicycle race.

Except for the famous marquee at the front entrance, the third Garden could easily be mistaken for one of the many warehouses or office buildings in the area. That marquee, which proudly displayed "MADISON SQ GARDEN" in capital letters on all three sides (the "Q" on the 49th street side was crooked), led to the main entrance which housed a Nedicks hot dog stand on the right and Adam Hats and Regal Shoes stores on the left.

The Garden could hold 15,284 spectators (15,925 including standees) for hockey but could only accommodate a 185-foot by 85-foot sheet of ice.

The building hosted everything from basketball and boxing to bowling, tennis matches, skiing competitions, animated bridge tournaments, rodeos, circuses, roller derby, and fire department exhibitions. It was where Marilyn Monroe famously sang "Happy Birthday Mr. President" to John F. Kennedy at a fund-raising event for the Democratic Party in May of 1962 and was used as a location for the 1962 film version of *The Manchurian Candidate* starring Frank Sinatra, Laurence Harvey, and Angela Lansbury.

In later years, the Garden was known for being a dark, smoky place with a lot of stairs. But what the old Garden lacked in creature comforts, it made up for in its rickety charm. The seats were wooden and sometimes broken and steel girders often blocked the view of the game, but most of the seats were so close to the ice that spectators could easily feel as if they were part of the game.

BOB NEVIN: "They had the balcony all around the ice and I was thinking one of these days somebody's gonna be falling over on to the ice."

Like the rest of the Original Six arenas, the Garden had it quirks and characters.

Fans with tickets for the balcony entered the building through a portal on 49th Street, where they then had to climb flights of stairs to reach their seats. Patrons who held tickets for the lower section and mezzanine entered through the main entrance on Eighth Avenue beneath the iconic marquee.

Ticket prices were very affordable by today's standards, and metropolitan area high school students could use their G.O. (General

Organization) card to buy balcony tickets at a discounted rate. Side balcony tickets were the least expensive since most of them offered an obstructed view of the ice. Because the Garden was originally built for boxing, the side balconies extended over the ice, making it impossible to see the action along the near boards unless you were sitting in the first two rows. In fact, for many years, side balcony seats were not assigned; there were no seat numbers on the tickets so it was first come, first served and fans had to race upstairs to get a good seat. Some sections were "controlled" by veteran fans that would arrive early and "save" the better seats which were then sold for monetary contributions. However a seat in the end balcony or corners usually provided a very good view of the ice.

The Garden also had its characters, in the form of devoted fans, that became familiar to the players and the rest of the crowd as well.

Sally Lark was a buxom, platinum blonde interior decorator from Brooklyn who was a fixture at the Garden during the 1940s and 1950s. Her seat was directly adjacent to the penalty box that, in those days, was used by both teams with players separated only by an attendant. Her location earned her the nickname "Sin Bin Sally" and provided her with significant television exposure. "My friends used to tell me I would like hockey," Sally told *Sports Illustrated* in 1957, "but I was only interested in baseball. They insisted I go with them to the opening game of the 1942 season. So, I went and, sure enough, they were right. From that day to this, I've missed only about ten of the Rangers home games." Since there weren't any glass partitions separating spectators and players in those early days, Miss Lark had ample opportunity to talk to the players while they were sitting out their sentence. "It's better not to talk to them at first," she said. "They're not in very good humor. But if a player gets a major penalty he usually has time to cool off before he leaves the box. Then, maybe, we speak."

Sally was the center of quite an uproar during the 1957 Stanley Cup playoffs. The Canadiens were playing the Rangers at the Garden and the games were being televised back to Montreal. Each time the camera zoomed in on the penalty box there was the lovely Miss Lark, seemingly planted there by the Rangers to distract the Habs. Canadiens fans were irate and wrote letters to the newspapers but were later calmed down when it was proven that Sally was indeed a devoted fan and season ticket holder and not a ploy to derail the Canadiens.

Herbert Khaury, better known as Tiny Tim of "Tiptoe Through the Tulips" fame, and a native of Washington Heights, was a huge Toronto Maple Leafs fan, and was a regular at the Garden during the mid-1960s. His disheveled appearance, falsetto voice, unkempt hair, and crammed shopping bags would often disrupt fans in the side promenade. The players used to call him "Alice" and being a Maple Leafs fan in the Garden wasn't pleasant either. "The fans used to throw beer at me when I sat in the balcony," he recalled in a 1969 interview. "But then I got a good seat by the ice where I sat with my big Leafs button and pennant."

And then there was "The Trombone Guy," otherwise known as John Gerecitano, who was a long-time season ticket holder. Wearing a gold lamé jacket and beret, Gerecitano would play a few bars on his trombone upon arrival to let everyone know that he was there. Then he would take his seat in the Ninth Avenue end of the Garden and not be heard from again unless the Rangers were losing by a lopsided score, in which case he would play "Taps." A tailor by trade, he designed his own clothing and ran John G. Originals on 48th Street in Brooklyn. He would also often toss bags of peanuts to nearby fans.

The final hockey game at the old barn was played on the afternoon of February 11, 1968. The Rangers invited sixty of the greatest players that appeared on the Garden's ice back for a pregame ceremony. Players such as Frank Boucher, Bill and Bun Cook, Ching Johnson, Leo Bourgeault, Davey Kerr, Bryan Hextall, Murray Murdoch, Andy Bathgate, Bill Gadsby, Lynn and Muzz Patrick, Wally Stanowski, Turk Broda, Eddie Shore, Ted Lindsay, Dit Clapper, Milt Schmidt, Maurice Richard, and Jacques Plante along with referees Bill Chadwick, Cooper Smeaton, and Frank Udvari donned sweaters from their old teams and took the ice to the cheers of the sellout crowd. Gordie Howe, who was playing for Detroit, the Blueshirts' opponents that day, was also introduced as well as former Montreal great Aurel Joliat, then sixty-seven, who delighted the crowd by skating figure eights at center ice. Bill Cook became emotional and told reporters, "So many of my memories are in these walls."

WALLY STANOWSKI, *Defenseman, 1948–51*: New York was a first-class outfit. Not like the Leafs who were always cheap and they didn't care too much about the players. At that closing ceremony, we all put our skates on and we were all introduced and skated out to the middle of the ice. And then we watched the game, the Rangers played Detroit and that same evening they opened up the new Garden. But that was the difference between the Leafs and New York. New York invited every hockey player who ever made the first or second all-star team and you could bring your wife if you wanted to and they looked after everything, the hotels and meals and everything and when they opened the new Garden we got seats that were $250 which was pretty high in those days. We were about four rows back. There was a boxing ring in the center and Jack Dempsey and Joe Louis were there and they were sparring and Bob Hope and Bing Crosby were there. And what a meal we had too. But the Rangers were a first-class organization."

The Rangers and Red Wings battled to a 3–3 tie. Jean Ratelle redirected a pass from Rod Gilbert to score the final goal in the old building, beating Roger Crozier. At the end of the game, organist Gladys Goodding played "Auld Lang Syne" and there wasn't a dry eye in the house.

That same night the new Garden opened with a gala fundraising event for the USO hosted by Bing Crosby and Bob Hope.

A week later on February 18, the Rangers played their first game in the new Garden, hosting the Philadelphia Flyers. Wayne Hicks of Philadelphia scored the first goal in the new building against Ed Giacomin. Phil Goyette scored the first Ranger goal against Doug Favell in the Rangers' 3–1 victory.

The new Garden was located on the corner of 33rd Street and Seventh Avenue. It was designed by Charles Luckman and built by Robert E. McKee of El Paso, Texas, at a cost of $123 million. It was the first arena to be built on a platform over an active railroad station.

Irving Mitchell Felt's vision for the new building was a multi-purpose complex in which a number of events could be held simultaneously, and he got what he paid for.

The new building was thirteen stories high and housed seven separate facilities, including the arena with approximately 20,000 upholstered seats (depending on the event). Other facilities included: the 5,000-seat Felt Forum, an art gallery, forty-eight-lane bowling center, exposition rotunda, a 486-seat cinema and the Madison Square Garden Hall of Fame. The complex also included a twenty-nine-story office building which was connected to the arena by a wide, glass enclosed mall.

As it turned out, the new Garden had everything except a press box. That not-so-minor detail was overlooked by the designers and apparently by everyone else until it was time to open for business. Hastily, the rear of the mezzanine section was set up for the press corps, but that location was very far from the ice. So another section near the organ on the Eighth Avenue end of the building was used for the team's local beat writers.

For the Rangers, moving to the new building meant playing their home games on the larger 200-foot-long rink, fifteen feet longer than the surface at the old Garden. The larger ice surface didn't worry Francis who told reporters, "If you've got good players, you can do well on any size rink. I don't care if it's a fish pond. We've always played well on the larger rinks."

The move to the new Garden also gave the Rangers the opportunity to enter the modern age of ice maintenance. Francis urged the Garden to purchase a Zamboni ice resurfacer and have it delivered to the new building before the first game. The machine was sent from California by air to New York but upon its arrival, sat idle because the arena employees were not sure how to operate it.

EMILE FRANCIS: "We always had the worst ice in the league and when we moved I said we're gonna get better ice. So, I bought a Zamboni for $60,000. So, we moved in February and I always remember the guys that used to push the wheel barrels around the ice, one of them looked just like Yogi Berra, it could have been his brother. So, it was the third game in the new Garden and in between the first and second period it seemed to be taking a long time. So, I went out to see what the hell was going on and here's the guys pushing the goddamn barrels around.

"So then the games over and I finish with the press and I run down to where the workmen were and one guy was Joey Mullen's father. So, I said, 'What the hell are you guys doing, I got a $60,000 Zamboni sitting there and you guys are still pushing those barrels around.' So, one of them says, 'Nobody knows how to drive it.' I said, 'Oh shit!' It never entered my mind who was gonna drive it. So, I had to bring in a guy from Canada to drive the Zamboni and be our equipment manager. And he taught these guys how to drive that Zamboni and you gotta know how to drive it. I remember one night I was scouting out in San Francisco and after the first period, I see this guy zooming around in the Zamboni and I said, that guy's gonna go right through the rink. Sure enough, at the end of the second period, he went right through the end of the rink. The game was held up for about thirty minutes. They had to get big plywood boards up to cover where he drove through."

A Day-Night Doubleheader at the Garden

Less than a month after the new Madison Square Garden opened, the building was the site of the rarest of rarities—a National Hockey League doubleheader.

The twinbill was made necessary when high winds blew part of the roof off of the Spectrum in Philadelphia, the home of the Flyers. The problems started a few weeks earlier on February 17 during an afternoon performance of the Ice Capades. A sudden gust of wind ripped away a 50-by-100-foot section of the Spectrum's roof and sent it crashing into the parking lot. The building was closed while the damage was assessed and repairs were made.

But two weeks later on March 1, the roof took flight again. This time Mayor James H. J. Tate, whose administration had been criticized for the sweetheart deal it awarded developer Jerry Wolman, shut down the building until a full investigation was made. Wolman had been one of the founding owners of the Flyers before selling his share to Ed Snider. He also owned Connie Mack Stadium and the Philadelphia Eagles of the NFL.

The Flyers co-tenants, the 76ers of the NBA, moved their remaining games to nearby Convention Hall and to the Palestra. The Flyers were not that lucky since neither of those buildings had ice-making facilities.

They were forced to hurriedly move their next home game against the Oakland Seals, which was being televised nationally, to Madison Square Garden.

Fans that had a ticket for that evening's Rangers–Chicago matchup were admitted to the Flyers matinee game for free. A crowd of 12,127 showed up for the Flyers' 1–1 tie with the Seals. The Rangers then shut out Chicago 4–0 in the nightcap.

The Flyers lost their next "home" game, 2–1, to the Boston Bruins, which was played at Maple Leaf Gardens in Toronto. The game featured a vicious stick-swinging duel between Flyers defenseman Larry Zeidel and Eddie Shack of the Bruins. Shack later said that Zeidel speared him while Zeidel claimed that he was retaliating for anti-Semitic slurs coming from the Bruins bench, but not specifically from Shack. Both players were badly bloodied and later suspended, Zeidel for four games and Shack for three. Both were also fined $300.

There had been bad blood between the two since the late 1950s when both were playing in the American Hockey League, Shack with Springfield and Zeidel with Hershey. During a preseason game Zeidel speared Shack multiple times and the pair got into a brawl and were ejected from the game. Later, while in their street clothes, the two got into another fight outside the locker rooms. The police were called and both spent the night in jail.

The Flyers finally set up a base of operations at Le Colisee in Quebec City, the home of their top minor league team at the time.

In total, the Flyers played seven "home" games at neutral site locations, posting a 3–2–2 record. They were permitted to return to the Spectrum by the opening round of the playoffs against the Blues on April 4.

Camille "The Eel" Henry

Camille Henry made his Ranger debut in 1953 and over time became one of the team's most popular players as well as their captain.

Born in Quebec City, Quebec, on January 31, 1933, Henry originally had hopes of becoming a professional baseball player, but that dream soon gave way to another when his outstanding hockey skills became apparent.

After rising through the local youth leagues, Camille moved up to the powerful and popular Quebec Citadelles of the Quebec Junior Hockey League where he was expected to fill the rather large skates of Jean Beliveau. Beliveau, a 6-foot-2, 195-pound center was so revered in Quebec that his popularity and grace were often compared to New York Yankees center fielder Joe DiMaggio. But what Beliveau had in size, the scrawny 5-foot-7, 138-pound Henry offered in brains, desire, and hockey sense, and he went on to lead the QJHL with 55 and 46 goals his last two seasons.

Camille's next step up hockey's ladder was to the Rangers in 1953–54 where he was used mostly as a power-play specialist. Henry made the most of every opportunity, scoring 24 goals and winning the Calder Trophy as the NHL's outstanding rookie, beating out Beliveau, who was then beginning his career with the Montreal Canadiens.

Late in that season, Camille scored four goals in a game against Detroit's legendary netminder Terry Sawchuk, who was considered by many to be the best goaltender to ever strap on a pair of pads. It was the first time any player had scored that many goals against Sawchuk in a single game. "That four goal night won the Calder trophy for me," Henry told reporters. "It also cost Sawchuk the Vezina Trophy and a first team All-Star berth. I ran into him a few weeks later. 'You little French baboon' he said to me. I guess I cost him a couple of thousand dollars." In addition, all four of Camille's goals were scored on the power play, a Rangers record that still stands today.

The next season, however, Camille got off to a slow start and was sent to the Providence Reds, who then loaned him to the Quebec Aces of the QHL. In 1955–56 he was back with Providence where he led the team with 50 goals in just 59 games and set a league record by scoring six goals in a game.

Cammy returned to the NHL for good in January of 1957 and won the Lady Byng Trophy the next season. Camille reached double digits in goals ten times as a Ranger and topped the 30-goal mark twice while never being called for more than eight minutes in penalties until the 1964–65 season when he amassed a total of 20 minutes in 49 games. He notched a career-high 37 goals in 1962–63 and was named captain of the Rangers in February of 1964 when Andy Bathgate was dealt to Toronto.

Henry specialized in deflections in front of the net and he had a deadly wrist shot, but his uncanny ability to use his small stature to avoid crunching body checks earned him the nickname "The Eel." Once when asked by a reporter which player he had ever hurt with a body check, Henry replied: "Camille Henry, that's who."

Cammy was one of the most popular Rangers of all time and Muzz Patrick was well aware of his publicity value. Once when Henry was in St. Clare's hospital recovering from an injury, Patrick had photographers present as he signed the winger to a new contract. Camille was also prominently placed in the Rangers' annual photo shoots with the ladies from the Ice Capades. Camille was married at one time to the famed Quebec singer/actress Dominique Michel.

Henry's Broadway run ended on February 4, 1965, when he was traded to Chicago with Don Johns, Wally Chevrier, and Billy Taylor for Doug Robinson, Wayne Hillman, and John Brenneman. He was later reacquired by the Rangers in exchange for Paul Shmyr in August 1967. Cammy was on the ice with Jean Ratelle and Rod Gilbert for the opening faceoff at the new Garden on February 18, 1968. But the NHL was getting bigger and Henry, one of the smallest players to ever make it to the big leagues, wasn't. He was once again traded away, this time to St. Louis with Bill Plager and Robbie Irons for Don Caley and Wayne Rivers in June of 1968. He retired following the 1969–70 season.

In 637 games as a Ranger, Henry recorded 256 goals, 222 assists, 478 points, and only 78 penalty minutes. Overall, he compiled 279 goals, 249 assists, 528 points, and 88 penalty minutes in 727 NHL games for the Rangers, Black Hawks, and Blues.

He became the first coach of the New York Raiders of the WHA and later moved behind the bench of the Kansas City Blues of the Central Hockey League. He also had a radio show in Montreal and worked at Ice World in Totowa, New Jersey. Unfortunately, his life took a downward spiral and he drifted from job to job and lived the last years of his life in virtual poverty.

Camille Henry was one of the few bright lights in many dismal Rangers seasons during the late '50s and early '60s. He beat the odds in making it to the NHL but in the end couldn't beat diabetes and other illnesses and the toll they took on his body. He died on September 11, 1997, at the age of sixty-four.

Big Ned

At 6-foot-2, 205 pounds, Czechoslovakian Vaclav Nedomansky was everything Emile Francis, as well as most of the other GMs in the league, was looking for in a center. He was big and strong, could skate, and possessed a wrist shot that was once clocked at over 90 miles per hour, faster than most slap shots in those days. By 1968, the twenty-three-year-old had accumulated 72 goals and 116 points over two seasons playing for Slovan Bratislava in the Czech League. He also registered 10 goals and 23 points in International competition including five goals and two assists while playing for the silver medal-winning Czechoslovakia squad in the 1968 Olympics. He was considered by many to be the best player in Czechoslovakia and perhaps in Europe.

EMILE FRANCIS: "Jackie McLeod, who played for the Rangers and played baseball for me, was a good pitcher who ended up as coach of the Canadian team and the years they didn't go to the Olympics they went to the World Championships. So I called him and asked him if when he was in Europe he saw any players that were capable of playing in the National Hockey League. 'Yeah, I did,' he said. 'A guy by the name of Vaclav Nedomansky from Czechoslovakia, that's the guy who stood out to me.'

"Back then we were allowed five guys on our negotiations list. So right away I pulled a guy off our list and put Nedomansky on there. Well now it's the next year and Czechoslovakia comes over to play Montreal's farm club at the Forum. I couldn't go because I was coaching but I sent three of our scouts up to watch him play. And they beat Montreal's farm team, 5–1, and he scored all five goals. So I said, okay, I gotta really get busy on this.

"So there was a guy I knew in Guelph who was from Czechoslovakia who was a real junior hockey fan, so when the Rangers were in Toronto I brought him in to talk to him. I said I gotta try to make contact with this guy because they were coming in to play eight games on a tour and their last game was in Kitchener, which was perfect for us because we had a junior team in Kitchener at the time and he lived about ten, twelve miles outside of Kitchener and he could speak the language and of course I couldn't.

"So he made contact and we had it all set up. The last game they played in Kitchener, the minute the game ended and he changed his clothes he was to come out the back door. We would have a car waiting and we'd take him to this guy's farm and we'd hide him out on the farm. So I told the guy, you call me at the end of the first period so I know all the details. Everything was perfect, the team came in to practice the day before and he had a chance to get Nedomansky on the phone to explain everything. So he calls me at the end of the first period, and says, 'Emile, we got a problem, he's not dressed. They didn't dress him and there's a guy on each side of him guarding him.' So, we never got him. But then when the WHA came along he ended up playing in Toronto. And then from there I think he played for Detroit. But he would have fit in with us very well. He was a good player."

Nedomansky eventually defected in 1974 and signed with the Toronto Toros of the WHA where he scored 135 goals for the Toronto/Birmingham franchise over parts of four seasons. In 1977 he signed with the Detroit Red Wings of the NHL and stayed there for five seasons, scoring a total of 108 goals.

Big Ned finally became a Ranger in September of 1982 when he was signed as an unrestricted free agent. He scored a power play goal in his first game as a Ranger and coach Herb Brooks was planning to use him on a line with Anders Hedberg and Ulf Nilsson. But due to an administrative error, the Rangers were forced to place Nedomansky on the waiver list where he was claimed by none other than Emile Francis who was then the GM of the St. Louis Blues. He played only 22 games with the Blues, scoring just two goals before being dealt back to the Rangers along with goaltender Glen Hanlon for Andre Dore in January of 1983. He played the remainder of the season with the Blueshirts, scoring a total of 12 goals for them and retired at the end of the year at the age of thirty-nine.

6

1968–69

The Year of the Rookies

THE BIGGEST CHANGE for the Rangers at the beginning of the 1968–69 season was behind the bench as Emile Francis stepped down and replaced himself with Boom Boom Geoffrion.

Francis had long admired Boomer's leadership qualities, so when the thirty-seven-year-old Geoffrion announced his retirement after a disappointing 1967–68 season (5-16-21 in 59 games), Francis quickly offered him the coaching position and Boomer was happy to have the opportunity. Geoffrion already had two years of minor league coaching experience, and he was determined to prove to his former employers in Montreal that they made a mistake in not hiring him to coach the Canadiens.

Following his initial retirement in 1964 Boomer had coached the Quebec Aces, Montreal's AHL farm club, for two seasons on the recommendation of Canadiens owner David Molson. Molson had told Geoffrion that if he spent two seasons coaching in Quebec, he would make him the next coach of the Canadiens. Boomer led the Aces to two first-place finishes and compiled an impressive 91–47–6 record. Unfortunately, the Aces were eliminated in the first round of the playoffs both years by the Rochester Americans, the top farm club of the Toronto Maple Leafs.

At the end of the second year Geoffrion was fired by Aces owner Gerald Martineau, presumably for the two first-round losses. He then went to see David Molson who had all but promised him the coaching job in Montreal. But with Toe Blake solidly ensconced behind the Canadiens' bench, all Molson could offer Boomer was a job coaching the Junior Canadiens at a significant cut in salary. Needless to say, Geoffrion was upset and greatly disappointed. It was then that he realized that he had wasted the previous two seasons and decided to resume his playing career.

Having played for only three coaches in his 16-year NHL career, Dick Irvin, Toe Blake, and Emile Francis (by comparison, Harry Howell played for 11 coaches in his 17 years as a Ranger alone), Boomer took away something from each of them. "Irvin was a very, very tough guy as far as discipline went," he told reporters. "But he was an understanding man and could get the players up for a game. He had to get after me a few times because I was relaxing too much, but he had a lot to do with making me a good hockey player. Blake had a knack for putting the right line on the ice at the right time. He was always fair to me. But I would put out more for Francis than the other two. Emile would never degrade you in the dressing room in front of the other players. The other two would do that. As far as I'm concerned Emile was the best I ever saw."

In the Rangers' only major deal of the summer, Francis reacquired Dave Balon by sending Wayne Hillman, Dan Sequin, and Joey Johnston to the Minnesota North Stars for the tough, grinding left winger. Balon was originally scouted and signed by the Rangers in 1958 and played parts of three seasons with the Blueshirts before being sent to Montreal as part of the trade that brought Phil Goyette, Don Marshall, and Jacques Plante to Broadway in 1963. After three seasons with the Canadiens, he was left unprotected in the expansion draft and was the first skater selected overall by the North Stars. The previous season he had scored 15 goals with 32 assists and 84 penalty minutes.

The Blueshirts also had two rookies in camp, Brad Park and Walter Tkaczuk, who would make their presence known to Rangers fans as the season wore on.

Walter Tkaczuk was a twenty-one-year-old, 6-foot, 185-pound center who was born in Emsdetten, Germany, and played his junior hockey for the Kitchener Rangers. He was big and strong and hard to knock off the puck. In 1967–68 he scored 37 goals with 56 assists for 93 points with Kitchener and was the league's fourth leading scorer. He made his Rangers debut during the 1967–68 season, seeing limited action in two games. An aggressive forechecker, Tkaczuk made an impression on Ranger scouts as well as team president Bill Jennings in training camp. When Jennings asked the scouts what Tkaczuk did during the offseason, he was told that Walter carried dynamite down to gold miners in northern Ontario. Jennings responded, "Well, shouldn't we get the lad a safer job?"

Tkaczuk began the 1968–69 season in Buffalo but was recalled after only five games with the Bisons when Orland Kurtenbach started having back problems. Tkaczuk was first told that he would only be with the Rangers for two weeks, but when it was determined that Kurtenbach needed season-ending spinal fusion surgery, Walter was in the NHL to stay.

Brad Park was a twenty-year-old, 6-foot, 190-pound defenseman who was the Rangers' first-round selection (second overall) in the 1966 amateur draft. The general consensus among NHL scouts was that Park would be the number one pick in the draft and so selecting in the second slot, the Rangers were lucky to get him. Boston had the first pick by virtue of their last place finish and Harold "Baldy" Cotton, their chief amateur scout pushed for the selection of Park. Instead, team management preferred to select a player from one of their sponsored junior teams and picked defenseman Barry Gibbs, who played for their team in Estevan, Saskatchewan.

Park played for the Toronto Marlboros in Juniors, but the Maple Leafs were unable to secure his rights by signing him to a "C" form because he was not yet eighteen years old. There had also been speculation that the Leafs passed on Park because of a feud between Park's parents and GM/coach Punch Imlach's wife, Dodie, whose son Brent also played for the Marlies and didn't like all the attention that Park was getting.

The Rangers liked Park because he had an accurate shot, was a deceptively quick skater, and was a very good all-around hockey player in addition to being tough and rugged.

Following the draft, Park played two more seasons with the Marlboros before attending training camp with the Rangers in Kitchener in September of 1968. He found himself battling both Allan Hamilton and Mike Robitaille for the fifth defensemen's spot on the roster. Hamilton had the edge because he was the most experienced and the Rangers had been grooming him for several years. Robitaille was the number one defenseman on the Rangers' junior team in Kitchener so he had his supporters as well. But Robitaille was sent to Omaha of the CHL early in training camp and Park was one of the final cuts, being sent to Buffalo of the AHL where he would be playing for Fred Shero.

Park's stay in Buffalo was a short one. After scoring two goals and 12 assists in 17 games he was recalled on November 29 as a replacement for the injured Rod Seiling, getting an assist in his first game. Park continued to make a favorable impression on Francis while Hamilton struggled and when Seiling returned to the lineup it was Hamilton who was shuffled off to Buffalo.

BOB NEVIN: "The first time I saw Tkaczuk and Park in camp, I thought, holy geez, these guys will really be able to help us. I could just tell that they had a couple of keepers there. So I knew they would be a big boost to the team."

EMILE FRANCIS: "Walter Tkaczuk came up through our sponsorship. He came out of Timmons, Ontario. When I took over the Rangers they had six sponsorship clubs and when I left they had sixteen. For each sponsorship, you would get twenty-five amateur cards. So, if you sponsored two junior teams then you had fifty amateur players whose rights you owned. Montreal had like eighteen. But when I got there I increased our sponsorships, I increased our scouts. I tripled everything. Walter came out of the team we were sponsoring in Northern Ontario. So, we just moved him from South Porcupine to Kitchener where we had our Junior A team in the OHA. You could tell in juniors that he was a strong guy. He'd just roll over people. One time I brought in an eye specialist in training camp to test everyone's eyes. I didn't want to embarrass the goalkeepers, so I got everybody's eyes checked. So, we're going over the results and he gets to Tkaczuk and he says, 'This guy can hardly see, we need to get him contact lenses.' I said, 'No, no, just leave him the way he is. He gets 25 to 30 goals and hits everybody in sight, he's fine the way he is.'

"But Brad Park was a different story. He was playing for a Toronto club but they didn't have him on their list. One of Jackie Gordon's responsibilities was to keep an eye on our Kitchener team. He kept telling me you gotta come up and see this guy. So, the first chance I got I went up and Holy Christ, you could see that this guy would be a hell of a player. So, we drafted him from Toronto. He was left unprotected so we took him. He was the best defenseman who ever played for me, I'll tell you."

Training camp in Kitchener, Ontario, got off to a rough start as veteran minor league winger Wayne Larkin of the Buffalo Bisons collapsed on the ice and died of an apparent heart attack during the team's first workout. Geoffrion and Buffalo trainer Frank Christie both attempted mouth-to-mouth resuscitation but could not revive the player. "It was an inexplicable heart death," said Dr. Felice Viti. "He wasn't under any particular stress; it was just an ordinary skating session."

Among the many players in camp was a goaltender by the name of Al Albert, who was the younger brother of team broadcaster Marv Albert. Albert had been invited to camp on a tryout basis. He had played goal for Ohio University's hockey and lacrosse teams and made an impression in camp with his quick reflexes and gutsy style of play. Unfortunately, on the same day that Emile Francis told him that he was good enough to play on the Rangers farm club in New Haven, he also got called for active duty in the US Army. Albert wound up playing for the Toledo Blades of the IHL the next season before retiring and going on to become a successful broadcaster in his own right.

Despite their recent regular season success, the Rangers still had not won a playoff round and their core group of veterans that included Phil Goyette, thirty-five, Harry Howell, thirty-seven, and Donnie Marshall, also thirty-seven, were getting older and needed to be replaced. And now with twelve teams in the league there were more players at all levels of hockey to keep track of. Francis hoped that with Geoffrion behind the bench that he would be able to spend more time on his growing duties as general manager.

Unfortunately, it didn't work out that way.

The Rangers got off to a great start, winning sixteen of their first twenty-three games, including a 4–2 victory over the Canadiens in Montreal in Geoffrion's first visit to the Forum as a coach.

However, the Blueshirts then went 0–6–2 in their next eight games and were 1–4–2 on the road in December and were not playing up to their potential or to the expectations of both Francis and Geoffrion. The stress was getting to the Boomer who had previously been diagnosed with bleeding ulcers and he told Francis that he was having health problems before leaving for a West Coast road trip.

EMILE FRANCIS: "He was doing good, he ran a good training camp and we were getting ready to move into our new practice rink in Long Beach and he called me up the night before. We were gonna practice that day in New Hyde Park and he says, 'Can I meet you half an hour before practice?' I said sure, no problem. So I went and sat in his car and he says, 'Emile, I can't go any longer, I've got bleeding ulcers. There are times I feel like I'm gonna pass out and I'm on medications.' So I said if you can't coach anymore that's fine but we want you to stay with us. I'll go back and coach and you'll go out and scout and help our younger players at the same time."

Boomer went on one more road trip and collapsed after the Rangers' 3–1 victory in Oakland on January 17, 1969, from a bleeding ulcer. He wound up in the hospital and had part of his stomach removed.

When Francis took over behind the bench the Rangers had a record of 22–18–3, but Emile was disappointed at the way the Rangers had been playing. Their next game was the following night in St. Louis and even though they would be arriving late at their hotel, Francis announced a mandatory practice at 9 a.m. the following morning. He put them through a grueling session without pucks. That night they played better in a 2–2 tie with the Blues.

That was the turning point of the season. Emile's return to the bench revitalized the team and they went on a five-game winning streak and posted a 19–8–6 record through the remainder of the season.

One of the first things Francis did when he stepped back behind the bench was to give more playing time to Tkaczuk and Park, both of whom saw little important ice time under Geoffrion. Tkaczuk centered a line that had Dave Balon on the left side and Bob Nevin on the right, while Park at first took a regular turn with veteran Harry Howell and later was paired with Arnie Brown.

BRAD PARK, *Defenseman, 1968–75*: "Boomer was very boisterous, great passion, very much a character. When Walter and I first got there, being that we were rookies, he had in his mind that we would get limited ice time and we did get limited ice time. But once he went down with that ulcer and Emile took over, Walter and I both saw our ice time increase."

ARNIE BROWN: "I played with Harry Howell most of the time until Park came along and then I played with him. With Park I started to get a few more points because he could throw the puck around pretty well, especially in the opposition's end. Sometime he'd move it across to me or sometimes he'd shoot. He had a great shot from the point. And I developed a pretty good shot because of that and started to score a few goals. With Harry, he was a left-handed shot playing on the right side and so he always moved the puck up the right side and of course his puck handling was always in the middle of the ice but he did not like to move the puck across the blue line because he would have to turn straight to move it across. So, I started to see more pucks coming my way when I started to play with Brad. And that helped me gain more confidence. I got the puck more and made more plays. I had a good time playing with him. He was a good guy, always up and never down."

Once they were sure that they had made the team, Park and Tkaczuk rented a three-bedroom duplex in Long Beach, where most of the Rangers lived in those days.

WALT TKACZUK, *Center, 1968–81*: "We were roommates in Long Beach at the time. Two young guys just coming out of juniors and getting into the league. Just happy to be there. We both went to the Buffalo Bisons and we had just gotten a house there and Emile Francis called me up and said that Orland Kurtenbach had a bad back and I had to come up for a couple of weeks and I ended up staying and a little while later Harry Howell was hurt and Brad came up and he stayed and we got a place in Long Beach."

BRAD PARK: "Walter and I really didn't know each other before training camp. He played for the Kitchener Rangers and I played for the Toronto Marlboros so we were rivals, but once we got up here together it was a very quick bond. Walter was very easy to get along with, a fun guy. He was going through the same things that I was going through; trying to establish ourselves and maybe get a full-time place on the roster and living with him was easy. To this day we're best friends."

Since both were signed to entry level contracts, money was tight, so they slyly talked Francis into paying one-third of their rent so that the Rangers could use their spare bedroom for players who were called up from the minors, instead of having to put them up in a hotel.

WALT TKACZUK: "We had a three-bedroom house in Long Beach on the water and I think it cost us $180 a month and what happened when other players would get called in from New Haven or wherever they would come and stay with us. It was better than having the new guys come up and getting a room. They would stay with us in the other bedroom. And this way the guys that came up were with us instead of all by themselves. We had a number of players who came up and we each paid sixty-five dollars a month rent."

BRAD PARK: "I think Walter was making $11,000 and I was making $10,000 at that time so we said maybe we can get Emile to pay for a third of the rent so that when he called somebody up he doesn't have to put them into a hotel. So we approached him about it and he said okay.

So it cost us about sixty-five dollars a month each. When you only make $10,000 a year, sixty-five dollars was a lot in those days."

WALT TKACZUK: "Brad would make supper once in a while. He thought he was a great cook. We didn't really eat at home that often. His famous thing was taking some pork chops and putting them in some cream of mushroom soup and that's how he cooked it. I was in charge of cleaning the dishes and he was always giving me heck saying, 'You gotta clean these dishes, there's no dishes left.' They were all dirty in the sink. We weren't too good at cleaning dishes."

Like most rookies, Park was tested by the veterans of the league and had a run-in with Gordie Howe in January of 1969.

BRAD PARK: "That was in Detroit. There was a point shot and Gordie was moving towards the net so I moved out to make sure he couldn't deflect it or screen the goalie and he threw an elbow at me and I went under it and I kind of picked him up and put him down, nothing malicious or anything. He got up and started to skate away and all of a sudden the stick comes and it was going to take my teeth out and I lift my head and it gets me in the throat. [Trainer] Frank Paice comes out and is helping me to the bench and I tell him to move from my left side to my right side because I was going to be closer to Gordie and I wouldn't have had to run over Frank to get to him. I went after him but there was a melee and I couldn't get to him. But I just wanted to let him know that wasn't going to happen again. Gordie was one of the guys that probably straightened out every rookie in the league."

One of the high points of the season was a 9–0 victory over Boston at Madison Square Garden in late February. The lopsided victory helped erase the memory of the Bruins' 4–2 win over the Rangers in the Garden on January 2, when they were physically intimidated by Boston at every turn. Tkaczuk, Marshall, and Gilbert each scored two goals in the lopsided victory and Dennis Hextall and Brad Park scored their first NHL goals. Park's goal was followed by a pratfall because after scoring he jumped into the air in celebration, but forgot to land and fell flat on his face. In addition, Nevin, Tkaczuk, and Park set a team record by scoring three goals in 38 seconds.

The Rangers finished the season in third place behind Montreal and Boston with a 41–26–9 record for 91 points and set team records for victories and points. They also set a record for home victories with 27 and tied a record set in 1939–40 with an 18-game unbeaten streak at home. In addition they scored the most goals in franchise history (231), and recorded the most assists (382) and scoring points (613).

Jean Ratelle led the team in scoring (32-46-78) while Rod Gilbert finished just a point behind him (28-49-77) despite missing ten games due to a broken bone in his ankle. Their linemate Vic Hadfield finished third in team scoring and set personal best marks with 26 goals and 40 assists for 66 points. Bob Nevin scored a career-high 31 goals and led the team with 11 power-play goals and Ron Stewart scored two of the Rangers' three shorthanded goals. Dave Balon scored the other. Jim Neilson recorded career highs in goals (10) and assists (34) and Arnie Brown scored 10 goals, doubling his total previous output in four full NHL seasons. Walt Tkaczuk finished the season with 12 goals and 24 assists in 71 games and Brad Park scored three goals with 23 assists and was third in the balloting for Rookie of the Year honors.

In goal, Eddie Giacomin led the league with 37 victories, a career high for the rapidly greying netminder. He also recorded seven shutouts (one shutout behind league leader Glenn Hall of St. Louis), posted a 2.55 GAA, and was named to the Second All-Star team. Giacomin also came close to scoring a goal against Montreal on November 17. With the Rangers leading 3–2 late in the third period, and Montreal on a power play. Eddie gloved a slapper from Yvan Cournoyer, dropped the puck at his side, and fired it toward the empty Canadiens net. The puck flew up ice headed for the center of the net but suddenly lost momentum and skittered harmlessly past the goalpost.

The Playoffs

The Rangers' opponents in the first round of the Stanley Cup playoffs were the powerful Montreal Canadiens, who had lost only 19 games during the regular season and won three of the last four Stanley Cups. But the Rangers had won the season series from Montreal, 4–3–1, and were also trying to avenge their four-game sweep at the hands of the Canadiens in the 1967 playoffs.

The series began in Montreal where the Canadiens won the first game, 3–1. The score was tied at 1–1 until late in the third period when Jean Ratelle hit the post behind Gump Worsley with a backhand shot. A few minutes later while killing off a penalty to Vic Hadfield, Brad Park shot the puck down to the Canadiens end of the ice. In an effort to keep the puck in the Montreal zone, Larry Jeffrey raced down and mistakenly touched the puck, making it a two-line pass. The puck was brought back to the Rangers end where Ralph Backstrom won the faceoff and got the puck to Bobby Rousseau, who shot towards the Rangers net. Rod Seiling was battling John Ferguson in front of the goal and pushed the big Montreal winger's stick down, but unfortunately right into the path of the puck, which deflected past Giacomin. The sequence of events was eerily reminiscent of the fourth game of the 1967 playoffs when Red Berenson's overtime shot beat Rogie Vachon but hit the post. Minutes later Ferguson put a rebound past Giacomin to win the series for the Canadiens. There was little love lost between Ferguson and Giacomin, who was upset earlier in the season when Ferguson had shot a puck at him after the whistle. Giacomin claimed that Ferguson had a habit of doing the same thing while both were in the AHL.

In the second game of the series, the Rangers got off to a 2–1 lead on goals by Seiling and Hadfield before the Canadiens stormed back with three unanswered goals by Rousseau, Yvan Cournoyer, and Jean Beliveau in a span of 8:31 in the second period and won by a 5–2 score.

The series then moved to New York for the third game which got off to a quick start when Montreal's Mickey Redmond scored 30 seconds after the opening faceoff on a pass from an unchecked Dick Duff behind the Rangers net. The Canadiens scored two more quick goals and led 3–0 by the twelve-minute mark of the first period.

Early in the first period a wild melee broke out when Ferguson and Jim Neilson started fighting. Brad Park quickly stepped in to help his teammate who was a much better defenseman than a fighter. This caused Worsley to leave his crease and enter the fracas. Seeing his counterpart involved in the fight, Giacomin skated the length of the ice and grabbed Worsley around the neck, putting him in a headlock as both benches emptied. Worsley was heard to say, "Stop choking me, I didn't start this," to which Giacomin replied, "I know, but you butted in, so I had to butt in. Why don't you go back where you belong?" "I will if you let me go, I'm not a fighter," Gumper said. "You can say that again," laughed Giacomin, "besides I don't want to hurt an old man." By then the pair were giggling at their predicament and separated as order was restored.

The Blueshirts had entered the contest riding an 18-game unbeaten streak at home. But that was the regular season and this was the playoffs and the Canadiens snapped the streak with a 4–1 win.

In a desperation move, Francis called Gilles Villemure up from Buffalo to start the fourth game, hoping that the Rangers would play better in front of a different goaltender. "They weren't scoring for Eddie," Francis told reporters. "I figured maybe they'd score for Gilles."

Although Villemure had seen action in 13 regular-season contests as a Ranger over three seasons, it was his first playoff game. Unfortunately, the change didn't work and despite the fact that Villemure played well, the Rangers still lost, 4–3.

Dick Duff scored 92 seconds into the game on a breakaway to put the Canadiens out in front and force the Rangers into catch-up mode. Jacques Lemaire and Henri Richard then added two more before the first period was over. When Yvan Cournoyer scored just 36 seconds into the second period it appeared that for all intents and purposes the game was over. But then the Rangers got a spark. Goals by Balon and Gilbert made the score 4–2 at the end of the second period. When Donnie Marshall scored early in the third, it looked like the Rangers may be able to tie it up. But that was as close as they got and once again the Rangers were on the wrong side of the post-series handshake line.

The Rangers outshot Montreal 114–104 in the series but were outscored 16–7. As Francis told reporters after the game, "We just didn't have their size and strength."

And after three consecutive postseason appearances, the Rangers were still looking for their first playoff series victory since 1950.

A Snowy Day in February

On Sunday, February 9, 1969, the Northeast was hit with a snowstorm that started in the Carolinas and moved rapidly up the coast. Weather forecasters confidently predicted that the precipitation would change to rain by the afternoon, but Mother Nature had something different in mind. Instead, the storm intensified and dumped more than seventeen inches of snow on New York City and twenty inches on Long Island.

It wasn't quite the storm of the century but it had quite an impact on the Northeast, the political future of John V. Lindsay, the mayor of New York City, and a hockey game between the Rangers and the Flyers that was scheduled to be played that night at Madison Square Garden.

These days the NHL would probably postpone the game due to the traveling conditions for both the teams and the fans. But back in 1969, if there was a game scheduled, they did the best they could to play it.

At the time, a large contingent of Rangers made their winter homes in Long Beach, a bedroom community about twenty-five miles east of Manhattan on the south shore of Long Island. Sensing that a heavy, stable vehicle would be needed, Arnie Brown commandeered teammate Orland Kurtenbach's station wagon and started the long trek to the city, picking up fellow Rangers along the way. Ron Stewart, Reggie Fleming, Dave Balon, Rod Seiling, Walt Tkaczuk, Brad Park, Vic Hadfield, and Jim Neilson all piled into the station wagon and ultimately took turns driving and pushing the car through the snow-covered roads. "A little snow never hurt anybody," Brown told reporters when he finally arrived at the Garden. "We rode over dividers, through snow banks, everything." "I never saw anything like it," said Balon, a native of Wakaw, Saskatchewan, that sees its share of snow each winter.

ARNIE BROWN: "Francis called and said we would have to forfeit the game and get fined if we didn't put a team on the ice. So I think we had eight guys in Kurtenbach's car going down the Long Island Expressway and we made it. It was a wild trip. I think it was the worst snowstorm I've ever seen."

ORLAND KURTENBACH: "We all lived in Long Beach on Long Island and I had back fusion surgery in December so I wasn't playing. There was this tremendous snowstorm, Philadelphia came into New York by train right into Grand Central station. And the guys didn't know how they were gonna get in. I had snow tires on my car. We had a station wagon because I think at the time we had three children. We all lived within about half a mile of each other and so they took my car and drove in. And whenever they got stuck, three or four guys got out and pushed and lifted the car to keep moving. When it came back to me, the shocks and springs had to be replaced. But Emile said it was well worth it. So the guys drove in and made it and I stayed home."

BRAD PARK: "We had a get to the city, they didn't cancel games in those days. The only two guys who lived in the city were Rod Gilbert and Bob Nevin and they even shut the trains down. So Orland Kurtenbach had a station wagon and we all piled in there and whenever we got stuck, Walter and I being the rookies, we had a get out and push. Not only did we have to do that but sometimes there were cars that were stuck in front of us and we had to get out and get them out of the way in order to get by them. It took us about three to four hours to get to the city to play that game. That's the way it was back then. They didn't cancel games, they didn't postpone them. There wasn't a lot of flexibility in travel and the schedule."

EMILE FRANCIS: "Finally at around six o'clock they all got to the Garden in Orland Kurtenbach's station wagon. It took them more than four hours! In the meantime they had pushed and pulled that car and by the time they got home again that night they burned out the motor. I had to buy him a new motor."

Meanwhile Donnie Marshall, Phil Goyette, and Harry Howell needed a police escort to make it from their Glen Oaks homes in Queens to the subway that took them to the Garden.

Backup goaltender Don Simmons came to the Garden earlier in the day before travel conditions became difficult. And city dwellers Rod Gilbert and Bob Nevin took a cab from their Upper East Side apartments.

But as the afternoon progressed, there was no sign of starting goal-tender Eddie Giacomin as well as Jean Ratelle and Larry Jeffrey. Sensing that he might not have the requisite two netminders available for the game, Francis signed himself to a one-dollar contract in case a backup for Simmons was needed. Francis was forty-two at the time and hadn't played since he retired in 1960, but this was an emergency and he was ready if needed.

EMILE FRANCIS: "The rules of the league at that time were that you had to have two goalkeepers. So, I had to call Clarence Campbell and tell him that I was signing myself as the backup goaltender and I meant it. If something had happened to Simmons I would have gone in there myself. So, he said, be sure to sign yourself to a good contract."

It turned out that at 3 p.m. Ratelle, Giacomin, and Jeffrey hopped on a Long Island Rail Road train bound for Penn Station, which was located right under the Garden. But they never made it. The train got stuck in Elmhurst, Queens, and they spent the night on the train until the tracks were cleared the next morning.

The Rangers' opponent that night, the Philadelphia Flyers had played in Boston the previous night and were experiencing their own travel problems. Their train was stuck at a frozen railroad switch north of the city.

So, at the usual 7:05 p.m. starting time, the visitors' locker room was empty. The Flyers eventually made it to the Garden by 8:00, but their equipment didn't show up for another thirty nervous minutes later.

The game finally started at 9:15 p.m. with 5,723 hardy souls in the stands.

Jean-Guy Gendron scored for the Flyers 5:27 into the first period, then Don Blackburn made it 2–0 in the second period and things looked bleak for the Blueshirts when Andre Lacroix made it 3–0 early in the third period.

But then the Rangers stormed back on goals by Tkaczuk and Goyette, making it 3–2 with about five minutes left. Francis pulled

Simmons and Bob Nevin scored with 42 seconds remaining to tie the game.

"What a night this has been!" Francis later told reporters.

"Okay, guys," Brown was heard yelling in the dressing room, "ready for the ride home?"

The Rangers' night might have been over but the fallout from the storm didn't end so quickly for the city or Mayor Lindsay. The city and suburbs were paralyzed for three days and the streets of Queens were snow-covered for a week causing a disruption in mail service, buses, milk and bread deliveries as well as trash collection. Lindsay was heavily criticized for not responding to the situation quickly enough and jeered when he tried to make a goodwill visit to Queens later in the week.

Later that year he lost the Republican mayoral primary, but ran as an independent and won re-election. However, he was never really able to shake what became known as the "Lindsay Snowstorm" and his political career, including a failed run for the Democratic presidential nomination in 1972, was never the same.

Hail to the Chief!

Jim "The Chief" Neilson was one of the most dependable yet under-rated defensemen the Rangers ever had.

Neilson wasn't flashy, but he got the job done and his teammates certainly appreciated his skill and steady approach to the game. When asked about Neilson, Rangers netminder Gilles Villemure once said, "He stops shots, He clears the puck. What else could you want from a defenseman?" Indeed, Neilson never shied away from blocking a shot and his strong skating and deft stickhandling skills enabled him to get the puck out of the Rangers zone and up to his forwards quickly.

Unfortunately, some fans and writers at the time wanted Jim to use his 6-foot-2, 205-pound body to rough up opposing forwards. But that was not Jim's nature. He was always a very smart player and knew that running around knocking people down would eventually leave him either out of position or in the penalty box. Although he preferred to finesse the opposition out of the play, Jim could also throw a crunching body check when needed and the word around the league was that when Jim hit you, you stayed hit.

Neilson also knew how to take care of himself when the going got rough on the ice. "I don't take any guff from anybody in this league," Neilson often told reporters. "I hand out as much as I take. If a guy gives me a hard, clean check, I'd never complain as long as it's clean. If a guy gets dirty with me, that's different. But I'm not going to take a stupid penalty to get even. I'll wait my turn and get him when it won't hurt the club."

Neilson was born on November 28, 1940, in Big River, Saskatchewan. His mother was a full-blooded Cree Indian and his father was a Danish fur trapper named Olaf Neilson. When Jim was just a boy his mother left her husband and three children and returned to the reservation. Because his father spent weeks at a time in the wilderness, Jim and his two sisters were placed in St. Patrick's Catholic Orphanage in Prince Albert, Saskatchewan, where he received a good education and played a lot of hockey.

Jim left St. Patrick's in his mid-teens and played for the Prince Albert Mintos of the Saskatchewan Junior Hockey League. He became an All-Star, notching 42 goals and 56 assists in three seasons. He was signed by the Rangers in 1958 and made his Blueshirts debut on October 11, 1962, against the Detroit Red Wings. His defensive partner that night was the legendary Doug Harvey, who was also the Rangers player-coach that season.

As a rookie, Neilson was full of youthful enthusiasm which, as expected, led to some on-ice mistakes, but Harvey and fellow veteran Harry Howell took the raw rookie under their wings and taught him the finer points of the game and to focus on playing his position. Years later, Jim would return the favor by tutoring Brad Park when he made his Ranger debut in 1968–69. Neilson's strong skating also led Harvey to give him an occasional shift at left wing, where he scored his first NHL goal against Eddie Johnston of the Boston Bruins. But Jim knew his role. "I'm a defenseman. That's what I'm paid to do. I don't go out of my way to score goals. If they come because I'm doing my job, then alright. I get a much better feeling when I break up a scoring play or block a shot."

Neilson spent many years teamed with another low-key but efficient defenseman, Rod Seiling, and came into his own during the 1967–68 season when he was named to the NHL's Second All-Star team. He also played in three All-Star games: 1966–67, 1969–70, and 1970–71. His highest point total came in 1968–69, while teamed with Park, when he notched 10 goals and added 34 assists for 44 points.

Injuries began to catch up with Neilson in the early 1970s. In February of 1970 he suffered a severe knee injury which limited his mobility. He broke his right foot twice during the 1972–73 season and missed twenty-six games. The next season he was plagued by knee and back problems and was sent to the California Golden Seals in June of 1974 as part of a three-team waiver deal that saw the Rangers acquiring Derek Sanderson from Boston with the Bruins getting Walt McKechnie from the Seals. Neilson played two seasons with the Seals and remained with the franchise when they moved to Cleveland. In 1978–79 he played in the WHA for the Edmonton Oilers and retired after the season.

In 810 games with the Rangers, Neilson scored 60 goals with 238 assists and 766 penalty minutes. Only three defensemen, Harry Howell, Brian Leetch, and Ron Greschner have played more games as a Ranger than Neilson. In 65 playoff games he tallied one goal with 17 assists and 61 penalty minutes.

Overall, in 17 seasons in the NHL and WHA, Neilson played in 1,058 games, scoring 69 goals, with 299 assists and 922 penalty minutes.

On the ice, Jim Neilson was a dedicated professional who never complained about injuries or bad calls. Off ice, Neilson was known to be one of the most decent, easygoing Rangers of his time.

Jim was elected to the Saskatchewan Sports Hall of Fame in 2010. However he was even prouder of being inducted into the Prince Albert Sports Hall of Fame in 1998. "That's the big one because that's where I grew up," said Jim. "That's the biggest honor."

Discipline

Emile Francis was a stickler for team rules and discipline. So he would often take the team on day trips to West Point for a tour of the campus, lunch with the cadets and an exhibition game against the Army's hockey team.

EMILE FRANCIS: "This was when I was drilling into the players how important discipline is. I took the Rangers to West Point for two or three years. The commandant of West Point was a Canadian. We'd always play an intersquad game with them. I'd give them Giacomin and five defensemen and I'd take their goalkeeper and five defensemen.

"We went in and had lunch with all the cadets and I'd never seen anything like it in my life. Three thousand cadets came in there, they ate and they were gone in thirty minutes. We sat down and started to eat and they were all gone. They were really disciplined. That's why I brought them up there so they'd get a taste of what it was all about. There was never a war won unless that army was disciplined. And a hockey team or any athletic team was no different. You gotta have discipline on the ice and off the ice believe me.

"I had team rules and a fine system. The players had to wear shirts, ties, and jackets, anything you did wrong there would be a fine. I didn't want their money, but I told them they represent New York and the Rangers and the National Hockey League. So I told them there will be no beards, no moustaches, and you'll keep your hair short. And furthermore when you're standing on that blue line and they're playing the national anthem I don't want to see anybody moving. You stand at attention to honor the flag of the country that you're playing in, and don't ever forget that. And if you don't, I'm gonna fine you and when the season's over whatever money we've collected, we go out and have dinner together. The night before training camp I went over all the rules with the team. I'm sure some players got sick of it because they had been there for ten years, but you go over the whole thing and have them sign it. And then I would file it with the Players' Association. So now you show up without a shirt and tie and a suit I'd fine you one hundred dollars, which was stated in the rules. If they complained I said, 'Hey, they've all been filed with the Players' Association and signed by both you and me. That's the team rules that you agreed to.'

"In all the years, Jean Ratelle never paid one fine. It was just how he was. He never did anything wrong. He was just a classy guy. Players would go out of their way to try to catch him. One day we were coming out of a game and he got within about ten feet of the bus and he didn't have his tie on. And the guys on the bus were saying, 'We got him now.'

But he stopped, took his tie out and put it on, stepped on the bus and said, 'How are you gentlemen tonight?' and sat down. I think he did that purposely."

Gerry Cosby, The Man Behind the Brand

To many fans, a trip to Madison Square Garden isn't complete without a stop at Cosby's, the iconic sporting goods store. Cosby's has long been considered the mecca, the place to buy Rangers jerseys, memorabilia, and hockey equipment. But what about the man behind the brand? How did the name Gerry Cosby become synonymous with sporting goods?

Finton Gerard David Cosby was born in 1909 in Roxbury, Massachusetts, and as a young man worked as an office boy and switchboard operator at the Boston Arena, the home of the Boston Tigers of the Canadian-American Hockey League. One day in 1928, Eddie Powers, the manager of the Tigers, fired their netminder because his drinking had made him too unreliable and asked Gerry, who was nineteen at the time, to be their practice goaltender. Keep in mind that Gerry had never played hockey, let alone goal, in his life, but he went down to the Tigers dressing room and gamely donned the pads and oversized skates, willing to give it a shot.

On the ice, however, Gerry's eagerness couldn't hide his inexperience and he expected the Tigers to bring in another goalie for their next practice. But Powers asked him to come back the next day and try it again and he played a little better. His play continued to improve each day and in time Gerry had a steady job as the Tigers' practice netminder.

The Boston Bruins also practiced in the Arena and Gerry caught the eye of Art Ross, their GM and coach, and he was soon seeing double duty as the practice netminder for both teams. Remember, this was back in the days when teams usually carried only one netminder, so having a reliable practice goaltender was a necessity. And although Gerry was not getting paid for any of these practice sessions, he was gaining valuable experience and being mentored by Bruins netminder Tiny Thompson, a future Hall of Famer.

In 1932, Gerry toured Europe with a group of American hockey players that was organized by Bruins president Walter Brown. A year later the United States entered a team in the World Championships in Prague, Czechoslovakia, with Gerry as their goaltender. Amazingly, after playing the position for only five years, he posted four consecutive shutouts against Switzerland, Poland, Czechoslovakia, and Austria and then beat a heavily favored Canadian team, 2–1, in overtime for the championship. It marked the first time that a Canadian team had been defeated in the World Championship games.

Gerry then moved to New York to take a job as a runner on Wall Street, but he didn't want to give up on his hockey career. So he called Rangers general manager and coach Lester Patrick and asked him if he could skate with the team and wound up becoming their practice goaltender.

Cosby then went to England to play for the Wembley Lions in the English Hockey League, where he was voted the MVP of the league and also managed to attend business college in his spare time. A year later he was invited to play on the United States Olympic team but declined because he had just gotten a new job with his former hockey teammate Stewart Iglehart's construction business.

During the late 1930s and early '40s, Gerry was a very busy guy, seeing duty as the backup netminder for the New York Rovers, the Rangers' Eastern League affiliate, as well as serving as the practice goaltender for both the Rangers and the New York Americans. Then during World War II when many players from all levels of hockey were overseas, Cosby was often called upon to tend goal for the Boston Olympics as well as the Rovers in the same week.

Gerry's involvement in the sporting goods business began while he was with the Rovers, when GM and Coach Tom Lockhart asked him to order some sticks. He found a company called Lovell Manufacturing, in Erie, Pennsylvania, that made hockey sticks, mouse traps, and washing machine parts and ordered six dozen at a good price. The sticks were delivered, Lockhart and the players liked them, and soon Gerry was placing orders for gloves and pads and the rest is history.

Cosby started getting orders from other teams in the Eastern Hockey League as well as the Rangers and the Americans. When he ran out of space in a store he had opened adjacent to his York Avenue apartment, he moved to a larger place at 12 West 48th Street, near Rockefeller Center.

Gerry briefly entered into a partnership with three other athletic suppliers but after a stint in the army as a pilot trainer, he once again assumed total control of the business. By this time Cosby's was a respected supplier of equipment and uniforms for all sports to the pros, colleges, and high schools as well as the general public, so a larger store was needed.

A chance encounter at his son Michael's football game with William Jennings led to Cosby asking the Rangers president about a vacant store adjacent to the old Madison Square Garden on the corner of Eighth Avenue and 50th Street. When Jennings told him it was available, Gerry drove down from Massachusetts the following Monday morning to sign the lease for the store which opened in 1959.

Gerry often said that the 50th Street store was his favorite. Being so close to the Garden was good for business and good for the Rangers who were frequent visitors, especially when a new batch of sticks came in. "They didn't have room upstairs in the Garden to keep the sticks." Michael Cosby recalled, "so when the Northland sticks came in the players would come in and we had a big rack in the back and they would go pick out the ones they liked." Former Ranger Dick Duff also recalled the store fondly: "The guys were always good to us in the Cosby's store down in the old Madison Square Garden. It was a nice store, nice family, and they loved hockey."

When the Rangers and Knicks moved into the new Garden on 33rd street and Seventh Avenue in 1968, Cosby's moved along with them, first to a street level location outside Penn Station, then into a space in the Garden's Esplanade. Today they are located at 11 Penn Plaza about half a block from the Garden. There is also a store and warehouse in Sheffield, Massachusetts, where most of the merchandise is designed, manufactured, and distributed.

Gerry was an innovator. He redesigned hockey jerseys to allow equipment to be worn comfortably underneath. He also added padding to hockey gloves and designed adjustable size and suspension features for helmets. He added Velcro straps to hockey pads and worked with stick manufacturers to create laminated stick shafts and fiberglass wrapped blades.

Sadly, Gerry Cosby passed away in 1996. He was inducted posthumously into the International Hockey Federation Hall of Fame in April of 1997 for his outstanding goaltending in International play.

Gerry Cosby's legacy is one of quality, service, and integrity and it is being carried on proudly by his son Michael and his grandchildren Christy and Matthew. Now in their eighth decade, Cosby's has provided quality equipment and service, as well as memories, to countless generations of fans with many more to come.

7

1969–70

A Great Start and a Wild Finish

THE RESTRUCTURING OF the Rangers front office, scouting department, and minor league system continued to pay dividends, producing several young players each season who were bigger and stronger and deemed ready for their NHL debut. And so, the 1969–70 season began with a number of significant changes both on and off the ice for the Blueshirts.

Gone were two of the Rangers steadiest and classiest performers.

Veteran defenseman Harry Howell underwent spinal fusion surgery in the summer of 1969 and Emile Francis offered him positions as assistant GM or assistant coach if he wanted to retire. Harry was thirty-six years old at the time and had undergone multiple surgeries and Emile had young defensemen that he wanted to bring along, including Allan Hamilton, Ab DeMarco Jr, Larry Brown, and Mike Robitaille. But Howell felt that he could still play. "I didn't go through these operations to sit behind a desk," he told Francis. So, when Emile asked him where he'd like to be traded, Harry chose the West Coast and he was sold to Oakland in June of 1969.

Harry also played for the Kings, as well as New Jersey, San Diego, and Calgary of the WHA before retiring in 1976 at the age of forty-three. He then moved up to the front office, becoming the assistant general manager of the Cleveland Barons in 1976. Harry became GM the following season, replacing Bill McCreary, and held that position until the Barons merged with the Minnesota North Stars in 1978. Howell coached the North Stars for 11 games in 1978–79 and then became the team's chief scout. He later was a scout for the Edmonton Oilers.

Howell holds the Ranger record for games played with 1,160, a mark that may never be broken. In addition, he recorded 82 goals and 263 assists for 345 points with 1,147 penalty minutes. Unfortunately, for the better part of Harry's career, the Rangers didn't make many playoff appearances, but he did manage to record three goals and two assists along with 30 penalty minutes in 34 postseason games.

Overall in 1,411 regular-season games over 22 NHL seasons, Harry scored 94 goals, with 324 assists and 1,298 penalty minutes. In 38 playoff games he scored three goals with three assists and 32 penalty minutes.

BRAD PARK: "When I first got there and my ice time increased, Harry was just wonderful, a terrific guy. He treated me like an equal. He gave me a lot of advice. There were a lot of discussions. We would go out for a beer after the game and really talk about the game and how situations should be handled. Harry's one of my favorite people of all time."

Howell was inducted into the Hockey Hall of Fame in 1979 and saw his number 3 jersey retired by the Rangers, along with Andy Bathgate's number 9, on February 22, 2009.

Phil Goyette was traded to St. Louis for the Blues' first-round pick in the 1969 amateur draft (Andre "Moose" Dupont). For six seasons Goyette had been a solid two-way performer, scoring 97 goals with 227 assists in 389 games. Known as the calmest player in the league, Phil knew how to slow the game down when the opposition had momentum. But injuries and age had slowed the thirty-six-year-old center a bit and

Francis had a few younger forwards who were thought to be ready for the NHL.

PHIL GOYETTE: "Well naturally I knew I was at the end of my career, I was thirty-six or thirty-seven years old. I knew I didn't have that many years left so I may as well capitalize on what I have left and get in as much as I can and that's it. I knew I didn't have the stamina anymore. But in St. Louis that was an expansion team and I ended up the fourth-leading scorer in the league. Nobody remembers that and I was thirty-seven years old! I don't know if there were many thirty-seven-year-olds who finished fourth in the league. I had my best year. But at my age, Scotty Bowman said we can't stick with just old guys, we have to rejuvenate the team so expansion came again, Buffalo and Vancouver, I think, and they put their protected list down and I wasn't on it. Buffalo needed some experienced players so that's where I ended up."

But that wasn't the last Rangers fans would see of Phil Goyette. Late in the 1971–72 season when Jean Ratelle suffered a broken ankle, Emile Francis brought Goyette out of retirement. Goyette played the final eight games of the season and 13 more in the playoffs as the Rangers reached the finals for the first time in twenty-two years.

Gone too was the muscle.

Reggie Fleming was traded in June of 1969 to Philadelphia for forwards Leon Rochefort and Don Blackburn. At thirty-three, Reggie had lost some of his effectiveness as a "policeman" and had worn out his welcome with a propensity for taking bad penalties. In addition, the Rangers, who were one of the smallest teams in the league when Fleming was acquired during the 1965–66 season, had drafted and recruited bigger players and weren't being pushed around quite as much anymore. Fleming did not go quietly, however, predicting to reporters that the Rangers would not make the playoffs without him. "Who've they got that can hit? No one on the defense. Not one of the forwards."

In the meantime, Francis brought in three younger forwards in hopes of replacing Goyette and Fleming.

Juha Widing was a 6-foot-1, 190-pound center who led the Central League in scoring with 41 goals and 39 assists for the Rangers' farm club in Omaha. The twenty-two-year-old was a native of Finland but was raised in Sweden. Widing also gave Francis another option in case Orland Kurtenbach was unable to come back after undergoing spinal fusion surgery.

Billy Fairbairn was a twenty-two-year-old, 5-foot-10, 170-pound right winger from Brandon, Manitoba. He was a solid two-way player who scored 28 goals and had 47 assists for 75 points for Omaha the previous season, making him the team's second-leading scorer behind Widing.

BILL FAIRBAIRN, *Right Wing, 1969–76*: "It was a very big change coming from Brandon to Omaha to New York. Playing in front of maybe three thousand people to seventeen, eighteen thousand was a very big change right off the bat, I guess. I was a little nervous for the first couple of months but then after that everything settled down and it was good.

"I was lucky right off the bat, when I came up to New York I roomed with Brad Park. We roomed that first year together. He'd been there a year and so he kind of took me under his wing and made me feel quite welcome. He knew his way around so I just kind of hung with him and saw the sights and everything else and got to the rink with him. He was the driver, he was a chauffeur for me but it was a good fit rooming together with him."

In an effort to replace Fleming's toughness, Francis traded Dennis Hextall and the recently acquired Leon Rochefort to Los Angeles for Real Lemieux, a twenty-four-year-old, 5-foot-11, 175-pound hard-nosed left winger who came with a reputation as a hitter. "I like to get hit my first time on the ice," Lemieux told reporters when the Rangers opened training camp. "Then I hit back and it puts me in the mood for a good night's work."

Francis also needed a replacement for backup netminder Don Simmons, who had retired at the end of the 1968–69 season. He had a young, promising goaltender named Gilles Villemure in the minors, but knowing that Giacomin would play the majority of the games, he didn't want Villemure languishing on the bench. So, he acquired forty-year-old Terry Sawchuk and minor league forward Sandy Snow from Detroit for Larry Jeffrey. Sawchuk's career was winding down but Francis hoped to get about ten games out of the veteran so that Giacomin would be a little fresher for the playoffs.

Off the ice, Bernie Geoffrion, who was forced to step down as coach the previous season due to ulcers, was named assistant general manager. Boomer had been offered the head coaching job in Minnesota by North Stars GM Wren Blair but after careful consideration decided to stay with the Rangers mostly due to heath concerns.

A Season to Remember

Like many that have come before and after, the Rangers' 1969–70 season was a roller coaster ride from start to finish. The Blueshirts got off to a strong start, posting a 32–11–11 record and spending the first three and a half months of the season in first place.

But as February rolled around a series of injuries to key players began to take their toll. The trouble began on Friday, February 13, in Oakland when Jim Neilson suffered a knee injury that sidelined him for almost a month and troubled him for the rest of the season. Less than a week later, Brad Park suffered a broken ankle when his skate got caught in the boards in Detroit. Later that month, veteran winger Donnie Marshall suffered a separated shoulder which basically ended his season. Then, in late March, the Blueshirts also lost Vic Hadfield for the rest of the season to a knee injury suffered in a 3–1 loss to the Bruins.

The injuries to Park and Neilson not only took two of the Rangers' better defensemen out of the lineup, but two of their tougher players as well. And as a result, the Rangers were beginning to get bullied again, especially by the Bruins. At the same time, Francis was becoming dissatisfied with the play of Real Lemieux, who was expected to replace Reggie Fleming as the Rangers enforcer. Lemieux had failed to retaliate when repeatedly pushed around by the Bruins in a 5–3 loss in Boston on February 26. At one point, Johnny McKenzie elbowed Lemieux in the mouth, breaking his dentures, but the Ranger winger skated away without fighting back. Francis knew then that he had to make a move, so two days later Lemieux and center Juha Widing were dealt to the Los Angeles Kings for Ted Irvine, a twenty-five-year-old, 6-foot-2, 195-pound left winger with a reputation for sticking up for his teammates.

TED IRVINE, *Left Wing, 1970–75:* "I was playing for the Kings and I got in a fight in St. Louis with Bob Plager and Noel Picard. I was fighting them both at the same time and Emile Francis happened to be at the game and he saw that I was on my own against those two big sluggos and he went and got me right away."

Francis tried to fill the void left by Neilson and Park by recalling Mike Robitaille and Ab DeMarco Jr. from the minors. Then he was able to acquire forty-year-old Tim Horton from the Toronto Maple Leafs on March 3 for future considerations (Denis Dupere).

Horton, 5-foot-10, 180-pounds was a veteran of 1,185 games and four Stanley Cup victories with the Maple Leafs and was considered by many to be among the strongest men in the league.

EMILE FRANCIS: "I remember we came into New York after a game and checked into the hotel. It was probably 2:30 in the morning by then and he put a dollar in the soda machine and nothing came out. So, he put another dollar in and nothing came out. So, he went back to the room and called the front desk. He said, 'I just put two dollars in your machine and didn't get any soda. I want you to come up here and either give me my money back or my soda.' The guy at the desk told him he was too busy. 'You're too busy are you' and he hung up. He went back out to the machine, picked it up and put it on the elevator and sent it down to the lobby. He got back on the phone and said, 'You're too busy to come up so I sent the machine down to you.' That's how strong he was."

Francis had only one misgiving about the deal—Horton's salary. He was making $75,000 at the time, more than anyone on the Rangers, so he talked to Rangers president William Jennings about it. "If it's the right deal, then make it," Jennings said. "Emile, you can't keep paying these guys $25,000 a year forever."

The Rangers suffered yet another loss during this time when their longtime surgeon Dr. Kauzo Yanagisawa died of a heart attack on February 22. Dr. Yanagisawa, fifty-five, had been the Rangers' surgeon since 1949 and had performed spinal surgeries on Rod Gilbert, Jean Ratelle, Orland Kurtenbach, and Harry Howell among others. He was replaced by one of the best known orthopedic surgeons in the country, Dr. James Nicholas, who had operated on John F. Kennedy's back and Joe Namath's knees.

Brad Park was able to return to action at the end of March but without him as well as the rest of his injured teammates the Blueshirts had gone into a 6–11–5 tailspin that included a nine-game winless streak. And as the season drew to a close, the Rangers were in danger of missing the playoffs for the first time in four years.

Entering the final weekend of the season, the Blueshirts were in fifth place, two points behind Montreal for the fourth and final playoff spot in the NHL's Eastern Division. The Rangers were scheduled for a home-and-home series against Detroit while Montreal had a pair of games against Chicago. If the Rangers could win both games against the Red Wings, and the Canadiens got less than three points out of their games with the Black Hawks, the Blueshirts would move into the final playoff spot.

But since nothing ever came easily for the Rangers, they were drubbed, 6–2, in Detroit, the Red Wings clinching third place with the victory. But as luck would have it, the Canadiens lost as well, 4–1 to the Black Hawks.

With just one game remaining, the best the Rangers could do was tie Montreal for the last playoff spot. But to do that, they would need to beat Detroit at the Garden on Sunday afternoon while the Canadiens would have to lose again to Chicago. That would put the two teams in a virtual dead heat with the same number of wins, losses and ties. The next tiebreaker would be goals scored and Montreal already had a four goal edge going into Sunday's game. The Rangers would not only need to beat Detroit, they'd have to score at least five goals and hope that Chicago would beat and also shut down the Flying Frenchmen. Quite a task indeed, but Francis wasn't giving up. "This game is slippery. It's played on ice," he told reporters. "We're not out yet, and we won't stop fighting until the last soldier is dead."

The consensus among the players was that if they could score nine goals, they would have a chance at finishing with more goals than Montreal. However, throughout the entire season the most the Blueshirts had scored in any game was eight goals (on November 7 at Oakland). Additionally, they had gone 3–10–7 in their previous seventeen games, while scoring only 33 goals, for an average of 1.94 goals per game.

The mood was somber as the players entered their dressing room at the Garden for the Easter Sunday matinee, which was being televised nationally. But Francis wasn't going down without a fight. "I've been in sports a number of years," he told the players, "and I've seen athletes with their backs against the wall and I've seen funny things happen. If you can score six, seven, eight goals, this is one of those times when funny things could happen." Francis then went around the room asking each player, "Do you think it's impossible?" and each player responded, "No it's not."

Eddie Giacomin and Ron Stewart started chattering, "C'mon guys, we can do it . . . Gotta get 'em early." Giacomin then started asking his teammates, "How many you gonna score?" "I got two goals," replied Dave Balon, "I'll take two," said Stewart. Jean Ratelle and Rod Gilbert each put themselves down for two goals apiece. "If we can get four goals in the first period, we can make it," Ratelle added.

The Rangers' intensity was evident from the opening faceoff. They swarmed the Detroit zone and Walt Tkaczuk nearly scored just 18 seconds into the game. Shortly thereafter, Rod Gilbert scored his first goal in over a month, slipping the puck past Roger Crozier and giving the Blueshirts a 1–0 lead at the 36 second mark. Crozier was in net because Marv Edwards, the Wings' regular starting goaltender, was in the dressing room on the trainer's table nursing a "headache." In fact, many Red Wing players were a little "under the weather" due to their clinching celebration the night before.

Bruce MacGregor, who was then a member of the Red Wings, remembers the game well.

BRUCE MacGREGOR, *Center, 1971–74*: "We had clinched a playoff spot the night before and we flew into New York and had to play the Rangers. It was an afternoon game and Sid Abel had decided to sit out a few guys. In hindsight, it wasn't a good thing to do because it took the momentum away and hurt our team. Obviously, the Rangers had a lot at stake. We didn't have anything to play for but you still go out and try to win the game. I think we left our goalie kind of in a bad spot and I don't think that went over very well with him. You know goalies take those things personally, trying to keep their averages down and things like that. But I remember it well it wasn't much fun being on the other side for sure.

"I don't think there was a party, maybe some guys went out, stuff like that has been known to happen. But knowing that we had a game the next day I think it was more about giving some players the day off, changing the lineup. The team wasn't ready to play that day for whatever reason but we didn't have a big party or anything."

Detroit managed to tie the score less than three minutes later, but then rookie Jack Egers, playing in place of the injured Vic Hadfield, scored on a power play. Balon followed with another power-play goal. Egers then scored again with two minutes left in the period. Unbelievably the Rangers, who had not scored as many as three goals in a period in two months, had scored four goals and outshot the Red Wings, 17–7.

The onslaught continued in the second period as Francis shortened the shifts from 90 seconds to a minute, to keep the Red Wings on their heels. Gilbert scored his second goal of the game 20 seconds into the period. Alex Delvecchio scored for Detroit at the 4:21 mark, but Ron Stewart scored twice, equaling his pregame prediction. Pete Stemkowski later scored for Detroit as the period ended with the Rangers leading, 7–3, having once again outshot the Red Wings, this time by a 22–8 margin.

In the third period, Francis shortened the shifts to 45 seconds as the Rangers continued to fire shots at Crozier from every angle. Balon scored his second and third goals of the game, making the score 9–3. With less than four minutes to play, Francis started pulling Giacomin for an extra skater in an effort to score even more goals. Gordie Howe and Nick Libett each scored into the empty net, making it a 9–5 final with the Rangers outshooting the Wings by a 65–22 margin, a team record that still stands today.

WALT TKACZUK: "The game prior to that we went into Detroit and they beat us and that clinched their position in the playoffs. So, the next day was a Sunday and because Detroit had clinched the playoff spot they sat out a couple of players, resting them for the playoffs. And we knew our main goal was that we had win, first of all, and we had to score a lot of goals. So we just sort of let our defensive game go by and kept putting the pressure on Detroit and we ended up beating them, 9–5. So that put the pressure on Montreal to win and score a lot of goals and they couldn't do it. I think they actually pulled their goalie in the second period so that they could get more goals."

EMILE FRANCIS: "We had to score at least six goals to have a chance. When we got ahead by 6–2 I think I pulled the goalkeeper. I figured what the hell, if they score I'll just put him back. Because goals-for was the tie breaker. We got a bonus in a way because it was an afternoon game and I'm sure the Canadiens were watching that game in Chicago and they were probably dying every time we scored. And that's another thing. Before that game started, the Garden wasn't half full. By the time we started the second period the rink was already full. They came from everywhere. By the time the game was over, the place was jumping, I'll tell you."

The Rangers did what they needed to do; win and score a lot of goals. The victory left the Rangers and Canadiens tied with 38 wins and 92 points each. However, the Rangers led in the goals-scored tiebreaker by a 246–242 margin. Now it was up to Chicago to beat Montreal while keeping the defending Stanley Cup champions off the scoreboard. If Montreal won or scored more than four goals, they would make the playoffs and the Rangers would be headed home.

Luckily for the Rangers, Chicago also had a big stake in the game as well. They were in a dogfight with Boston for the top spot in the Eastern

Division. If the Black Hawks won, they would finish in first place. If they lost and Boston won their game against Toronto, Chicago would finish in second place. Either way, the Black Hawks had made quite a turnaround after finishing dead last the season before.

That night both players and fans alike tried to keep tabs on the Chicago-Montreal game the old-fashioned way—with their transistor radios. Since the Chicago station didn't start broadcasting the game until the second period, most fans listened to the Montreal station with Danny Gallivan doing play-by-play, but only if they could find the right spot and hold the radio's antenna at the right angle. Even then reception was poor.

Most of the players were either able to listen to the game or arranged to telephone each other with developments. Vic Hadfield and Tim Horton took their wives to see Tom Jones at the Copacabana that night but had to keep going outside to check the score from Chicago.

Rangers president Bill Jennings made an arrangement with *New York Times* sportswriter Gerald Eskenazi to have details of the game relayed to him by telephone,

GERALD ESKENAZI: "The critical factor of whether they would make the playoffs or not was what happened that night with the Canadiens. I went back to the Times building and we had what they called the radio room. Nowadays an iPod probably has more power than that thing had, but we had this huge contraption there with all kinds of bulbs and lights, it must have been six-foot high. Because we had correspondents all over the world and we had to get radio broadcasts from all over the world at the *New York Times*. So, I set up a thing where the head of the radio room was able to get the broadcast of the Montréal game. I had this open line on the phones and I had Bill Jennings on the other end. I would tell Bill what was going on. I would tell him the score, if there was power play or something like that and then, of course, he would relay that to Emile. It was really one of the strangest games in National Hockey League history because the Canadiens had pulled the goalie in the first period when I think they were down two-zip because it didn't matter whether they won or lost at that point as long as they scored a certain number of goals they would be in the playoffs and the Rangers would be out, and of course that tactic backfired. And I remember Emile telling me he had been reading General George S. Patton's autobiography, *Ordeal and Triumph*. And he took the book when it was over and flung it across the room. He had been reading the book to sustain himself during the last couple weeks of the season. It was a very emotional season as it wound down. So that's the story. I was getting the results of the game and feeding them to Bill Jennings and Jennings was feeding them to Emile. It was kind of primitive in terms of radio.

"But even to this day, of all the events I've covered and I've been to four Olympics, I've been to more than twenty Super Bowls and that game, and it wasn't even a championship game; it was just a goddamn game to get them into the playoffs, that game was the greatest sports event I have covered. Actually, I also covered the US Olympic hockey team when they beat the Soviets on the way to winning the gold medal, the Miracle on Ice game, that day with the game against Detroit and subsequently the game that night was the most thrilling sports event that I've ever been involved with."

JACK EGERS, *Right Wing, 1970–71, 1973–74*: "That was a Sunday afternoon game at the Garden. I'll never forget it. We knew we had to score as many goals as we could. It didn't matter how many were scored against us because that was the tiebreaker—goals for. After that season it was changed. So fortunately I was able to get a couple and we ended up beating Detroit, 9–5, and then we had to sit around to see how Montreal did that night against Chicago. I think Montreal had to score five goals to knock us out but they couldn't do it. I think they lost 10–2 in Chicago."

BRAD PARK: "I had come back within a week or ten days before the game. We were in the playoff hunt but we weren't guaranteed anything and if we won our last two games against Detroit home and home we were in the playoffs. But we lost in Detroit which guaranteed them a playoff spot and then we went home and we knew that the next criteria was goals-for and we knew that we were five goals behind Montréal and we would have to score over five goals. We had to hope that Montreal wouldn't win and not score a lot of goals. That Sunday afternoon in the first period there were about 7,500 people in the stands and we were up,

4–1, by then. By the end of the second period, there were about 12,500 in the building and then when we came out for the third period the Garden was full.

"We pulled Eddie. We got nine goals which put us even in points and put us ahead of them in goals and then it was a matter of waiting for the game in Chicago that night. We went out for a bite to eat in a restaurant called Mr. Laffs and we couldn't get anything on the Chicago game. One of the guys said, 'I've got a mother who lives in Chicago,' so he called her up and I got on the phone with her and she put the game on the radio and I sat in the back of the restaurant's bar listening to it and reporting out to my teammates who were having dinner."

BILL FAIRBAIRN: "That was kind of a weird situation we got put in there having to win the game and score so many goals and Montreal having to go into Chicago to lose a game or not get enough goals. It ended up that we got what we needed and we waited to see what went on with Montreal. We were all together waiting to see if they would be able to beat us out but they didn't. And I think it was the first time that they missed the playoffs in a number of years, so it was kind of a happy moment for the whole team. And we were a team. We were like a family, we stood together pretty well all the time. Even after practice in Long Beach we would go out for lunch as a group. I had never been on a team like that. I can say that they were all kind of like brothers to you and the Cat was the father because it was like one big family. We backed each other up right from the get-go."

In Chicago, the Canadiens jumped out to a 1–0 lead on a power-play goal by Yvan Cournoyer. The Black Hawks tied it up a few minutes later and scored another goal as the period ended with Chicago leading, 2–1.

In the second period, the teams each scored a goal and Chicago still led at the end of the period by a 3–2 score. Between periods, the Black Hawks learned that Boston had beaten Toronto, so they knew that they had to beat the Canadiens to finish in first place.

The Black Hawks came out storming in the final period and Pit Martin scored two goals to make the score 5–2. Montreal coach Claude

Ruel decided to pull goalie Rogie Vachon for an extra skater in an effort to score the three goals needed to overtake the Rangers. The move backfired badly as Chicago scored five empty-net goals and won, 10–2.

When the dust had settled, the Rangers made the playoffs, Chicago finished in first place, and the Canadiens missed the postseason for the first time in twenty-two years. Montreal and much of Canada was in a state of shock. As a result, the tiebreaker was changed at the beginning of the 1970–71 season. Under the new system, if there was a tie for a playoff berth, the team that won the season series between the two clubs would be in. If the season series ended tied, then the team that scored the most goals in games between the teams would make the playoffs. Had that system been in effect in 1969–70, the Canadiens would have nosed out the Blueshirts for fourth place.

Television and radio stations broadcast the news: "The Rangers make the playoffs." Some stations even interrupted regular programming with the story. As Francis told reporters, "It was like we won the Stanley Cup."

The Rangers top producers that season was the Dave Balon, Walter Tkaczuk, Billy Fairbairn line, which was called "the Bulldogs" because of the way they played. Together they recorded 203 points, second only to Detroit's trio of future Hall of Famers Frank Mahovlich, Alex Delvecchio, and Gordie Howe. Balon had a career year with 33 goals, 37 assists, and 70 points and led the team in goals. Tkaczuk led in assists (50) and points (77) while Fairbairn, who joined the line when Bob Nevin suffered a knee injury, finished the season with 23 goals and 33 assists which set a team record for assists by a rookie.

BILL FAIRBAIRN: "I played with Walter and we clicked right off the bat and if I hadn't started off with him I wouldn't have been run up for the rookie of the year. We just sort of jelled when we went to training camp and then when we started playing there Emile took us both aside and said look you guys are the young guys on the team and we're going to have you killing penalties so the extra ice time really helped me during that year."

Jean Ratelle scored 32 goals, including a team-leading 10 on the power play, but linemate Rod Gilbert had an off-year, finishing with only 16 goals and 37 assists. It was the first time Gilbert scored fewer than 20 goals since he underwent back surgery during the 1965–66 season. Bob Nevin also had a subpar season with only 18 goals, down from 31 the year before.

Ed Giacomin had a fine season in goal, posting a 2.36 GAA, his lowest average in five seasons with the Rangers. He also recorded six shutouts. Terry Sawchuk appeared in eight games, going 3–1–2 and posting a solid 2.91 GAA with one shutout.

The Playoffs

Unfortunately, the momentum from the Rangers' frantic finish didn't carry over into the playoffs where they met the second-place Boston Bruins.

The two clubs had split the season series, 4–4, with the Blueshirts going 3–1–0 at home and 1–3–0 in Boston. The series began in Boston and it didn't start off well for the Rangers.

The Bruins jumped out to a 2–0 lead halfway through the first period of the opener, but a goal by Jack Egers at the 19-minute mark got the Rangers back into the game. But then the roof fell in. The Bruins scored five unanswered goals in the second period, including shorthanded goals by Bobby Orr and Derek Sanderson just 44 seconds apart. Phil Esposito recorded a hat trick and Bobby Orr scored twice in the 8–2 rout. Ed Giacomin was replaced by Terry Sawchuk at the start of the third period. The game was chippy from start to finish as referee Art Skov called 88 minutes in penalties, including 66 in the third period.

Looking to spark his team, Francis started Sawchuk in the second game. It was the veteran's 105th playoff appearance, tying Glenn Hall's record. However, Brad Park (knee) and Rod Seiling (shoulder) were forced to sit out due to injuries. They were replaced by rookies Larry Brown and Ab DeMarco Jr., meaning that along with Allan Hamilton the Rangers would be playing with three defensemen who had little or no Stanley Cup playoff experience.

The Rangers led, 2–1, at the end of the first period, but the Bruins once again scored four unanswered goals and won, 5–3. It was the Blueshirts' tenth straight playoff defeat, tying an NHL record.

Surprisingly compared to the series opener it was a quiet game as referee Bruce Hood called only 10 minutes in penalties the entire evening.

The fireworks started almost immediately when the series moved to Madison Square Garden for the third game. Early in the first period, at the first faceoff in the Rangers zone, Giacomin skated out of his crease towards centers Derek Sanderson and Walter Tkaczuk who were preparing to take the faceoff. Sanderson and Giacomin began shouting at one another and Sanderson later told reporters that Giacomin had tried to get under his skin by telling him, "We're getting a bonus to take care of you tonight," to which Derek was supposed to have responded, "Cool, man."

On the ensuing faceoff, the puck went into the corner with Balon and Sanderson in pursuit. Sanderson jumped Balon and started punching him. Park and Tkaczuk attacked Sanderson as the rest of the players joined the melee. Sanderson and Balon were ejected and four other skaters were given fighting majors by referee John Ashley. It took 19 minutes to play the first 91 seconds of the game. A few more scraps developed through the rest of the period and a total of 132 minutes in penalties were assessed in the first period alone, setting a Stanley Cup playoff record.

DEREK SANDERSON, *Center, 1974–75*: "Everybody thinks the Rangers were out to get me and they were. But it was not over the thing with Eddie Giacomin, good guy by the way, when I went to the Rangers, Eddie said, 'Thanks, that made me famous.' Eddie came out to the circle, he liked to move around. He was a very skittish, nervous guy. And he came out and he said to Walter, don't let him shoot. He'll try to shoot. But everybody thought he was talking to me. So I said, 'Fuck you, get back in the net.' He said 'Fuck you.' So now the two of us are going back and forth and everybody thinks that the Rangers are waiting for me. But they drop the puck and I still got a shot off, it just missed the corner of the net, it just missed the post and went into the far corner. So I get there and boom they start hitting me. Park, Balon, Tkaczuk. We looked like the Keystone Cops we all got piled up. And I snuck out from underneath. And the Cat was flippin' out and [Bruins coach Harry] Sinden was too.

"So they throw me and Balon out of the game. And Harry Sinden went ballistic. Standing on the boards, he wanted to go on the ice and Emile just the same. Two of the greatest coaches in the history of the game. But the reason the Rangers wanted to get me was the game before in Boston, we were winning late in the third and I jumped Billy Fairbairn. I suckered him and he just flipped out so we had a scuffle. And I said, that's for nothin' see what you get for somethin'. I'll see you in New York and he said you're fuckin' right. Everybody liked Billy Fairbairn. Billy Fairbairn was quiet, he hit, he worked hard, he took his hits and he played up and down that wall. And you could trust him every step of the way. You knew what he was gonna do and he didn't play dirty, he was a good guy. So that's why they were after me. It had nothing to do with Giacomin.

"So when they threw me out of the game I was in the dressing room and there was no one else there with me. But for some reason they let [singer] Paul Anka in. But then all of the reporters came in to see what Giacomin said. I didn't know what to do. But I used to play with the press all the time. My dad always said, listen, they've got a job to do and if you don't help them, they won't help you when they write about the way you play. The man's got a job to do, he's got a deadline, pay attention to him, it's entertainment. You've got to take care of the people who make the game important to the fans. So all these reporters came rushing in and they were so eager. So I said, I shouldn't tell you this but Giacomin said that [Rangers president Bill] Jennings had put a bounty on me. To maim me. A $5,000 bounty. So, they printed it."

WALT TKACZUK: "I was right there. Eddie came up to him and said something, there was a big rivalry between Boston and New York, and Eddie was a fierce competitor and he said something to him. I don't know what it was. It didn't seem like much of a conversation and then Eddie went back in the net and all of a sudden everything just blew up. The puck went into the corner, somebody hit somebody and everybody just dropped their gloves. I don't know what was said, even to this day. I was Eddie's roommate and I don't even remember him ever telling me what he said."

BRAD PARK: "The Rangers and the Bruins in the early '60s were probably the two worst teams in the league. With the New York-Boston rivalry we didn't like each other very much. I remember we went to Boston for the first game and we lost then the second game we lost but then with about a minute and a half left, Derek Sanderson jumps Dave Balon and beats him up and 'Bozey' was not a fighter. So then when Derek goes out through the Zamboni entrance, he puts both his arms up and makes a victory sign and goes off the ice. So we go back to New York and we have our meeting getting ready and the last thing the Cat says in the meeting was, 'This is our building. We run the show and there ain't nobody giving the victory sign in our building.'

"So my second shift was Derek's first shift and the faceoff was to the right of the net and Eddie Giacomin goes by me and said something to Derek. And then they finish up with F-you F-you. The puck went in the far corner and Derek went in the corner and all five Rangers went in after him, not only to prove a point and to take exception to what happened in Boston but to get ourselves back into the series.

"The funny story about that is that when Derek went off the ice the press ran down after him. I had asked Eddie, 'What did you say to him?' He said, 'I told him keep his head up,' but Derek told the press that we had put a bounty on his head. So the next day was an offday and Derek was on *The Tonight Show* with Johnny Carson. Derek is a great promoter, I'll tell you."

Billy Speer scored midway through the first period for the Bruins but the Rangers came back with goals by Ratelle and Tkaczuk for a 2–1 lead. They increased that lead to 4–1 early in the third period, but the Bruins made it interesting, scoring two goals and pressuring the Rangers right up to the final buzzer. The 4–3 victory broke the Rangers' ten-game playoff losing streak and Ed Giacomin's personal eight-game losing skid. A total of 174 penalty minutes were assessed by John Ashley, setting another playoff record.

In the fourth game, Rod Gilbert scored two goals early in the first period to give the Rangers a quick 2–0 lead by the five-minute mark. Phil Esposito cut the Bruins deficit in half with a goal at 11:30 of the second period, but Dave Balon scored an unassisted goal 22 seconds later to restore the Blueshirts' two-goal cushion. Bobby Orr scored a power-play goal nine minutes into the third period but Walt Tkaczuk put the game away with a goal at 11:16 of the period and the Rangers were able to hang on for a 4–2 victory.

With the series tied at two games apiece the teams returned to Boston for the all-important fifth game.

Bobby Orr and Jack Egers swapped goals in the first period and Orland Kurtenbach gave the Rangers the lead midway through the second period. But the turning point of the game and perhaps the series occurred at 15:33 of the second period when Phil Esposito accidentally cut the left side of Jean Ratelle's head with his stick, drawing blood as well as a five-minute major. Unfortunately, with their top center and leading power-play scorer in the dressing room getting stitched up, the Rangers could muster only one shot on goal while they had the man advantage. Tim Horton was later called for holding, nullifying the man advantage. Esposito then scored two goals in the third period to give the Bruins a 3–2 lead. "We were leading 2–1," Francis later told reporters. "But what good was the power play with Jean not being able to be in it? He was the guy who was moving us best. But he couldn't do much the rest of the game."

The Rangers had one final chance to tie the game when Bobby Orr was called for slashing at 19:53 of the third period. But Boston Garden timekeeper Tony Notagiacomo didn't hear the whistle to stop play and let the clock run down. Francis had to run out onto the ice and argue with referee Bruce Hood to get the seven seconds put back on the clock.

Francis pulled Giacomin for an additional skater and sent Ratelle out to take the draw, deep in the Bruins zone, hoping to get one last shot on goal. But Fred Stanfield won the faceoff and the Bruins skated off with a 3–2 victory, one game away from eliminating the Blueshirts.

The series moved back to New York for the sixth game where Brad Park got the Rangers on the board with a power-play goal in the first period. But that was all the Garden fans had to cheer about that night as the Bruins scored four unanswered goals over the next two periods and won the game by a 4–1 score. Art Skov called only 18 minutes in penalties in the game, but the Rangers and Bruins set an NHL record for penalty minutes in a Stanley Cup series by two teams with a total of 375 minutes.

For the fourth year in a row, the Rangers had made the playoffs but once again failed to advance past the first round. Rod Gilbert led the Rangers in scoring in the series with four goals and five assists. Rookie Jack Egers, who was in the lineup in place of the injured Vic Hadfield, surprised many by scoring three goals. By comparison, Bobby Orr racked up seven goals and three assists for the Bruins, followed by Phil Esposito who scored six goals with four assists. Balon (32), Horton (28), and Kurtenbach (24) accumulated the most penalty minutes for the Rangers while, not surprisingly, Derek Sanderson (68) and Wayne Cashman (39) led the Bruins.

Ed Giacomin had a poor series, allowing 19 goals in 4 2/3 games for a bloated 4.13 GAA compared to his 2.50 GAA (with one shutout) in the eight regular-season meetings with the Bruins.

Many felt that "Steady Eddie" could not be expected to play nearly the full schedule of regular-season games and still be fresh for the play-offs. A comparison of Giacomin's regular season and playoff statistics up to that point in his NHL career showed that he did indeed seem to be stronger during the regular season than in the playoffs. Over the previous four seasons Giacomin led all NHL netminders each season in games and minutes played and posted an overall 2.49 GAA in the regular season. Yet for those same four seasons his goals against average in the playoffs rose to 3.38, nearly a goal a game more than in the regular season.

Gerry Cheevers, Eddie's counterpart in the Boston net, played in only 41 games during the regular season, posting a 2.72 GAA. He then appeared in 13 playoff games and recorded a 2.23 GAA for the Bruins who swept past the Black Hawks and St. Louis Blues to win their first Stanley Cup in twenty-nine years.

The Tim Horton Trade

The trade that brought Tim Horton to the Rangers has been the subject of much debate over the years primarily because it's hard to believe that the Leafs' GM Jim Gregory would let Horton go for a only a minor leaguer named Denis Dupere. Even if the Leafs were looking to dump Horton's salary, considering how desperately the Rangers needed to shore up their defensive corps in the wake of injuries to Brad Park and Jim Neilson, they certainly could have gotten a lot more for the forty-year-old veteran.

The Rangers' 1970–71 "Blue Book," the team's popular media guide, listed the Horton transaction as including winger Guy Trottier as well as Dupere. Gerry Eskenazi also reported in the June 10, 1970, issue of the *New York Times* that Trottier had been sent to Toronto to complete the Horton deal.

Other sources reveal a more complex deal that involved Jacques Plante and the St. Louis Blues. Andrew Podnieks's *The Blue and White Book*, billed as "The Most Complete Toronto Maple Leaf Fact Book Ever Published," lists Plante and Trottier as well as Dupere as going to Toronto for Horton. Apparently, when the trade was made the Rangers were still owed an unnamed player from St. Louis to complete an earlier trade. Emile Francis had that player to be named later transferred to the Leafs as part of the deal. That player turned out to be Plante, who was going to be left unprotected by the Blues anyway. In addition, Guy Trottier had a great season for the Buffalo Bisons of the AHL that year, scoring 55 goals with 33 assists. The Buffalo Sabres would be joining the NHL in 1970–71 and their GM Punch Imlach, who had been dismissed by the Leafs the previous season, would be sure to claim him. But the animosity was so great between Leafs owner Harold Ballard and Imlach that the Leafs would have wanted to grab Trottier just so Imlach couldn't have him.

EMILE FRANCIS: "The Leafs were gonna get Jacques Plante from St. Louis. I had made that deal with St. Louis. Horton came to me and I had to get Plante at the end of the year and send him to Toronto. I was supposed to send Sawchuk to St. Louis but then when that accident happened and he died I had to send Plante instead."

Road Woes: Bumped by the Stones, Beaten at the Buzzer, and Grounded by a Strike

Road trips are an accepted aspect of a hockey player's life, part of the schedule that takes teams from coast to coast during the course of the long NHL season. Most road trips are uneventful: you win, you lose, you tie (until 2004), you go home. But sometimes the road hits back, presenting a team with challenges and difficulties that it would have never faced in their home arena.

On Saturday, November 8, 1969, the Rangers were scheduled to play the Kings in Los Angeles at 8 p.m. However, unbeknownst to the Blueshirts or the NHL, the Kings had moved the starting time of the game up to 2 p.m. that afternoon because their owner Jack Kent Cooke had scheduled the Rolling Stones for two performances at the Forum that evening. The concerts were expected to rake in over $250,000 for Cooke and the Forum. It was also an important booking for the Stones, who hadn't played in the United States in three years. The concerts were booked in October but in the excitement, Cooke and the Kings had failed to notify the league and the Rangers of the time change.

Emile Francis discovered the change when preparing for a three-game road trip which would take the Rangers to Chicago, Oakland, and then Los Angeles in the span of four days.

EMILE FRANCIS: "We had a guy named Tommy Barnwell, we called him 'Tom the Bomb.' He was like a runner for us. He was delivering the mail and he comes in my office. He said, 'Cat you asked me to go on a trip with you out to California didn't you?'

"I said, 'That's right.'

"He said, 'Well, what time is the game in LA?'

"I said 'It's a night game.'

"He said, 'Oh no, it's not gonna be a night game.'

"I said, 'What do you mean?'

"He said, 'I just got mail promoting a Rolling Stones concert in Los Angeles on the Saturday night we're supposed to be there.'

"I said, 'What?'

"So he shows me the flyer. I said who the hell are the Rolling Stones, what team do they play for? So right away I called Clarence Campbell. I said, 'Mr. Campbell, I've got a flyer sitting in front of me here and I wanted to know if you knew anything about it. Evidentially, Jack Kent Cooke out in LA is bringing in the Rolling Stones and our game has been changed from a night game to an afternoon game.' I said, 'First of all, he's gotta get permission from us to agree to the change in time which I'm not gonna do. Second of all, he should tell you because you're in charge of the league and you have to assign the referees and linesmen.' He said, 'No, I never heard anything about that.' I said, 'Well neither did I until about half an hour ago when our mail boy delivered this thing to me.' So, I faxed it to him."

The problem for the Rangers was that they were playing in Oakland the night before the Kings game and would have to make a scheduled flight to Los Angeles at midnight. It also meant playing an afternoon game fifteen hours after a night game, which Francis would never had agreed to considering how taxing the West Coast trips were for teams from the Eastern Division.

The NHL had by-laws against teams arbitrarily changing game times and Francis knew that he could force the Kings to forfeit the game. It would have been the first pregame forfeit in NHL history, but he played his hand carefully.

EMILE FRANCIS: "So a couple of hours later I got a call from Jack Kent Cooke. 'Mr. Francis, I just got off the phone with Mr. Campbell. He said I had to go through you get the approval to move the game and then the league because they have to assign the officials. I'm sure that being a businessman like you are that you will agree that if I can get the Rolling Stones in here for a couple performances on Saturday night that it would put a lot of money in our pockets and that would help us out because we don't have a very good hockey team to fill the building like you do in New York. I need all the help I can get financially. And being the type of guy that you are I'm sure that you'll agree with me to change the time.'

"I said, 'No, I don't agree with you and we're not gonna change the time.'

"He said, 'What?'

"I said, 'You heard me. We play in Chicago on Wednesday night and in Oakland on Friday night and get into LA about three in the morning and you want to schedule a game for two o'clock in the afternoon? No, I'm not gonna agree to that.'

"So he says, 'I can't believe that you won't make a change.'

"I said, 'suppose it was your team. What would you do?'

"So he said, 'Well, I'm sorry we wasted our time with you.'

"But he didn't give up. The next day he called again. He said, 'I gotta have that concert. We've sold out all our tickets. Do you know how much it means to me?'

"I said, 'I know what it means to me—two points! Two points that we may need at the end of the season.' And don't you know that's exactly what happened.

"So he said, 'What can I do to get you to agree to the change?'

"Well, I said, 'there's only one way we could do it and it'll cost you some money.'

"So he says, 'what's that?'

"I said, if you have a charter there waiting after the Oakland game and get us out of there we can probably get to LA by about one-thirty. You pay for all the expenses and meals on the plane, steak dinners after the game like we normally have and you have busses waiting to take us to the hotel, I'll agree to the time change.'

"So he says, 'Let me think about that.' He called back later and said, 'Okay, I'll do that.' And that's what we did. We took the charter and flew right out and it saved us a lot of money. So he called before the game and asked how the flight was. 'I got the best I could for you.' I said, Only one more thing, Jack, now we need two points.' But we won, 4–1.

"And when we came out of that building that night I never saw so many people waiting to go in. But it was a funny thing with Cooke. When Muhammad Ali had his first fight after he was locked out because he wouldn't go in the army, the fight was in Madison Square Garden and guess who promoted the fight—Jack Kent Cooke. So I knew our players wanted to go but we didn't have any tickets and the Garden didn't have anything to do with it. He was just promoting the fight out of the Garden. So I just took a chance and called him. I said, 'Jack I've got twenty-two players here and they're after me to call you to get tickets for the fight. Any chance we can sneak those guys in? He said, 'You'll have your twenty-two tickets and you won't have to worry about sneaking anybody in,' and that's what he did."

An even more compelling drama played out the next time the Rangers visited the Kings in LA on January 28, 1970.

The Kings were leading the Rangers, 4–3, very late in the third period when Bob Nevin scored with 71 seconds remaining to tie the score.

As the seconds ticked away, the Kings' Ross Lonsberry launched a desperate 25-foot drive just as the buzzer sounded to end the game. The puck entered the net just as the green light came on signifying the end of the game. The goal judge, ironically former Ranger Dutch Hiller, pressed the button signaling a goal. But the red goal light which should have been disabled when the green light was activated came on anyway. That's when the fun started.

Emile Francis rushed out onto the ice yelling at referee Bob Sloan that the lights had malfunctioned and the goal should not be allowed. Both teams mobbed Sloan and Kings owner Jack Kent Cooke and GM Larry Regan also somehow made it onto the ice and were talking to the referee, which infuriated Francis even more.

After about fifteen minutes Giacomin overheard Sloan tell his linesmen, "Let's call it a tie and get the hell out of here." But then Sloan reversed himself and allowed Lonsberry's goal, giving the Kings a 5–4 victory. This set off a wild scene as Giacomin rushed at Sloan, pushed him against the glass and threw a punch at him. Apparently, Sloan had been assured by Cooke and Regan that the lights were wired properly, so the red goal light had to have been turned on before the green light came on.

Later in the arena parking lot, Francis called Rangers president Bill Jennings and told him that he was going to appeal the ruling. Protests were not allowed in the NHL, but Francis thought that an appeal based on the rules would be his only recourse.

Francis knew that the lights were not wired correctly and was upset that it took Sloan that long to make a decision. If the referee wasn't sure, he should have called it a tie. Emile was also upset that Cooke and Regan were also on the ice talking to Sloan.

Jiggs McDonald was broadcasting Kings games back then and he remembers that evening very well.

JIGGS MCDONALD, *broadcaster*: "It was a nightmare that night. By the time I got downstairs, the screaming and yelling was still going on.

Emile was just livid. They had to close the door in the hallway between the dressing rooms which was very seldom done. But Jack Kent Cooke convinced the officials that the scoreboard and clock were wired so that when the clock hit triple zeroes the red light couldn't come on. And so, it was a goal.

"However, Emile wanted that checked. But Mr. Cooke said, 'Emile, calm down. Come back tomorrow morning and I'll show you exactly how it works.' He did a masterful selling job, 'come back in the morning, Emile'. So Emile settled down and left the building. But in the meantime, Cooke sought out the building engineer and the electrical people and they spent the night making sure it was wired properly. They worked all night to make sure that the next morning when the clock hit zero, there was no chance of that red light coming on."

However, according the Gerry Eskenazi's book *A Year on Ice* which followed the Rangers through the 1969–70 season, the lights still weren't wired correctly. Francis was in the Forum bright and early the next morning with assistant trainer Jim Young testing the system that ran the red and green lights. As the clock wound down to 00:00, the green light came on as it should, but when Young pressed the button to signify a goal, the red light which should have been disabled came on as well.

EMILE FRANCIS: "I went back there in the morning and the guy who was the building manager didn't know who I was. So I asked him, 'Could you do me a favor? I'm thinking of building a new rink and I like the way your lights are set up. Could you put that clock back to the five minute mark and just run it down. I just want to see how it works.' He says, 'No problem.' So guess what? It gets to the zero mark and both lights came on. So I told Clarence Campbell about it. He sent Scotty Morrison [supervisor of officials] right down there and they made them change their whole system."

At the same time, Ranger executives were in the studios of WOR-TV in New York reviewing the tape of the game. The frame-by-frame review of the tape revealed the same sequence of events, but it also showed the puck entering the net with one-sixth of a second remaining in the game. The goal was legitimate! The puck crossed the goal line before the game ended but with no video replay, Sloan could not have known that at the time.

The Kings were forced to fix the goal light system and for his part, Sloan did not mention anything about Giacomin's punch in his game report, sparing Eddie a hefty fine and a lengthy suspension.

Thankfully, the Rangers' final visit to Los Angeles that season on February 11 was an uneventful 6–2 victory for the Blueshirts.

But the Rangers' road woes weren't over.

Friday, March 27, 1970, started out as a normal getaway day for the Rangers. They were scheduled to fly to Montreal for a game the next evening against the Canadiens. It was the first game of a home-and-home series against Montreal and an important weekend for the Blueshirts, who were desperately trying to overtake the Canadiens and Red Wings for a playoff berth.

Following their morning practice at Skateland in New Hyde Park, the Rangers traveled by bus to Kennedy Airport for a typical late afternoon Air Canada flight to Montreal. But what followed was anything but typical.

Upon arrival at JFK, they discovered that their 4 p.m. flight was cancelled due to an ongoing labor dispute involving air traffic controllers in Montreal. No problem. Francis was used to itinerary changes after all his years of traveling with hockey teams and promptly summoned another bus that would take the team to Montreal. The trip would be longer, but it would also give the team a chance to relax and bond with some of the newer players who were acquired late in the season.

The new bus arrived and the players promptly boarded and settled in for the long trip to Montreal. Francis was among the last to board and noticed that seated in the first row, directly behind the driver, was a woman who was in her mid-thirties. "Who's that?" Francis asked the driver. "She's my wife, she's going to Montreal with me," the driver replied. "Not on this bus she isn't," snapped Francis. "You'd better drop her off somewhere."

The driver took the bus to 46th Street and Queens Boulevard in Sunnyside, where he and the woman got off . . . and never came back.

"We were really stuck," Francis said later. "The guy left the bus running, and none of us could even turn the damned thing off."

Emile found a phone booth in a nearby candy store and called Campus Coach for yet a third bus. "We've got no one to drive the damn bus," he yelled into the phone. "Get someone the hell over here." Francis returned to the bus and told his players, "They said if the other driver shows up, not to let him touch the bus. They're sending another driver. They said it would be at least a half an hour."

Most of the players then left the bus and wandered into a local deli, ordering sandwiches for what was obviously going to be a very long ride. The deli owner could hardly keep up with the orders while veterans like Ron Stewart and Terry Sawchuk smuggled six packs of beer back onto the bus.

Pretty soon, word spread throughout the neighborhood that the Rangers bus was on Queens Boulevard. "They knew who we were, and we drew a crowd," Francis remembers. One local fan stuck his head inside, and said "What are you guys doing here?" "We're on a tour," cracked Eddie Giacomin.

Finally, a driver arrived but told Francis that he had already worked an eight-hour shift and could only bring the bus back to the garage. There the Rangers boarded another bus and awaited the arrival of their third driver. The new driver stuck his head into the bus and recognized Frank Paice. "Hey Frank remember me? I used to drive the Rangers to Lake Placid," he said. The third bus was old and the driver couldn't get it to go over 55 miles an hour. The trip took ten hours, and the Rangers didn't get to Montreal until 1 a.m. the next morning. But they tied the Canadiens that night, 1–1, for a critical point in the standings.

"One thing that whole mess taught me," said Francis, "was that we needed a new bus company!"

The Terry Sawchuk Tragedy

Terry Sawchuk was one of the greatest goaltenders in NHL history. During hockey's "Golden Era" of the six-team league, Terry's records stood above those of his netminding brethren that included Glenn Hall, Jacques Plante, Johnny Bower, and Gump Worsley.

Terry played for 21 seasons in the NHL. He started out in Detroit where he won the Calder trophy as the NHL's Rookie of the Year in 1951. He then went to Boston, returned to Detroit, moved to Toronto, went to Los Angeles in the expansion draft, returned to Detroit for a third time, and finished his career as a New York Ranger.

In the summer of 1969, Rangers GM Emile Francis was looking for a backup for Ed Giacomin to replace Don Simmons, who had retired at the end of the previous season. Sawchuk seemed to be the perfect candidate. On June 17, 1969, Francis swung a deal that sent winger Larry Jeffrey to Detroit for the forty-year-old Sawchuk and minor-leaguer Sandy Snow.

EMILE FRANCIS: "The best goalkeeper I ever saw in the National Hockey League was Terry Sawchuk. He's my number one guy. I picked him up at the end because I was developing Gilles Villemure. I knew I was going to use Giacomin in about sixty games and I didn't want Villemure sitting around playing ten or twelve games, we were playing seventy-six games back then. So I left Villemure in Buffalo to develop and I brought in Sawchuk, because I knew it would probably only be for a year."

Emile was surprised by Sawchuk's physical condition when he reported to training camp that September.

EMILE FRANCIS: "When I first played against him, he weighed two hundred and twenty pounds, but when I picked him up in New York, he weighed one hundred seventy pounds. He had been sick and lost a lot of weight and had a lot of family problems. But he was a great goalkeeper. The first year he played with the Red Wings they won the playoffs in eight straight games and he had four shutouts. His goals against average was 1.00 [actually, 0.62]."

Physical condition aside, Terry did not let Emile down. He played eight regular-season games, posting a 3–1–2 record with a 2.91 goals against average. He also recorded the 103rd shutout of his storied career on February 1, 1970, in a 6–0 win over the Penguins at Madison Square Garden. "I'm old and tired but I try my best" Sawchuk told reporters after the game. Some of his teammates good-naturedly kidded that the shutout might have been Sawchuk's last. Unfortunately, they were right. Ironically, Sawchuk's very first shutout also came in New York at the old Garden, in a 1–0 victory over the Rangers on January 15, 1950, shortly after making his NHL debut with Detroit.

Sawchuk, "Ukey" to his friends, due to his Ukrainian heritage, also made three appearances in the playoffs that season, totaling 80 minutes and posting a 4.50 GAA. His final appearance as a Ranger came on April 14 in Game Five of the quarter-finals against the Bruins in Boston. With the Rangers trailing in the third period, Francis wanted to slow the pace of the game and replaced Giacomin with Sawchuk. After allowing Terry the league-mandated warm-up period, Giacomin returned to the net following the next faceoff. The Rangers ultimately lost the game, 3–2, and the series in six games.

Six weeks later, Terry Sawchuk was dead.

At the start of the season Sawchuk had rented a house with teammate Ron Stewart in Atlantic Beach, Long Island, where most of the Rangers stayed during the season. The two were old friends, having previously won Stanley Cups and rooming together in Toronto. They had a lot in common. Both were divorced, liked to drink, and were known to lose their temper when drinking.

The problem started on April 29, thirteen days after the Rangers were eliminated from the playoffs. Stewart and Sawchuk were drinking at the E & J pub, a local hangout that the players frequented. The pair began to argue about whose responsibility it was to clean the house before returning the keys to the owner. Stewart also claimed that Sawchuk owed him some money for household expenses. They began pushing each other in the bar and were asked to leave. The argument continued outside the bar until the bartender told them to go home. They each drove separately back to the house at 58 Bay Street where they started arguing again on the lawn in front of two witnesses, Stewart's girlfriend Rosemary Sasso, a registered nurse, and Ben Weiner, a friend of Sawchuk's. Sawchuk moved to grab Stewart, but was pulled back by

Weiner. Unfortunately, the two men stumbled and both fell on Stewart. It is not known whether Sawchuk fell on Stewart's knee or a barbeque grill, but he immediately doubled over in pain. Seeing that Terry was in trouble, Sasso called Dr. Denis Nicholson who found Sawchuk pale, in shock, and with very low blood pressure.

Sawchuk was taken to Long Beach Hospital where tests revealed that he had suffered damage to his gall bladder and liver. He then underwent surgery to remove his gall bladder. A few days later he had another operation to repair his liver.

Terry was in the hospital for three weeks before it became known to the public. The story was broken on May 22 by Gerry Eskenazi of the *New York Times*. There were rumors of a cover-up but in actuality, Terry didn't want anyone to know because his father had been in an auto accident and was in a Detroit hospital, so he didn't want him to worry.

Sawchuk took a turn for the worse on May 29 and was transferred to New York Hospital, which specialized in acute illnesses. Tests found internal bleeding and he once again underwent surgery to further repair his liver.

Following the surgery, Sawchuk regained consciousness briefly but died in his sleep from a blood clot on May 31.

EMILE FRANCIS: "The whole Sawchuk affair was one of the toughest things I had ever faced in my whole life. I was out scouting in Quebec and I had to go to the hospital. He underwent a five hour operation that lasted until midnight and the doctor came out and said, 'you might as well go home because there's nothing you can do here. We'll call you if anything changes'. They called me at six in the morning to tell me he died.

"I'll never forget it was Memorial Day weekend in New York and I had to go to get his body from the morgue on Second Avenue. And honest to God, there were thirty people lying on the floor in bags like we carry hockey sticks in. The guy that took me down there, I could tell he'd been drinking, I could smell it. He said, 'Okay which one is the body you came to claim?' I mean I could have nailed him right there. I looked over and I see Terry's head sticking out from one of the bags with a tag around his neck to identify him. God damn, that's where he ended up, on the floor in a morgue in New York City on Memorial Day weekend. And I said to myself, *If this guy only knew that's the greatest goalkeeper ever.* I mean I was sick, believe me."

Stewart took the news very hard and now faced criminal charges. The Rangers hired noted attorney Nicholas Castellano to represent him, but a grand jury in Mineola, New York, eventually found no reason to bring charges and the case was closed.

Francis also felt bad for Stewart who, at thirty-eight, was on the down side of his career. Rather than release or trade the veteran winger and make him feel like an outcast, he brought him back to play the next season with the Rangers. "It was the right thing to do," Francis told reporters at the time, "and I would do it again." Francis eventually chose Stewart to coach the Rangers at the start of the 1975–76 season.

Despite the notoriety of the case, the press left Stewart to himself and didn't make an issue out of the tragedy. Francis recalls only one incident of anyone ever confronting or taunting Stewart.

EMILE FRANCIS: "Stewie was still playing for us and a guy in Toronto poked his head into our bus behind Maple Leaf Gardens and called Stewie a murderer. Vic Hadfield pounced off the bus and threw the guy into a snow bank."

Overall, Sawchuk played in 971 regular-season games in the NHL, posting a 447–330–172 record with 103 shutouts and a 2.51 GAA. In 106 playoff games he went 54–48 with 12 shutouts and a 2.54 GAA. He won four Stanley Cups and four Vezina Trophies and was elected to the Hockey Hall of Fame in 1971.

EMILE FRANCIS: "Terry was one of the greatest, maybe even the greatest, but you just never know in real life. It was a tragedy that far transcended hockey."

Remembering the Boomer

As assistant general manager, one of Boom Boom Geoffrion's responsibilities was scouting. This meant that he received his assignments from Dennis Ball, the Rangers' chief scout. Ball served the Blueshirts from 1950 to 1975 in a number of administrative and scouting roles. Ball was a true character and loved pulling pranks, especially on the Boomer. Ball would usually arrange for Geoffrion's seat for a college game to be directly in front of the school's band. "Once the Boston College tuba guy damn near blew Boomer out to center ice," Ball recalled. Dennis would also mislead Boomer as to weather conditions on the road. He would tell Geoffrion "Omaha is like the tropics at this time of year, bring your golf clothes." Geoffrion would then pack lightly and arrive in Omaha in January to a blizzard with Arctic-like conditions.

In 1972 Geoffrion was elected to the Hockey Hall of Fame and left the Rangers to become coach of the Atlanta Flames. He stayed behind the bench for two and a half seasons before moving to the broadcast booth with Jiggs McDonald.

JIGGS MCDONALD: "Da Boom and Jigg McDonalds, as he always called me. What a team that was. You have to give [Atlanta GM] Cliff Fletcher a lot of credit. He hired a salesman, he hired a motivator and I have to think he knew what he was getting, the personality he was getting. A lot of us in the business wondered what he was doing. Boom had that history of illness and didn't have a very good coaching record as I recall. But in Atlanta, the Boomer was accepted by the populous, the people of Atlanta and the South. Yeah, he played in New York, but he was not a Yankee. He was French Canadian. The outpouring of love and support for Boom was incredible.

"From the hockey standpoint, there are a lot of Boom stories. I don't think that too any players would tell you that he was good with the X's and O's or the strategy of the game, but he could certainly motivate. There's a great story about Boom saying, 'There's tree ting to dis game, tree ting. Skate and Shoot.' 'But Boom, you said three things.' Boom said 'Yeah, skate . . . and . . . shoot.'

"The guys used to tell the story of a game against the Boston Bruins and Boom was going through the Bruins lineup before the game. 'Who dem guys got? Nobody der dat I would want on dis team. All you guys better than dem. Well maybe dat H-Orr (pronounced hoar) but all you guys better dan de Bruins.' He was a funny individual.

"He had a presence; he demanded an audience and commanded the audience. But when it came to the dressing room it was done through motivation. I think the majority of the guys would tell you that they pretty much coached themselves and he got them ready to go out there.

"The day that he resigned as coach, we had played the Minnesota North Stars. We were flying back, commercial of course. Cliff had the aisle seat, I had the middle seat, and Boom by the window. And there was hardly anything said back and forth, there was no conversation. That afternoon, I got a call from Jim Huber who was our PR guy that there was a press conference at six at the Omni, be there. 'Oh geez, we've been away, we just got home, there's no reason for me to go down there. What's going on, Hube's?' 'Boom quit.'

"He had taken the team to the playoffs that second year and now into the third he recognized that they weren't going to get there. And he was gone. He was out of there. That's when Fred Creighton came in. Cliff always seemed to have a safety net. He was well aware of Boom's history of either illness or of walking away. The tendency to get out from under a bad situation. And the team wasn't very good and wasn't going to make the playoffs and this was his escape.

"We were over at the house one day and I had a company car but he didn't like our family car. He said, 'Why you drive dat shitbox?' I said, 'Well it depends on where I'm going and what I'm doing.' But that's basically my wife's car. He said, 'Oh, you shouldn't be driving dat, I get you a big Lincoln.' I said how are you gonna get me a Lincoln. He says no problem. So we're doing a tag line, just a tag line about the Lincoln Mercury dealer and sure enough I got a car to drive and it was a Lincoln. It wasn't even a lease; it was a loaner, I guess. But I kept saying, 'Boom, how do you do this?' He said, 'Oh, dey like me, Jiggs.' And his whole MO was to get it 'on the cuff.' 'I get dat Jiggs, no problem. It fall off a truck.'

"He took great delight in telling everyone that he wasn't French-Canadian, he was Sicilian. 'You have a car?' he'd ask. 'Don't start it,' he'd warn. We were on a cruise with him and Marlene one year, he had the entire crew of that ship in the palm of his hand. Everywhere he went the crew would be saying, 'Don't start it.' He had a presence; he demanded an audience and commanded the audience. But when it came to the dressing room it was done through motivation. I think the majority of the guys would tell you that they pretty much coached themselves and he got them ready to go out there."

In 1979, Boomer realized a life-long dream by becoming the coach of the Montreal Canadiens. Once again, however, he was forced to step down due to stomach ulcers.

On March 11, 2006, the Canadiens retired Geoffrion's number 5 sweater. The date had been selected by Geoffrion because it held a special significance for his family. When Geoffrion's father-in-law, the great Howie Morenz, died in 1937, his casket was placed in the Forum for public viewing on March 11. Unfortunately Geoffrion never made it to Montreal that night or saw his sweater raised to the rafters. The Boomer died that morning in Atlanta of cancer at the age of seventy-five.

JIGGS MCDONALD: "His death was almost like it was orchestrated, he always had that element of show business about him. It was a shock, the timing of his passing. I had spoken to Marlene earlier that week and also to Linda and was aware that there wasn't a whole lot of time left. And Marlene had kept me up to date on the trip to Montreal for the raising of the banner and how they were looking forward to it, and just hoping that Boom would be able to make it. But to have him miss it by a day, but he probably wouldn't have been able to go as it turned out but they were sure hoping that he would be there.

"We went to Atlanta for the funeral. The only member of the Canadiens to be there was Jean Beliveau. It meant a lot to Marlene. There were flowers from the Canadiens but Jean was the only representative of the Canadiens fraternity."

Playing for a Tie

During the 1969–70 season the Philadelphia Flyers set an NHL record with the most ties in one season with 24. It is a record that still stands today. The Flyers and Rangers met six times that year and each game ended in a tie. Following the last Ranger tie, the one that set the record, the Spectrum message board displayed, "Yes we have a pretty sister" and the Flyers' hostesses handed out more than 2,000 ties to commemorate the occasion.

Ned Braden on Broadway?

Michael Ontkean is probably best known among hockey fans for his portrayal of minor league hockey player Ned Braden in the 1977 cult classic *Slap Shot*. But many fans may be surprised to learn that Ontkean was actually a pretty good collegiate hockey player who turned down an offer for a tryout with the Rangers in 1969 to pursue an acting career.

Ontkean was a three-time all-star right winger for the University of New Hampshire, scoring 63 goals and 111 points in his collegiate career.

Ontkean grew up in Montreal and played for the Montreal Canadiens' Junior B team before moving to Western Canada where he starred for New Westminster's Junior A club. He received hockey scholarship offers from twelve schools around the country but selected the University of New Hampshire because he felt they had a good program and had just earned full Division I status.

The future actor played on a line with Bob Brandt and Rich David and in 1967–68 the trio recorded a total of 163 points (73 goals, 90 assists) that led the nation. That same season Ontkean scored 30 goals and 54 points which led the ECAC as well as the nation.

After graduation Ontkean was invited to a tryout by the Rangers. But he had taken acting courses in his senior year and took part in several productions put on by the theater department. He had caught the acting bug. He moved to Hollywood and played semi-pro hockey with the Los Angeles Blades at night and attended auditions during the day. His first regular role in a TV series was as Officer Willie Gillis in *The Rookies* from 1972 to 1974. He is also known for his role as Sheriff Harry Truman in *Twin Peaks*. But among hockey fans he is most famous for portraying Ned Braden, the Charlestown Chiefs' college-educated winger who refused to fight. "At the time I thought the combination of wild satire, sexual bravado, and general anarchy might be too much for any major studio to release," Ontkean once told a reporter. "I'm glad I was wrong."

8

The Blueshirts on the Air

NO REVIEW OF the Emile Francis era would be complete without a chapter dedicated to the announcers who brought the games into our homes, our cars and our lives. Over the years each of these men became like family as they shared the joys and disappointments of being a Ranger fan with their audience.

Radio

The first radio voice of the Rangers was Hamilton, Ontario, native John "Jack" Filman. Filman began broadcasting New York Americans home games in 1925 and added the Rangers when they joined the league in 1926. The games were broadcast over WMSG, formerly WWGL and located at 1420 on the AM dial. The station was purchased by MSG boss Tex Rickard for the purpose of carrying every event that took place in the Garden. Filman, known for his rapid-fire delivery, had coached both hockey and lacrosse and was considered an authority on both sports.

Hockey was presented much differently on the radio than it is today. The games usually started at 8:45, but the radio coverage began at 10 p.m., just in time for some third period play-by-play and a wrap-up. This abbreviated coverage remained the order of the day until 1940.

The broadcasts moved to WMCA in 1930 because they had a stronger signal. Filman died in 1940 at the age of forty-three and was replaced by Bertram Lebhar Jr., otherwise known as Bert Lee. The games moved to WHN and it was only then that the Rangers were given full opening faceoff to final buzzer coverage. Lee worked with Dick Fishell and Marty Glickman in the early years but teamed up with Ward Wilson in 1944 and the pair stayed together until 1955–56.

Coverage was sporadic for the next ten years with Win Elliot, Bud Palmer, Les Keiter, Jim Gordon, and even future game show host Monty Hall taking turns behind the microphone.

Marv Albert

Marv Albert grew up listening to sports on New York radio. There was Marty Glickman and Les Keiter calling Knicks games; Vin Scully, Al Helfer, and Connie Desmond working Dodgers games; and Ward Wilson and Bert Lee broadcasting the Rangers. They were his idols and his inspiration, and he knew from an early age that broadcasting sports on radio and TV was the career path that he wanted to pursue.

As a youngster growing up in the Manhattan Beach section of Brooklyn, Marv played roller hockey, basketball, and baseball. And when he wasn't actively involved in the game he would do play-by-play from the sidelines on his own imaginary radio station, WMPA (Marvin Philip Aufrichtig, later changed to Albert). His father took him to New York Rovers Eastern League hockey games at the old Madison Square Garden where he would try to stand as close to the radio announcers as he could and quietly do play-by-play to himself. But when Marv was thirteen, his dad bought him a tape recorder which gave him a chance to save and critique his own work. The machine was big and bulky but Marv lugged it to all of his "games."

When he got to high school, Marv wrote a letter to Herb Goren, the Rangers PR director and fellow Brooklyn native, asking if he could interview one of the players for his school newspaper. Goren supplied Don "Bones" Raleigh, who was one of the Rangers best players at the time. As luck would have it, Howard Cosell overheard the interview and offered young Marv a spot on a new kid's sports show he was launching on WABC radio called *All League Clubhouse*. Marv seized the opportunity and appeared on the show for two years. One of the guests on the program was Fresco Thompson, who was then a vice president of the Brooklyn Dodgers. When the show was over Marv asked Thompson if they needed any summer help, and thus landed a job as an office boy with the Dodgers.

It was Marv's first opportunity to rub elbows with the players and executives of professional sports teams. One of the perks of the job was a pair of tickets to the press box for every home game, so Marv would usually bring one of his brothers along as well as his tape recorder and do play-by-play and then review the tapes later that night.

Albert was also an avid Knicks fan and started a fan club for Jim Baechtold, who was his favorite player at the time. Marv's efforts drew the attention of Knicks executives who encouraged him to expand the scope of the club to include the entire team. The New York Knicks Fan club soon took shape with Marv as president and editor of its official newsletter, *Knick Knacks*.

This was another big break for Marv—not only did he get to know the players, but he began to be recognized by members of the Knicks' front office as well. One of those men was John Goldner, who got Marv a job as a ball boy. He also allowed Marv to sit in the press box during Rangers games where he continued to work on his play-by-play technique.

In 1959, Marv enrolled at Syracuse University which had one of the best communications programs on the East Coast and was Marty Glickman's alma mater. While at Syracuse, Marv took as many on-air jobs as he could, working as an announcer for a classical music station as well as a rock 'n' roll DJ. He also called the school's basketball games as well as Syracuse minor league baseball.

After his junior year at Syracuse, Marv was offered a job with WCBS in New York working for Glickman and Rangers broadcaster Jim Gordon as a producer/writer and backup announcer. He jumped at the opportunity and finished his education at NYU.

Marv's first big professional break came in January of 1963 while still attending NYU. He got a call late one Saturday night from

Glickman saying that he was stuck in Paris and wouldn't be able to make the Knicks game the following day in Boston. Marv and his brother Al took the midnight train out of Grand Central Station to Boston arriving about 4 a.m. Since neither could sleep they bought all the Boston newspapers and prepared their notes for the game. However, in his rush to get to Boston, Marv had failed to bring his press credentials and a guard near the press entrance wouldn't let the pair into the Boston Garden. In desperation Marv opened his briefcase to show the guard his prepared notes. The guard must have been impressed because he made some calls and finally Knicks coach Eddie Donovan came out to vouch for the twenty-one-year-old Albert and his younger brother.

In March of 1963, a few months after his Knicks debut, Marv was in Detroit to call another Knicks game and since the Rangers would be in town the following night, the station manager suggested that he stick around and call the hockey game as well. It was another dream come true for Marv, but he was nervous and unfortunately the visiting team's broadcast booth in the old Detroit Olympia was as small as a closet, and in order to see the scoreboard or the clock, he needed to look through a periscope. But Marv got through it and did a few more Rangers games that season.

A short while later he moved to WHN where he became sports director and in 1965 convinced station management to broadcast a partial schedule of Rangers games. As it turned out, not only was it partial coverage of the schedule but for some of the individual games as well. WHN was a music station at the time and didn't want to disrupt their format too drastically, so on Sunday nights the station only aired the final five minutes of the first two periods and the entire third period. Fortunately, that arrangement only lasted one season. The next year the station still broadcast only a partial schedule, but the individual games were covered in their entirety.

For those first two seasons Marv worked alone, providing play-by-play, analysis, and between-period interviews. In 1967, former NHL referee Bill Chadwick was brought in as the color man. In 1972, Chadwick was moved over to the television broadcast and Gene Stuart provided analysis for one season. Sal Messina, whom Marv nicknamed

'Red Light,' was brought in the next season and the duo formed a very insightful and entertaining combination.

Albert's hockey play-by-play style was influenced by Danny Gallivan, who broadcast Montreal Canadiens games. One of Marv's strengths as a hockey announcer was his ability to modulate his voice according to the action on the ice. When the puck was in the neutral zone, his voice was calm and steady. But as the action moved towards the goal, his call would become quicker and more intense. Marv also set the geography of the rink and the game as it progressed. For example, at the start of each period, if he said the Rangers were skating from left to right, you knew that their goal was to the left and the opposition's net was to the right. The play could be "along the near (or far) boards." And so if his call was "Park over the blue line along the near boards" you knew that Brad Park had the puck and was skating over the blue line along the boards closest to Marv's broadcast position. And of course, "Kick save and a beauty" was self-explanatory.

As the years went by, Marv became a hot commodity and took on more jobs outside of the realm of Rangers hockey. He was moved to Knicks TV broadcasts and became the voice of the New York football Giants. He became the sports anchor for WNBC-TV and when NBC bought the rights to NBA games he became their primary announcer. He has also worked on major league baseball, college football and basketball, boxing, and tennis broadcasts.

As his workload increased, Marv's work on Rangers broadcasts became more infrequent, as Spencer Ross, Sam Rosen, Howie Rose, his brothers Al and Steve, and his son Kenny, who had also joined the family business, filled in beside Sal Messina.

Albert did find time to broadcast the Rangers' Stanley Cup victory over the Vancouver Canucks on June 14, 1994. As the final buzzer sounded and the Rangers ended their fifty-four-year Cup drought, Marv captured the moment perfectly. "And it's all over," he said. "The New York Rangers have won the Stanley Cup, something most people didn't think they'd hear in their lifetimes."

Marv officially left the Rangers following the 1994–95 season and was replaced by his son, Kenny.

Sal Messina

In 1973 Sal Messina became the color analyst on Rangers radio broadcasts alongside play-by-play man Marv Albert. It was the natural progression for the Queens native who had been involved in hockey and the Blueshirts for most of his life.

Sal grew up listening to Bert Lee call Rangers games on radio. "Bert Lee got me hooked on hockey," Sal told author David J. Halberstam in the book *Sports on New York Radio.* "In our neighborhood in Astoria, kids grew up baseball and basketball fans. I would roller skate; it was hard to get ice time. Lee was theater. I envisioned the NHL by listening to his broadcasts. He really started me on hockey."

Young Sal became a goaltender, playing for Metropolitan League teams throughout the New York area as well as the Long Island Ducks of the Eastern Hockey League. He also had brief stints with the New York Rovers and Philadelphia Ramblers.

SAL MESSINA: "We had a pretty decent senior league over in New Jersey and at the time the Rovers had a team and everyone on that team was from Canada. So near the end of the season someone got hurt and they needed a goalie and Stan Fischler had written a couple of articles about me, so they called me up and I played a few games, a couple of good ones. The Rangers automatically put me on their list and Muzz Patrick signed me to a C-Form.

"I went to two training camps with the Rangers. The first training camp I went to was right after they traded Gump [Worsley] to Montreal in 1963. The team was good; Red Sullivan was a great guy. The thing is that they didn't have first dibs on Canadian players, except the guys they signed early and sent to Guelph. They got lucky with those guys. I played in training camp games. I played for the Rangers and against the Rangers. In fact, Leo Reise scored a goal against me. I'll never forget that. That was a good bunch of guys, very close-knit. But they just didn't have the overall talent that the Red Wings or Leafs or Canadiens had. But it was a great bunch of guys."

Back then teams were only required to carry one netminder, so Sal was able to stick around with the Rangers as a practice goaltender. He also had to be ready to play in case their regular goaltender got hurt and couldn't continue.

SAL MESSINA: "For a year and a half I was traveling with the Rangers. I would sit in the stands even on the road. I would sit in the stands with Muzz or Emile and they would announce your name as wearing number 23. They used to have house goalies at that time but by Muzz having me travel with the team I would have gone in instead of the other team's house goalie if our guy got hurt.

"I almost got into a game once. Jacques Plante was hurt or sick. We had taken the train up to Montreal, and that morning we got off the train and Jacques told me that he didn't feel very well. He hadn't beaten the Canadiens all year and the Rangers weren't going to make the playoffs. When we got to the rink, I skated with the guys who weren't playing. But when I got to the rink that night they had my equipment out and all the guys were giving me the needle. But Jacques came into the dressing room and they made him play. I think they threatened to fine him and so he played and I think they won the game, 3–1. That was the closest I ever got to getting into a game except for training camp.

"Players were treated differently then. They weren't making a lot of money and a lot of them worked over the summer. The minimum was $7,000 so that was one hundred dollars per game. I remember Larry Cahan got traded out to Oakland, and came back to the Garden for a game. I was working in the penalty box and he was bragging about his $10,000 a year contract."

In addition to his role with the Rangers, Sal also continued to play amateur hockey on teams in New Jersey.

SAL MESSINA: "We had a bunch of ex-college players who didn't even get a look in those days because everybody was Canadian, the American weren't even looked at and there were only six teams. I think the first player from Europe to see any action was Ulf Sterner. He was in one of the training camps that I was at. He was good but he was a Swedish kid and he was a little different. It was a grinding game and he wasn't used to that. It was different then. They were good players but the league was really tight. There were only six teams and I think they only dressed sixteen or seventeen players and a goalie."

One of the highlights of Sal's career was traveling to Russia with a team comprised of EHL players.

SAL MESSINA: "One year the Eastern Hockey League was sending a team to Russia. That was the highlight of my career. Wearing the USA jersey in Russia and Czechoslovakia was a thrill. We played in Prague but we didn't do very well because the Russians were better than anybody thought they were."

When his playing career ended, Sal became an off-ice official at the Garden, serving as a goal judge, official scorer, and penalty timekeeper. Then one night he bumped into Bill Chadwick, who had just been moved up to the television booth.

SAL MESSINA: "In 1972 Bill Chadwick was the radio announcer and I was a minor official. The Rangers would have two preseason games in the Garden before the season started. Bill was moved to television. So I saw Bill before one of the games and congratulated him and asked him who would be doing radio, not even thinking about me doing it. So he said, 'well, why don't you give it a try?' I said, 'Me?' He said, 'Call Marv Albert.' So I went in the penalty box that night and I thought, *Well I can talk about hockey, that's not hard. I'd been involved in it all my life practically.* So I called Marv and he said come on in.

"So I go in and he said, 'Okay, we're gonna talk about a couple of plays.' And that went all right. But then he says, 'Interview me, I'm Gilles Villemure,' and I'd never interviewed anybody in my life and I didn't do a good job. They had already hired Gene Stuart, he was the play-by-play guy for the Rangers' New Haven team at the time. So

The Cat.

Earl Ingarfield (10) and Reggie Fleming (9) battle Montreal's Claude Larose.

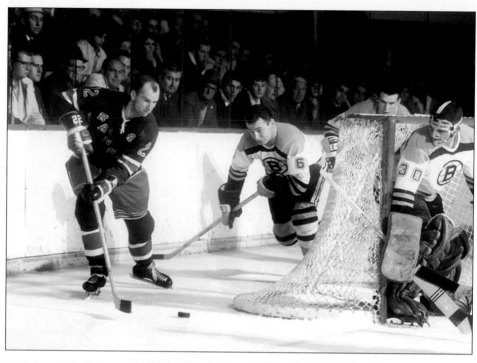

Donnie Marshall skates away from a falling Ted Green as Bernie Parent hugs the post.

Bernie "Boom Boom" Geoffrion.
Photo courtesy of the New York Rangers.

Ed Giacomin (1), Arnie Brown (4), Red Berenson (with helmet), and Harry Howell (3) surround Bobby Orr.

Arnie Brown grabs a hold of Bobby Orr.

Walt Tkaczuk (18) and Dave Balon (17) close in on Dallas Smith.

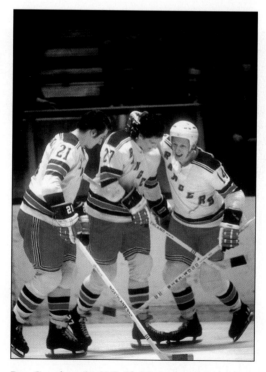

Pete Stemkowski (21), Teddy Irvine (27), and
Bruce MacGregor (14) celebrate a goal.

Billy Fairbairn (10) outraces Dallas Smith for the puck.

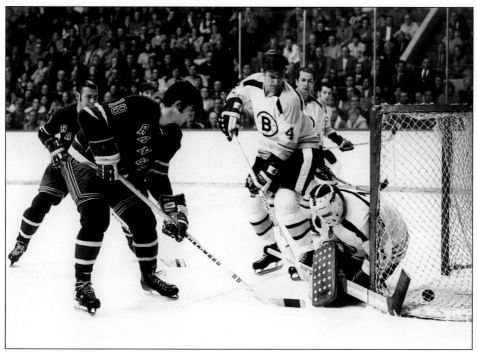

Walt Tkaczuk puts a rebound past Eddie Johnston as Dave Balon, Bobby Orr, and Dallas Smith look on.

Gilles Villemure stops a shot by Wayne Cashman (12) and Bob Nevin chases the rebound while Brad Park, Vic Hadfield, and Tim Horton follow the play.

Ted Irvine (27) and Ken Hodge chase a loose puck.

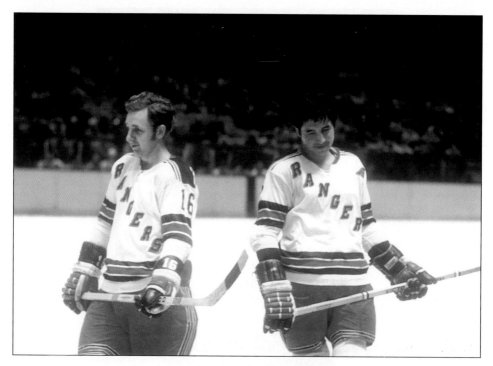

Defensive partners Rod Seiling (16) and Jim "The Chief" Neilson (15).

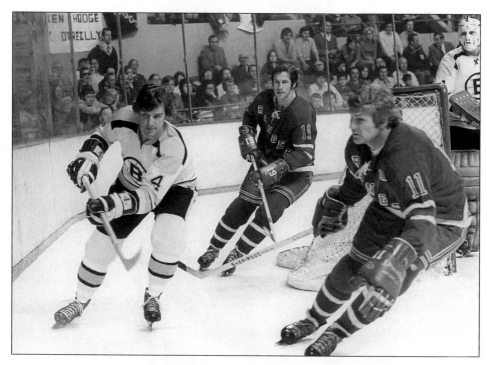

Jean Ratelle (19) and Vic Hadfield (11) try to corral Bobby Orr.

Former teammates Bobby Orr and Derek Sanderson.

Longtime public relations director
and historian John Halligan.
Courtesy of the New York Rangers.

Brad Park, Rod Gilbert, Jean Ratelle, and Vic Hadfield at
Ratelle's 1981 retirement ceremony.

they used him that season. But I knew a lot of people from my days as a player, Red Sullivan, Jacques Plante, Freddie Shero. I knew a lot of people on other teams. So Marv said that I should ask questions. So before each game I'd interview Freddie Shero, they'd come into the Garden five or six times a year. I'd interview all kinds of people. Then I'd submit these tapes to Marv and he'd critique them. And so they gave me the job the next year.

"Funny story about Freddie Shero, every time he came in I'd meet him in the press room and we'd talk for fifteen, twenty minutes. So now it's the first year he's coaching the Rangers. So before the opening game I went up to Freddie and said, 'Let's do an interview.' He said, 'Sal, you know I don't do interviews.'"

Of course, down deep Sal was a Ranger fan but on the air he was as quick to praise an opponent as he was to point out a Rangers mistake. He told the fans exactly what was happening on the ice and didn't pull any punches. Even Marv Albert, who often made Sal the butt of his disparaging sense of humor, called him "vastly underrated and one of hockey's most incisive color commentators." But it was Albert who gave Sal the nickname "Red Light."

SAL MESSINA: "We were out in Oakland one time, the Rangers had played in Toronto and from there they were going to Oakland. Dunc Wilson was in goal and the fans were calling him "Red Light." After the game Hugh Delano put that in the *Post*. Now every goalie was called 'Red Light' at one time or another, even back when we played with chicken wire instead of glass. So, Dunc says to Delano, 'You shouldn't put that in the papers, my wife will think I'm fooling around.' So, then Delano finds out about the other meaning of 'Red Light' and we had a big laugh. So, he tells that story to Marv in Oakland while we were having lunch. That night we go on the air and he says, 'This is Marv Albert with Sal "Red Light" Messina.' And from that day on whenever we went on the air that's what he called me. Nobody else called me that, not Kenny Albert, or Sam Rosen. Just Marv. But it stuck."

During the course of Sal's nearly thirty years behind the microphone, Rangers broadcasts moved up and down the radio dial and he worked with eighteen different play-by-play announcers including Albert's brothers, Steve and Al, as well as Marv's son, Kenny. But the one constant that held the broadcasts together was Messina. Sal was also often called upon to provide play-by-play on the occasions when Albert arrived at the Garden late from his duties as radio voice of the New York Giants.

Few fans realized that in addition to broadcasting Rangers games, Sal also had a full-time job as vice president of sales for a Port Washington-based manufacturer of aircraft parts. Many times Sal would arrive home from a Rangers road trip at 3 a.m. and be at his desk the next morning at 7:30. In fact, in 1987 when the Rangers became the last team in the NHL to broadcast their entire schedule on radio, Sal had to use some of his vacation time in order to work the additional games. But by 2002 with two years left on his contract, Sal knew it was time to retire.

SAL MESSINA: "Even though I retired with a couple of years left on my contract, I had enough after thirty years. I was selling aircraft parts so I traveled for them for a lot of years. I was doing both, working for the Rangers and was VP of sales for W. S. Wilson on Long Island. So every September I had to go to Europe for two weeks right before training camp. When we'd go to Montreal I'd visit Air Canada. So I'd mix it in. But after thirrty years of doing both, it was time. I was tired. But I still have the Dish and I watch every game."

In 2005, Sal was awarded the Foster Hewitt Memorial Award presented by the Hockey Hall of Fame for his outstanding work as an NHL broadcaster. He lists that award as well as the Rangers' 1994 Stanley Cup victory as the highlights of his broadcasting career.

SAL MESSINA: "When they won the Cup and of course getting into the Hall of Fame, were the highlights. That whole series, going out to Vancouver, Rangers were up 3–1 and then coming back to the Garden and getting blown out in Game Five, going back out to Vancouver and winning the Cup at home. It was a great time."

Part of Sal's charm was that he never took himself too seriously. New Yorkers could identify with him as a local guy who made good. Sal made the job of color analyst seem easy but behind his success was a lot experience, perseverance, and hard work.

He may not have been good enough to make it to the NHL as a player, but, as a broadcaster, Sal Messina made it all the way to the Hall of Fame. And it couldn't have happened to a nicer guy.

Television

The Rangers made their television debut on February 25, 1940, in a 6–2 victory over the Montreal Canadiens at Madison Square Garden. It was the first NHL game to be televised in the United States. The game aired on W2XBS, an experimental station, with Skip Walz, known at the time as "Bill Allen" doing the play-by-play. The telecast was only available to the few hundred homes and bars in the New York area that could afford to own a TV set.

The Blueshirts also made broadcasting history on January 5, 1957, when their 6–1 victory over the Black Hawks at the Garden was featured on the first nationwide hockey telecast on CBS. Former Knick Bud Palmer did the play-by-play and Fred Cusick provided color commentary.

The Blueshirts appeared sporadically on local television throughout the 1950s and early 60s, usually on WPIX-Channel 11 until 1965 when they were picked up by WOR-Channel 9 which covered most of their Saturday night road games.

Win Elliot

Very often our first memories of a sport are accompanied by the faces and voices that brought that sport into our homes. For many fans, Win Elliot was one of those faces and voices.

Before the days of national mega-buck broadcasting contracts, cable, 24/7 coverage, or any of the advanced broadcasting techniques available to us today, New York Rangers fans considered themselves lucky to see the Blueshirts in action on their home TV screens once a week. Those rare games on WPIX or WOR were usually on Saturday nights and often on tape delay as part of the Schaefer Circle of Sports. "Schaefer, the one beer to have when you're having more than one," was their motto. And one of the voices that brought them into our homes belonged to Win Elliot, who alternated with Bob Wolff depending upon the station that held the rights to the broadcast and the sponsor.

Win Elliot was born Irwin Elliot Shalek in Chelsea, Massachusettes, but changed his name early in his career. A zoology major and hockey goaltender at the University of Michigan, Elliot took a communications class to get the credits he needed to graduate, and an impressed professor suggested sportscasting as a career.

During his heyday, Win was one of the busiest announcers in the business, anchoring World Series and Super Bowl pre- and postgame shows, covering boxing and horse racing and hosting radio call-in shows as well as his work on the Schaefer Circle of Sports on television. He also reported for Sports Central USA on the CBS Radio Network as well as hosting early television game shows such as *Tic Tac Dough* and *On Your Account* and the radio variety show *Borden's County Fair*.

But it was Elliot's nearly twenty years as the voice of the Rangers on both radio and TV that he is best remembered by New Yorkers of a certain age.

In those black and white, single camera days, Win *was* the Rangers to many of us, serving as play-by-play announcer and color analyst as well as the between-period host.

Elliot's warm, friendly, almost folksy manner made him a welcomed guest in our living rooms on those long-ago wintry nights. Despite the fact that the Rangers racked up a lot of losses during Win's time in the booth, he still made the games exciting and enjoyable to watch. He was a storyteller, always imparting a bit of hockey lore into each broadcast. "The game of hockey was invented by Canadian Indians," Win would say. "And the game was named after the word the Indians would shout after getting hit with a frozen road apple—ho-gee, which meant 'It hurts.'" He also recounted the tale of former Rangers netminder Steve Buzinski who, after making a glove save, flipped the puck behind the net only to discover he had misjudged his position and tossed the puck into his own goal instead.

Between-period interviews were conducted from the penalty box or the Rangers bench using the lone press box position camera on a long shot. And in the era before videotape and replays, Elliott, with bow tie, glasses, and crew cut, would re-enact goals on screen using just the gifts that he was born with, his voice and body movements. Yes it was all very primitive, but it was all we had and we loved it and looked forward to it every week. It was the earliest form of "appointment viewing" for New York hockey fans.

Bob Wolff worked with Win and remembers him fondly. "Win loved hockey and for many years we worked as a team together and I enjoyed that tremendously. One year I found out that his job was in jeopardy for a very unusual reason and I was very happy that I could come up with a solution to keep his career going. It was not a question of Win's talent; it was a question of his honesty. The people who hired him at the Garden didn't listen to him calling the Rangers home games because they were at the games. So, they only heard him when he was on the road. And all good sports announcers go up with the crowd's roar and stay silent when there was no noise. The problem was that on the road, Win was going up with the crowd's roar when the Red Wings or Leafs scored but was silent after the Rangers scored, and the people at the Garden were asking, 'Doesn't Win love the Rangers anymore?' So, I told him, 'Win, when you're on the road you've got to get equally or more excited than the crowd when the Rangers play well than when the home team does well.' Win realized that I was right and after that it was smooth sailing. It was funny because nobody was more passionate about the Rangers than Win was."

Win's brother, Biff Elliot, also went into show business and became the first actor to play Mike Hammer on film. But Win also had flair as a showman. "One day Win was walking down the street with me in New York and he was wearing this funny looking beret on his head," Wolff recalled. "I said, Win, why are you wearing that beret? He said, 'It helps'. 'How does it help?' 'Well, people stand and look at me don't they? It's cheaper than an ad in *Variety*!'"

Win passed away in September of 1998 at the age of eighty-three.

When asked how he wished to be remembered, the father of ten children responded simply, "As a great dad." But to those of us old enough to remember, he was also a great announcer and storyteller and a reminder of a simpler time and long-ago, cold winter nights.

Author's note: Away from the arena Elliot was friendly and approachable. I was fortunate enough to meet him on a number of occasions, once while walking up Eighth Avenue towards the old Garden with my father. Here I was, this kid bothering Win while he was rushing to work, munching a hot dog, yet he patiently answered every question I had.

Bob Wolff

Bob Wolff is a legend among sportscasters. He began his professional career in 1939 while attending Duke University and broadcast Washington Senators baseball games on radio and TV from 1947 to 1960. He also did television play-by-play for the Detroit Pistons, Baltimore Colts, Washington Redskins, and Cleveland Browns. He called the baseball *Game of the Week* on NBC TV and worked several World Series for NBC and the Mutual Radio Network. He announced Don Larsen's perfect game in Game Five of the 1956 World Series as well as the 1958 NFL Championship Game, the Colts' overtime win against the Giants which has come to be known as "The Greatest Game Ever Played."

But he is also well known in New York for his work with the Rangers and Knicks on radio and TV as well as cable.

BOB WOLFF: "In 1954, I became the Garden announcer. I did the Rangers on TV, the Knicks, tennis, gymnastics, horse shows, dog shows. I did the play-by-play for everything except wrestling.

"I always thought hockey was a great game to watch but hard to televise because you couldn't feel the quickness or see the colors back then."

Like many of his listeners, Bob's first exposure to hockey was on the streets of New York City.

BOB WOLFF: "As a kid growing up I played roller hockey in our back-yard and it was a big treat every once in a while to go to the Garden to see what these guys could do on ice and how fast they could skate.

"But when I was in Washington they had a team called the Washington Hockey Lions in the Eastern Hockey League. They played in the Uline Arena, where I worked for the Washington Capitols, one of the original teams in the Basketball Association of America.

"I watched the hockey team and got to know some of the players. They didn't make a lot of money in those days. One of my first realizations was that the players were living on 'stitch money'—they had insurance policies that paid them ten dollars a stitch. So they used to line up and tell the doctor or trainer, 'Give me a couple more stitches, doc. I want to eat well tonight.' That's the first I knew about hockey wages in those days."

One of the toughest jobs for any announcer is to gain the respect of the listeners by being knowledgeable about the sport they are covering. So one of the first things Bob did when he began broadcasting Rangers games was to find a mentor who could explain the finer points of the game to him.

BOB WOLFF: "I had to start recognizing the nuances of the game so I could sound like an authority and not just a guy describing the game. So, I started palling around with my good friend Andy Bathgate, who was just a learned, brilliant hockey guy. When we'd go on road trips I'd sit beside Andy and ask him questions and I kept a book of my questions and his answers. Over time I just accumulated more and more books, and I think he appreciated my interest in the sport. So one day I asked him, 'Andy, all these things you've been telling me about hockey, does everyone know these things? He said, 'No Bob, this is just what I do.' So, I said maybe it might be fun to see if we could get this published, your secrets of hockey so kids could learn from you.

"So I went out to a couple of publishers and Prentice Hall said, sure we'll publish it. So there I am co-author with Andy of *Andy Bathgate's Hockey Secrets*. And Andy went out with an amateur cameraman, and we took some shots of how you hold the stick, how you get the shot off correctly, all the techniques of the sport. Lo and behold that became the best selling hockey book in Canada. And when they saw my name on the book, they thought, boy I was the authority on the sport, when all I knew was what Andy had been telling me and what I picked up watching games.

"But the book got big in the United States, it even got big in Sweden. So, I became very well known for my hockey expertise via Andy Bathgate. A funny thing happened with that. I thought a great cover would be a picture of Andy in a Ranger uniform. He was the captain of the team and a very popular player, good looking guy and just a whiz on the ice. That worked well for sales until he was traded to Toronto. But the publisher was very kind to me. They changed the cover of all the books they had left to a picture of Andy in a Maple Leaf uniform. And that did well until he was traded to Detroit. Then they said they'd be going with the old cover for the books they had left. So, our sales stopped shortly thereafter."

Because of his various broadcasting duties, Bob traveled a great deal between games which caused more than a few anxious moments.

BOB WOLFF: "My heart was always in my throat because if the plane was late or anything I'd miss the game and they'd fire me because I was the only announcer on the game, they didn't use a color man back then. I'd usually stay over in New York so I had a bag with my game notes some clothes and I always asked to bring my bag on the plane with me because then I could go directly to the game. If the plane was late and I had to check my bag I'd be in trouble.

"But they always made a big fuss that the bag wouldn't fit under the seat. They had this little box and if the bag fit in the box it was okay. So, I said I'll prove to you that it can fit in that little space under the seat. I opened the bag and opened all the compartments and put my shirts in one, my socks in another, my shaving kit, etc. So, then my entire bag was depleted and I could just pack it down under the seat. So, they said OK you win, and I got to bring the bag on the plane with me.

"One time when the Rangers were in Boston, I did a Penn State college football game in the afternoon and rented a single engine plane to fly me into Boston. I called for a taxi to meet me at the gate to get me to the Boston Garden and got to the broadcast booth one minute before the game started.

"I liked doing games from Montreal, Toronto, and Detroit because there was so much history in those places. The Garden always had the roar of the crowd. I was in Chicago when Bobby Hull first passed the fifty-goal mark. I did an interview with him on the ice after the game. I did the Stanley Cup Final in Detroit. That was a thrill because I had previously done the World Series, NFL Championship, NBA Championship, and then I was able to add the Stanley Cup Final to make it the four major sports. And my color commentator was one of my very best friends, Emile Francis, who was a real pepper pot. He was always up for every game. He got really passionate about it. He was a lot of fun to be with."

Traveling with the team allowed Bob to get to know the players, which led to some lighthearted moments, such as the time he invited the entire Ranger squad over for their pregame meal in his home.

BOB WOLFF: "In the early 1960s the Rangers were asked to come down to Washington for a benefit game for a local reporter who got hit with a puck and lost an eye. So since I was doing all these events at Uline Arena, I offered to help out. I got a bus company to donate a bus to pick them up at the airport. I told my wife we'd be having a few people over for lunch today, so we have to order something from a catering service. She asked how many, I said at least twenty-five. So that afternoon before the game we had the whole team and all the officials for dinner. Then after lunch they wanted to take their pregame naps. So there they were. One was in the bathtub, some were on the floor, three were in my bed. Some were in the backyard on lounge chairs. They were sleeping all over the house. It was an unusual experience and I think it really cemented my relationship with the Rangers."

Bob's career has spanned more than eight decades. He is one of only two broadcasters to be honored by both the baseball and basketball Halls of Fame, the other being Curt Gowdy. He has also been inducted into Madison Square Garden's "Walk of Fame" and has been recognized by *The Guinness Book of World Records* as having the longest career as a sports broadcaster.

Now in his mid-nineties, he can still be seen on News 12 Long Island where he is the senior sports correspondent and commentator.

Bill Chadwick and Jim Gordon

Separately, Jim Gordon and Bill Chadwick were each very good at their jobs, but together they were great and formed one of the most popular broadcasting teams in Rangers history.

Gordon was the straight man, the professional broadcaster of the duo.

A Brooklyn native, ex-Marine and graduate of Syracuse University, Jim Gordon began his broadcasting career in Syracuse, New York, with WNOR radio in 1948 calling games for the Syracuse Nationals of the old N.B.L. He also broadcast minor league baseball for the Syracuse Chiefs of the International League as well as the Syracuse Warriors of the American Hockey League. "The first hockey game I ever broadcast was the first hockey game I ever saw," he told David J. Halberstam in *Sports on New York Radio.*

Gordon broke into the New York sports scene in the mid 1950s when he hosted Brooklyn Dodgers pre- and postgame radio shows. In 1954 he began working for Madison Square Garden, sharing Knicks broadcasting duties with Marty Glickman. He began working Rangers games in the 1959–60 season with color analyst Monty Hall, who went on to greater fame and fortune hosting game shows including *Let's Make a Deal.*

Gordon started out getting $75 a game, which was good money in those days. "I was living with my wife and kids in my parent's basement in Rego Park and that was more money than I had in my bank account at the time."

Jim broadcast Rangers games on radio periodically until the 1973–74 season when he was teamed with Chadwick on television.

Gordon was also a news anchor for WINS Radio and served as the news director for WABC-AM and WNEW-AM. While at WINS he held the coveted early morning drive-time slot. His usual day began at 1 a.m. when he would leave his Putnam Valley home for the ninety-mile drive to the WINS studio near Grand Central Station. He would then write his own copy and take the air from 3 to 10 a.m. After home games, Gordon would often go directly from the Garden to the WINS studio and sleep on the floor to be there for his 3 a.m. shift. He would then return home after his work day ended and get up the next morning and do it all over again. It was a hectic lifestyle and he didn't get to spend much time with his wife and five children during the season.

Gordon also became known as the radio voice of the New York football Giants, calling their games from 1977 through 1994, including the Giants' first two Super Bowl seasons in 1987 and 1990.

John Halligan, former Ranger PR director, remembered Gordon fondly: "Always a very sweet man, but that didn't mean he wasn't a hard-bitten newsman. If the lines went down because of a storm or something—something that even the technicians couldn't fix—Jim would be wiring alligator clips to the phone lines, whatever it took to stay on the air. Once, in Minnesota, there was a transmission problem and Jim got to work. The play-by-play got back to New York about ten seconds after the video, but it got back to New York. When viewers in New York heard Jim holler, 'Score!' the guy who scored was already skating back to the bench."

Gordon always looked upon sports broadcasting as just another form of news reporting. "I never considered myself a sports expert at all. I wasn't even that serious a sports fan. I liked sports but news broadcasting was what I most wanted to do, news has made me a better sports announcer."

Bill Chadwick, a native New Yorker, began his hockey career in the old Metropolitan League before earning a spot on the Ranger-sponsored New York Rovers, an amateur club in the Eastern Hockey League in the mid-1930s. Chadwick was declared legally blind in his right eye in 1935 when he was struck by an errant puck during a Met League All-Star game played at the Garden. Undeterred, Bill later continued to play but after another close call he "wised up and got into officiating."

Chadwick reached the NHL as a linesman during the 1939–40 season, becoming the first American-born official in league history. A year later Bill was promoted to full-time NHL referee, a position he held from 1940 to 1955. During that time, he created a series of hand signals so that fans in the stands would know what type of penalty was being called—a practice that continues to this day. Few people knew about his vision problem but when fans or players complained that he was blind, he was known to tell them that they were "only half right."

In 1964, nine years after his retirement, Chadwick was inducted into the Hockey Hall of Fame in the Referees/Linesman category. Ten years after that, he would become the first referee ever inducted into the United States Hockey Hall of Fame.

Chadwick was working in private business when Emile Francis called him in 1967. Emile wanted him to begin working Rangers radio broadcasts, first doing between-period interviews and then working with play-by-play man Marv Albert as a color analyst. He moved to the television side in 1972–73, working with Sal Marciano. In 1973–74 he was teamed with Jim Gordon and the duo clicked and stayed together until the end of the 1980–81 season, calling more that 650 regular-season and playoff games together.

"Bill was a natural for broadcasting even though he wasn't formally trained in it," said Francis. "He and Jim Gordon got more mail than some of our players."

Chadwick truly put the "color" in the role of color commentator. Outspoken and opinionated, he was never afraid to say what was on his mind, even during the course of a game.

Nicknamed "The Big Whistle" by Rangers statistician Arthur Friedman, Chadwick was known for his colorfully honest appraisals of Rangers players as well as their opponents. He also had his own unique way of pronouncing names. For example, defenseman John Bednarski was always Ben-dar-ski and Chris Kotsopoulos became Kos-top-oulos. It makes one wonder how he would have fared in today's truly international NHL. Even when addressing his broadcast partner, Jim Gordon, most of the time it was "Chim," as in "Chim, watching Dave Silk handling the puck is like a cow trying to handle a gun." Or, "Chim, I've seen Bobby Clarke start a lot of fights but I haven't seen him finish one yet!"

Gordon often said that he worked with a lot of color men, but Bill was his only real partner in the booth. He was the perfect foil for Chadwick, who once proclaimed that the Rangers' flashy forward Gene Carr "couldn't put the puck in the ocean if he was standing on the edge of the pier." So after Carr had been traded to the Kings, he scored against his former team in a game in Los Angeles. "I thought you said Carr couldn't put the puck in the ocean," Gordon asked slyly. "Well, Jim," Chadwick responded, "it's a bigger ocean out here."

While Gordon tried to be impartial, Chadwick wore his heart on his sleeve. He was a Rangers fan and sometimes when they played well his excitement got the better of him. One of those times was in the 1973 playoffs when the Rangers ousted the Boston Bruins in five games. Chadwick blurted out that the Rangers would be flying back to New York that night and would be landing at LaGuardia Airport. It seemed like a harmless comment, but when over 5,000 fans stormed the runway it got serious. Chadwick grabbed a bullhorn and stood on a table, pleading with the fans to let the players get to their cars. It became a frightening scene when Ed Giacomin's car was almost overturned and the next day Emile Francis issued a memo forbidding the broadcasting of the team's itinerary.

And like many fans, Bill was frustrated with the Rangers' inability to score on the power play even with Barry Beck on the point. He implored Beck to "Shoot the puck Barry, shoot the puck!" when he thought the big Ranger defenseman was passing up shots to dish the puck to teammates. Chadwick's cry soon became a chant that Beck heard whenever he had the puck in the offensive zone.

Chadwick was a great storyteller and knew practically everybody in hockey. His between-period interviews with former Maple Leaf Howie Meeker and especially King Clancy were classics, filled with a lot of laughter and good-natured bantering.

"Jim and Bill weren't big on rehearsals," Halligan recalled. "They'd be in Boston, Denver, wherever. They'd get in the booth, the light would go on, they'd say where they were, then they'd say, 'These two teams don't like each other.' That's how every telecast began."

Chadwick was replaced by Phil Esposito following the 1980–81 season. He stayed as a special assignment reporter for one more season and then retired in 1982 at the age of sixty-six. He then teamed with Steve Vickers and John Halligan to organize the first Rangers Golf Classic to benefit the Rangers Alumni Association. Gordon worked with Esposito for three seasons and was replaced by Sam Rosen in 1984. He continued to broadcast New York Giants football games until 1994.

Sadly, both men are gone now. Jim Gordon died in February of 2003 at the age of seventy-six, and Bill Chadwick passed away at the age of ninety-four in October of 2009.

But they will long be remembered as one of the Rangers' most colorful and entertaining broadcast duos of all time.

They also served:

Tim Ryan also called Ranger games on television for two seasons from 1970 to 1972. Local TV sports anchor Bill Mazer and reporter Norman MacLean provided color analysis.

9

1970–71

A Record-Breaking Season

IN 1970–71, THE pieces began to come together for the Rangers as they enjoyed their most successful campaign thus far under Emile Francis.

Once again the season began with the phasing out of older players, replacing them with younger prospects that were coming out of the Rangers' fertile farm system. The transition was at least partially due to the league's addition of the Buffalo Sabres and Vancouver Canucks that necessitated an expansion draft in which the Rangers lost veterans Donnie Marshall, Orland Kurtenbach, and young defenseman Allan Hamilton.

Marshall, thirty-eight, had suffered a separated shoulder the previous February and missed the remainder of the season except for a brief appearance in the Rangers' final playoff game against the Bruins. Donnie's best season as a Ranger was in 1965–66 when he scored 26 goals with 28 assists. In 479 games with the Rangers over seven seasons, Marshall scored a total of 129 goals and added 141 assists while accumulating only 40 penalty minutes. He also added three goals and two assists in 15 playoff games.

Marshall was claimed by Buffalo in the expansion draft and retired in 1972 after playing in Toronto for a year. In 1,176 games for Montreal,

New York, Buffalo, and Toronto, Donnie scored 265 goals with 324 assists and accumulated 127 penalty minutes. In 94 playoff games he recorded eight goals and 15 assists along with 14 penalty minutes.

Kurtenbach, thirty-four, had been hampered the previous two seasons with back problems and while he still provided toughness he was being pushed aside by younger, speedier forwards. Originally a product of the Rangers organization, Orland made his Broadway debut during the 1960–61 season. He then saw action with Boston and Toronto before returning to New York in 1966–67. In 198 games as a Ranger Kurtenbach recorded 30 goals, 61 assists, and 191 penalty minutes. In 15 playoff games he scored two goals, with four assists and 50 penalty minutes. Big Kurt was claimed by the Vancouver Canucks where he became team captain and recorded consecutive 20-goal seasons. However, injuries began to slow him down and Orland retired following the 1973–74 season.

EMILE FRANCIS: "Orland had come to me and said, 'I don't imagine you're gonna protect me so I'd appreciate it if you could get me out to Vancouver because I spent some time out there when I first started playing and I'd like to make that my home.' So I arranged to send him to Vancouver."

ORLAND KURTENBACH: "There was a draft that year and Emile called me in and told me, 'I absolutely cannot protect you.' And I really didn't play much for the two years prior to that. One year I had gone to Omaha to try to get into shape. But I could not skate. I couldn't bend over and push off. So then I had the back fusion surgery prior to Christmas. I was in a back brace for six months. Then I started getting in shape. I ran every day. I went to training camp and I was a step behind everybody. And Emile played me with the Rangers one night and Buffalo the next. This went on for two weeks and camp broke and I went back to Buffalo for two weeks and I didn't start getting my legs back until the end of the season and then Emile started playing me again.

"So I talked to Emile. There were two clubs coming in. I had played for [Buffalo Sabres coach] Punch Imlach in Toronto and gotten along well with him but he had me playing in more of a defensive role and the other team was the Canucks and I had played for Bud Poile in San Francisco [in 1962–63] and got lots of ice time, I think I led the team in scoring. So I told Emile I wanted to go to Vancouver to make my home. My wife was from there and that's where we wanted to bring up our family and it really worked out well for me."

Hamilton, twenty-four, was left unprotected because the Rangers' farm system was producing a number of young prospects and they couldn't protect them all. At 6-foot-2, 195 pounds Allan had the size and was also a right-handed shot which has always been a coveted attribute for a defenseman. However, he was never able to crack the lineup and steadily moved down the depth chart. Selected by Buffalo in the expansion draft, Hamilton jumped to the WHA's Alberta (later Edmonton) Oilers in 1972–73. He spent eight seasons with the Oilers before retiring in 1980.

To fill the void at forward, Francis brought in center Syl Apps Jr. from Omaha of the CHL. Apps was the son of Hall of Famer Syl Apps who enjoyed a 10-year career with Toronto in the 1930s and 1940s. Drafted in 1964, Apps chose to study at Princeton and Queen's University before resuming his hockey career.

Jack Egers was also given the opportunity to stick with the Rangers based upon his late 1969–70 season performance when he scored six goals in 11 games including the playoffs.

There were also changes in the crease as Ed Giacomin acquired a new goaltending partner in Gilles Villemure. The thirty-year-old rookie had been in the Rangers organization since 1962, playing for Blueshirts' farm clubs in Vancouver, Baltimore, and Buffalo. He made his Rangers debut during the 1963–64 season when he played five games in place of the injured Jacques Plante. He also saw action during the 1967–68 and 1968–69 seasons. Villemure spent the 1969–70 season backstopping the Buffalo Bisons of the AHL to regular-season and playoff championships. He was named the league's MVP for the second year in a row, posting eight shutouts and being named to the league's First All-Star team. Gilles, who spent his offseasons as a harness racing driver and trainer, was considered by many to be the best goaltender not playing in the NHL.

GILLES VILLEMURE, *Goaltender, 1964, 1968–69, 1970–75*: "It was hard to break into the league but the last two years in Buffalo I thought I was ready because we had won a championship and I was the MVP of the league and I thought I was playing well. I thought I was ready after that and Emile gave me a chance."

Giacomin also began wearing a mask in 1970, leaving Gump Worsley and Andy Brown as the only barefaced netminders in the league. Giacomin had worn a mask in practice in past seasons but finally decided to wear it during league games as well. "I just reached the point where I thought the mask became part of the goaltender's equipment," Giacomin explained to reporters. Eddie began by wearing a basic mask made by assistant trainer Jimmy Young. But by mid-season Giacomin had moved up to a more protective model made by Ernie Higgins, who was gaining a name for himself among netminders, especially on the East Coast.

The preseason also featured a holdout by four of the Rangers' best players, Brad Park, Walter Tkaczuk, Jean Ratelle, and Vic Hadfield. The four players were represented individually by Pro Sports, Inc. It was the agency's first foray into hockey having previously represented NFL, NBA, and MLB players.

Park and Tkaczuk were coming off of their entry-level contracts while Hadfield and Ratelle were up for renewals. Hockey players as a group were being vastly underpaid compared to their peers in other sports and the four Rangers were no exception. During the holdout it was learned that Mike Riordan, a second stringer for the New York Knicks basketball team, had made $35,000 the previous season, more than any of the Rangers except for Rod Gilbert and Tim Horton. The situation was exacerbated when the newly minted Vancouver Canucks signed their No. 1 draft pick Dale Tallon to a $60,000 contract, more than any of the four Rangers were making.

Hadfield and Ratelle came to terms with Francis before the season began. But Park and Tkaczuk who both made $12,000 in 1969–70 missed the season opener, a 3–1 loss in St. Louis. Two days later, Park and Tkaczuk met privately with Francis at his home. They watched *Monday Night Football*, had a couple of beers and came to an agreement on their contracts which would pay them each $30,000 plus bonuses.

EMILE FRANCIS: "I wouldn't talk to agents. But after a while Bill Jennings came in and said, 'You know, Emile, we're getting a little concerned. Everybody's entitled to representation and we could get sued.' It figures that Jennings who was with one of the biggest firms in New York would think like that. So I said let me think about it. So later on I said to him, the problem with agents is that they go back to the player and say he said this and he said that. I'll talk to an agent, but he's got to have the player in there with him. That way I can look them both in the eye and there's no bullshit and the player can hear what I'm saying. So Jennings says, 'Yeah, that'll work.'

"They tried to get Giacomin to join the holdout and said if we can get Giacomin we got 'em right by the balls. But I brought them all into New York and I said look we're getting close to training camp and I'll give you one more meeting and that's it. So they come in on a Friday and they were trying to sell me on deferred salaries. You know you pay him $90,000 but you only give him $50,000 and defer $40,000. So they talked for about three hours. When they were finished, I said well, I'll have to bring in my financial adviser. So I call my assistant Dennis Ball who was also my chief scout. I said, 'Mr. Ball, would you come in here please, I'd like you to meet some people.' So he comes in smoking a big cigar and carrying a yellow legal pad. So I said to them, 'Okay, I want you to repeat what you just told me because if I try to tell him I might miss one or two things.' So they went through it again quick and after about an hour they were huffing and puffing. So I let them go for about an hour and then I stood up and said, 'I'll tell you what. You pick up all your papers and get out of this office. I never want to see you again. So I threw them all the hell out.

"So now we go to training camp and they all showed up and now we're ready to play our first exhibition game against Toronto in Peterborough. So we practiced and then I went to my room and I get a telegram from these agents, 'These players that we represent will not be going to Peterborough tonight to play.' So I had a note placed in every one of their rooms telling them that they were suspended—check out of this camp. Then I called Frank Paice, I said, 'Frank, these guys are gonna be looking for their skates, so lock them up. Those skates belong to the New York Rangers.' So about an hour later I get a phone call from Jean Ratelle. Now Jean Ratelle was the nicest guy you could meet. In all those years I never heard him swear once. He says, 'Mr. Francis, we all came to the rink to get the skates and they won't give us the skates.' I said, 'That's right. Those skates belong to the New York Rangers. You guys want to make $100,000, buy your own skates,' and I hung up.

"Now we finish training camp and we opened the season on the road and we're getting ready to leave and the lawyers sent us a funeral wreath. So we went on the road and when we got back the first guy to call me was Jean Ratelle. He says, 'Can I come in and see you. I wanna play, I've been with you all these years, give me the contract you offered and I'll sign it.' So he says, 'What happens if one of these other guys sign for more money?' I told him that at the end of each season I rate each player one through twenty and I make sure that they're paid according to that order. And I've got you listed as number one and that's where you'll stay, no matter what happens with the other guys. Well eventually I got everybody signed. And then those lawyers, within a month they sent them a bill for about $20,000. So the players said they wanted to meet with me and they showed me the letter. What do you think about that? I said give me that letter and I ripped it up and threw it in the wastepaper basket. I said you'll never hear from them again because if the other players find out what they're trying to do they'll never get another client. A couple months later those guys called me and said that American Express wanted to use me in one of their commercials, and then they said we'll take our usual 20 percent. I said go shit in your hat!"

WALT TKACZUK: "Brad and I had signed a two-year contract and it was time to renegotiate. Brad had become one of the key defensemen on the Rangers, had been selected as an All-Star and he and Bobby Orr were the two best defensemen in the league at the time. And I had just come off a good year, I think I led the Rangers in scoring. I think we were making $12,000 a year. So we went in and said we wanted $21,000. So it wasn't huge money we were asking for but at that time, that's the way it was. We sat out two or three games and we ended up finally settling and signing for about $21,000 for one year and $23,000 for the second year, something like that. But those contracts that we signed I hung up on the wall in the golf club and tube slide we have here in St. Mary's and people look at them and they see this one page contract and they're amazed how simple they were in those days."

BRAD PARK: "Basically I had made $10,000 my first year and $11,000 my second year and made the First All-Star team with Bobby Orr. We were considered the two best defensemen in the game, not that I felt that way but reputation wise. So with that we were trying to get a deal done and move up in salary. I had met a guy named Larry Rauch, who was a lawyer and I asked him to be my agent. But he said that he didn't have enough experience, so we ended up meeting with a company called Pro Sports which was Marty Blackman and Steve Arnold. At that time nobody was using agents and Emile didn't want to talk to any agents. So by the time we got to training camp we didn't have a deal and we left training camp. We asked for some kind of insurance, we would have come back to camp but we needed insurance in case we got injured because we didn't have a contract.

"Eventually, Vic and Ratty negotiated a deal and the last day before the season started Emile called Walter and myself and asked if we would sign the contract in front of us and I said no. He said, 'Well it looks like we're stuck in the mud.' Yeah, deep in the mud and Walter didn't agree to what they offered him and the team left for St. Louis and Walter and I went home. Now we didn't have a pot to piss in and we're renting a place but we're still holding out. And the team loses in St. Louis so we were unhappy about holding out but at least the team missed us.

"So when the team came back Walter came over and said, 'Let's go talk to the Cat.' I said I don't want to talk to the Cat. And he said, 'NO—let's go talk to the Cat!' So we called him up and went to his house and we ended up negotiating a deal. I think Walter and I had such a loyalty to the team and the guys that we wanted to get back playing. It wasn't that we disliked the Cat or anything but it was business."

With Park and Tkaczuk back in the lineup the Rangers won their home opener against the Buffalo Sabres, 3–0. The victory began a 24-game unbeaten streak (17–0–7) at the Garden. This streak coupled with two consecutive victories at the end of the 1969–79 season ran the unbeaten string to 26 games (19–0–7), a record that still stands today. The streak ended on February 3 with a 4–2 loss to the Black Hawks. Overall, the Blueshirts posted a 30–2–7 record at home, setting franchise standards for most home victories and most home game points (67), two records that also have yet to be matched. The Rangers also rode multiple winning streaks of five, six, and seven games and never lost more than three games in a row.

However, the season was not without its setbacks.

Jack Egers sustained a severe concussion on November 22 when hit by North Stars rookie defenseman Fred Barrett as he got off a slap shot from the blueline. The sound of Egers's head hitting the ice could be heard throughout the Garden. Unfortunately, Egers was knocked unconscious and had swallowed his tongue. Only the fast action of Ranger trainer Frank Paice who used forceps to free the tongue from the young winger's throat saved Egers's life. Egers returned to the line up a few weeks later but the effects of the concussion bothered him the rest of the season.

JACK EGERS: "I don't remember any of it. My wife Wendy filled me in about what happened. I was carted off on a stretcher, I guess, but I know Barrett caught me with an elbow coming out from a slap shot and I don't remember anything after that. I went to the hospital overnight for observation and then a couple of days later I was practicing. But the only precaution taken back then was that I had to wear a helmet for a couple of weeks. That's just the way it was back then. But now, mandatory helmets came in the '80s and I wouldn't be surprised if visors become mandatory before too long. The concussion protocol, once the NFL started getting lawsuits against them, the NHL picked theirs up real quick. But now they have to get checked out by a doctor. It was a different era, a different time. But I know I had symptoms like numbness at the ends of my fingers and toes for the rest of that year and didn't play that much."

Billy Fairbairn also missed twenty-two games when he came down with mononucleosis and was less than 100 percent for the remainder of the season.

BILL FAIRBAIRN: "I thought it was the flu and that I would shake it off. But I had it for quite a while. I think we were in Oakland and Teddy Irvine was my roommate and I just told him I can't go to practice this morning; I can't get out of bed. And that's when they flew me back to New York and found out that I had mono. Where it came from I had no idea. I went to Lenox Hill and I was in the hospital there for quite a while."

At the same time that the Rangers were sitting near the top of the standings, the once-proud Detroit Red Wings were languishing near the bottom under the mismanagement of coach Ned Harkness. Harkness had great success at Cornell University but his collegiate approach to hockey didn't work with NHL veterans, and the Red Wings were in turmoil. As Harkness began cleaning house in Detroit, Emile Francis was ready to take full advantage of the situation, making three trades with the Red Wings that brought three players that would play important roles for his Rangers, while giving up little in return.

Pete Stemkowski was one of the first to go. Stemmer, a twenty-seven, 6-foot-1, 195-pound center, was big and durable and a very good hockey player who won a Stanley Cup with Toronto in 1967. But he was also "the Polish Prince" and his locker room pranks didn't sit well with the stern Harkness. So, on October 31, 1970, Pete was traded to the Rangers for spare defenseman Larry Brown. Stemkowski was thrilled with the trade, telling reporters, "Emile is a good coach and GM and I don't want to let him down. The Rangers have a good system, they're well coached and disciplined. The center is the key on the ice."

EMILE FRANCIS: "I'll tell you how I got Stemkowski. Pete was a real character. Ned Harkness was coaching at the time and had come from Cornell University, and so the trainer came out and told the players that Ned's tied up and won't be here for a half hour or so. So Stemkowski goes in and gets Ned's Cornell cap and he took the whistle and he said, 'All right, gather round me' pretending he's Ned Harkness. And who comes skating on the ice behind him but Ned Harkness. So Pete turns around and looks at him and says, 'Here you go, coach. I got 'em warmed up for you.' Next day he was gone to New York, cause I had been trying to get him."

But Francis wasn't finished. In February, he sent Arnie Brown, Mike Robitaille, and Tom Miller to the Red Wings for right winger Bruce MacGregor and defenseman Larry Brown, who had begun the season with the Rangers before being traded for Stemkowski. MacGregor was placed on a line with Stemkowski in the middle and Ted Irvine on the left side. The trio clicked and became a valuable checking line for the Blueshirts. Arnie Brown, however, was not happy to be leaving New York and heading to Detroit.

ARNIE BROWN: "I was pissed off when Emile traded me but that's the game. You get over it. I was home and I got a call from Francis. "Arnie, I just traded you to Detroit and they're expecting you to be there tomorrow night." It just knocked the wind out of me when that happened. I had never had any feeling that I was gonna get traded. Detroit was a bad scenario. Ned Harkness was there and he was a college coach and he was an absolute nut. He just destroyed the team. You could see Howe and Delvecchio were there and they had a bad season because Harkness was such a jerk. That started the downswing for me. I started getting my knees hurt and stuff like that.

"I was playing with Park and we'd move the puck and Parkie gave me a lot of good setups to shoot the puck hard. I don't know if Francis appreciated the goals or not. He didn't think that defensemen should be up the ice that much. I think he saw me as a defensive defenseman and not an offensive defenseman and he didn't like it when you were up the ice."

BRUCE MacGREGOR: "I'd been in Detroit for ten years. It wasn't the best of times for sure because things obviously weren't going that well in Detroit. I knew that they were making a lot of changes but it was still kind of a shock. I kind of always expected that I would end my career there to be honest. The word around the league was that New York wasn't the easiest place to go to if you had a family, so you gotta consider all those things. I think it's more of a shock factor trying to figure out what you were going to do with your family and everything. So there was a period of time there where I was trying to weigh what my options were and I obviously didn't have a lot of options so it took a few days to sort everything out."

Ironically, MacGregor's first game as a Ranger was against his former team.

BRUCE MacGREGOR: "That was a weird feeling to be honest with you. I remember going downtown and having lunch and meeting the Ranger players. I really didn't know anybody and then going to the game that night and having to be sure that you walk into the right dressing room and that kind of thing. Yeah that was a tough day, with all the emotions you're going through and having family at the game, having to put on another jersey. But the guys on the Rangers were very receptive."

But wait—there's more!

In March, Francis pulled off yet another trade with Harkness, sending minor-league winger Jim Krulicki to the Red Wings for Dale Rolfe. Rolfe, thirty, 6-foot-4, 210 pounds, was a speedy, smooth-skating defenseman with a long reach and the ability to get the puck out of the defensive zone and up ice to a waiting forward. Rolfe was eventually paired with Brad Park who called him the "best defensive partner I ever had."

EMILE FRANCIS: "I was always in good standing with Ned because when he was coaching at Cornell I brought his team in for the holiday tournament at the Garden. So then he became the general manager and he started dealing everybody. Anybody that he didn't like or stepped on his toes they were gone. So I was right there to get Stemkowski, Dale Rolfe, and Bruce MacGregor."

DALE ROLFE, *Defenseman, 1971–75*: "I think Harkness was in way over his head. He should have stuck with college hockey because he could bullshit the kids but he couldn't bullshit the pros. In my opinion he ruined the Red Wings. We had a pretty good hockey team there and he came and traded everybody away. Never did like the man, had no respect for him.

"I was very happy to be traded to the Rangers. It was the best thing that ever happened to me actually. Getting traded from LA to Detroit was one of the highlights of my career because I didn't like LA and I figured that once you got to an Original Six team, you had made it to the NHL. I was twenty-seven years old before I broke into the NHL, put it that way."

Francis also found a trading partner in Pittsburgh. Taking advantage of the Blueshirts' depth at center, he sent little-used fourth line center Syl Apps and defenseman Sheldon Kannegiesser to the Penguins for the agitating presence of Glen Sather who was expected to add more toughness upfront.

EMILE FRANCIS: "Well there was Sather and another guy who played for Pittsburgh, Bugsy Watson. Those two guys had the balls of a thief and I wanted them both. They were both competitors and they both got their noses in there and there would never be any one of our players being taken advantage of with those two guys around. I'll never forget we were playing Philadelphia and they had this big guy Rick Foley, six foot something and about thirty pounds overweight. I was giving him shit because he was running our guys on the ice and there was a faceoff right near our bench and Glen Sather happened to be sitting right in front of me. So I was yelling at this guy and he tried to spit at me. I said, 'You're so goddamn fat you can't even spit over your chin.' And he made a beeline for the bench to come at me and Sather jumped up and hit him in the goddamn teeth and knocked him right out. But Sather was like a bulldog, he never complained if he wasn't getting any ice. He was a good penalty killer and a good defensive player. I put him on a checking line and he worked his ass off. He was as determined a hockey player as you ever want to see. I wanted Watson because he was a defenseman and was the same as Sather. I thought if you ever put those two guys out there at one time you may have a riot. But I couldn't get Watson no how. But I gave up a good player in Syl Apps to get Sather. But when you're trying to build a team it's like a jigsaw puzzle, you know, you need this, you wanna get that.

"One year the Knicks were playing Philadelphia in the playoffs and somehow someone got into the Philadelphia dressing room and stole everything that they had; watches, rings, money. So the NBA passed a rule that every team had to have a safe in the building and that applied to us. So we had a big meeting with the top brass from Madison Square Garden and our trainer Frank Paice was there along with the Knick trainer. So they give the combination to Frank and the Knick trainer and tell them to make sure that nobody else gets the combination. So we're playing one night at the Garden, we came back in from warmups and I walked into the room with the safe and here's Glen Sather sitting on his ass in front of this big vault that they had and he's manipulating the dial, click - click – click. All of sudden he must have hit the right combination because he opens the door. And then who walks in but Frank Paice. Well, Frank starts yelling at him, 'What the hell are you doing? You think that's a toy? Get the hell out of this room.' So they had to take the safe away and get another one. But he was always full of mischief."

In goal, the tandem of Eddie Giacomin and Gilles Villemure provided the Rangers with the best goaltending in the league as they won the Vezina Trophy. Giacomin played in only 45 games (27–10–7) and posted his best statistics with a 2.16 GAA and eight shutouts.

Villemure got off to a great start, going 14–1–3 in his first eighteen games and surrendering only 30 goals. Overall, Gilles played in 34 games (22–8–4), posting a 2.30 GAA with four shutouts.

Their styles were very different. Giacomin was a very acrobatic netminder and roamed from the net while Villemure was a classic stand-up netminder who played the angles very well. There was also another key difference between the two: Giacomin caught the puck with his left hand while Villemure caught with his right.

EMILE FRANCIS: "It was great when I had Villemure and Giacomin because one guy was a lefty and the other a righty and the other team was always all screwed up as to where they should shoot. They were both great that year. But I had to keep telling the reporters, 'We don't have a number one goalie and we don't have a number two goalie. They're both number one goalies.'"

Villemure agreed with Francis, telling reporters, "Eddie and I are team-mates, not rivals. I ask Eddie a lot about shooters since he knows the league so well. He's a big help to me. We always perk each other up before a game."

Ultimately Giacomin and Villemure gave up a combined 173 goals for a 2.22 GAA, edging out their nearest competitor, the Chicago Black Hawks, who finished with a 2.33 GAA. It was the Rangers' first Vezina Trophy since Davey Kerr won the award in 1940. "I guess Emile knew what he was doing, right?" Eddie asked reporters. "Not playing every game and getting an occasional rest helped me. I felt sharper, more relaxed and found it easier to concentrate."

Giacomin sealed the deal with a 6–0 shutout of the Red Wings at the Garden in the final game of the season. After the final buzzer Giacomin was mobbed by his teammates. Even Arnie Brown, who was then with Detroit, skated the length of the ice to congratulate his former teammate.

ARNIE BROWN: "Well, if someone deserves an accolade you should give it to him. I played a lot of hockey games in front of him and him behind me and it was a team effort. We played hard, we had nothing to be ashamed of."

EMILE FRANCIS: "The Rangers were always a team that had a lot of goals scored against them, but the fourth year I had them we won the Vezina Trophy. Eddie Giacomin got eight shutouts and Gilles Villemure had four. So they had twelve shutouts between them. And I was proud of the players, because I remember the last game, it was gonna be a race for the Vezina and we were winning the game, 3–0, but the whole last half of that game they were yelling 'check-check-check' from the bench. They wanted to win that Vezina for those two guys."

Upon winning the Vezina, Giacomin and Villemure split the $1,500 cash award and took their teammates and wives out to dinner at a Manhattan restaurant.

The Rangers ended the regular season in second place with a 49–18–11 record for a team record 109 points, finishing 12 points behind the first place Boston Bruins.

They also set new team records for: most victories (49), most game points at home (67), most home (30) and road (19) victories, most goals scored (259), most goals scored at home (150), most assists (427), most total scoring points (686), most power-play goals (60), most 20-goal scorers (7), fewest home losses (2), longest home non-losing streak (24), home sellouts (38), and home attendance (672,432).

Walt Tkaczuk led the team in scoring for the second year in a row with 26 goals and 49 assists for 75 points. Jean Ratelle finished three points behind Tkaczuk but was given the Bill Masterton Trophy by the Professional Hockey Writers Association in honor of his perseverance, sportsmanship, and dedication to hockey.

Winger Dave Balon led the team in goals with 36, the most he had scored in his career. Ed Giacomin's eight shutouts were the most in the league and Brad Park reached career highs in points (44) and penalty minutes (114) while Ted Irvine scored 20 goals for the first time in his career.

Unfortunately, 1970–71 was a record-setting season for the Boston Bruins as well.

The Bruins racked up the most victories (57), most home wins (33), and the longest home unbeaten streak (27) in their history. They also scored 399 goals, 140 more than the Rangers and 108 more than the Montreal Canadiens. They registered 697 assists and 1,096 scoring points. Phil Esposito set a new NHL record with 76 goals, breaking Bobby Hull's record of 58. Espo also set a record for most points with 152, passing his own mark of 126. He also set a record with 550 shots on goal. Ten different Bruins notched 20 goals or more and Bobby Orr's 102 assists and 139 points set records for defensemen.

The Playoffs

The Blueshirts had great expectations going into the 1970–71 playoffs. It was the fifth straight year that they made the postseason under Francis, with a record-setting season and a second-place finish. Not a bad year at all. But the playoffs are always a different story for the Rangers.

Their first-round opponent was the fourth-place Toronto Maple Leafs whom they had beaten in the season series, five games to one.

The Blueshirts won the series opener, 5–4, on April 7 when Walt Tkaczuk powered his way past Leafs defensemen Bobby Baun and Jim Dorey to score what proved to be the game-winner. Jacques Plante was in goal for the Leafs and did not have a good game. It was a rough game with Brad Park being knocked unconscious by a Billy MacMillan check.

BRAD PARK: "I remember when Billy MacMillan hit me. The interesting thing was that I never missed a shift and with about four or five minutes to go I turned to Frank Paice, the trainer, and I said, 'What's the score?' He said 4–3 I believe [actually, 5–4] and I said, 'For who?' In those days, concussions weren't treated like they are now."

But it was in the second game, on the following night, that the fireworks really started. The game began with a chippy first period, as Ted Irvine and Brian Spencer fought early. Goals by Garry Monahan and Paul Henderson gave the Leafs a 2–0 lead. Dave Keon scored early in the second and tensions mounted as Vic Hadfield took on Bobby Baun and then Jim Harrison. Tim Horton scored for the Rangers late in the period but Paul Henderson put the game away for the Leafs early in the third period with an unassisted goal.

But then all hell broke loose. With 4:42 left in the third period, Hadfield and Harrison went into the corner to the left of the Leafs net and came out fighting, with Hadfield getting the better of Harrison. As the players paired off in the corner, Leafs goalie Bernie Parent wandered over to lend a fist. Seeing the mismatch in manpower, Eddie Giacomin quickly left his crease to join the fray, discarding his stick and gloves as he raced the length of the ice. Referee Lloyd Gilmour tried to keep

Eddie away but Giacomin pushed him aside and grabbed Parent. After about ten minutes it seemed that things were beginning to quiet down when Hadfield pushed Harrison and the players paired off once again. In one of the more humorous scenes of the night, Gilmour attempted to break up Darryl Sittler and Brad Park, who had been wrestling and pulling each other's sweaters all the while.

BRAD PARK: "So we get to Game Two and I got into it with Darryl Sittler in the first altercation and got thrown into the penalty box. In the second altercation, this was all with about three and a half minutes to go, we had two bench-clearing brawls. I hate to think what the league would do now. It was mayhem out there.

"I knew that I was in trouble when Darryl and I came out of the penalty box and I didn't want to do anything else that would lead to a suspension in the series so Lloyd was yelling at us, 'Break it up! Break it up!' So I rested my arm on him and said, 'Lloyd, take it easy!' And when he did his write up for the game we didn't get as bad a write up."

Order was finally restored but somewhere along the way, amid the litter of gloves and sticks on the ice, Hadfield had snatched Parent's mask and flipped it into the crowd, leaving the netminder wandering around looking for his mask and becoming more upset and agitated by the minute.

Garden police flooded that corner of the arena, searching for the mask. Leafs vice president King Clancy made his way into the corner of the stands and was seen leading the search party and screaming at the referee and the Rangers, especially Hadfield.

The mask was passed through the Garden and ended up in the blue seats. Public address announcer Pat "The Hat" Doyle pleaded with the fans to return the mask but their response were rhythmic chants of "Keep the mask" and "Don't give it back."

EMILE FRANCIS: "I'll never forget seeing that guy running up the stairs with that mask. I never talked to Vic Hadfield about what compelled him to throw the mask into the crowd like he did. I remember hearing that Punch Imlach sent King Clancy out to chase the guy down. By the time Clancy got there the guy was out of Madison Square Garden."

HOWIE ROSE: "Every high school in New York had at least one kid who claimed to have the mask."

Since Parent had brought only one mask on the trip he couldn't continue and was replaced by Jacques Plante. When asked later why Parent had brought only one mask, Leafs GM Jim Gregory explained, "Why bother bringing another mask, nothing can happen to them. You can drop a building on one and it wouldn't break."

On the very next faceoff, the puck was sent into the opposite corner and Ted Irvine and Jim Dorey went at it again. Plante charged into the mix and once again Giacomin sped up ice like the Lone Ranger and slammed Plante into the boards. Both benches emptied and Park and Sittler left the penalty box to join the party as a couple of fights also broke out in the stands. After another long delay, order was restored and the remaining minutes of the 4–1 loss were played without incident.

In the wake of the brawls, NHL president Clarence Campbell fined the Rangers and Leafs a record total of $16,500. Both teams were fined $5,000 and fourteen players from each team were also fined. Vic Hadfield got off relatively cheaply with only a $250 fine for a misconduct penalty and getting tossed out of the game.

But what happened to Parent's mask you may ask? A few days after the game it was hand-delivered to the Rangers office by a private messenger, who was prepaid in cash, so there was no way of tracking where the mask had been and who had it. Emile Francis then sent it back to Parent.

Gilles Villemure started the third game of the series in Toronto but the Rangers lost, 3–1, despite outshooting the Leafs by a 34–24 margin. Bernie Parent played extremely well for Toronto while wearing a new, custom-made mask that was manufactured at Jacques Plante's factory near Montreal and had arrived at three o'clock the morning of the game.

Giacomin was back in net for the fourth game and the Rangers scored three goals in the second period on their way to a 4–2 victory that tied the series at two games apiece. It was their first road victory in the playoffs since 1958, having lost fifteen straight.

The series returned to New York for the fifth game, where Ted Irvine put the Rangers on the board at the 34-second mark of the first period. That first goal was important for the Rangers because the Leafs had scored the opening goal in each of their victories so far in the series. "We need that first goal for our system of play," Rod Gilbert later explained to reporters. "When the other team gets it first, we have to open up and that's not our game. We start to press." Hadfield and Nevin also scored as the Rangers coasted to a 3–1 win.

Toronto coach John McLellan tabbed Plante to start in place of Parent as the teams moved back to Toronto for the sixth game. Bob Nevin's second-period goal stood up until Jim McKenny tallied with less than three minutes left in the third period, sending the game into overtime. Nevin then scored his second goal of the game and fifth of the series midway through the first overtime period to give the Blueshirts their first playoff series win in twenty-one years. The victory was especially sweet for Giacomin and Nevin. For Giacomin, it was his first series victory in five tries as a Ranger and Nevin was able to gain some retribution against the team that traded him.

BOB NEVIN: "We were winning, 1–0, with about three minutes to go and Jim McKenny made a solo rush up the ice and scored. And I said, *Oh Geez, it would have been nice to knock out my old team.* Then about nine minutes into overtime I was on the ice and put one past Plante and we won the series."

The Rangers' next opponent was the Chicago Black Hawks, who had finished first in the Western Division with 107 points. The teams had split the season series with three wins apiece but Chicago had swept the Flyers four games to none in the first round so Bobby Hull, Stan Mikita, Tony Esposito, and company were well rested.

The Rangers won the first game of the series, 2–1, in overtime on a goal by Pete Stemkowski just 97 seconds into the extra session. Jean Ratelle had tied the game late in the third period when he stuffed a rebound of a Vic Hadfield shot past Esposito. The Blueshirts' victory was a testament to the toughness and determination of their goaltender Eddie Giacomin, who suffered a freakish injury in the second period when Bobby Hull inadvertently skated over his catching hand, opening a gash that needed five stiches to close. Giacomin refused to leave the game and was stitched up at the end of the period.

In the second game of the series, the Blueshirts failed to create a sustained attack and lost, 3–0, while being badly outplayed by the Black Hawks. Tony Esposito stopped all 32 Ranger shots to earn his first NHL playoff shutout.

The series shifted to New York for the third game and the Rangers bounced back from their poor performance in Game Two to beat the Black Hawks, 4–1. The G-A-G line led the way as Vic Hadfield recorded the Rangers' first playoff hat trick in twenty-one years and only the fourth in their history. Rod Gilbert also tallied and Jean Ratelle was credited with two assists.

As good as the Rangers were in the third game, they were that bad in the fourth, which was televised nationally on Sunday afternoon, April 25. Chicago led, 6–0, before Dave Balon could put one past Esposito as the Blueshirts were routed, 7–1. Giacomin, whose hand had become infected, was replaced by Villemure at the start of the third period.

The teams returned to Chicago for the fifth game, which turned into a tight defensive battle. Goals by Pat Stapleton and Chico Maki put the Hawks up, 2–0. But Vic Hadfield and Rod Seiling scored for the Blueshirts to tie the score at two. Hadfield's goal was his eighth of the playoffs, tying a team record set by Cecil Dillon in 1933. Ratelle recorded his eighth assist, setting a team record. The game went into overtime and about six minutes into the first extra session, Walt Tkaczuk lost a faceoff to the right of Giacomin to Chicago's Pit Martin. The puck went back to the blue line where Bobby Hull launched a 40-foot slapper past Giacomin's glove hand. It was Hull's first goal of the series and his first career overtime winner.

After five games the Rangers were down three games to two and on the brink of elimination. As the crowd filed into the Garden on April

29 for Game Six, they had no idea that they were in for a long but memorable night.

Dennis Hull opened the scoring late in the first period and when Chico Maki made it 2–0 early in the second, things looked bleak for the Blueshirts. But Rod Gilbert scored in the second period and Jean Ratelle tied it up early in the third to send the game into overtime.

The series had already seen two overtime thrillers, with Pete Stemkowski scoring the game winner in Game One and a Bobby Hull slapshot ending Game Five.

The first overtime period was a real nail-biter as both teams sped up and down the ice and each Chicago shot could mean sudden summer for the Rangers. But both Eddie Giacomin and Tony Esposito were sharp and after 80 minutes of play, the score was still tied at two.

Perhaps the most frightening sequence of the night occurred during the second overtime. Stan Mikita ripped a rising shot that caught Giacomin square in the face, knocking him down. The puck bounced over the net and off the boards and came back out to Mikita near the left faceoff circle. As the dazed Giacomin scrambled to his feet, Mikita passed to an open Bill White whose shot hit the left post. The rebound came back to Mikita who had an empty net to shoot at, but hit the right post. Finally, defenseman Rod Seiling was able to clear the puck for an icing. While Giacomin went to the bench for repairs, Mikita slumped against the Rangers net shaking his head at the golden opportunity he had just missed.

It was a warm night at the Garden and between periods, both teams needed oxygen to revive them for the next stanza. But the players weren't the only ones feeling the effects of the evening. As Marv Albert later revealed in his book *I'd Love to But I Have a Game*, because of the length of the game and between-period interviews he had a very urgent personal need prior to the third overtime and no time to leave the broadcast booth. His problem was remedied by a bucket fetched by a production assistant and placed discretely beneath his covered broadcasting table.

Marv was lucky; the rest of us had to wait, but as it turned out, not too much longer. Early in the third overtime session, Tim Horton skated the puck out of the Rangers end and dumped it into the corner, to the left of the Chicago net. Ted Irvine played the puck off the boards and shot towards the net where Esposito made the save but as he was known to do, kicked the rebound right out in front. There was Stemkowski, steaming towards the crease to slam home the rebound. And so at 1:29 of the third overtime period, two minutes before midnight and four hours and 23 minutes after the game had started, the Blueshirts had won one of the most exciting games in their history. The Rangers jumped off the bench to mob Stemkowski. Emile Francis and trainer Frank Paice ran onto the ice to join the celebration as the exhausted Garden crowd went wild. On the radio, color analyst Bill Chadwick excitedly told the fans, "There no stopping this Rangers club now after a victory like that!"

PETE STEMKOWSKI: "Well, it was late, approaching midnight, and we were pretty much going on emotion. But the adrenaline was flowing pretty good. Tim Horton shot the puck in and Ted Irvine went for it in the corner and it came out to me. It was a thrill, it prolonged the series but then we went back to Chicago and lost. It's a goal that I remember. A lot of people remember where they were and what they were doing; they still come up to me on the street and tell me that they remember that game, so that's a special feeling for me. It was a personal achievement but we had a good team here and playing for Emile Francis and the Rangers was an honor, I still maintain friendships with those people and that's something that you just can't replace. Those are the memories I cherish more than anything else."

TED IRVINE: "I had pretty good speed and I got in the corner pretty quickly. Most of the time, out of the corner of your eye you knew where your centerman was. I threw it to the front of the net and Stemmer deflected it in. It was just one of those bang-bang plays. But interestingly enough, outside Madison Square Garden there's a picture of all of us crowded around Dale Rolfe and Stemmer and when my son, Chris Jericho, who's a former wrestler with the WWE wrestled at the Garden, he would always show the guys the picture on the wall as you leave the dressing room. 'There's my dad, he set up this goal.' But you never see me in that picture; all you see is my skate with the number twenty-seven on it. So they always kid him and say, 'Where's your dad?' and he says, 'There's his skate.' But that was very special. Those were the type of games where they'd tap you on the shoulder and say your line was up next and you say, 'Oh my goodness.'"

WALT TKACZUK: "People always asked if you were really tired. You weren't. You were just waiting for your next shift. After the game, of course, everybody just kind of vegged out after that."

BRAD PARK: "That was an exhausting game; our backs were against the wall. We were down, 3–2 in the series and if we lost that game it's over. In the first overtime it was very simple—'Let's go get a quick goal and get out of here and go back for Game Seven.' When that period dragged on and all of a sudden we're in period two and that goes the distance we were pretty tired puppies because in those days we would dress five defensemen and play four. So myself and Dale Rolfe were going out there every other shift and the other pair, Tim Horton and either Rod Seiling or Jimmy Neilson, were going every other shift. So when the third period began, I started the game and I got to the bench after my first shift and Stemmer scored. It was such a great relief, it was unbelievable. But we didn't have any time to celebrate because we had a go back to Chicago for Game Seven."

EMILE FRANCIS: "The concession stands had nothing left. They were sold out, they had been there for so many hours. I came in after the second overtime and said would somebody put the puck in the net so we can get out of here. So Stemkowski pipes up and says, 'Yeah, it'll be too late to get a beer,' and guess who scores the winning goal? Stemkowski! Stemkowski was the best player you'd ever want to see under pressure. That series against Chicago he got two winning goals. The more pressure, the better he played."

The seventh game was another defensive battle. Tied 2–2 early in the third period, Lou Angotti won a faceoff deep in the Ranger zone and got the puck back to Bobby Hull. Hull's slapper beat Giacomin, who was screened on the play. It was almost the same play that beat the Rangers in overtime in the fifth game of the series, except for the fact that Pit

Martin won the faceoff instead of Angotti. Chico Maki added an empty net goal late in the period, and that was all she wrote.

HOWIE ROSE: "The seventh game in 1971 was the toughest loss I ever experienced as a Ranger fan. Losing the seventh game in Chicago was devastating. When the Bruins were eliminated in the first round by the Canadiens I thought it was clear sailing, we're gonna win it. But that seventh game in Chicago still haunts me.

"The unfortunate reality is that as much as we love that team they did not have the level of star to compete with or to outshine or outplay Hull or Mikita in Chicago, Orr and Esposito with the Bruins. When it came to beating the Black Hawks or the Bruins, although they did eventually beat them both, they just seemed to be a little short."

The loss to Chicago was a one tough to swallow. Many Rangers did not participate in the traditional handshake line at the end of the game, but Francis said that he was "proud of every man in that Ranger uniform." The Blueshirts had broken nearly every franchise regular-season record and had advanced to the second round of the playoffs for the first time since 1950, but once again the season had ended a few weeks too early. However, it was clear that they were headed in the right direction and for once there was real hope for the future.

Frank Paice Honored by Hockey Writers

In 1970–71 Rangers trainer Frank Paice was honored by the Metropolitan New York Hockey Writers for "Long and meritorious service to New York Hockey." That season marked his 25th year in New York and 23rd as the Rangers trainer.

Born in Montreal in December of 1913, Frank got a job in the Forum as the visiting team's stickboy at age eleven. He then worked for the Montreal Maroons in various positions until the team folded in 1938. After a stint in the Canadian Air Force during World War II, Frank joined the Rangers organization in 1946, becoming the trainer for the minor-league New York Rovers. Two years later he moved up to the Rangers when their trainer Tom McKenna took a job in baseball with the Jersey City Giants of the International League. (McKenna later served as trainer for the New York Mets in the 1970s.)

Paice was a jack-of-all-trades for the Rangers. In addition to his duties as the team's trainer, he was also their equipment manager, traveling secretary, and chief cheerleader.

EMILE FRANCIS: "Frank Paice was so dedicated to the Rangers for thirty years. I'd have to put him under wraps. He'd be yelling at the ref and I'd tell him to sit back down there and shut up. If you ever get a bench penalty for our team I'll fine you $200 for crissakes. Shut up!"

Hall of Fame referee Bill Chadwick was a frequent target of Frank's. Chadwick once recalled the time Paice chided him for gathering (and pocketing) the coins that fans at NHL arenas sometimes threw on the ice. "He would always yell, 'Chad, you'll never die poor as long as you keep this job.' In truth, I put all those damn coins into my daughter's piggy bank, and it was a pretty big piggy bank."

As a trainer, Paice was as old school as they came, often telling players to "tape an aspirin" to an injury. When asked by a reporter how he decided whether to use ice or heat to treat an injury, Frank replied in all honesty, "I try one, if that doesn't work, I try the other."

He always packed an oversized equipment bag full of everything players would need but sometimes lose. Socks, suspenders, gloves, gum, Band-Aids, everything was in Frank's "grab bag." The bag weighed over twenty-five pounds and also contained medical supplies as well as an assortment of ointments, balms, salves, and pill bottles labeled "pain" and "shits."

Paice was a fixture at the Garden and well known by the fans, so much so that Topps issued a Frank Paice hockey card in 1962, the only trainer to be included in the set of cards that year.

Paice retired in 1977 after twenty-nine years with the "big club" as he would say and moved to Florida with his wife Anita. He passed away in 1996 at the age of eighty-two.

Tom the Bomb

Thomas Patrick Barnwell, otherwise known as "Tom the Bomb," spent more than thirty years catering to the needs of hockey players and officials at both Madison Square Garden and the Nassau Coliseum. Barnwell, who had eleven brothers and sisters, began working for the Rangers in the late 1960s. His first job was to take care of the officials and their dressing room at the Garden but he soon took on more responsibilities and his role was expanded. He did a little bit of everything, from delivering mail to handling tickets and traveling with the team. Basically he was there to help in any way he could. He also worked at Gerry Cosby's sporting goods store right outside of the Garden.

Tommy was always quick with a joke to keep the players loose and every now and then he would prove his value to Emile Francis in an unexpected way.

EMILE FRANCIS: "That guy had a great memory I'll tell you. It was at the end of the year and the players had to file for whatever they had coming as far as their pension and that. And each game they missed during the year, they had to write down why they missed the game. So Walter Tkaczuk couldn't come up with why he had missed a game. He kept saying, 'Cat, I didn't miss a game.' Just then Tommy came in. I said, 'Tommy we can't remember what game Walter missed.' 'Oh yeah, I'll tell you what game he missed. One night he got hurt in LA and he sat out the next night against Oakland.' Sure as hell he was right and he had it right off the bat. But that's the way he was, he had such a great memory."

One of Tom's unofficial duties was to supply the players on the visiting team with postgame beers, especially if the team was departing on a charter flight for a game the next night. The routine was simple. Late in the third period of a game, Tom would stuff a couple of cold ones into the players' travel bags. One night, however, he stuffed a couple of beers into the unmarked bag of Montreal coach Scotty Bowman and caught hell about it from the future Hall of Fame coach the next time the Canadiens were in town.

Tom later performed the same type of duties for the New York Islanders for many years and was part of their organization during all their Stanley Cup victories. Tom "The Bomb" passed away at the age of fifty-eight on October 12, 2007.

10

1971–72

A Trip to the Finals

FOLLOWING THEIR RECORD-SHATTERING 1970–71 season, the Rangers had great expectations as they opened training camp in the fall of 1971.

As always there were a few new faces in the lineup replacing a number of old favorites.

In May, captain Bob Nevin was sent to the Minnesota North Stars for a player to be named following the NHL's intra-league draft. The timing of the deal allowed the Rangers to protect one of their younger players while still getting value for Nevin, who at thirty-three had been moved to the fourth line due to the progress of Billy Fairbairn and the acquisition of Bruce MacGregor. In 505 regular-season games with the Rangers, Nevin scored 168 goals and added 174 assists. In 33 playoff games he recorded six goals and 12 assists. His best season as a Ranger was in 1965–66 when he led the Blueshirts in goals (29), assists (33), and points (62) and was named the team's MVP. He was also named an All-Star in 1967 and 1969. After two full seasons with the North Stars, Nevin was dealt to the Kings where he played for three additional years. He then moved to Edmonton of the WHA before retiring at the end of the 1976–77 season.

Two weeks after the draft, speedy forward Bobby Rousseau came to the Rangers to complete the Nevin deal. Rousseau, thirty-one, 5-foot-10, 180 pounds, could play right wing or center but Francis wanted his cannon-like slapshot at the right point of the power play.

Rousseau had spent 10 seasons with the Montreal Canadiens where he won four Stanley Cups, scored 200 goals, added 322 assists and was named the NHL Rookie of the Year in 1962. He was dealt to Minnesota in 1970 and was coming off a disappointing year where he scored only four goals with 20 assists.

BOBBY ROUSSEAU, *Right Wing, 1971–74:* "It was a matter of being maybe four or five years from retiring and I had gotten a concussion and I got a phone call the next afternoon asking me to go and play. I decided not to go because I was still having headaches and from then on my relationship with Sam Pollock [Montreal GM] was not good. So he traded me that summer for Claude Larose.

"In Minnesota I was not called for practices, I was not called for hockey games, I was pushed away. I was never told why. Wren Blair was the GM and he was doing some scouting in Europe during the Christmas holidays and when he came back he started having meetings with all of the players to go over their performance. So Blair told me that he was going to get me out of hockey and I said, look your job is not to get me out of hockey but to have me play hockey.

"One game in Minnesota we were finishing warm-up and the Rangers were going on the ice and I thought to myself, *I'm going to look Emile Francis right in the eyes.* The Rangers were going towards the rink and we were going back into our dressing room and I looked Emile right in the eyes and tried to convey to him that he should come and get me. By the next summer I was a member of the New York Rangers. These things happen. I was very happy to be traded to the Rangers, the guys that were there were great teammates. I enjoyed my stay with the Rangers very much."

EMILE FRANCIS: "I always liked Rousseau. He could play right wing, left wing, center, and he was good on the power play and I needed to improve our power play. When I got him, I put Brad Park on one side and Rousseau on the other."

The Rangers also lost defensemen Larry Brown (Philadelphia) and Tim Horton (Pittsburgh) in the intra-league draft.

Emile also made a deal that summer that wouldn't bear fruit until a couple of seasons down the road when he sent minor league goaltender Peter McDuffe to St. Louis for their first pick in the 1971 amateur draft, who turned out to be Steve Vickers.

With Nevin gone, Francis needed to name a new captain. So while at the NHL draft in Montreal, Emile called Vic Hadfield at his golf course, telling him that he had to talk to him about something important and didn't want to do it while Vic was "selling golf equipment." Hadfield, thinking that Emile wanted to talk about his contract, flew to Montreal and arrived in the afternoon. When he got to Emile's suite, some of the Rangers scouting staff were there, so Francis pulled him into an adjacent room and told him that he was making him the captain of the Rangers. Hadfield, whom Francis often called the "Duke of Paducah" due to his stylish clothing, was known to have great leadership qualities both on and off the ice. "He'll be a fine representative for the Rangers," Francis told reporters. As it turned out, being named captain was just the beginning of a great year for Hadfield.

After starting the season with a tie in Montreal and a split of a home and home against Boston, the Blueshirts went on an 11–0–3 tear. They held the top spot in the NHL's Eastern Division until the middle of January when they fell to second behind the Bruins.

Despite their early season success, Francis still took every opportunity to make the team stronger and fill holes in the lineup.

Dave Balon, who led the team in goals the previous season, had gotten off to a slow start and was experiencing weakness in his legs and arms. As it turned out, Balon was in the early stages of multiple sclerosis which wouldn't be diagnosed until after his playing career was over.

To fill the void, Francis made two moves, sending Jack Egers, Andre Dupont, Mike Murphy, and future considerations to St. Louis for Gene Carr, Jim Lorentz, and Wayne Connelly on November 15. The next day he sent Balon, Wayne Connelly, and Ron Stewart to Vancouver for Gary Doak and Jim Wiste.

JACK EGERS: "Yeah, they traded me the day my daughter was born. My wife Wendy gave birth to my daughter and the Cat called me that afternoon and I thought he was calling to congratulate me on my daughter being born. He said, 'I heard it's been a big day for you' and I said 'It sure has, Cat.' So, he says, 'Well, I've got some more good news for you, you've been traded to St. Louis, they want you in Detroit tomorrow night.' So, I had to fly out the next morning to Detroit.

"It was a different era, a phone call and you were gone. I knew guys that found out they were traded when they reported to training camp, like if they went away for the summer. I remember Paul Curtis came back to St. Louis and didn't know he'd been traded. I guess they didn't know how to get a hold of him. He left his car with me to look after because he was going back to Texas where his wife was from. He called to see how the car was and I said, 'Gee, I'm sorry to hear about you getting traded to Buffalo.' He says 'What? I've been traded?'"

Gene Carr was a speedy center/left wing with long flowing blond hair who had been the Blues' first-round pick in the 1971 amateur draft. He had gotten off to a pretty good start in St. Louis with three goals and two assists in 15 games and was surprised by the deal.

GENE CARR, *Center/Left Wing, 1971–74:* "I had no idea what was going down. It just happened, one day after practice I was on my way to New York. It hit me very hard that St. Louis gave up on me so to speak after a month and after playing junior hockey and being one of the better players in Canada and then being traded like that, I think it had a negative impact on me. And of course then when I went to New York I was playing with guys that were icons, guys that I had watched on TV. So it kind of set me back on my heels because I didn't even get my feet wet so to speak.

"Emile put me on left wing with Walter and Billy and the thing is that I had never played wing, I was always a centerman. And it's like a whole different way of life when they put me on left wing. Emile said he did it because he wanted someone with speed for Walter to get the puck to so that was another obstacle I was going through because when you've been a center since you were two years old and you did all your good stuff at center and then you're put on left wing, believe it or not it wasn't easy to play a whole different position. It's not easy to start switching positions when you're young and trying to make it in the league."

Trading Andre "Moose" Dupont was a move Francis always regretted:

EMILE FRANCIS: "We had a lot of good prospects coming along but we always had a problem with our protected list over the years. The first year you get an exemption and the second year you had to protect them or they were gone. Andre Dupont fell into that category, where we couldn't protect everybody. So, I traded Dupont to St. Louis with Jack Egers and Mike Murphy for Gene Carr, who was a first-round pick, with Jim Lorentz and Wayne Connelly. Now when I made a deal with St. Louis it was always under the condition that they couldn't trade them to anyone else unless they offered them back to me. It was like I had another farm club. But Dupont got a real bad concussion in St. Louis and he hadn't played for two months. So, they called me and said that they had a deal for Dupont and did I want him back? I told them to give me twenty-four hours to think about it. So, I checked with the doctors and I said go ahead and trade him. They traded him to Philadelphia and he never had another concussion and he played great and he could have helped us in the playoffs against the Flyers because he was a real tough defenseman. So that's the one I regret."

JACK EGERS: "Moose got traded to Philly and we were in there playing a regular-season game and he'd been playing well and I was lined up to take shots in warmups and I asked him, what happened to you, you've been playing so well. So he says 'I could never read the clock so they took me and got me these contact lenses and now I can see.' If you remember Moose in New York he made a lot of blind passes right up the middle, right onto the other teams sticks and I guess he just couldn't see that well. So Shero figured it out pretty quickly in Philly, got him contacts and he had a great career."

The twenty-year-old Carr made a big splash in his Garden debut on November 21, notching two goals and two assists in the Rangers' 12–1 drubbing of the California Seals. The 12 goals were the most any Rangers team had scored in a single game. The Rangers also set records for largest winning margin (11), most assists in one game (23), most scoring points in one game (35), and most goals in one period (8) in the one-sided defeat of the Seals. Jean Ratelle had a four-goal night, Ted Irvine scored a pair, and rookie Pierre Jarry set a team record by scoring twice within eight seconds. Following the Rangers' ninth goal, Seals coach Vic Stasiuk mercifully replaced netminder Gilles Meloche with backup Lyle Carter. Meloche had tears in his eyes when he came to the bench.

The Tkaczuk-Fairbairn combination became the Blueshirts' best penalty killers. One January night in Los Angeles, the pair along with defensemen Brad Park and Dale Rolfe put on a display of the art of penalty killing in which they controlled the puck for nearly the entire two minutes.

At the 10:47 mark of a scoreless first period, Vic Hadfield was called for a holding penalty and Emile Francis sent Tkaczuk, Fairbairn, Park, and Rolfe out to nullify the Kings' two-minute advantage. What followed was a textbook clinic in penalty killing that had been rarely seen in the NHL before or since.

The Kings initially retrieved the puck and got off a weak shot. But the Rangers immediately gained possession of the puck and played keep-away for the next minute and twenty seconds. They made no attempt to take it into the Kings zone, passing it around among each other instead. Even with the extra skater, the Kings could not intercept or even deflect the puck. Finally one of the Kings managed to grab the puck, but the Rangers got it right back and kept it until the penalty was over. At the time it was estimated that the Rangers controlled the puck for 110 seconds of the two-minute penalty.

The Blueshirts' almost-flawless penalty killing even drew applause from the 7,814 Kings fans at the Forum that evening.

Fairbairn later scored a pair of goals and Hadfield, Pete Stemkowski, and Bruce MacGregor added three more and the Rangers left town with a 5–1 victory.

WALT TKACZUK: "It was incredible. What happened was we won the draw and Dale Rolfe and Brad Park were on defense. We got the puck back to Park and Rolfe and they were both good skaters and smart players of course, and they got the puck and sort of drew the Kings towards them.

"Instead of just shooting it down the ice, they passed it back and forth and we kind of came in but we didn't come in too deep and Brad or Dale would pass it up to us and we would skate up to the Kings defense and they would kind of back up towards their net and we'd cross the blue line and instead of going all the way in we would just turn around and go back to center ice. Our defense would stay back and there was a big gap between their forwards and our defense and it went on and on. I felt embarrassed. I felt so bad, like 'What's going on here?'

"Everybody on the ice as far as the Rangers were concerned knew exactly what we were doing. And we just kept that gap between their forwards and our defense wide enough so that we had room to maneuver and we just didn't give the puck back to them until I think the last five or ten seconds of the penalty. It was just a combination of the defense, Brad Park and Dale Rolfe and Billy Fairbairn and myself keeping that gap wide enough so that there was room for us to play.

"What we did when we killed penalties in New York through the early years, if we had the puck we tried not to just throw it away. We tried to keep control of it as long as we could and then when we saw that we were in danger of causing a problem in our own zone we would throw it down to the other end."

BRAD PARK: "Walt and I talked about it and we kind of felt bad for Los Angeles. But we'd be in practice and we had the power play going and Walter and Billy were out there and they would get the puck and hold it and hold it and the only way we could get back was Emile had to blow the whistle and tell them to give it back to us. So, when we were killing that penalty Walter and Billy started doing it again and Dale and I would just hold it until somebody came and then we would pass it to one of the open guys. We just kept doing that. All four guys felt very comfortable with the puck and nobody was going to panic with it."

BILL FAIRBAIRN: "We were on the ice for the full two minutes. We just worked the puck around. We didn't want to give it up. We never did give the puck up that much like they do now. As soon as they get it they shoot it down. But we killed it off as long as we could before we shot it down."

"I've never seen anything like it," said Emile Francis. "Neither have I, in all the years I've been watching hockey," added broadcaster Bill Chadwick. "The last group I saw that could do a thing like that was Neil and Mac Colville and Alex Shibicky," Chadwick continued. "They scored more goals shorthanded then they gave up." "The Colvilles?" said Francis, "that was long before my time." "Don't believe him," Chadwick laughed.

In the meantime, the rookie Carr was being introduced to big city life.

GENE CARR: "When I first went to New York I lived out in Long Beach where all the married players lived. After a couple months out there, I said that I wanted to live in the city. Rod Gilbert was the only other guy living in the city and I remember going into Emile's office one afternoon, me and Rod. I basically wanted to get Emile's blessing to live in the city and that was a big deal. So, we had a meeting after practice one day and Rod told Emile, 'I'll look after the kid, don't worry,' and so I packed up and moved to the city and got an apartment on Seventy-second and York and Rod and I lived about five blocks from each other and we became very close friends."

Despite being under the watchful eye of Gilbert, Carr still managed to find a little bit of trouble on the streets of Greenwich Village.

GENE CARR: "Here I am a kid from Flin Flon, Manitoba, small-town Canada where you know, you trusted everybody and I went down to the Village because I wanted to check it out. I wanted to look at some pictures for my apartment that I just got. So somebody approached me and in broken English said he had to meet a guy at this hotel but he can't read English and if I could just get the number of the hotel in the phone book, you know back then they had phone booths like Superman, so I said yeah, sure I can do that for you, no problem.

"There must've been a neon light above my head saying this kid's from small-town Canada and he's an easy mark. So, while I was looking in the phone book all of a sudden the guy in perfect English this time says, 'Hey, I want all your money and don't give me any trouble.' So I looked at him and I thought to myself, well I'll be a son of a bitch, and I'm thinking this guy's not going to get a penny of my money because I'm going to come across with an elbow and knock the shit out of him, of course you know being young and strong. Anyway, just as I was going to give him the elbow and run of course, because that was my split-second game plan, I looked to the left a little bit and there's another guy standing on the other side of the phone booth blocking the way on the left side. So that's when I decided you know what, I had a couple hundred bucks or whatever on me and I just gave it to him. I said look, this is all I've got take it and leave me alone. Which they did and then it took me, it seemed like forever to bum a quarter so I could call my attorney to come and get me because I was seventy or eighty blocks from my apartment. So that was one of my first experiences of big city life."

In February, Francis made another deal that he ultimately regretted, sending spare forward Pierre Jarry to Toronto for hard hitting defenseman Jim Dorey. Dorey played one game for the Rangers and separated his shoulder. He missed the remainder of the season, made one playoff appearance, and jumped to the rival WHA that summer.

The G-A-G line of Hadfield, Gilbert, and Ratelle was the most potent line in the league and the trio became the first linemates in NHL history to each score at least 40 goals. But the Blueshirts suffered a crushing blow on March 1 when a Dale Rolfe slap shot from the point broke Jean Ratelle's ankle. Ratelle, who was having a career year with 46 goals and 63 assists and was only one point behind Phil Esposito in the scoring race, missed the rest of the regular season and most of the playoffs.

DALE ROLFE: "That was an unfortunate incident. It cost us the Stanley Cup. But that's hockey, you take a shot and it hits your player. That's just the way it goes. Nothing you can do about it. You can't pull it back."

Now in need of an experienced center to take Ratelle's place, Francis sent cash to Buffalo for the rights to Phil Goyette, who had retired earlier in the season. He also re-acquired Ron Stewart from Vancouver for cash and the loan of Mike McMahon for the remainder of the season.

EMILE FRANCIS: "We lost Jean Ratelle in March. We were on a power play and he passed the puck to Dale Rolfe and he went to the front of the net and Rolfe's shot broke his ankle. So we lost a key guy. And I thought the closest guy that I could get that could play like Ratelle who knew our power play and our system was Phil Goyette who had played for us for seven, eight years. So, I called Punch Imlach. I said, 'I need a favor, Goyette retired last year and he's not playing but I lost Ratelle, he's got a broken ankle. You've got him on the voluntary retired list. Could you take him off the list and trade him to me?' He said sure."

PHIL GOYETTE: "I had had enough with Buffalo my second year there. I was thirty-nine and I just said 'that's it.' I just couldn't do it anymore. So, I decided to retire around January. But then Emile needed a centerman because Ratelle had gotten hurt and they had a good chance to win the Cup. So, he made a deal with Punch Imlach and bought my contract from them. So, Emile called me and said I'd like to talk. So, we met and I gave him a price, I didn't think he'd take it but he did. So, I came back for the rest of the season and my deal was honored. We did pretty well. I know I helped them get to the finals and I scored some points that were helpful and we ended up in the finals."

Goyette played in eight of the Rangers' final fifteen games, scoring one goal and adding four assists.

Francis was forced to juggle his lines in order to find a compatible center for Hadfield and Gilbert. He first tried Goyette and then

Tkaczuk but soon moved versatile Bobby Rousseau into the center spot on the line. Francis also moved Pete Stemkowski onto the Tkaczuk-Fairbairn line as a left winger and put Gene Carr in the middle of Ted Irvine and Bruce MacGregor. He ultimately moved Stemkowski back to his regular spot on the third line and inserted Glen Sather on the left side of Tkaczuk and Fairbairn.

With their leading scorer out of the lineup, the Rangers went 6–6–3 in their last fifteen games and were winless in their last six games leading up to the playoffs.

There was one more highlight to the season and that came in the final game, a nationally televised Sunday matinee against Montreal at the Garden.

Vic Hadfield entered the game with 48 goals as well as a dislocated right thumb and torn ligaments in both hands. Vic's goal total as well as those of his linemates Ratelle and Gilbert had already surpassed Andy Bathgate's 40 goals in 1958–59, but no Ranger had ever scored 50 goals in a season. Hadfield naturally wanted to reach that plateau. Vic also wanted to play because Montreal was the team they would meet in the first round of the playoffs and he couldn't let them know that he was injured. Doctors taped the thumbs to the adjacent fingers to stabilize them, making it necessary for him to cup the stick instead of gripping it in the usual way.

Hadfield scored his 49th goal of the season in the second period off a pass from Rod Gilbert. Then with 5:14 left in the third period, Rod Seiling saw Vic streaking towards the net from the left wing and hit him with a pass which Hadfield redirected past Montreal netminder Denis DeJordy. As Seiling was coming down the ice he also saw Phil Goyette alone on the right side of DeJordy. "Phil didn't have a snowball's chance in hell of getting that pass with Vic going for number fifty," Seiling later told reporters. Hadfield became only the sixth player in NHL history to score 50 goals in a season, joining the ranks of Maurice Richard, Bobby Hull, Phil Esposito, Johnny Bucyk, and Boom Boom Geoffrion.

Hadfield was mobbed by his teammates and received a long standing ovation from the Garden crowd. Following the game, he told reporters, "First I've got to thank my teammates for the season and I've got to thank the doctor (Dr. James A. Nicholas) who bandaged me so I could play."

Montreal won the game, 6–5, and the Rangers finished the season in second place with a 48–17–13 record for 109 points, 10 points behind the first-place Bruins and one point ahead of the third-place Canadiens who they would meet in the playoffs.

Once again they also set a number of team and individual records, including most road victories (22), fewest losses (17), most road points (50), most goals scored (317 in 78 games), most goals scored at home (173 in 39 games), most goals scored on the road (144 in 39 games), most assists (531), most scoring points (848), most short-handed goals (14), most power-play goals (60—tied record set in 1970–71), most 20 goal scorers (7—tied record set in 1970–71), most penalty minutes (1,008), and season attendance (672,750).

The G-A-G line also set many team marks both individually and collectively.

Vic Hadfield's 50 goals were the most ever scored in a season by a Ranger. He also set records for assists (56) by a left winger as well as power-play goals (23). Jean Ratelle set records for points (109), assists (63), goals (46) and assists by a center. Ratelle also tied a record for the longest consecutive point-scoring streak at 13 games. Ratelle scored 16 goals and 12 assists during the streak which ended on March 1 when he suffered the broken ankle. Ironically, Rod Gilbert also had a 13-game point-scoring streak in 1968 that ended when he too suffered a broken ankle. Gilbert set a record for goals by a right wing with 43. As a line they set a team marks for points (302) and goals (134).

Brad Park set a record for goals (24), assists (49), and points (73) by a defenseman. Walt Tkaczuk set a mark for most assists in a game with five and Billy Fairbairn tied a record set by Ron Stewart with four short-handed goals. Ed Giacomin set records for most assists by a goaltender in one game (two) and most assists in a season (three).

The Playoffs

The Rangers' first-round opponents were the Montreal Canadiens from whom they had won the season series, 3–1–2.

Despite entering the playoffs with a six-game winless streak, the Rangers won the opening round four games to two. It was the first time the Blueshirts had won a playoff series from the Canadiens since 1950.

Bill Fairbairn led the Rangers with five goals and three assists. Bobby Rousseau, who was skating in place of Ratelle, had two goals and four assists against his old club and Vic Hadfield, still playing with a pair of bad thumbs, finished the series with four goals and one assist. However, Rod Gilbert had a disappointing series, recording only a single assist.

Ed Giacomin had an excellent series, playing in all six games and posting a 2.33 GAA. Eddie made several outstanding saves throughout the series, including an unbelievable stop of a Frank Mahovlich shot late in the third period of the sixth game to preserve the Rangers' slim one-goal lead. Giacomin was guarding the left post when the puck came out to Mahovlich who was storming in from the right side. The big Montreal winger immediately fired the puck towards the open side of the net but Giacomin lunged to his right and blocked the shot with his body. As the play went back up ice, Mahovlich stood staring at the net and shaking his head. "Damn it!" Mahovlich was later overheard in the locker room saying, "How could he have made that save? There was absolutely no way he should have stopped that puck." Even Montreal netminder Ken Dryden was impressed, telling reporters that it was one of the greatest saves he had ever seen a goaltender make.

Giacomin also came within inches of scoring a goal with 78 seconds left in the third period of the sixth game. Jim Neilson was in the penalty box and Montreal pulled Dryden to give them two extra skaters. Jacques Lemaire took a low shot towards Giacomin who made the save and shot the puck the length of the ice, barely missing the open net.

As the final buzzer sounded, Giacomin let his emotions take over. He fell on his back in the crease and kicked his legs in the air, whooping it up.

The unsung hero of the series was Gene Carr, whose job it was to shadow Yvan Cournoyer who was Montreal's leading goalscorer with 47 during the regular season. Carr's speed and superb checking limited "The Roadrunner" to just two goals and an assist in the series. Considering that two of the Rangers' victories were by one-goal margins, limiting Cournoyer's offensive output was a huge factor. The other two Rangers wins were also one-goal games late in the third period but Ted Irvine scored an empty net goal in each of the contests to seal the deal for the Rangers.

GENE CARR: "I've talked to Emile and other players about that series and it's funny when you get into the heat of the action and when I was doing that I really didn't comprehend the full extent of how good that was to shut Yvan down. It was my job. I mean before the game Emile sat me down and said, 'Look if Cournoyer jumps up and goes to the bathroom, I want you to follow him.'"

Next up were the Chicago Black Hawks, who had finished in first place in the Western Division by 21 points over the second-place Minnesota North Stars. Led by perennial 50-goal scorer Bobby Hull, the Hawks posted an impressive 28–3–8 record at noisy Chicago Stadium and their goaltending tandem of Tony Esposito and Gary Smith won the Vezina Trophy. They had swept their first-round opponents, the Pittsburgh Penguins, so they were well rested when the series began.

The Rangers prevailed again, beating the Black Hawks four games to none for the first playoff series sweep in team history. Once again it was a matter of keeping the opposition's big guns off the scoreboard. This time it was Bruce MacGregor, Billy Fairbairn, and Ron Stewart, who was playing with possibly broken ribs, taking turns closely checking Bobby Hull and limiting him to a single goal in the series. Hull had scored 50 times during the regular season and added three goals in the sweep of the Penguins.

Rod Gilbert snapped out of his opening round slump to lead the Rangers in scoring with three goals and four assists while his linemates Bobby Rousseau and Vic Hadfield each recorded two goals and five assists. Walt Tkaczuk scored a goal and added four assists while Brad Park chipped in with two goals and an assist.

But the long road to the finals was beginning to take its toll on the Blueshirts. Ed Giacomin injured his knee late in the first game and missed the remainder of the series. Gilles Villemure was outstanding, allowing only seven goals in three games. Jim Neilson suffered a broken finger in the first game blocking a Bobby Hull slapshot and did not play the rest of the series. Ron Stewart also missed the last two games of the series with cracked ribs.

The trip to the Stanley Cup Finals was the Rangers' first in twenty-two years. Their opponent was the Boston Bruins, who had dominated the league with a 54-13-11 record and scored a league-leading 330 goals in the process. The Bruins had steamrolled through the first two rounds of the playoffs, beating Toronto four games to one and then sweeping St. Louis, 4–0, and scoring 46 goals in those nine games while surrendering only 18. The Bruins had also overpowered the Blueshirts during the regular season, winning the last five meetings between the two clubs and finishing with a 5–1–0 record against their longtime rivals.

The Rangers were off for a full week before the finals began, giving them time to get some of their injured players back in the lineup including Jean Ratelle, who was limited to spot power-play duty and recorded only a single assist in six games.

The series opened in Boston and the Rangers lost both games, 6–5 and 2–1. Both teams played poorly defensively in the first game especially the Blueshirts, who allowed two shorthanded goals by Ken Hodge and Derek Sanderson 45 seconds apart in the first period. The Rangers had also allowed the Bruins to score two shorthanded goals in the first game of their 1970 series when Sanderson and Bobby Orr scored 44 seconds apart.

But the Blueshirts came back from a 5–1 deficit on goals by Gilbert, Hadfield, Tkaczuk, and MacGregor to tie the score at five. However, with only 2:16 left in the third period, Garnet "Ace" Bailey raced down the left side past Gilbert and Park and beat Giacomin with a high shot to give the Bruins a 6–5 victory. Hodge recorded a hat trick and Phil Esposito assisted on all three of his goals. Jean Ratelle returned to action for the first time since he suffered a broken ankle in March but was used only on the power play. Unfortunately, defensive forward Ron Stewart, who was already nursing cracked ribs, suffered a broken jaw when he crashed into Johnny Bucyk's knee and missed the rest of the series.

EMILE FRANCIS: "After we swept Chicago, Bill Jennings came in and said, 'Congratulations but you made one mistake, you won it too fast.' I said, 'Let me tell you something. In hockey, you better win it when you can.' You don't even think about prolonging any series. But it really hurt us because we had to sit there for seven days. I practiced them hard, I scrimmaged like it was a game but you gotta play because you've got it rolling and those seven days off really hurt us. The first game in Boston, they had us 5–1 midway through the second period. And don't you know we tied that game up and we didn't let them out of their end the last four minutes. And then with about a minute to go Ace Bailey came down the left wing, cut in and scored a bad goal between Giacomin and the goalpost. The next year Ratelle was healthy and we beat them out in five games but we didn't have a layoff and it made all the difference in the world. And of course, what helped too was when Ron Harris hit Esposito and put him out."

Gilles Villemure replaced Giacomin in goal in the second game which was more of a defensive struggle. Johnny Bucyk opened the scoring for the Bruins thanks mostly to the unique configuration of the Boston Garden, the only rink in the NHL besides the Montreal Forum that had the penalty box close to the home team's bench. Bucyk was on the bench when Carol Vadnais and Glen Sather were sent off for fighting at 14:08 of the opening period. About a minute later Gary Doak of the Rangers was whistled off giving the Bruins the man advantage. When the first penalties expired, Vadnais quickly got to his bench and was replaced on the ice by Bucyk, who dashed down the left side, received a pass from Orr, broke in on Villemure and scored.

The teams were tied, 1–1, after the second period, but Ken Hodge's goal with both Walt Tkaczuk and Bruce MacGregor in the penalty box midway through the third period proved to be the game-winner. But the game did not end without controversy. With the Rangers pressuring the Bruins late in the third period, the Blueshirts were ruled offside with 54 seconds left. Apparently everybody in the building heard the whistle except for timekeeper Tony Notagiacomo, who let an additional four seconds tick down before stopping the clock. Notagiacomo, the same timekeeper who let time run out in the fifth game of the Rangers-Bruins 1970 playoff series, claimed that he didn't hear the whistle. "When I saw the players standing around and realized the play was dead, I stopped the time," Notagiacomo told reporters after the game. NHL president Clarence Campbell later said that "the seconds were not restored because in the opinion of the timekeeper, there was no need to."

The series moved to New York where the Rangers won the third game, 5–2. Brad Park notched two goals and two assists and became the first defenseman to score two power-play goals in the same period in the playoffs. Rod Gilbert also scored a pair of goals and added an assist and Ed Giacomin was strong in goal. But the win was costly as Jim Neilson strained his knee and Ab Demarco suffered a deep cut behind his knee when sliced by the skate of Ace Bailey. He missed the rest of the playoffs.

In the fourth game the Bruins jumped out to a 2–0 lead on a pair of first-period goals by Bobby Orr and hung on for a 3–2 victory. It was a rough game as referee Bruce Hood called 104 minutes in penalties including 72 minutes in the first period alone when Orr and Park and later McKenzie and Sather squared off against each other. Jim Dorey made his first appearance since he separated his shoulder in February, replacing the injured Ab DeMarco in the lineup. Dorey only played a couple of shifts and did not dress for the rest of the series.

Down three games to one, the Rangers returned to Boston and won the fifth game, 3–2. Gilles Villemure was outstanding in goal, stopping 36 of the Bruins' 38 shots including 17 in the third period. Boston led, 2–1, going into the third period but a pair of goals by Bobby Rousseau put the Blueshirts on top. Rousseau had been bumped down to the third line centering Ted Irvine and Bruce MacGregor as Jean Ratelle was ready to take full shifts between Hadfield and Gilbert. The Rangers had a four-minute power play in the first period but could not manage a single shot on goal. The turning point of the game came in the second period when the Bruins had a two-man advantage for a minute and 29 seconds but could not score. Phil Esposito took six of his total of eight shots in the third period but could not put the puck past Villemure and could be seen shaking his head in frustration.

BRAD PARK: "When we went into Boston for Game Five we were down three to one in the series and we walked by this room, I think it was the Celtics dressing room, and we looked in and they had the banners, the signs and the napkins. It was one thing to have everything there saying that they were the Stanley Cup champions but they had the date on it which was that day. And we kind of took exception to that. Bobby Rousseau scored two goals and we ended up forcing game six back in New York."

GENE CARR: "Word had gotten around the room there that they had champagne and that they were all ready to go. And so that gave us a little bit of extra incentive, like we can't let this happen."

The Rangers had a lot of scoring chances in the sixth game but could not convert on any of them. Aided by his pals, the goalposts, Gerry Cheevers turned away all 33 Rangers shots, blanking them, 3–0, as the Bruins clinched the series at Madison Square Garden. Captain Johnny Bucyk was presented the Stanley Cup at center ice but declined to take a victory lap for fear of "getting hit in the head."

BRAD PARK: "We had a very tight hockey game, one-nothing going into the third period. I spoke to Gerry Cheevers, who is a good friend of mine about that game, and he said, 'Never have I had so many pucks go by me that didn't go in the net.' We hit two or three posts in that third period. With a little luck, we would have forced a Game Seven."

Many Rangers took a beating in what was a very physical series. Ron Stewart suffered a broken jaw in the opener and Ab DeMarco sustained a deep gash behind his knee that nearly ended his career. Vic Hadfield, who was already nursing two dislocated thumbs, also suffered a dislocated shoulder as well as torn rib cartilage. Most Rangers insisted that the outcome of the series would have been different had Jean Ratelle been healthy. But the real difference in the series was made by Bobby Orr who, despite sore knees, finished with four goals and four assists and was awarded the Conn Smythe trophy as the playoffs MVP as well as a Dodge Charger from *Sport* magazine for being the top player in the finals. Phil Esposito, who had scored 66 goals during the regular season, was held scoreless but recorded eight assists and Ken Hodge led the Bruins in scoring with five goals and three assists. Ed Johnston played very well for Boston, surrendering only six goals in three games while Gerry Cheevers gave up 10 goals in three games and recorded a shutout. For the Rangers, Gilles Villemure had a good series, giving up only seven goals in three games while Ed Giacomin's performance was disappointing, allowing 11 goals in three games. Rod Gilbert led the Rangers in scoring with four goals and three assists followed by Brad Park who scored two goals and added four assists.

Each Bruin received $15,000 as the winner's share and each Ranger received $7,500.

PHIL GOYETTE: "Emile didn't play me in the last game because Ratelle came back. Maybe that's why they didn't win the Cup that year, eh? I kid him about it but it was a decision anyone would make, Ratelle was younger and he was one of their top players. I laugh too, I don't know if I would have made any difference, but who knows? You don't know, right?"

DALE ROLFE: "I still say we were the best team that never won a Cup. But there was a guy in Boston, number 4 who had a lot to do with it too. Bobby Orr was the best, it's that simple. The best hockey player in history, bar none. We worked hard, we tried hard, there were mistakes made on both sides, but we made one too many. It just wasn't meant to be."

BRUCE MacGREGOR: "That was a heckuva hockey team we had but losing Jean, especially when you get into the finals and the way that line had played and what he meant to the team, I think that was a big reason why we couldn't win that thing. When you looked at our team that year I think that was as good a team that I'd ever played with, because we didn't have many weaknesses at all. It was a good hockey club but when you take one player out of the lineup that meant so much to the team I think it equalized things a lot and I always thought that that was a big factor why we didn't win the Cup."

GENE CARR: "That damned Bobby Orr. If it wasn't for him, we would have won that Cup. That's what I've always said. I don't know how many reporters have asked me who was the fastest skater in the league, because you're one of them and I would say without a doubt Bobby Orr. There was nobody faster than Bobby. He was faster than Cournoyer, he was faster than me. He had like these after-jets. After about three or four strides skating with him, and I did it many times, all of a sudden I don't know where it came from, but he would just take off. It's something that you can't teach. You can't teach a kid how to do that. I don't care how good he is or how great a skater he is, you've either got it or you don't.

"It's like a pro golfer when he hits a ball about two hundred eighty yards it gets like these after- jets and it scoots another fifty or sixty yards. I asked these guys many times, how the hell did you do that? When I hit a ball it will go three hundred yards or whatever and that was it. You didn't see it take off like that.

"Emile would put me on left wing when Orr was out there just so when he made that rush down the right side I'd be racing down there with him. I'd take a quick peek to see where the play was developing and just in that quick split-second where I would have a look and look back, Orr was four or five strides ahead of me. That was the reason why we ended up losing the Cup."

Because they had played an additional round compared to previous Rangers teams that had made it to the finals, the Blueshirts set team playoff records for victories (10), goals (52), assists (87), scoring points (149), penalty minutes (275), and goals in a playoff round (41) and goals against (41). Vic Hadfield tied a team mark for most goals in a game (three) while Brad Park, Bobby Rousseau, and Rod Gilbert each equaled team records for points in a game with four.

"We'll be back next year," an always upbeat Francis told reporters, "and next year we'll win it."

Play the Man

In the spring of 1970, noted hockey writer Stan Fischler asked Brad Park if he would be willing to collaborate on a diary-type book that would cover the 1970–71 Rangers season. A few years earlier Jerry Kramer, an offensive lineman for the Green Bay Packers, had worked with Dick Schaap to produce the bestseller *Instant Replay* that chronicled the daily life of a professional football player. Both Fischler and his publisher thought the idea would work for hockey and selected Park because he was young, smart, and a member of one of the league's most popular teams.

Park agreed to do the book and dutifully dictated his thoughts into a tape recorder daily during the season.

The result was *Play the Man* which hit bookstores in the fall of 1971. The book detailed Park's holdout in training camp as well as presenting an honest account of key events and milestones throughout the 1970–71 season. He was also not shy about expressing his opinion of opposing teams and players which caused more than a few problems for both himself and the Rangers.

In a chapter titled "Boston's Big, Bad Bruins," Park outlined the roots of the Bruins-Rangers rivalry and then tore into some current Bruins, the Boston Garden, as well as their fans. He called venerable old Boston Garden "downright grubby, without question the worst rink in the NHL." He wrote that "Boston is like a schoolyard bully, push a little guy around as long as the little guy won't fight back. But when the little guys fight back, the bully doesn't know what to do."

He said that Derek Sanderson "throws two or three punches then backs off because he got his shots in and knows he can't handle most guys after that." He called Ted Green "a hatchet man" and accused Bobby Orr of taking "cheap shots." Of winger John McKenzie, he said "his bag is running people from behind."

But he saved the best barbs for Phil Esposito, saying, "Esposito is an extraordinary stick handler and superb shooter but he doesn't have any guts. He's carried in that department by the animals with the Boston team. Esposito runs people from behind."

"Esposito gets annoyed more than any other player when he's taken out of the play," Park continued. "Maybe he thinks he's too good to be touched."

The Bruins were not amused and took it out on the Rangers by winning five straight games from the Blueshirts after the book was published.

When Park played with several Bruins in the All-Star game that January in Bloomington, Minnesota, he was snubbed by them. Johnny McKenzie complained about sharing a dressing room with "that creep Park." "His presence took all the joy out of being an All-Star."

"The book gave our guys extra incentive to beat them" said Bruins coach Tom Johnson. "I wonder if Park realized how much some of the things he said in the book can hurt him and the Rangers."

BRAD PARK: "My comments on the Boston Garden were how old and dingy it was. There were rats in there and it could always use a coat of paint, which was probably the truth. But the Boston fans thought it was an attack on them. There was also a quote about Bobby Orr that was taken out of context so it looked like I was attacking the Bruins. Stan Fischler wrote the book with me and it was supposed to be like a year-long diary but it seemed to be generated more towards the Bruins, so I was public enemy number one. I would get hate mail threatening my life to the point where I showed the letters to Emile Francis and the next thing I know, the next time we go to Boston I've got the FBI walking me to and from the ice. It was a very difficult time."

11

1972–73

The Islanders, the WHA, and the Fat Cats

THE PROFESSIONAL HOCKEY landscape changed dramatically at the start of the 1972–73 season. First, the Rangers had a new rival, the expansion New York Islanders who joined the NHL along with the Atlanta Flames. Then the World Hockey Association also opened for business in the fall of 1972, offering players a new market for their services and forcing NHL GMs to either pay their players inflated salaries or risk losing them to the new league.

The Birth of a Rivalry

The New York Islanders were born in 1972 in an attempt to keep the WHA's New York Raiders from setting up shop in the brand-new Nassau Veterans Memorial Coliseum in Uniondale, Long Island. The Nassau County government did not consider the WHA to be a major league and didn't want any part of them. But the only way to legally deny the Raiders' bid would be to get an NHL team to play there instead. So

William Shea, who played a major role in bringing the Mets to New York in 1962, was enlisted to lobby the NHL for an expansion team.

Shea quickly found allies in NHL president Clarence Campbell and Rangers president William Jennings. Campbell didn't want a WHA team in New York, while Jennings, more of a pragmatist, knew that if the Raiders wanted to play in New York, it would have to be at the Garden where he would be happy to charge them exorbitant rental fees while in effect controlling their destiny by offering them bad dates and times for their home games. It was a "win-win" situation for Jennings.

EMILE FRANCIS: "I had made a deal when they were building that Coliseum. I was gonna move our farm team there. It would have been ideal for us, but then the WHA came along and I was told that they were gonna get an NHL team, so forget about a minor-league team."

Clothing manufacturer Roy Boe, who also owned the New York Nets of the American Basketball Association, organized a group of nineteen investors to buy the franchise for $6 million. He also had to pay the Rangers a territorial indemnification fee of $4 million—another "win" for Jennings.

Boe's wife, Deon, designed the team's original uniforms with a green and black color scheme that was soon changed to the now familiar royal blue and orange.

Designer John Alogna was given only a weekend to produce a logo before the team's initial press conference. He came up with a simple but effective design featuring a silhouette of Long Island and a large NY with a hockey stick, all within a circle.

Bill Torrey, who had worked for the California Seals, was named general manager. Torrey would ultimately become one of the most respected GMs in NHL history but his choice of a coach for the fledgling team was former Ranger Phil Goyette and unfortunately that didn't work out so well. Goyette posted a 6–38–4 record and was let go after forty-eight games. He was replaced by another former Ranger, Earl Ingarfield, who didn't fare much better.

PHIL GOYETTE: "When I look back on it today I should never have gone there. I should have waited and learned the trade a little bit more in an organization and then worked up to that point. But I wasn't there for the draft meetings; they only hired me after the draft and then three quarters of those guys jumped to the WHA. The only NHL player I had of any consequence was Eddie Westfall, the others were all out of juniors.

"So I told them, 'What do you want? You don't have any players.' They even had to look for players for training camp. But that's a team that got in the league too fast and wasn't organized from the base up. They said, 'Don't worry, you're gonna be with us for a long time.' But if you don't win, you can't get rid of the players, they didn't have any. So, they got rid of the coach.

"They wanted me to stick around and be an assistant to Bill Torrey, but that meant that I would be running around all over the league, scouting and whatnot. So, I said that's not for me. Just give me whatever you owe me and we'll just say goodbye. Unfortunately, I would have loved to have what they had after, I mean the following year they started to get guys like [Mike] Bossy and [Bryan] Trottier and [Denis] Potvin and they started getting a team. So, Al Arbour came in and had some good hockey players and they won four Cups in a row."

EARL INGARFIELD: "I was scouting for the Islanders when they let Phil go and Bill Torrey asked me to come in and take over for that first season. He actually asked me to stay on for the next season, but I didn't think I was ready for it. And we had just retired in 1971 from playing in Oakland and we had a young daughter and I just didn't want to move again at that time. And then they got Al Arbour which turned out to be great for the Islanders. I thought it worked out quite well. The sad part of it was that back then in expansion they certainly didn't leave many players available that you could build a team around. It was difficult, but I certainly enjoyed the time there. It was a great experience for me and I thought the players we had worked hard for me but we just didn't have the skill."

The undermanned and overmatched Islanders finished with the worst record in the league at 12–60–6 that first season. They also lost all six meetings with the Rangers, being outscored 25–5 in those games. But for the first time since the New York/Brooklyn Americans folded in 1942, the Rangers had local competition and a great rivalry was born. The Islanders would also play a huge role in altering the course of Rangers history just a few years down the road.

The WHA and the Fat Cats

The Islanders were the least of the Rangers' problems going into the 1972–73 season. The World Hockey Association was set to begin playing that season and was looking to steal the best players in the NHL including several Rangers.

The new league was the brainchild of two Californians, lawyer Gary Davidson and Dennis Murphy, a born promoter who knew nothing about hockey but knew how to sell sports franchises to wealthy businessmen. Davidson and Murphy had started the American Basketball Association in 1967, luring players from the NBA with big bucks and contracts that didn't include a reserve clause.

The reserve clause was a part of every standard contract used by professional leagues in all major sports. It basically bound a player to the team they initially signed with until they were traded, sold, or retired. The California duo along with Don Regan, who was one of Davidson's legal associates, used the same business model in 1971 when they began the WHA. Some of the owners that they had sold ABA franchises to found themselves shut out by the NHL expansion and were more than willing to fork over the $25,000 franchise fee to join the new league.

The WHA was never a threat to overtake the NHL as the elite hockey league in North America, but they still made life difficult for the established league by offering players an alternative to the NHL.

EMILE FRANCIS: "It was very difficult because up until that time we never signed a guy to a two-year contract or signed questionable players to one-way contracts. But they were coming in with offers that would blow your socks off. And a lot of teams really got hurt because they were losing minor league players because they were giving them one-way contracts and we had them on two-way contracts. So I would say that those nine years that the WHA was in business were the toughest years I ever had in hockey. Because after we expanded we figured it would take us five years to get back to having the same caliber of hockey as the league had before we expanded in 1967. And just about the time where we felt we were back to when we expanded in 1967, bang—in comes the WHA.

"Hockey really changed there for a few years. And the worst part was they started signing guys seventeen, eighteen years old and our draft was twenty year olds. So, we had to change the draft because if we didn't drop down to 18, the WHA would have ended up with all the young players. So, we dropped the age to eighteen and that made it even tougher because not many players can come into the league and play at eighteen. When it opened up, it opened up real good. And it opened up because Birmingham started signing all those kids and they sued on the grounds of the right to work law and they were right. The judge said they were right. You've got the right to work in this country at eighteen years old so we had to change right away or we would have been sued. It was like a war and in a war nobody wins. It was costing everybody money."

In February of 1972, the WHA held a general player draft in which teams selected players from other leagues, most notably the NHL, that they would try to sign. Many NHL players were reluctant to jump leagues, fearing financial instability. But when the WHA owners banded together and raised enough money to lure Bobby Hull away from the Chicago Black Hawks to play for the Winnipeg Jets it opened the flood gates. The Montreal Canadiens lost defenseman J. C. Tremblay and the Toronto Maple Leafs lost Bernie Parent. The notoriously tightfisted Boston Bruins were hit especially hard, losing Derek Sanderson, Gerry Cheevers, Ted Green, and Johnny McKenzie.

The Rangers were targeted by Cleveland Crusaders owner Nick Mileti who had applied for one of the two expansion franchises that were to join the NHL for the 1973–74 season but lost out to a Kansas City group that included Jeff Jennings, the son of Rangers president William Jennings. Mileti then launched a financial assault on the Rangers, contacting Brad Park, Vic Hadfield, and Rod Gilbert and offering them long-term deals worth more than $1 million each, a far cry from the approximately $50,000 they were making at the time.

Francis and Jennings saw what Mileti was doing and had a decision to make. Did they want to risk letting three of their core players jump to the new league and have to start a rebuilding project when they had already come so far? They knew the team couldn't win without Park, Hadfield, and Gilbert so they anted up, starting with Park, whose salary was increased to $250,000. They also knew that once they gave Park, Hadfield, and Gilbert raises, everybody else on the team would need to be increased appropriately as well. Ed Giacomin's salary tripled when he signed a three-year contract for $150,000 a season, up from the $50,000 he made the year before.

EMILE FRANCIS: "The first guy they came after was Brad Park. And I told them, they're not going to be able to afford to sign more than one guy and if we lose one guy we lose one guy and if we give in to him it'll be the next guy and the next guy. It'll just keep going. In war there are no friends and it was a war."

By the time all of the renegotiations were finished, the Rangers' payroll had more than doubled from $750,000 to almost $1.75 million. Maple Leafs owner Harold Ballard complained that the Rangers were "trying to buy the Stanley Cup." But the Rangers were not the only team feeling the pressure from the new league. The average NHL salary was raised by 400% as each team in the league tried to hold on to their key players.

BRAD PARK: "Steve Arnold, who was my agent in 1970, was now working with Nick Mileti who was the owner of the Cleveland franchise in the WHA and they came to Toronto to talk to me. Larry Rauch was my agent at that time and we had thrown a number at them of a five-year deal at $300,000 a year. And they took an hour and then they came back to us and he said you got it. So I said okay that's great but I said, listen I have to go and talk to the Cat and they said no you don't. And I said I owe it to the Cat.

"So Emile flew into Toronto and we met at the Royal York Hotel. I said, 'Emile this is what the offer is,' and he said, 'Well I'm not going to match that. So, I told him I'd like to stay in New York so I would take $250,000 a year to stay in New York. So, he says, 'I'll be right back' and I told him that we had to make a deal that night or I'd be going to Cleveland the next day for a press conference. So, he goes in the other room and I guess he called Bill Jennings and the Cat told him not to do the deal. But Bill Jennings said to do the deal and he comes back in the room and says, 'Okay, we got a deal.' Then when I told Cleveland that I'd agreed to stay in New York for $250,000 they upped their offer to $400,000 a year! But I said no I can't do that and they said why not? I said because I gave the Cat my word. So, I ended up signing in New York. I loved New York while I was there."

As a result of Mileti's assault, the Rangers became the highest paid team in the NHL and were labeled "fat cats" due to the fact that in the eyes of most hockey observers, they were "overpaid underachievers." It was a moniker that would stick with them for the rest of the Emile Francis era.

The 1972–73 Season

The Blueshirts lost only three players in the expansion draft, all minor leaguers. Norm Gratton and Morris Stefaniw were selected by the Atlanta Flames and Bryan Lefley was picked by the Islanders. The Isles later selected Don Blackburn from the Rangers' top farm team in Providence in the inter-league draft. In November, veteran Ron Stewart was sold to the Islanders for cash. Although many players have played for both teams, the Rangers and Islanders have never made a player-for-player trade.

Francis made two preseason deals of note, sending tough guy defenseman Steve Durbano to the Blues for future considerations which turned out to be winger Curt Bennett and goaltender Peter McDuffe. Bennett was a big (6-foot-3, 195 pounds) twenty-four-year-old who had been in the St. Louis system for two seasons after graduating from Brown University where he was used strictly a defenseman. The Blues signed him following graduation and made him a winger. In 35 games over two seasons with St. Louis, Curt recorded five goals and five assists along with 30 penalty minutes. McDuffe had originally been acquired by the Rangers from Phoenix of the WHL in 1969 then dealt to St. Louis in May of 1971 for the Blues' first-round draft pick that year. That pick was then used to select Steve Vickers. But there was much more to the deal than originally met the eye.

EMILE FRANCIS: "I was carrying three goaltenders and I couldn't trade McDuffe anywhere and I didn't want to carry three goaltenders. I was looking to get a first-round draft pick for him and St. Louis was one of my favorite trading partners at that time. So, they agreed to take McDuffe for their first-round draft choice but with one little consideration. They said, 'Whoever you take with that first-round draft pick, if at the end of next year we decide we don't want to keep McDuffe we can give him back to you for the guy you took with our draft choice.'

"So at that point in time I thought that was about the best deal I could make so I traded McDuffe to St. Louis. So McDuffe played there all year and at the end of the season [Blues owner] Sid Salomon's son, who was making all the deals with me said, 'Well, we had a deal with you and you took Steve Vickers with our draft choice.' We had Vickers playing in Omaha and he was playing great. He said, 'There's only one way we would consider not taking Vickers back. You've got a big, tough defenseman down in Omaha named Steve Durbano.' So, when he said Durbano, I thought, 'What the hell?' So, I said, 'Well, I can't trade him. Christ, if I trade him they'll run me right out of New York. He's a big tough guy, just what we're looking for.' So, he said would you give that some thought? So, I said, 'Yeah, let me think about it and I'll get back to you tomorrow.'

"So I called my manager in Omaha, Jake Milford, and I said, 'Jake, has St. Louis had anyone around scouting?' He said, 'Oh yeah they've been following us around for about a month. Yeah, they sent a scout down here and he goes behind our goal when we're at one end moves down to the other end of the ice when we go down there.' So, I said, 'Well, shit, he can't be looking at the goalkeeper because he's not going to the National Hockey League, so they were looking at Durbano.'

"So I went back to them the next day and said I've been thinking about your deal for me to trade Durbano. I'm going to need more than McDuffe. I need Curt Bennett and a cash outlay of twenty grand and Vickers. He said you've got it. I thought, 'Holy shit, I got Vickers back, Curt Bennett, twenty grand, and McDuffe for Steve Durbano. So now the next season, the first time St. Louis comes into the Garden, Vickers has a hat trick. So, I spent extra time with the press because I knew that Salomon was going to be waiting for me. I finally leave the press room and I hear 'Emile!' So, I turn to my left and there's Sid Salomon Jr., the acting general manager and his dad, who's a fine guy and he says, 'That Vickers is quite a hockey player, isn't he?' So, I said, 'Well, we had a lucky night tonight. He's playing with two great players, Tkaczuk and Fairbairn.' So, he says, 'Oh is that right?' So, I got the hell out of there. But we had a deal and he could've gotten Vickers back from me but when he sprung Durbano on me I had to take a couple of steps back."

Francis also traded Gary Doak and Rick Newell to Detroit for Joe Zanussi and the Red Wings' first-round pick in the 1972 amateur draft which the Rangers used to select Al Blanchard. Some drafts work out better than others.

Forwards Jerry Butler and Steve Vickers as well as defenseman Larry Sacharuk were among the new faces in camp, but it was Vickers who made the biggest impression on the front office. The Rangers selected Vickers in the first round of the 1971 amateur draft following an eye-opening junior career with the Toronto Marlboros of the OHA. In his final season with the Marlies, Vickers was one of the league's top scorers with 43 goals and 64 assists. Then in his first season as a pro, Steve scored 36 goals with 23 assists in 70 games for the Omaha Knights of the CHL.

STEVE VICKERS, *Left Wing, 1972–82:* "Emile drafted me in 1971. At the time, I really didn't want to be drafted by the Rangers because I knew they had a set team and I knew I wouldn't have a chance of playing much. But they did take me and I had to spend the first year in Omaha. I was a little disappointed, I was a first-round pick but I think they brought me along the right way. If I was the GM I probably would've done the same thing. In retrospect, it was probably the best thing to happen to me for my career because I had always lived at home and I learned how to live on my own and learned what being a professional hockey player meant and not just a junior hockey player. A lot of these kids come along at eighteen. I can't imagine playing in the NHL at eighteen. You have to be really, really gifted to do that. I certainly wasn't ready for that. Maybe I could've played as a part-time player at twenty, but at eighteen, forget about it.

"We didn't have a very good team in Omaha but I think I grew a little there. Emile, through his scouts, told me that he wanted me to play left wing instead of right wing which was my usual position. I always played the off wing. But he said we needed left wings not right wings, plus he didn't think I was fast enough as a right winger to go around the outside. It was a little bit of a wake-up call but it made sense to me after a while because I could still score goals from left wing."

The Blueshirts got off to a slow 1–3–0 start as Ed Giacomin surrendered 19 goals in his first four games. Gilles Villemure then took over between the pipes for the next eight games and helped to get the Rangers back on track, going 6–1–1.

The team began to hit its stride in late October, going on a 9–1–0 run and moving up to second place in the standings. By then however, injuries to key players began to take their toll. Jim Neilson missed a total of twenty-six games when he broke his right foot on two separate occasions. Bruce MacGregor also missed nine games early in the season with a knee injury and then suffered a broken ankle later in the year. Brad Park suffered the same fate, missing eighteen games with knee problems early in the year and then eight more as the season wound down. Ted Irvine also missed fourteen games with strained knee and ankle ligaments.

Due to the injuries to Neilson and Park, Francis was forced to shore up the blue line, sending Curt Bennett to Atlanta for Ron Harris in November. Francis also made three deals in early March to give him more options for the playoffs. First he reacquired forward Mike Murphy from St. Louis in exchange for spare defenseman Ab DeMarco Jr. Then he traded future considerations (Steve Andrascik) to Pittsburgh for defenseman Sheldon Kannegiesser. And finally he sent cash and future considerations (Dave Hrechkosy and Gary Coalter) to California for veteran defenseman Bert Marshall.

In addition to the injuries there was the continuing problem of finding a left winger for Walt Tkaczuk and Billy Fairbairn. The search for the third member of the Bulldog line had been going on since 1971 when Dave Balon was traded to Vancouver. Gene Carr had been playing regularly on the line but it wasn't a perfect match. In the season opener in Detroit, Carr was having trouble handling the puck, so rookie Steve Vickers, who had started the game on a line with Pete Stemkowski and Bruce MacGregor, was moved up to the coveted left wing spot. The trio clicked and Vickers scored on his first shot on goal in his first NHL game.

STEVE VICKERS: "It was a loss in the old Detroit Olympia. It was my first shot actually I think I had four or five shifts. I was on the fourth line, just waiting my turn. It wasn't until a month into the season that they decided to put me with Walter Tkaczuk and Bill Fairbairn."

But Francis had made a major investment in Carr, sending Jack Egers, Andre Dupont, and Mike Murphy to St. Louis for Carr, Jim Lorentz, and Wayne Connelly, and he had a lot riding on the speedy winger. So Gene was back on the Tkaczuk line for the next game and Vickers once again became a spare part. The two players alternated at left wing on the line for about a month. Carr was flashy and had great speed but couldn't put the puck in the net, while Vickers developed chemistry with Tkaczuk and Fairbairn and the results were record-setting. Steve scored a hat trick against Gary Edwards and the LA Kings on November 12 and repeated the feat in the Rangers' next game against Michel Belhumeur and the Flyers. It was the first time in NHL history that a rookie had recorded back-to-back hat tricks. It was also the first time the feat had been accomplished by a Rangers player. Vickers gave full credit to his linemates. "Playing with Walt Tkaczuk and Billy Fairbairn has to be the easiest way for a left wing to break into the

NHL," he told reporters. "They're doing all the work and I'm getting the goals." A week after Vickers's record-setting hat tricks, Vancouver's Bobby Schmautz had a three-goal night followed by a four-goal night. "That's something!" Vickers remarked. "And he did it without Tkaczuk and Fairbairn."

STEVE VICKERS: "Both games were at the Garden and the puck was just going in. I was getting the chances. Billy and Walter were setting me up and I made the best of it. I always had a high scoring percentage because I scored most of my goals from in tight. I didn't have a good slap shot coming down the wing, I wasn't a great skater, I was a strong skater but not a great skater. Those two guys were unselfish, they didn't care who got the goals, who got the points, as long as we won. They took me in and accepted me as a linemate. And I guess it helped when I scored the back-to-back hat tricks playing on their line. It showed that I could play not only with them but in the National Hockey League."

But Francis still wanted to give Carr every opportunity to succeed. That was when fate stepped in. On December 20 Carr suffered a broken collarbone and the Bulldog line was reborn with Vickers on left wing. The previous version was pretty successful as well with Dave Balon at left wing. In fact since Balon had been traded in November of 1971 as many as sixteen left wingers were tried on the line until Vickers came along.

GENE CARR: "[St. Louis's] Bob Plager caught me coming along the inside, going around the defensemen and he came all the way across the ice as I was going around the other defenseman on the board side and he nailed me. I didn't see him and he drove my shoulder up to my head, snapped it in two. I guess Bob was thinking well, he's a rookie and I'll nail his ass. It was pretty severe.

"Steve was a great winger, he was perfect for that line. He grew up in junior hockey in Canada playing left wing so when I got hurt, he fit into that line. He was there for years. He was the perfect winger for them like Vic Hadfield was the perfect winger for Jean and Rod. It was a perfect line. So then when I got healthy and came back they weren't going to move Steve off that line. Steve went on to be Rookie of the Year. At the time I was upset that I couldn't get back into the lineup but you know what? Good for Steve. He became a good friend and he's a great guy he deserves everything he got, that's for sure."

STEVE VICKERS: "They had made a big trade for Gene Carr. He was supposed to be the next Bobby Hull but it just didn't turn out that way. He had trouble scoring and then when Bill Chadwick came out on the air and said he couldn't put the puck in the ocean if he was standing on the pier that didn't help the situation. It didn't help his credibility in the eyes of the fans."

GENE CARR: "Chadwick used to jump on me about putting the puck in the ocean and I don't know why he attacked me. He had no idea how that affected me mentally. I used to just cringe when I heard them say something or they would bring up my name. I wish I could've talked to Bill before he passed away. I would have asked him, 'Why did you attack me like that? I didn't do anything to you.' That's a lot of years ago but people still talk to me about Chadwick. Anytime he would come into the dressing room or whatever I would just walk by him because I just couldn't bring myself to even say hello to the guy."

BILL FAIRBAIRN: "Balon and Vickers were both good goalscorers. They were magic with the puck around the net there and it was pretty much up to me and Walter to get them the puck. They were the 'go to guys' Dave and Steve both because they were natural goal scorers and they were close to the net all the time so they weren't too hard to find. Steve especially because he was always right off the post there and he stayed away from the defensemen and if you could get him the puck he made sure it went in. The same with 'Bozey,' he was a hustler. We were called 'The Bulldog Line' because we worked hard to get the puck and when we got the puck Dave or Steve would find a way of putting it in. I enjoyed playing on the line. I played most of my career with Walter. It was very enjoyable; it made hockey fun to play.

"We were the checking line. We were put out against the top lines and we'd kill penalties and we were second on the power play. Ratty,

Rod, and Vic were the number one power play line but we were second up so we got a lot of ice time and it helped me and Walter because we were chunky guys and we needed the extra work out during the game to stay in shape.

"I liked going along the boards. I didn't go off my wing too often but if I could get the defensemen to take the body on me then Walter would be wide open and then there'd be a two-on-one with either Steve or Davey. I didn't mind taking the hits but I'm starting to feel them now. Back then I didn't feel them. Now the aches and pains are coming out in the hips and shoulders and everything else but that's old age setting in too."

STEVE VICKERS: "I learned quickly that when I went to the net, at any level, that the puck would usually end up there, either from a pass or rebound so that's where the action was. Yeah, sometimes you'd take a little beating but all in all it was worth it. Pete Stemkowski's nickname for me was '3.5'—that was the average length of my shot. But I never had a coach tell me not to score from that close in.

"It was wonderful playing with those guys. It was the Bulldog Line. We were the second line of course; the big line would score more goals. I think we were more defense oriented. I think we prided ourselves on our defense. We were more upset about being scored against than elated about scoring a goal. We didn't like to get scored on. I think we went nine or ten games once without being scored on.

"The only negative thing about playing with Walter and Billy was that in those days the penalty killers were out there for a minute and a half and then another forward twosome would go out and mop up the rest of the penalty. I didn't kill penalties so I didn't get a lot of ice time. They didn't keep track back then but I probably only got about twelve minutes per game. And we weren't on the power play obviously because that was the G-A-G line. Maybe we'd get an occasional shift out there, but that was the only negative thing about playing with those guys. Other than that, I really enjoyed playing with Walter and Billy."

Vickers also brought something to the line that Balon couldn't: Toughness. Although Steve wasn't the type to go looking for a fight, he could take care of himself and be counted on to stand up for his team-mates. "Vickers is tough," said Francis. "It takes a lot to get him riled up but when he does, look out!" Rangers scout Steve Brklacich put it this way: "He doesn't start fights, he finishes them."

By early January the Rangers started playing well and went on a sixteen-game unbeaten streak which included a ten-game winning streak and three consecutive 6–0 shutouts over the Islanders (two) and Atlanta (one). The streak propelled them into second place but a late 6–6–2 stretch dropped them back into third place in the tight Eastern Division standings. They wound down the season on an 0–4–1 slump while being outscored 19–8.

The Blueshirts finished the season in third place with 102 points, five points behind the second-place Bruins and 18 behind the first-place Canadiens. After six seasons of steady improvement, the Blueshirts had taken a step backwards. Compared to the 1971–72 season the Rangers won one fewer game, lost six more, and tied five fewer games, earning seven fewer points than the year before. They also scored 20 fewer goals and allowed 16 more than the previous season.

Jean Ratelle led the team with 41 goals and added 53 assists followed by Rod Gilbert with 25 goals and a team-high 59 assists. Vic Hadfield, who had reached the 50-goal plateau the previous season, scored only 28 but also missed fifteen games due to injuries.

Despite missing three weeks due to a knee injury, Vickers finished the season with 30 goals and 23 assists, then added five goals and four assists in nine playoff games against Boston and Chicago. His impressive season earned him the Calder Trophy as the NHL's Rookie of the Year, the first Ranger to win the award since Camille Henry in 1954. Vickers's linemates also compiled impressive numbers that season. Walt Tkaczuk scored 27 goals with 39 assists and Billy Fairbairn had a career year, reaching the 30-goal plateau and adding 33 assists.

STEVE VICKERS: "Winning the Calder Trophy was nice. Another feather in the cap. Especially after missing seventeen games right after I got the back-to-back hat tricks. I hurt my knee and I missed five weeks. I had stretched ligaments so I never had to get cut. The doctor told me it was a good thing I was twenty-one instead of thirty-one because it would come back faster and it did. I was up against Bill Barber and he had more points and a lot of people thought he deserved it and maybe they were right. But I think scoring thirty goals in New York, the media capital of the world helped a lot. I would've traded it for Stanley Cup but unfortunately that never happened."

BILL FAIRBAIRN: "I don't know how I got the goals because I had one of the worst shots in the league. I think the goalies were kind of surprised when I shot the puck because when I let it go it was like a changeup in baseball and that would be my hard shot. I wasn't known for hard shot. As a matter fact, once in practice Eddie said, 'Give me your best shot,' so I came over the blue line and let a slapper go and he threw off his trapper and caught it in his bare hand. That's how slow my shot was, but it was accurate and I had help from my two wingers to get the thirty goals that year. As a line we really clicked well. I could never have played on a better line for myself. Steve ended up getting Rookie of the Year that season."

Ed Giacomin played in 43 games and posted a 2.91 GAA, his highest since his rookie season in 1965–66. But he also recorded four shutouts, surpassing the team mark of 40 set by Davey Kerr. Gilles Villemure appeared in 34 games, posting a 2.29 GAA with three shutouts.

Brad Park was named to the Second All-Star team and played in the midseason game along with Giacomin, Villemure, and Ratelle.

The Playoffs

The Rangers' first-round opponent in the playoffs were the Boston Bruins. The teams were evenly matched, having split the season series with three victories each. But the Bruins were the defending Stanley Cup champions and despite losing many key players to the WHA, they still played with a lot of pride and still had a defenseman named Bobby Orr. But with the loss of Gerry Cheevers to the WHA the Bruins were weak in goal, relying on thirty-seven-year old Ed Johnston and forty-four-year old Jacques Plante, a late season acquisition from Toronto.

Health-wise, Bruce MacGregor was still not fully recovered from a broken ankle and Vic Hadfield was experiencing dizzy spells from a concussion that occurred when he took a puck in the face in late February. Both were ready to play but the Rangers would be without Rod Seiling, who had sustained a broken collarbone late in the season.

ROD SEILING: "I had made a great pass to one of our players and foolishly was watching it and [Minnesota's] Freddy Barrett was on the ice and he upended me and I happened to land on my collarbone. It was kind of a freak accident because you landed on your shoulder many, many times in the course of the season and nothing happened. But it was just a freak break. It was my own fault for watching my pass and not paying attention."

While watching films of the Rangers' last two games against the Bruins, Francis devised a plan to stop Bobby Orr, or at least wear him down. The idea was to quickly put two men on Orr whenever he started a rush out of his defensive zone. This would either force him to pass the puck or make him work harder and put more pressure on his knees which had always been a problem. The third man on the line was supposed to try to anticipate the pass and intercept it. Francis also noticed that Orr's defensive partner, Don Awrey, would usually rush at an attacking forward, with Orr backing him up. This left open ice to Orr's left which Ranger forwards were alerted to.

In order to avoid distractions and prepare for the playoffs, Francis took his team out of town, to the Thunderbird Motel in Fitchburg, Massachusetts, about fifty miles west of Boston. The move ruffled a few feathers in the small town because the Rangers took over the local rink and barred the public from watching practice or public skating sessions. "We were told this was going to be a great thing for Fitchburg," said one resident. "But now the kids can't even skate in the public sessions. The Rangers won't let them." Francis also barred the press from the workouts.

The series opened in Boston, where the Rangers easily won the opener, 6–2, putting four unanswered second period goals past Plante, who did not have a good night. Walt Tkaczuk and Brad Park each scored twice. The turning point of the game came early in the first period when Ken Hodge slammed Giacomin against the boards while the Rangers' netminder was attempting to clear the puck. Ted Irvine immediately intervened with fists flying to protect his goalie. "Teddy's the guy that got us going," Giacomin later told reporters. "He did the most to help us win." "Nobody's going to run our goalie while I'm on the ice," said Irvine. "For what Eddie means to this club, I'd risk a fine to come off the bench if a guy ever took a cheap shot at him."

In the second game, Steve Vickers, Ted Irvine, Pete Stemkowski, and Walt Tkaczuk pumped four more goals past Plante as the Rangers won, 4–2.

In the second period, Boston's Ken Hodge fell on Giacomin, injuring the netminder's shoulder. Eddie was replaced by Gilles Villemure but returned 40 seconds later at the next stoppage. Between periods, however, Giacomin's shoulder stiffened up and Villemure played the third period. Giacomin was diagnosed with a pinched nerve in his right shoulder and neck.

The loss was especially costly for the Bruins. In the third period, Ron Harris caught Phil Esposito with a low hip check. Esposito suffered torn ligaments in his right knee and missed the rest of the series. The loss of Esposito was a huge blow to the Bruins. Espo had been their leading scorer against the Rangers during the regular season (6-4-10) and had also led the league in goals (55), assists (75), and points (130). "I wasn't trying to hurt him," Harris said after the game. "I would have tried to hit any other guy the same way." Bobby Orr agreed. "He hit Espo clean. There was nothing dirty about it."

Ed Johnston replaced Plante in the Bruins net when the teams moved to New York for the third game of the series. The Rangers could generate little offense and lost, 4–2. Francis juggled his lines and benched Rod Gilbert in the third period, replacing him with Bobby Rousseau, hoping that the speedy winger's forechecking ability would result in Bruins turnovers.

In the fourth game, Eddie Giacomin recorded his first playoff shutout as the Blueshirts beat the Bruins, 4–0. It was the first time the Rangers shut out an opponent in the playoffs since 1950 when Chuck Rayner blanked the Canadiens. Vic Hadfield (concussion) and Dale

Rolfe (swollen hand) both sat out due to injuries, joining Rod Seiling, who had missed the entire series with a broken collarbone. Gilbert, Stemkowski, Rousseau, and Vickers scored for the Rangers.

Late in the third period, Carol Vadnais whacked Giacomin with his stick on his already sore neck. Giacomin chased Vadnais but Ron Harris intervened and took the Bruins defenseman down. At the time, Giacomin was nursing a shutout and took off after Vadnais before the whistle had blown. But even with an empty net the Bruins couldn't get control of the puck long enough to take a shot. At the final buzzer with the Garden crowd chanting Eddie . . . Eddie, Giacomin grabbed the game puck and raised it to the crowd.

Down three games to one and facing elimination, the Bruins switched goalies yet again, this time starting Ross Brooks, who had no previous playoff experience. Steve Vickers scored on the Rangers' first shot of the game and later added two more goals for a hat trick as the Rangers coasted to a 6–3 victory. Brooks pulled a muscle in the first period and was replaced by Johnston. The victory eliminated the Bruins, giving the Rangers a measure of revenge for their loss to the Bruins in the finals the previous spring.

Billy Fairbairn led the Rangers in scoring against the Bruins with no goals but eight assists. Steve Vickers (5-1-6), Pete Stemkowski (4-2-6), and Brad Park (2-4-6) were all tied for second behind Fairbairn. Gregg Sheppard (2-1-3), Derek Sanderson (1-2-3), and John Bucyk (0-3-3) were the leading scorers for the Bruins who really missed Esposito, especially on the power play. The Bruins scored only one goal with a man advantage in twenty attempts.

"Ron Harris made the difference in this series," Derek Sanderson told reporters following the deciding game. "He was the best player on the ice. He hit every guy we had who went near him. He was super sensational."

Next up were the Chicago Black Hawks who, despite losing arguably their best player in Bobby Hull to the WHA, were still a very formidable team. They finished atop the Western Division with 93 points, 18 points ahead of second-place Philadelphia. They were led by winger Jim Pappin, who scored 41 goals with 51 assists, Dennis Hull, who fired home 39 goals and 51 assists and, of course, Stan Mikita, who added 27 goals and 56 assists.

The series began in Chicago where the Rangers won, 4–1. The game was tied at one after the first period, but a goal by Hadfield and a pair by Tkaczuk in the third period put the game away for the Rangers. Hadfield's goal was his first of the playoffs. He was still suffering from severe headaches as the result of a concussion suffered at the end of February and was only playing sporadically.

Perhaps the most valuable member of the Rangers was their assistant trainer and skate sharpener Jim Young. Early in the third period with the Blueshirts trying to protect a 2–1 lead, first Walt Tkaczuk and then Brad Park needed their skates sharpened quickly. "Jim got them back quick," Francis later told reporters. "Each only missed one shift. Years ago, some clubs on the road used to depend on the home team's skate sharpener. If we had to do that instead of having Jim with us, we'd have gotten Tkaczuk and Park back on Saturday instead of them missing only one shift."

Chicago won the second game, 5–4. Ed Giacomin had an off night, surrendering three goals on eight shots in the first 12 minutes of the opening period. The first two goals were scored by defenseman Pat Stapleton. Gilles Villemure replaced Giacomin at the start of the second period. In the third period with the Hawks leading, 5–4, Villemure made three saves in succession on shots by Dennis Hull, Lou Angotti, and Mickey Redmond within moments of each other and another stop on a point blank drive by Pit Martin to keep the Rangers close. Bruce MacGregor had the Rangers' best opportunity to tie the score when he broke in on Esposito who deflected the shot which then ricocheted off the post. Chicago defenseman Keith Magnuson suffered a broken jaw when he tried to block a Brad Park slap shot. "He slid out into it as I shot," Park later explained. "I got pretty good wood on the shot but his head was on the wrong side."

The series shifted to New York, but the Black Hawks prevailed once again winning, 2–1, in a tight defensive battle. Stan Mikita scored the game-winner, knocking a rebound of a shot by John Marks past Giacomin early in the third period.

The Rangers came out flying for the fourth game, outshooting the Black Hawks, 39–21, but were turned away repeatedly by Tony Esposito. Dennis Hull scored a pair of goals and the Hawks won, 3–1.

The teams had a five-day layoff between the fourth and fifth games to allow the Montreal-Philadelphia series to catch up. The delay gave some of the injured players a chance to mend, including Chicago's Keith Magnuson, who had suffered a broken jaw while blocking a Brad Park slap shot in Game 2.

Chicago won the fifth game, 4–1. Stan Mikita scored late in the first period and Dennis Hull and Rod Gilbert swapped goals in the second. But the Black Hawks wrapped it up in the third period on goals by Mikita and Cliff Koroll.

Tony Esposito was the difference in the series. In the last three games, the Rangers took 106 shots at the Chicago goal but only managed to get three past Esposito. With all of their firepower, the Blueshirts couldn't score when it was needed most. The result was another disappointing end to a season. "We threw everything at them," Brad Park said following the game. "We did the best we could, but they played it tight. They didn't panic."

STEVE VICKERS: "I don't know what happened there. We were riding high. We beat Boston in five games. They had a pretty good team with Esposito and Orr and all those guys. We just ran over them. They had beaten the Rangers the year before, I didn't play but maybe we were looking for a little bit of revenge.

"I don't know what happened in Chicago. Tony Esposito was a big factor, especially against me. I know personally I really, really had a lot of trouble against Tony. Not so much the other top goalies, I scored against them occasionally. But I think I scored one goal my whole career against Tony, it was my 200th goal. He was stoning me, he was stoning everybody. We won the first game handily in Chicago, then we got into a shootout with them in the second game and lost, I think 5–4. And then Tony had his way with us in the two games in the Garden. So I think mostly it was Tony. But in those days, they were a real tight checking club, clutching and grabbing, in those days you could do that. And they had big defensemen that could tie you up in front of the net like Bill White and Keith Magnuson. We should have been able to adapt to it but we were frustrated by Tony. So, that was a big reason why we didn't win that series."

If the plan was to buy the Stanley Cup as Harold Ballard had suggested, it clearly wasn't working.

Hadfield Bolts Team Canada

In September of 1972 a team of Canadian NHLers played the Soviet National team in an historic eight-game exhibition series. The first four games of the series were played in Montreal, Toronto, Winnipeg, and Vancouver, while the remaining games were played in Moscow. The Canadian team was coached by Harry Sinden and his assistant John Ferguson and was composed of thirty-five of the best players in the NHL including Rod Gilbert, Jean Ratelle, Vic Hadfield, Brad Park, and Rod Seiling of the Rangers.

Although Canada seriously underestimated the skill of the Russian players, they managed to win the series four games to three (there was one tie) on a late third period goal by Paul Henderson in the final game.

Rod Gilbert played in six games scoring one goal and adding three assists and nine penalty minutes. Gilbert's lone goal came in the third period of Game 7, giving Team Canada a short-lived 2–1 lead. Later in the third period of the same game Gilbert set up Bill White's only goal of the series which tied the score at three goals apiece. Surprisingly Gilbert was also the only Team Canada player to get into a fight, squaring off with Yevgeni Mishakov who allegedly kicked Gilbert in the leg.

Jean Ratelle also played in six games, notching a goal and three assists. Two of those assists came in the crucial final game which Team Canada had to win to save face within their own country.

Brad Park played in all eight games, recording a goal, four assists, and two penalty minutes. Teamed with Gary Bergman of Detroit, Park was especially dominant in Moscow. He along with Paul Henderson were named players of the game in the all-important finale, quite a feat for Brad considering that Phil Esposito had two goals and two assists in the game. The series was particularly meaningful to Park because his son James was born between Games One and Two.

Rod Seiling was paired with Boston's Don Awrey for the first game in Montreal. Coach Harry Sinden called the duo his best defensive pairing but the Soviets' speed proved to be their undoing. Both defensemen only saw spot duty after that with Seiling appearing in a total of three games and Awrey two.

Vic Hadfield was another story altogether. Hadfield took a regular shift on the left side of Ratelle and Gilbert in the first game in Montreal but the entire line was scratched for the second game in Toronto. When questioned by the trio, Sinden told them that he had thirty-five guys to pick from and the lineup for the first game didn't work out and he was changing it. Gilbert and Ratelle took the move in stride, but Hadfield took it personally, thinking that Sinden was trying to embarrass him in his hometown. Hadfield confronted Sinden and threatened to quit the team. According to Ferguson's book *Thunder and Lightning*, Sinden's response was succinct and to the point. "This team is going to be what John Ferguson and I want it to be," Sinden told Hadfield. "Not what Vic Hadfield wants it to be." Hadfield was also scratched for the third game in Winnipeg, but played in the fourth game in Vancouver.

Following the four games in Canada, the team flew to Sweden for an exhibition series to become accustomed to the larger European rinks. Hadfield was back in the lineup on the left of Ratelle and Gilbert. But when the team settled in Moscow, Hadfield was back on the sidelines and wasn't happy. When his name was inadvertently omitted from any of the line combinations at practice, Hadfield stayed near the boards and watched as the rest of the team went through their drills. Ferguson noticed the idle Hadfield and asked Sinden who Vic should be skating with. Sinden told him to tell Hadfield to "spell" the other left wingers, but not on a regular line. When Fergie relayed the message to Hadfield, Vic told him "he didn't have to take this crap" and left the ice, sat on the bench and read a newspaper.

A few days earlier Sinden had also mistakenly left Dale Tallon's name off the practice list, but it was corrected and nothing came of it. But Hadfield was already on the edge and when Ferguson told him what Sinden had said, he reacted.

Sinden confronted Hadfield and ordered him back onto the ice. When the Rangers captain refused, Sinden told him, "Well, you might as well take your stuff off. There's no sense in you just sitting here and making us all look foolish." But Hadfield wasn't finished. "Why did you bring me here?" he shouted at Sinden. "Like everybody else, to play hockey," Sinden replied. "And like everyone else Vic, the player decides who plays on this team by the way he plays."

Hadfield left the ice, but after talking to NHL Players' Association chief and series organizer Alan Eagleson, he returned for the rest of the practice. However, despite the pleas of Gilbert and Park to reconsider, Vic packed his bags and headed home. Canadians scorned him for his actions, but Vic, always a no-nonsense kind of guy, did what he thought was best for his family, himself, and the Rangers.

The 1973 All-Star Game

On January 30, 1973, the Rangers hosted the NHL All-Star Game for the first time in their history. They were represented on the East squad by Ed Giacomin, Gilles Villemure, Brad Park, and Jean Ratelle.

It was a low-scoring game by today's standards that ended with the Eastern Division winning by a 5–4 score. Bobby Schmautz of the Vancouver Canucks, who had been waived out of the league the previous year, scored the winning goal. Greg Polis scored two goals for the losing side and was named the MVP of the game. Gilles Villemure, who had appeared in the 1971 and 1972 All-Star Games and had not been scored upon, finally gave up a goal at the 55 second mark of the second period. The goal which was scored by Polis, ended a 79 minute, 21 second shutout streak, the longest streak recorded in All-Star history. In a total of 88 minutes in three All-Star games, Gilles surrendered only one goal. His 0.68 All-Star GAA is still the lowest of any netminder who has made at least two All-Star Game appearances.

GILLES VILLEMURE: "In those years, the 1970s, the game was not the same as it is today. Now it's wide open, but back then we played a regular game with low scores, now they're 9–8, 10–8, whatever. It's all offense now, nobody wants to get hurt."

12

1973–74

Francis Tries to Take a Step Back

FOLLOWING THEIR SECOND-ROUND ouster from the 1973 playoffs, criticism of the Rangers by fans and media alike was at an all-time high. They had the highest payroll in the NHL with little to show for it. At least seven of their players were signed to long-term contracts that paid them well over $100,000 a year, yet they lacked the intensity and aggressiveness needed to win in the postseason.

In an effort to bring a fresh perspective to the team and spend more time on his mounting duties as general manager, Emile Francis decided to hand the coaching reins over to forty-two-year-old Larry Popein. The new coach had spent 21 of his 22 years in professional hockey as a member of the Rangers organization. And like all Rangers coaches up to that point, "Pope" had also played for the team, scoring 75 goals with 127 assists in 402 games over six-plus seasons mostly centering a line between Andy Bathgate and Dean Prentice.

Francis originally installed Popein as the player-coach of the Omaha Knights of the CHL in 1968–69 and from there Larry moved up the coaching ladder with stops in Seattle and Providence. Overall, his minor-league coaching record was rather unimpressive. He coached Omaha to the Central Hockey League championship in 1969–70 but finished out of the playoffs the next two seasons in Seattle and once again with Omaha. In 1972–73 "Pope" moved up to Providence of the AHL and finished in fourth place, but the Reds were then swept in the opening round of the playoffs by Nova Scotia. Overall, Popein's minor league coaching record was 153–159–52.

The hiring of Popein was Emile's second attempt to replace himself behind the bench, having previously named Bernie Geoffrion to coach in 1968. Geoffrion lasted all of forty-three games before a bleeding ulcer forced him to step down. Ultimately, Popein didn't last quite that long.

The Regular Season

The Rangers began the regular season with a 3–0–1 record but quickly fell into a slump, gaining only a single tie in their next seven games.

It was right around that time when the trouble with Popein began, following a run-in with Rod Gilbert over a missed team meeting. Gilbert was the only Ranger to live in the city at the time and so usually when returning from a road trip the bus from the airport would leave Gilbert off near his Upper East Side apartment and then bring the rest of the players to a hotel near the Garden. On this occasion Popein moved the time of the next days' team meeting up to 10 a.m. from its customary eleven o'clock start. However, he made the announcement after Gilbert had left the bus and no one thought about calling Rod and telling him about the change. So the next day when Gilbert showed up for the meeting at the usual time he was an hour late and Popein suspended him, keeping him out of the game that night at the Garden against the Kings. The rest of the team nearly mutinied.

Gilbert, of course, was very upset and offered to pay a fine rather than miss the game. But Popein would have none of it. He thought that Gilbert was challenging his authority and that he needed to make an example of his star right winger.

Upon hearing of the suspension Vic Hadfield, Brad Park, and others told Popein that if Rod wasn't going to play, neither would they.

Once again the coach stood firm telling them, "Do what you have to do, but it's not open for discussion." Eventually Emile Francis had to come down and talk his team into taking the ice. Gilbert even asked for a trade, sensing that the rift between him and Popein would be a continuing problem, but Francis assured him that he would deal with it. Following the game, reporters repeatedly asked Popein about the Gilbert benching but the coach would only respond with a curt "my decision." It was not even a quarter of the way into the season and Popein had already lost his players.

BRAD PARK: "Larry was very different from the Cat. I guess you could say he was introverted and it just seemed that the Cat was a much more inspirational guy. But Larry was very demanding. It started early when he suspended Rod Gilbert. I went up to Emile and complained. I told him I wasn't going to play if Rod didn't play. I wasn't gonna play but then I changed my mind. I wasn't going to hurt the team even though Rod's not playing was going to hurt the team."

EMILE FRANCIS: "Larry had a real dry disposition, not too much of a personality, but a good player, a serious guy, gave everything he had. They were coming in from the airport by bus and Rod didn't go back to the hotel because he lived in the city. So he got off the bus and when the bus got to the hotel Larry changed the time of the meeting in the morning and Rod didn't show up until the meeting was over. But he didn't know that the time had been changed and nobody thought to tell him. So now it's about 5:30 at night before our game at the Garden and they had a meeting and he told Rod that he wasn't dressing because of what had happened that morning. So now Vic Hadfield comes up to me and says, 'I don't know if you've heard but Larry just told Rod he wasn't playing tonight because he didn't show up for the team meeting.' So, I said okay and I called down and got a hold of Larry and I told him to come up because I wanted to talk to him.

"So I asked him, 'What's this about Gilbert not playing?' So he explained to me what happened. I said, 'Did you ever think that maybe he didn't know that you changed the time?' So he says, 'That's his problem to find out.' So I said to him, 'This is going to be a bad thing to have happen. I'll stand behind you. If that's what you want, that's what you're gonna get. But I gotta warn you, do you remember when you were playing with the Rangers and one night before you got out of the rink Phil Watson brought you guys back onto the ice and kept you out there for thirty minutes going back and forth from one side to another. Is that right?' He said, 'Yes that's right.' I said, 'What happened?' And Larry said, 'He lost the team.'

"'Well that's what I'm afraid of Larry, because the same thing could happen to you. Gilbert's one of the most respected guys in that dressing room. The game comes first over and above everything else.' I told him, 'You can decide what you want to do on your way back to the dressing room. If you change your mind go in and tell him to dress. If you don't change your mind, it's up to you. I'll stand behind you. I'm not gonna tell you what to do. You make up your own mind. But I'm just warning you what could happen.' And he lost the team. He had seen it happen with Phil Watson. I mean you gotta be strong but you gotta be fair too. He changed the time and nobody told Gilbert, and then later when I took over the team we won nine straight right off the bat. But I wanted to get away from taking over because there was so much to do. And that was right when we were in the middle of that war with the WHA too."

The situation quickly worsened. On November 15, the Rangers had a terrible night defensively and were blown out in Boston by a 10–2 score. Unfortunately, Popein kept Giacomin in goal for the entire game. Usually a coach would pull his netminder to save him from the embarrassment and humiliation. But when asked about it later, Popein told reporters that he never considered pulling Giacomin. After Boston scored their sixth goal, Giacomin's frustration got the better of him. He threw his stick in the air and kicked the puck to center ice. Following the game, Eddie was irate, he had never given up 10 goals in a single game in his career.

It was also a bad night off the ice for a couple of other Rangers as well. Following the game, Gene Carr and Mike Murphy were injured in a taxi cab accident. The pair was in Derek Sanderson's bar, Daisy Buchanan's, getting something to eat following the game. When they were finished, they hailed a cab to take them back to the team's hotel. Unfortunately, the cab was T-boned by a police cruiser racing after a stolen car. They were both injured when their heads hit the cab's Plexiglas divider. Bloodied and possibly in shock, Carr and Murphy were wandering around looking for a hospital when they were picked up by none other than Derek Sanderson who had been tipped off about the accident by the police. Both sustained upper body injuries and concussions and were sidelined for a few weeks.

GENE CARR: "I never thought about how severe it was and how close I was to being killed in that car accident. I was with Mike Murphy and we were headed back to the hotel for curfew. We had gone out to have something to eat and then we were headed back to the hotel and this cabbie, he wasn't exactly going very slowly, it was winter and there was snow on the ground, but we had a green light and apparently this black-and-white was in pursuit of a stolen car and he went through a red light and T-boned us. The cabbie was injured really badly and of course so was Murphy and I. I mean our heads hit that Plexiglas probably at Mach One speed. We hit that Plexiglas and it knocked us silly. All I remember was I was helping Murphy in the cab and there was his blood like everywhere. It was spurting out of his head and I had blood all over me too. I remember Murph and I trying to get to the hospital. We were walking from the accident. We were just so out of it, I didn't even know my own name and I was holding Mike and I knew I needed to get him to the hospital. We got picked up by Derek Sanderson who recognized us and stopped and drove us to Boston General and tried to explain what happened.

"I didn't realize how severe that was on my body. I don't think I ever recuperated from that body trauma because it seems like I had nothing but physical problems after that. My back, I mean to this day I've had five back surgeries and I just had another neck surgery two months ago and now I'm trying to decide whether I should have another back surgery because these guys, the orthopedic doctors for the Kings out here [in California] are telling me that basically I could get rid of my crutches. See, I can't walk without my crutches, that's how bad I am now. I can walk maybe five or ten feet with difficulty but anything more than that I need crutches to get around. That accident in the cab was the beginning of a lot of physical problems that I developed over the years."

Following his recovery, Murphy was eventually dealt to the Kings in November along with Tommy Williams and Sheldon Kannegiesser for burly defenseman Gilles Marotte, known as Captain Crunch, and former Ranger Real Lemieux in a trade that was expected to add a bit of toughness to the Rangers lineup.

EMILE FRANCIS: "Gilles Marotte could have been a mistake on my part. The guy had plenty of natural ability but I think his problem was that he couldn't think fast enough. I should have known because when we were playing Los Angeles I'd sit with the Ratelle line and tell them, 'Shoot the puck in Marotte's corner and Jean you go right to the front of the net.' The puck was dropped and shot into Marotte's corner, he turned around and put it right on Ratelle's stick and he scored. He had that tendency of giving up the puck. He was a strong guy, he could hit, but his weakness was coughing that puck up. It wasn't the best deal I made, that's for sure."

Francis also made another deal at the end of October, sending Glen Sather and minor leaguer Rene Villemure to St. Louis for Jack Egers. Sather had only seen action in two games so far that season and was deemed expendable. In 186 games for the Blueshirts, the thirty-year-old winger had scored only 18 goals with 24 assists but had added some much-needed grit to the Rangers lineup, racking up 193 penalty minutes. He also recorded a pair of assists and 47 penalty minutes in 38 playoff games. Egers, a former Ranger (1970–72), played for Popein in Omaha during the 1969–70 season, scoring 42 goals. He had a couple of pretty good seasons in St. Louis, where he scored 45 goals with 50 assists. Unfortunately, he also had knee problems that limited him to only 28 games in his second tour with the Rangers, scoring one goal with three assists.

JACK EGERS: "I really think that Pope was behind me coming back to the Rangers. I had a couple of twenty-plus goal seasons in St. Louis but I had a slow start to the season because I had knee surgery in the summer for a torn cartilage. I didn't know it at the time but I just found out in the last few years that when the Cat would trade his young players like myself, Mike Murphy, and Andre Dupont he had a deal with St. Louis or whatever team he was trading with that if they were ever going to trade one of us, that the Rangers had the right of first refusal. And at that time Pope was brought in to coach and he wasn't doing very well. I think because I played so well under him in Omaha that I think he wanted me back. Let me put it this way, when my name came up that St. Louis wanted to trade me, I think Larry went to the Cat and told him I would like to have Jack back. Unfortunately, when they got me back I had a knee problem and had to have surgery again. It was one of the injuries that plagued my career all the way through. So that year I had to recover from knee surgery and then I played on the fourth line and didn't get a lot of ice time.

"Larry Popein was great for me. I had nothing against him at all. He was a disciplinarian. You did it his way or you didn't play. But it was good for young kids. The Central Hockey League was a training ground for young kids coming out of juniors and Pope was a good guy to have because you didn't stray too far from the way he wanted you to play. And I think young guys like myself needed that. But Pope didn't know how to handle the stars. He treated everyone the same and I think you gotta give them a little leeway."

The players complained that Popein's practices were boring and his game plans seemed to be more suitable for pee-wee league games. One Ranger told *Sports Illustrated* that season, "Larry spent 20 minutes before the game telling us that he wanted us to fire the puck down our right side and make [Philadelphia defenseman] Moose Dupont handle it. He had coached Moose in Omaha and he knew that Moose panics when he touches the puck. I didn't think it was a very good idea in the first place, but what happened was that Dupont didn't even play in the game."

The Rangers got sloppy. They stopped playing the tight defensive style that had been so successful in previous seasons. Defensive coverage broke down, resulting in an extraordinary number of breakaways and odd men rushes against them. Overall, Ranger netminders faced 78 breakaways in 78 games. Giacomin saw the most breakaways, facing 60 in 56 games, and stopping 47 of them.

Finally, on January 11, 1974, the day after a 7–2 shellacking by the Sabres that dropped the Blueshirts to fourth place, Francis fired Popein and once again took over the coaching reins. The players had spent the night in Toronto before flying to Vancouver and Francis informed them of the coaching change on the bus taking them to the airport. Francis told reporters that he had been considering making a change for some time but hoped that Popein could work out the problems. But following the debacle in Buffalo, Emile knew that the time had come.

Popein's biggest fault was that he couldn't communicate with the players, which had been a problem in the minor leagues as well. In Providence the previous year, Popein had angered both management and players with his failure to communicate. "Popein was not the right man to coach the Rangers," said one rival general manager. "If Francis had been able to follow Popein around for a week last season he would have seen what we all knew." Popein was also a disciplinarian whose harsh tactics might scare younger players fresh out of juniors but didn't work on seasoned NHL veterans who were earning much more than his $35,000 a year salary.

BRUCE MacGREGOR: "Because I had been through the thing in Detroit with Ned Harkness and I saw what happens when you bring a new guy in, it was kind of like the same song, second verse type of thing—new guy coming in trying to make changes on an experienced hockey club. I actually liked Larry Popein, I thought he was a pretty good coach but sometimes it doesn't work. But I didn't have a big problem with him. Everybody has their own ideas of coaching, in the way of practicing and that kind of thing. When a new guy comes in and tries to implement those things, sometimes it works and sometimes for a lot of reasons it doesn't."

ROD SEILING: "Pope was a very tense, uptight guy. The team didn't perform as well as it could have or should have for him."

BOBBY ROUSSEAU: "The year when Emile was not coaching, Larry Popein didn't know who Bobby Rousseau was I guess and I didn't know who he was and I was not getting much ice time. The people started yelling 'Rousseau, Rousseau' so it was a great complement for me. Of course the Ranger fans saw me play for ten years with Montreal so they knew what I could do on the ice on a line and on the power play, so if I wasn't on the power play the fans wanted me out there. It was a nice complement."

Francis did his best to stay away and give his new coach some breathing room. He stayed in his office or traveled on scouting trips. "I figured that if I wasn't around too much, Larry would have a better chance," Francis said later. "If I had been around, people would have said that I was calling the shots, so I stayed away." Popein didn't exactly see it that way. "I knew I was going into the bees' nest with the queen bee still around," he told reporters. "I had my doubts when I was offered the job, but how in hell do you turn down a chance to coach in the NHL?" Popein was kept on the payroll as a scout.

But in the end, these were Emile's Rangers. He had put the team together and he knew how to get the most out of them. "Francis understands us and we understand him. It's really his team because he brought us all together," said Gilbert. "He can relate to us and we can relate to him. The Cat knows how to project his thoughts and ideas to us. He can tell us we're playing awful and do it in a way that doesn't make us mad."

It was the third time Francis had fired a coach and the second time he had to dismiss one that he had handpicked and he wasn't happy about it. "I'm going to crack down on these guys," Francis told reporters. "We'd better make the playoffs and you can underline the word *better*." The players knew the Cat wasn't kidding. The general feeling around the club was that if they didn't start producing, someone else would be leaving and it wasn't going to be Francis.

At the time of Popein's dismissal, the Blueshirts had an 18–14–9 record and were in fourth place. But once Emile stepped back behind the bench they went on a 17–2–3 run including winning streaks of eight and five games and they lost only ten of their final thirty-seven games.

One Ranger who welcomed the coaching change was Steve Vickers. "Sarge," who scored 30 goals the previous season and was named the NHL's Rookie of the Year, had not scored in Popein's final fifteen games and spent a lot of time on the bench. As soon as Francis took over, he reunited Vickers with Tkaczuk and Fairbairn and Steve responded with five goals in ten games.

STEVE VICKERS: "I had Larry in the minors in Omaha and I guess it was my second year he got to New York. We had no negative words towards one another. Unfortunately he couldn't get his message across. We went on the road and I think in three games we had twenty goals scored against us and he only lasted half a year. I never had anything negative against him; he might have had some negative thoughts about me. But it was probably half my fault, I was probably in a slump and maybe I wasn't prepared for a new coach."

Once back behind the bench, Francis was better able to determine which players were helping the club and made two deals that could be classified as addition by subtraction. In January, he sent the recently acquired Real Lemieux to Buffalo for minor leaguer Paul Curtis and then in February he sent the much-maligned Gene Carr to the Kings for their 1977 first-round draft pick. Unfortunately, Francis wasn't around by that time but John Ferguson used that pick to select Ron Duguay.

GENE CARR: "My situation when I left there didn't have anything to do with Emile. I just wanted to go somewhere where I could play fifteen to twenty minutes a game like I should have but after I got hurt and each player on the team was so great it was tough as hell to break back into the lineup. I remember approaching him a couple of times and saying, 'Hey, you have to play me. You can't play me for a couple of shifts in the third period. I can't do that.' I'm not Glen Sather. Glen Sather could sit on the bench and go out there in the third period and look like he never missed a shift but I couldn't do that. I didn't have the confidence. I told him, you got to play me. But he couldn't do it because the guys who were making half a million a year and were scoring fifty goals, they had to play.

"He was in a tough situation and finally I remember talking to Emile one night after a game in Philly. My contract was up at the end of the year and I said, hey I'm done, you either trade me now or I'll sit for the next few months or I'll go sign with the World Hockey Association and you won't get anything for me. I didn't even let my attorney handle that. I just told him after the game I need to go somewhere where I can play all the time because I'm too good to be sitting here and I'm losing my confidence and I've got to get it back.

"Emile was under pressure to win now! He couldn't wait for me to develop like [Guy] Lafleur and [Marcel] Dionne and the rest of those guys that I was drafted with. They were brought along right. They were worked into the lineup.

"I liked Emile, to be honest with you. I liked him very much. So many times he would be on the bench there and I would kind of chuckle to myself when he used to put that right foot there up on the boards from the bench to yell at the referees. To me that was Emile Francis. If there was ever a picture to describe the man, that was it. He had a great system, he was good with the guys, and all the guys liked him. He would talk to you. He was under a lot of pressure to win because the club he had put together was the best club in the league other than Boston without a doubt. You wanted to play for the guy. Emile had that knack for making the players dig down and give that something extra."

The Blueshirts finished the regular season by losing eight of their last fifteen games and wound up in third place, five points behind the second-place Canadiens and 19 points behind the first-place Bruins. Their 94 points was their lowest total in four years, eight points less than last season's 102 and 15 behind the record setting 109 of 1970–71 and 1971–72. Their 40 victories were also seven less than the previous season. Clearly as a group, the team had peaked and was on a downhill slide.

Individually Brad Park, Pete Stemkowski, and Ted Irvine each had the best years of their careers up to that point. Park became the first Rangers defenseman to lead the team in scoring with 25 goals and 57 assists for 82 points. He also led the club with 148 penalty minutes. Stemmer notched 25 goals and 45 assists for 70 points, 11 more than his previous high of 59. Irvine scored 26 goals with 20 assists for a career-high 46 points.

However, Walt Tkaczuk's production dropped slightly, mostly due to a broken jaw he suffered against Chicago in the middle of March.

WALT TKACZUK: "I got hit around center ice. I was carrying the puck and I made a quick turn and I turned right into Pit Martin and I hit his hip and I broke my jaw. I went down to my knees and tried to get up but every time I tried my legs were too shaky. I ended up losing about seventeen pounds in three weeks with my jaw wired and I came back wearing a helmet with a bar in the front."

Ed Giacomin played in 56 games, posting a 30–15–10 record with five shutouts and a 3.07 GAA, which was his highest since his rookie year. Gilles Villemure injured his knee in a collision with Dennis Hull in December and saw action in only 21 games, going 7–7–1 with a 3.53 GAA. Peter McDuffe also appeared in six games (3–2–1, 3.18 GAA).

The Playoffs

The Rangers' first-round opponents were the second-place Montreal Canadiens. Montreal had won the season series four games to two and were favored to win the opening round. The Canadiens, however, had surrendered 240 goals during the season, the most in team history and with the retirement of Ken Dryden, their three netminders—Wayne Thomas, Michel "Bunny" Larocque, and Michel Plasse—did not have a single game of playoff experience between them.

The series began in Montreal where Steve Vickers, Bruce MacGregor, Dale Rolfe, and Brad Park scored as the Rangers outshot the Canadiens 31–24 and skated away with a 4–1 victory. In the second period, Giacomin wandered into the corner to retrieve a loose puck and was slammed into the boards by Steve Shutt. Rod Seiling, usually a non-combatant, took exception to this and started pummeling Shutt. Both players received fighting majors. Then later in the third period, Pete Mahovlich roughed up Giacomin while he was out of the crease and had to answer to Brad Park for his actions.

In the second game, Bruce MacGregor opened the scoring for the Rangers in the first period and Steve Shutt tied it early in the second. A short time later, Steve Vickers had a goal disallowed which would have given the Rangers a 2–1 lead. But then the game turned into an Yvan Cournoyer highlight reel. The aptly named "Roadrunner" scored the next three goals, two on breakaways and one on a two-on-one rush. In total, Cournoyer took seven of the Canadiens' 31 shots, while the Rangers could only manage 19 at Bunny Larocque and lost by a 4–1 score.

Game Three was played in New York on April 13 which marked the 34th anniversary of the Rangers' last Stanley Cup victory in 1940. Goals by Pete Mahovlich, Steve Shutt, and a pair by Yvan Cournoyer gave the Canadiens a 4–0 lead going into the third period. Stemkowski and Ratelle scored for the Rangers in the third period but it was too little, too late as Montreal skated away with a 4–2 victory and led the series two games to one.

At this point the media and the fans began to get on the Rangers for their poor showing. Calls of "Fat Cats" were once again heard and Brad Park for one took it personally.

BRAD PARK: "There was a *Sports Illustrated* article that came out showing a bunch of us on the cover and the headline was 'Emile's Fat Cats.' So in this playoff game we didn't perform very well and the crowd got into a huge chant of 'Fat Cats . . . Fat Cats . . . Fat Cats.' And at that time, I think I was the highest paid guy and I took real exception to that. We went out to Gallagher's after the game and I said to my wife, I'll be back and walked out onto 33rd Street. I walked up to a bar named McAnn's and I went in and had a beer because I wanted to cool down a little and I didn't feel too much like socializing. So a couple of fans recognized me and said you look upset and I said yeah, that chant of 'Fat Cats,' I took real exception to that. I said, look, I'm not in these playoffs for the money and I'll prove it. Tomorrow morning I'll announce that any money I make in the playoffs I'll donate it to charity and those couple of fans loved that idea and the next day I made the announcement."

All well and good, but when Steve Shutt scored just 46 seconds into the first period of the fourth game it looked like the Blueshirts were once again headed down a slippery slope. However, Ron Harris, who had been moved up to wing in place of the injured Vic Hadfield, tied the score midway through the period with his first goal since November. Hadfield had injured his ankle and the prognosis was that he would miss the next seven to ten days.

Pete Mahovlich reclaimed the lead for the Canadiens with a goal late in the period and his brother Frank added to it with another marker early in the second. But then the Rangers came alive. Goals by Rod Gilbert and Ted Irvine tied the score at three going into the third period.

Irvine scored his second goal of the game early in the third but Serge Savard tied it at the 13:57 mark. Bruce MacGregor then scored the game-winner less than two minutes later and Pete Stemkowski put the game away with an empty-netter.

In the fifth game, MacGregor was assigned to cover Cournoyer and held "the Roadrunner" scoreless for the remainder of the series. Montreal once again got off to a quick start when Henri Richard scored just 49 seconds into the first period. But MacGregor tied it at the 12:43 mark of the period.

After a scoreless second period, Murray Wilson gave Montreal the lead with a goal early in the third that stood up until late in the period. With less than a minute to go in regulation and Giacomin pulled for the extra skater, MacGregor knocked the rebound of a point shot by Park past Bunny Larocque to send the game into overtime. The Blueshirts dominated the extra session, outshooting the Canadiens 5–0 and Ron Harris scored the game-winner with a 45-foot wrist shot at 4:07. Pete Stemkowski was instrumental in both the tying and winning goals, taking both faceoffs deep in the Montreal zone and getting the puck to Park and Harris respectively.

BRUCE MacGREGOR: "Emile tried to keep me out there against Cournoyer and I had to change wings and go over to the left side. A lot of times I played with Ratelle and Gilbert so I always kidded Vic after that series and I had scored a few goals and I said I could've scored fifty goals playing with those guys. That was the only time I played with Ratty and Gilbert because Rod and I played the same position. But I have to give Emile credit because it was his idea. He said that's what I want you to do and with the help of everybody else we really shut him down a little bit and it worked out pretty well.

"That's what Emile did, he thought the game out and he tried to find ways that we could win and he wasn't afraid to make changes and move guys around. If it was going to help it was worth taking a shot at it."

In the sixth game, back at the Garden, Montreal once again got on the board first when Henri Richard scored almost midway through the opening period. Steve Shutt then added to the lead early in the second. But then the Rangers scored five unanswered goals, including MacGregor's sixth of the series and two empty-netters by Stemkowski to close out the series with a 5–2 victory.

The victory over Montreal marked the third straight season that the Rangers had eliminated the defending Stanley Cup champions. But the Blueshirts had little time to savor their victory, having only one day off before meeting their second-round opponents, the Philadelphia Flyers who were well rested. The Flyers had swept the Atlanta Flames in four games and had been off for almost a week waiting for the Montreal-New York series to end.

The Flyers were a young, hungry team on the rise, finishing in first place in the NHL's Western Division with a 50–16–12 record. They had a potent offense led by Bobby Clarke, Rick MacLeish, and Bill Barber and a steady group of defensemen that included Ed Van Impe, Jim and Joe Watson, and Barry Ashbee. The Flyers also relied heavily on the superb netminding of Bernie Parent, who posted a 47–13–12 record and a 1.89 GAA with 12 shutouts and shared the Vezina Trophy with Chicago's Tony Esposito.

Parent was a product of the Bruins organization and was selected by the Flyers in the 1967 expansion draft. He was traded to Toronto in February of 1971 and jumped to the WHA in 1972. After a season in the rival league Parent gained his release and wanted to return to the NHL but did not want to play for Toronto. The Flyers acquired Parent's NHL rights from Toronto in a May 1973 deal that sent their first-round draft pick and future considerations (Doug Favell) to the Leafs.

EMILE FRANCIS: "Parent was brought up in the Boston Bruin organization and then he went to Philadelphia in the expansion draft and then after two or three seasons they traded him to Toronto. Then in 1972 the WHA came along and he signed with the Miami Screaming Eagles, who never got off the ground. So he played one year for the Philadelphia Blazers and then became a free agent, but Toronto owned his NHL rights. That's when I started negotiating with Toronto because I always liked Bernie Parent. I'd seen him as a junior. At the time I had Eddie Giacomin but Eddie wasn't really that successful in the playoffs up to that point. But the odds were against us getting Parent because he had met a guy in Philadelphia who was his agent and I'm sure that agent was paid off to get Parent back to Philadelphia. So Toronto was forced to make a deal with Philadelphia. Because I had offered Toronto a better deal than what they got. I offered them four players off the Rangers roster. But Toronto's hand was forced."

Nicknamed "The Broad Street Bullies," Philadelphia was also the most physically intimidating team in the league with tough guys like Don "Big Bird" Saleski, Bob "Hound" Kelly and Dave "The Hammer" Schultz, who led the league with 348 penalty minutes. Shultz set the tone of the series early by telling reporters that he was "glad to be playing the Rangers because they always seem to choke in the playoffs."

The Rangers had won the season series from Philadelphia, 2–1–2, and were 20–6–12 against them since their inception in 1967. Rangers fans knew very well that regular-season records tend to be meaningless once the playoffs begin, however.

The series began in Philadelphia where Parent recorded his first playoff shutout by beating the Rangers, 4–0. The Blueshirts didn't take a shot on Parent until the 13 minute mark of the first period and managed only two more for the rest of the stanza. In fact, they only got off seven shots during the first 45 minutes of the game. The Rangers also played very poorly defensively and only Giacomin's acrobatic goaltending kept the final score respectable. The Flyers dominated throughout the game and broke free for five breakaways in addition to three three-on-ones and a pair of two-on-ones. Giacomin also had to contend with Gary Dornhoefer, one of the best in the league at screening and interfering with goaltenders, setting up shop in front of his crease. Eddie was also checked and interfered with whenever he went behind the net or into the corners to clear loose pucks.

The Flyers continued their intimidation tactics in the second game as referee Dave Newell whistled 40 minutes in penalties in the first period alone. Just 19 seconds after the opening faceoff, Bob Kelly dropped his gloves and pummeled Jerry Butler, who did not play the rest of the game. Bobby Clarke scored the only goal of the period, which took more than an hour to complete.

In the second period, Ed Van Impe took a long shot that was deflected by Rod Seiling. The puck glanced off Giacomin's shoulder, but Eddie appeared to grab it before it crossed the goal line. Unfortunately, goal judge Charles Zavorka, who was brought in from St. Louis, thought differently and signaled a goal. Giacomin went ballistic, slamming his stick against the glass in front of the goal judge and pounding his fists on the ice where he said he stopped the puck. Longtime Rangers fans had never seen Giacomin so upset. Referee Newell asked Zavorka several times whether it was indeed a goal, but the judge refused to change his call. Francis replaced Giacomin with Villemure in order to give his goaltender a chance to cool down. Villemure played only 22 seconds until the next faceoff when Giacomin returned to the game. Jack Egers got the Rangers on the board later in the period.

In the third period, Ross Lonsberry scored a shorthanded goal at 7:54 which was quickly answered by a goal by Park 16 seconds later. But that was all the offense the Rangers could muster. MacLeish scored late in the period and Lonsberry added an empty-netter as the Flyers won, 5–2.

The series moved to Madison Square Garden where the Flyers had not won since December of 1968. Goals by Rick MacLeish and Andre Dupont gave the Flyers a 2–0 lead but Billy Fairbairn cut the lead by one with a goal near the end of the first period. Gary Dornhoefer scored a power-play goal midway through the second period to restore the two-goal lead. Steve Vickers answered with a power-play goal less than two minutes later and Hadfield tied it late in the period. Unfortunately, Hadfield, who was playing his first game of the series due to an injured ankle, twisted the ankle on the play and did not see action again until the seventh game of the series. Park and Gilbert then scored in the third period, making the score 5–3 and putting the game away for the Rangers, who outshot the Flyers, 39–15. Referee Bryan Lewis whistled a total of 109 minutes in penalties including three game misconducts as once again the Flyers tried to intimidate the Blueshirts.

In the fourth game, Joe Watson opened the scoring with a goal late in the first period. The Flyers held onto that one goal lead until Bobby Rousseau scored on a power play with less than two minutes left in the second period. Parent had made the initial save, but the puck popped up into the air behind the Flyers netminder. Parent reached back and appeared to knock the puck out of the net in midair. However the goal judge, Frank Daigneault from Montreal, ruled it a goal and referee Lloyd Gilmour agreed.

Rod Gilbert then evened the series at two games apiece with a goal 4:20 into overtime assisted by Tkaczuk and Vickers. Rod was deep in the Flyers zone and had not yet gotten off the ice for a line change. Vickers saw him near the left post and passed the puck, which Gilbert deflected between Parent's legs. The Rangers may have had too many men on the ice at the time, but the officials missed it. Once again the Rangers outshot the Flyers by a wide 37–20 margin. On a tragic note, just before Gilbert's game winner, Flyers defenseman Barry Ashbee was hit in his right eye by a slap shot from Dale Rolfe. He was carried off the ice and never played another game in the NHL.

In the fifth game, Pete Stemkowski got the Rangers on the board early in the first period and the Blueshirts controlled the game by forechecking relentlessly, holding the Flyers to just five shots in the first period. But during the first intermission, Flyers coach Fred Shero conferred with his assistant, Mike Nykoluk, and made a strategic change in his game plan, telling his defensemen to get rid of the puck quickly and ordered his forwards to come back deeper to help out. The move worked as Tom Bladon and Rick MacLeish scored in the second period and Simon Nolet added a goal early in the third. MacLeish scored an empty-netter late in the third period to ice the Flyers' 4–1 victory.

Back at the Garden for the sixth game, Don Saleski opened the scoring for the Flyers with a goal early in the first period. About halfway through the stanza, Giacomin swung his stick at Dornhoefer out of frustration and wound up fighting with Ross Lonsberry. Giacomin received four minutes in penalties and Lonsberry two for the skirmish. The Flyers would have come out of the altercation with a power play but Bernie Parent had skated up ice and was given two minutes for leaving his crease. Brad Park scored for the Rangers near the end of the period to tie the score at one.

After a scoreless second period, Ron Harris put a wrist shot past Parent at 4:10 of the third. It turned out to be the game winner. Ted Irvine provided an insurance goal less than two minutes later and Steve Vickers added an empty-netter as the Rangers evened the series with a 4–1 win.

After six extremely hard-fought battles in which each team won their respective home games, it all came down to Game Seven played in the Spectrum on Sunday afternoon, May 5, 1974.

The game was scoreless when one of the most debated incidents in Rangers history took place at the 11:55 mark of the first period. With arguably six of the Rangers' best players on the ice—Rod Gilbert, Jean Ratelle, and Vic Hadfield up front, Brad Park and Dale Rolfe on defense, and Ed Giacomin in goal, the Flyers' Dave Schultz took Rolfe into the corner to the left of the Rangers net and proceeded to pummel him mercilessly, even going so far as to grab handfuls of Rolfe's hair to hold him up. It was a planned attack with the Flyers hoping to draw one of the other Rangers into taking a third-man-in penalty and therefore being ejected from the game. Schultz even paused at one point to see if anyone was coming to Rolfe's aid. But no one did. Flyers coach Fred Shero called it the turning point of the game and many fans and members of the media felt that the incident demoralized the Blueshirts and ridiculed them for allowing their teammate to take that kind of beating and not try to intervene.

Brad Park addressed the issue with reporters during the run up to the Rangers-Flyers 2012 Winter Classic. "Let's get it straight once and for all," Park said. "We did not meekly stand by; we were forced to stand by. It was Game Seven, the league had brought the third-man-in rule, so someone would have gotten thrown out of the game with a game misconduct for intervening, so who did you want to lose—Rod Gilbert, Jean Ratelle, Vic Hadfield, or myself? I did finally decide to go, but Dale looked me in the eye and said to stay out of it. Sorry you weren't on the ice to hear it."

BRAD PARK: "I think in those days Philadelphia brought in premeditated fighting and Schultz was actually coming for me when Dale grabbed him. It was the seventh game and Orest Kindrachuk had slashed Eddie Giacomin and I punched him and I turned around because I knew Schultz was coming and Dale grabbed him so that I wouldn't end up off the ice. And the press was saying that no one went to Rolfe's aide but they brought a new rule in that season, the third-man-in rule. So we're in the first period and it's myself on the ice with Giacomin, Ratelle, Hadfield, and Gilbert. Now who would you like to see get thrown out of the game in the first period of the seventh game? And to this day it bothers me that the stereotype of the team was that we lost because nobody stood up for Dale Rolfe. The only reason why Philadelphia won was that Bernie Parent stopped everything. What do you think the media would have done if I got tossed for being the third-man-in? They would have said it was a stupid decision. The game was more important. Philadelphia had last change. We put out the G-A-G line with Rolfe and I and Shero puts out Kindrachuk, Saleski, and Schultz.

"Schultz wasn't interested in playing hockey. It was, 'Who do I get off the ice and how quickly.' The last couple of years I was his target. He used to get on the ice his first shift and say, 'I want you, let's go' and I go back and say I'm not mad yet."

DALE ROLFE: "I made a mistake, I shouldn't have grabbed him. I don't know what really happened, I can't even think about it. It was just part of hockey, it don't mean shit. There's two ways of looking at it, maybe somebody should have jumped in, maybe they shouldn't.

Because if they did they would have been the third man in and got kicked out. So, I think what transpired was perfect because Schultz and I got penalties and we kept all our better players in the game."

Many expected Hadfield to come to the aid of Rolfe. After all, protecting his teammates was what got him into the NHL in the first place and later earned him a spot on the Rangers' top line. But as it turned out, Hadfield who was already hobbled with a bad ankle was nursing a broken thumb as well.

EMILE FRANCIS: "The last game of the year, Vic gets into a fight and breaks his thumb. So now we play Montreal and we beat them out in six games. I had put Bruce MacGregor on the line with Ratelle and Gilbert because Vic was hurt. He played very well but he wasn't a physical player like Hadfield. So now we play Philadelphia and it was a brutal series, because that was the type of team they were. They were like a rat pack, when they were separated they weren't worth anything but together they played very well. In Game Six at the Garden we kicked the shit out of them. So, I put out MacGregor, Ratelle, and Gilbert for the last shift of the game. And they put out their goons including Schultz, so I pulled Gilbert off and put Ron Harris on. So Schultz skates by the bench and says, 'You're a wiseguy.' I said, 'Go fuck yourself.' And he didn't do a thing.

"So we practiced Friday and Saturday and we had the afternoon game in Philadelphia on Sunday. When we got to Philadelphia I sat down with Vic and told him I know exactly what's gonna happen. They're gonna go out there and go after somebody. I don't know who, it could be Brad Park it could be Ratelle or Gilbert. And I asked Vic if he thought he could play. He said he could. I didn't ask him to fight or anything, because you never had to. Well it's an afternoon game so we'll have a team meeting at 10 a.m. You think about it and see me at 9:30. Because I don't know how you'll feel, I don't know how your thumb is. [Hadfield had also missed three of the previous six games with an injured ankle.] You think about it and tell me Sunday morning. So I see him on Sunday morning and he says he'd like to play. Okay, you're our captain, you're in the lineup.

"Well, the puck was dropped and shot into the corner. So Park goes into the corner and Schultz goes right for Dale Rolfe in front of the net. But I just think that Vic knew his thumb wasn't right but he wanted to play so badly, because he had been such a great player for us. But neither Rolfe nor Hadfield were the same players for the rest of the game. But the key was that we lost Jerry Butler who had more guts than a slaughterhouse, who had taken on that whole team on Thursday night. He had three fights. He would take on anybody, anywhere. So what happened, his line went out for the next shift, Ted Irvine, Pete Stemkowski, and Jerry Butler. So the puck goes towards him and he fell down and couldn't get up! What happened was that in one of those three fights he ruptured his intestine. When we got back that night his wife rushed him to the hospital. They had to operate on him or he may have died."

TED IRVINE: "Well as you look back at it, I think we should have cleared the bench. That wasn't our style back then, but it all happened so quickly. Dale always said that he was handling himself okay, but it looked worse afterward and when we saw the replay we didn't feel good about it because that was your teammate. But I think it was one of those reactionary things that happened when you played Philadelphia. You never knew where they were coming from and we'd cleared the bench before against Toronto. But for some reason it just didn't happen. But looking back we should have definitely gone over the boards. But at the time it just didn't seem to be as bad as it turned out to be."

WALT TKACZUK: "A lot of people made a lot out of it but I never made too much out of it. It was just an incident that happened. Schultz was trying to start a fight and Hadfield had a bad hand and he couldn't get involved and Brad had mentioned to me, because he was on the ice, that Dale had told him just stay back 'I'm okay,' he said. We had all our key players on the ice and if any of them would have jumped in they would have been tossed out because of the third-man-in rule and so I think they did the right thing. Dale told Brad, 'I'm fine' but the media made a big issue out of it."

BILL FAIRBAIRN: "I don't know what happened it was so quick. I don't even think he was going after Rolfe. I guess somebody could have tried to get in there, but nobody did. A lot of people think that lost us the series but I don't think it did. The bad part was that he had Rolfe by the hair and was swinging at him. If he hadn't done that I'm sure Rolfe could have held his own with Schultz. I'm sure of that, but when you've got somebody who's got you by the hair moving your head around you can't do much. All you need is one shot in the head and all of a sudden you can't defend yourself. I think that's mainly what happened because Rolfe was fairly tough, too and he was a big man. Everybody on the ice would have gone in except maybe Ratty, but you don't want him to go in anyway, he's your leading scorer."

HOWIE ROSE: "Years later I asked Emile on the air, "When you look back at that do you wish that someone would have jumped in?" And he immediately said, 'Yeah, Hadfield.' He said because Hadfield was playing hurt and he wasn't much use to us and if he had been thrown out of the game so be it.

"But even after Rolfe got pummeled, the game was scoreless and a few minutes later the Rangers scored the first goal of the game. So for everybody who conveniently over forty years has said that the Rangers were cooked as soon as Schultz beat Rolfe to a pulp, well a few minutes later the Rangers took the lead in that game. So I don't know if that was the turning point that people have made it out to be. I think there's a little distortion or revision of history going on with that."

GERALD ESKENAZI: The Rangers had always had a reputation of not being tough guys, in fact Emile was always looking for some big guys, big beefy guys. Of course in those days if you were six foot and 180 pounds you were a big guy. But the way the Rangers were standing around while Rolfe was getting the shit kicked out of him symbolized that. Even though Emile had done a good job with the team and the team had come back and established itself as a contender, there was something so symbolic about the actual beating. You could also say that maybe they were disciplined but the guy was getting the crap beat out of him. It was really one of the most shocking things I've seen in hockey."

JACK EGERS: "That seventh game, and I still haven't talked to the Cat about why he sat me out, I'm not gonna say I was a tough guy or anything, but I would fight and I still wonder why he didn't dress me. I don't know if he was afraid I was gonna take penalties or what but he sat me out that game. So I had to watch that fight on television sitting in a security office because I couldn't even stand outside and watch it because of the fans.

"My thoughts on that were that Dale was playing very well and Schultz was sent out to get him out of the game. I never thought Dale would be stupid enough to drop his stick because he wasn't a fighter. But he must have dropped his stick and what happened after that is just hockey, right? When there's a fight going on everybody grabs somebody and obviously Schultz was a fighter and Dale wasn't. But it certainly took a lot out of the team, I know that. Philly won those Cups on fisti-cuffs and intimidation and bullshit, not on skill, that's for sure. When you went into Philly there was a lot of intimidation."

Once the dust had settled, Billy Fairbairn and Rick MacLeish swapped goals and the first period ended with the game tied at a goal apiece.

Second period goals by Orest Kindrachuk and Gary Dornhoefer gave the Flyers a seemingly safe two-goal cushion. But instead of sitting on the lead, they wore the Rangers down with relentless forechecking and outshot the Blueshirts, 37–19, over the first two periods. Only the spectacular netminding of Ed Giacomin kept the game from turning into a rout.

The Rangers came to life in the third period when Steve Vickers scored from the slot at the 8:49 mark. But the Flyers got the goal back 12 seconds later when Lonsberry grabbed a loose puck and fed Dornhoefer, who rifled a shot over Giacomin's shoulder and into the net.

Pete Stemkowski brought the Rangers back to within a goal when he beat Parent on a rebound at 14:34. The Blueshirts then spent the rest of the period shooting from every angle, desperately looking for the tying goal. However, in the final minute while Giacomin hurried off the ice for an extra skater, linesman John D'Amico called the Rangers for having too many men on the ice at 19:09. The Rangers vehemently argued the call to no avail.

Captain Vic Hadfield was sent to serve the penalty and it was there while sitting in the penalty box with his team frantically trying to score the tying goal, that he was caught on camera laughing. It was later explained that a fan had joked with Vic and offered him a liquid refreshment and that the camera had caught Hadfield at the moment he was about to hurl an insult back at the spectator. But Rangers management was not amused.

HOWIE ROSE: "For the first split second I thought well I guess that's kind of cool, the season's going down the toilet and he's got the presence of mind to be able to smile. Then I said wait a minute! What the hell is he laughing about? I feel like putting my foot through the television and this guy's the captain of the team and he's laughing?

"So the next day, I knew Marv Albert pretty well by then, and I called him because he had done the game on radio and it was televised on NBC, I guess Tim Ryan did that game. So, I called Marv and asked him, 'Did you happen to notice Hadfield laughing in the penalty box?' I didn't know enough about how things worked then. I didn't know if he would have seen NBC's feed on his monitor. And in his inimitable way Marv said, 'Well Emile and [chief scout] Dennis Ball were up at NBC watching the tape today. They saw it and let's just say, they did not appreciate it. And a couple of weeks later Hadfield was sent to Pittsburgh."

BRAD PARK: "What happened was Vic had his thumb in a cast and we ended up getting a penalty in the last couple of minutes which kind of put us out of the game because we were one goal behind. So they had to pick someone to go to the penalty box and since Vic had his thumb in a cast he was the guy who was designated to go to the penalty box. As the game wound down, Vic had an interaction with a fan and the camera was on him and he probably laughed at the fan or something like that and that was taken out of context by the press and they said, look he doesn't even care and it got blown out of proportion."

The Flyers won the game, 4–3, outshooting the Rangers, 46–34. The two teams set a record for penalty minutes in a playoff series with 405 and Philadelphia set a single team record with 252 minutes. One of the Rangers' major problems in the series was their power play, or lack thereof. The Blueshirts only managed to score four power-play goals in fifty-three opportunities and failed to score in their last twenty-three chances. Certainly a few more power-play goals could have turned the series around or at least made the Flyers think twice about manhandling the Blueshirts.

But overall the difference in the series was Bernie Parent, who would go on to win the Conn Smythe Trophy as the MVP of the playoffs. A couple of weeks later, the Flyers beat the Bruins becoming the first expansion team to win the Stanley Cup. The Flyers would go on to win the Cup again in 1975 and continued to be a contender throughout the rest of the decade.

Following the game, Parent questioned the Rangers' commitment. "The Rangers have to be the biggest mystery in all of hockey. Maybe they are overestimated and not as good as they or their fans think they are," Parent told reporters. "They pay them a lot of money but they cannot win in the playoffs. There has to be something really wrong with them as a team." Many fans also wondered how the Rangers could allow the Flyers to get off 37 shots in the first two periods and 46 overall in a crucial seventh game.

The Rangers, who scored 21 goals against Montreal in a six-game series, only managed 17 against Philadelphia in seven games.

Brad Park (3-2), Steve Vickers (3-2), Bill Fairbairn (3-2), and Walter Tkaczuk (0-5) led the Rangers with five points each. Rick MacLeish led the Flyers with seven goals and three assists. Overall in 13 playoff games, Park (4-8-12) and Pete Stemkowski (6-6-12) led the Blueshirts in playoff scoring, followed by Dale Rolfe (1-8) and Bobby Rousseau (1-8).

Ed Giacomin surrendered 37 goals in 13 games and finished with a 2.82 GAA.

EMILE FRANCIS: "It was a hell of a game. We lost, 4–3, but the guy called a penalty on us with a minute to go in the game. It was a horseshit call. But a lot of referees when they went in to Philadelphia they went into the tank. It was tough to lose that way.

"But I knew at that point in time that it was time to start making some moves and rebuild. We were good enough for five or six years to win the Stanley Cup but we didn't. Because you have your team and you build it up to the point that you should win and when you don't you know you have to start over again."

New Blood

A week after the Flyers ousted the Blueshirts, Garden president Mike Burke and new Garden Corporation chairman Alan Cohen discussed the Rangers' future with team president Bill Jennings and Emile Francis over lunch. The Rangers had made the playoffs for eight consecutive seasons but had also failed to win the Stanley Cup or finish first overall. "Sure, we're disappointed," Burke later told reporters. "We all expected this to be the Rangers year. Some new blood, younger blood is a requirement and it's a question of how to achieve it. We didn't get into specifics of executing, but we discussed how to approach the problem."

Burke, who came to the Garden in 1973, had been an executive with CBS in the early 1960s when he suggested that the company buy the New York Yankees who were on a downward slide at the time. CBS bought the fabled franchise in 1966 for $13.2 million and put Burke in charge, tasked with rebuilding the team and renovating aging Yankee Stadium. In 1972 after threatening to move the Yankees to the New Jersey Meadowlands, Burke made a deal with New York City Mayor John V. Lindsay to keep the team in the Bronx and in return the city would rebuild the stadium, a move that cost taxpayers more than $100 million. Burke had less luck rebuilding the Yankees' on-field product, however, and in 1973 the team was sold to George Steinbrenner for $10 million, with CBS absorbing an overall operating loss of over $11 million.

GERALD ESKENAZI: "Mike Burke was an interesting guy. He had run the circus for a while and didn't do well at that, he had run the Yankees and didn't do well with them either. His leadership ability just went so far. I mean you could be theatrical and you could dress fancy and have beautiful shirts, he had this great aura about him. He was very suave; he was great with the press and he was very theatrical and I think that the Garden was trying to go into some new direction and so they hired him. I think when he said 'new blood' what he was really thinking was theatrics because he had a showbiz background. Everything with him was to put on a show and that was completely opposite of Emile Francis. So I think that Jennings and Francis felt pressured into doing something dramatic because of Burke and hockey was the last sport that a Mike Burke could succeed in. Yeah, maybe he could have succeeded in Philadelphia but in New York you can't have a lot of bullshit. I really liked Mike but I think he really wanted to bring kind of a showbiz mentality to the Rangers and anyone who knew Emile Francis knew that that was not going to happen."

Cohen was also new to the Garden. He had been an executive vice president for Warner Communications, dealing with record labels. He later became part of a group that purchased the New York Cosmos soccer team. Neither man knew much about hockey, but Cohen in particular would have an unfortunate impact on the Rangers in the very near future.

Goodbye, Vic

Emile Francis was not at all happy with Vic Hadfield's behavior during the Rangers' seventh game loss to the Flyers and acted quickly. Just twenty-two days after the series finale, Hadfield was sent to the Penguins for defenseman Nick Beverley, a twenty-seven-year-old, 6-foot-2, 190-pound defenseman.

Hadfield was the highest-paid left winger in the league at the time and was in the third year of a five-year deal that paid him $175,000 a season. But Vic was thirty-three years old and injuries to his hands and legs had taken their toll as his production had dropped dramatically from his record-setting 50-goal season in 1971–72.

Hadfield, who had spent 13 seasons with the Blueshirts, took the news in stride, albeit with a trace of bitterness. "You don't win a Stanley

Cup with a trade like that," Hadfield told reporters. "I believe it was pressure from above. You make a deal that you figure will help the club, but I figure there was pressure to get rid of the older guys, the high salaried players. But that's the way it goes, this is the profession I chose and these are the handicaps that come with it."

In 839 games with the Rangers, Vic scored 262 goals and added 310 assists along with 1,036 penalty minutes. His point total ranks him in ninth place on the Rangers all-time scoring list and he is also fifth on the Blueshirts' all-time penalty minutes list. He still holds the Rangers record for assists (56) and points (106) by a left wing in a single season (1971–72). In 61 playoff games he scored 22 goals with 19 assists and 106 penalty minutes. Overall in 1,002 NHL games, he registered 323 goals with 389 assists and 1,154 penalty minutes.

Why Not Shero?

Fred Shero had coached in the Rangers' minor league system for six years before joining the Flyers in 1971. His teams had finished in first place four times and won two championships. Yet Shero was bypassed three times as Emile Francis made changes behind the Rangers bench. In 1965 when Francis replaced Red Sullivan as coach, Shero was not considered. However, in this case it is understandable because Francis needed to get firsthand knowledge of his team. But in 1968, Francis had an opportunity to bring Shero in twice, once when Bernie Geoffrion was named coach and later when he was forced to step down due to health reasons.

But Shero had a well-known drinking problem and Francis didn't want any part of it.

When interviewed by Jay Moran for his book *The Rangers, the Bruins, and the End of an Era,* former Rangers PR director John Halligan said, "He would've been the coach many times, if he had that under control, but you know Freddy was indeed 'The Fog.' We used to see him all the time in training camp and he was spacey, but he did win, there's no question about that. Now could he have done it at the NHL level at that time? I'm not sure, but he did come in and we went to the Finals in 1979."

In 1971, Flyers GM Keith Allen was looking to replace coach Vic Stasiuk and asked the Rangers for permission to speak to Shero. Freddie had been with Omaha in the Central Hockey League where his team won the league championship with a 45–16–11 record. Francis gave the Flyers permission and Shero jumped at the chance. "There wasn't an opportunity for him with the Rangers then," Francis told reporters. "I wasn't planning a coaching change in 1971."

Shero had been uneasy about being in the minors for so long. He felt that the coaching apprenticeship prior to the majors should be five years and he had already spent more than that coaching in the minors. "Emile told me last year that I'd move up to coach if he moved up to assume only the general manager's duties." said Shero. "Francis told me that I'm always free to leave the Rangers organization to better myself. At the time, Emile told me if you can't wait for the Ranger job you better take the Flyer job."

EMILE FRANCIS: "I had played with him in New Haven, the Rangers, and Cleveland and I thought he was good with the minor leaguers but I had my doubts about him in the National Hockey League because Freddie was a loner. He was always by himself. He was a hard guy to keep track of, if you know what I mean. I knew about his problems. I'll never forget his first year coaching Philadelphia, they were beaten in the playoffs, I think by Buffalo, and who calls me but Keith Allen. He said 'you probably know Freddie Shero better than anybody. I was walking with him after losing and all of a sudden I turned to say something to him and he wasn't there. We haven't seen him and his wife hasn't heard from him for three days. Do you have any idea where he might be?' I said Keith I haven't got a clue. Believe me. He did a good job coaching. But to me it would be too easy to get lost in New York."

13

1974–75

The Beginning of the End

CHANGES WERE DEFINITELY in the wind as the Rangers opened training camp in Kitchener in September of 1974. The core group of Blueshirts was getting on in years and it was time to say goodbye to a few old favorites and welcome some new faces to the Rangers.

Brad Park had been named captain of the team, replacing Vic Hadfield, who was dealt to Pittsburgh following their playoff loss to the Flyers in May. Park was initially reluctant to take the position, feeling that Rod Gilbert, who had been with the club the longest, should be next in line. But Gilbert as well as Jean Ratelle gave their blessings and Park became the fifteenth captain of the Rangers on August 9. As far as Francis was concerned, the choice was an easy one. "When Vic was traded, Park was the automatic choice," the GM told reporters. "I had no one else in mind for the captaincy. Brad played the most, he played the hardest. He was a key guy on the team and the other players respected him. Even Vic Hadfield, the man Park replaced as captain, agreed. "He'll be a good captain," said Hadfield. "He has the ability and respect of every guy on that club."

BRAD PARK: "Basically, I wasn't very happy about it. Emile Francis had approached me at Rod Gilbert's wedding and I said no, I don't want it. Rod was the senior member of the team and he's the guy who should have been captain and Emile just said no I'm not going to make him captain and if you won't take it, I'll find somebody else. So I said well let me go talk to Rod and he encouraged me to take it. And so I kind of looked at the team and tried to figure out where the Cat might go. So I went back to him and said okay, Rod gave me his blessing and accepted it."

The Washington Capitals and Kansas City Scouts joined the NHL in 1974–75, necessitating a realignment of the league as well as another expansion draft. The now eighteen-team league was broken up into two conferences, named after Clarence Campbell and the Prince of Wales. Each conference contained two divisions, the Patrick and Smythe divisions in the Campbell Conference and the Norris and Adams divisions in the Wales Conference. The Rangers were moved to the Patrick Division along with Philadelphia, the Islanders, and the Atlanta Flames.

The Rangers weren't hurt too badly in the expansion draft, losing only winger Jack Egers to Washington while third string netminder Peter McDuffe and minor leaguer Doug Horbul went to Kansas City. In two separate tours of duty on Broadway, Egers had scored a number of important goals for the Blueshirts, both in the regular season and the playoffs but unfortunately, back problems hampered him during the 1973–74 season and Francis had no choice but to leave him unprotected.

JACK EGERS: "Washington drafted me and in the twelfth game of the season I herniated a disk and had to have surgery. Then they screwed up, putting me on the ice too soon and I re-herniated it and had to have another back surgery and then I tried to come back from that but I couldn't. I was done in the '75–'76 season."

The Caps wanted Jack to go to the minors to work himself into condition but he refused. Egers then hired an agent named Richard Sorkin to settle his contract with the Caps. Unfortunately, Sorkin gambled away Egers's settlement as well as the accounts of at least fifty other athletes that he represented. Sorkin was found guilty of grand larceny in 1978 and sentenced to prison. No restitution was ever made to any of Sorkin's victims.

Also gone was right winger Bruce MacGregor who had jumped to the WHA, signing with his hometown Edmonton Oilers. MacGregor had been a valuable member of the checking line along with Pete Stemkowski and Ted Irvine. In 220 games over four seasons in New York, MacGregor scored 62 goals, including six short-handers and added 73 assists. He also contributed 10 goals and 14 assists in 52 playoff games and was masterful at keeping the opposition's top players such as Yvan Cournoyer off the scoreboard.

BRUCE MacGREGOR: "That was the year that they opened up the Coliseum here in Edmonton, the new building in the WHA. So I had to make a decision about what we wanted to do as a family. I guess more than anything else I had the opportunity to stay with the Rangers which was tough because I really got to enjoy the team and Emile and so it was a hard decision. But I think it was based on coming back here to Edmonton and the opportunity to settle down and not make a big move every year back and forth between Edmonton and New York.

"The one thing I want to say about Emile was that he really had the knack of knowing what to do to make people feel comfortable in New York. He tried to make it as easy as he could, not only on the player but he also cared about their families. And I think that was a big part of why our team was so close and why we had that camaraderie between everybody. He was tough and he was the boss but he was always fair and he treated everybody with respect and got respect back from everybody. I admired him a lot for the way that he handled the Rangers and all of us and our families. And he did such a good job with systems. He put a lot of time into it as well. I think that's a big part of it, the way he handled the team. I think the guys admired it. He was such a competitor himself that nobody hated to lose more than he did and I think it rubbed off on everybody because he took a loss as hard, maybe harder than anybody. The 'compete level' for him never changed.

"To me, you look at those teams, the difference between winning and losing was pretty slim. When I look at the makeup of the team with Brad and Jimmy Neilson and Rod Seiling and Dale Rolfe on defense, we had all the ingredients but sometimes it doesn't work out the way you think it should. To me we were as good as any team in the league. We came up short but I don't think it was because of personnel or the way the team was coached or any of those things. It was just the way things go sometimes, you just don't win. We had that in Detroit. We had some great teams and we got to the finals a few times, but sometimes it's the bounce of the puck or a crazy goal or whatever. But I thought the teams Emile built in the '70s were as good as any team in the league for sure."

On the same day as the expansion draft, Francis engineered a three-way deal that brought longtime nemesis Derek Sanderson to the Rangers. First he left veteran defenseman Jim Neilson unprotected in the intra-league draft, allowing him to be selected by the California Golden Seals. Under league rules, the Seals then owed the Rangers a player or cash. Francis opted for a player and selected forward Walt McKechnie, who he then sent to Boston for Sanderson.

Sanderson had jumped to the WHA's Philadelphia Blazers in 1972, but was subsequently bought out by the team making him a free agent. He then returned to the Bruins but was hampered by colitis and back problems and played in only 54 games over two seasons.

DEREK SANDERSON: "The Bruins made a mistake when they protected me in the expansion draft. They were trading me to Vancouver and I didn't want that. So I was in Las Vegas and called up Emile Francis. 'Need a centerman?' He said yeah. So, I said give Harry Sinden something for me and I'll come to New York. So, he says great! But I wasn't going to Vancouver. I ended up in Vancouver at the end of my career. I was there for 163 days and it rained 140 of them. My God! And you were always in an airport. This was in the days before charters, you know? It was four to six hours to anywhere. Terrible travel."

Sanderson, of course, came with a lot of baggage. His off-ice troubles with drugs and alcohol were well known to most people in the hockey community, but Francis respected him as a player, especially as a faceoff man and penalty killer. Grateful for the opportunity Francis had given him, Sanderson wanted get off on the right foot with his new teammates, so he arrived in camp a week early, driving his father's station wagon instead of his Rolls Royce.

BRAD PARK: "With Derek's history and everything I wasn't very excited about it and Emile said he's going to go to rookie camp and prove himself and show how dedicated he is, so I took a wait and see attitude. He gave us another centerman that teams had to worry about. He was very good on the penalty kill and things like that so he had a very good year. He established himself and was a strong teammate."

BILL FAIRBAIRN: "I always hated him, but yet when he was on our team I became friends with him, like he was a good guy. I never thought I would do that, you know, change that quickly. I couldn't stand him when he was in Boston, I just hated him, but then when he came to us he was just like one of the guys, he wanted to win. At first I didn't think it was a good move but then after a while it turned out that it was. There's nothing wrong with a guy who played his heart out and tried to win."

Francis also hoped to beef up his top forward line by acquiring left winger Greg Polis from St. Louis in exchange for young defenseman Larry Sacharuk and the Rangers' first-round pick in the 1977 entry draft. Polis, twenty-four, had been Pittsburgh's first-round pick in the 1970 draft and scored 88 goals for the Pens over four and a half seasons. He was also named the MVP of the 1973 All-Star Game held at Madison Square Garden. Polis had been traded to St. Louis in January 1974 but managed only eight goals in 37 games for the Blues. At 6-feet, 195 pounds, Francis thought that the native of Westlock, Alberta, had the size and skills to replace Vic Hadfield on the Ratelle-Gilbert line.

During the early stages of training camp, Gilles Villemure surprised everyone by walking out due to a contract dispute. He later returned but left again, threatening to quit in order to devote more time to his harness racing interests. But once again he returned.

GILLES VILLEMURE: "I thought Emile promised me more money, but I came back and it was nice of him to take me back. That's the bottom line. Those years, we weren't making much money."

The Rangers also had two rookies who stood out in training camp that fall, both of whom would have long NHL careers in front of them, Rick Middleton and Ron Greschner.

Rick Middleton was selected by the Rangers in the first round of the 1973 amateur draft. He had been named the Ontario Hockey Association's MVP and led the league in scoring with 67 goals and 70 assists while playing for the Oshawa Generals in 1972–73.

He then spent the 1973–74 season with Providence of the AHL where he won Rookie of the Year honors and earned a First Team All-Star berth, scoring 36 goals with 48 assists despite missing 13 games due to injuries. He also led the Reds in playoff scoring with nine goals and six assists in 15 games.

Ron Greschner was the Rangers' second-round pick in the 1974 amateur draft. The slick-stickhandling, smooth-skating defenseman played his junior hockey for the New Westminster Bruins of the WCJHL where he scored 56 goals and 126 assists over three seasons. At 6-foot-2, 185 pounds, the tall, rangy nineteen-year-old made an impression on Francis very quickly. "I knew after the first few days of training camp that he was ready for the NHL and that we would have to make room for him." Francis told reporters. And true to his word, Francis made room for Greschner as soon as possible.

EMILE FRANCIS: "In that 1974 draft we could pick a seventeen-year-old player, but it had to be with your first pick. So here's Ron Greschner. He's nineteen and he's playing junior hockey with New Westminster. So we were going over all the reports and I went to see Dave Maloney play and they were the two guys at the top of the list. So, I'm thinking, if we take Maloney, who was seventeen, in the first round, Greschner's gonna be gone by the time we pick in the second round. So I'm thinking how am I gonna get around this. Well I took a chance. I'm gonna have to start a rumor. Vancouver was in the World Hockey Association at the time and here he is playing thirty minutes away from Vancouver in New Westminster. So, about a month before the draft I started this rumor that Greschner had already signed with Vancouver. I spread the word that he's already gone, so don't waste your draft pick. And I'm sitting there all through that first round with my fingers crossed and we took Maloney with the first pick and don't you know we come to our second-round pick and there's Greschner still there for us. I grabbed him so quick. I couldn't believe how we got out of there with those two guys, two real fine defensemen.

"When Greschner came in, he looked like he had been playing in the NHL for two or three years already. He was like a proven pro when he stepped on the ice for the first time. And I knew his dad. I had never met him but there was a friend of mine who was a priest and they were having a dinner for him in Goodsoil, Saskatchewan. So that's where I met Greschner's dad. He owned half the town. He owned a car dealership, a grocery store, a hotel. He came from a very fine family. His mother and dad were great people but he was a terrific hockey player."

At the conclusion of training camp, Greschner was initially sent to Providence of the AHL where he scored five goals with six assists in seven games. At the same time in New York, veteran defenseman Rod Seiling was getting tired of hearing boos and catcalls from the fans at the Garden. Seiling was never a fan favorite because he wasn't a physical defenseman, but he was effective in more subtle ways. However, he became the fans' scapegoat for the Rangers' mediocre play at the start of the season. In an interview with the *New York Post*, Seiling blasted the fans, saying that they didn't understand or appreciate the game of hockey. He also said that the fans crossed the line by abusing his wife and children. At that point, there was no turning back and Francis was forced to move him. Seiling was placed on waivers and claimed by the Washington Capitals, who turned around and sent him to Toronto.

ROD SEILING: "The fans were booing me and blaming me for things that happened when I wasn't even on the ice. It became a problem for me when it started to have an impact on my family, especially my two boys who were getting hassled in school. I thought it was very unfair and inappropriate to say the least and I needed to stop it because I would protect my family at any cost. And I wasn't prepared to accept it anymore so either the team had to step in and defend me or do what they did. That's life. Two young kids should not have to bear the brunt for what their father is doing."

Seiling came to New York in the blockbuster 1964 deal that also brought Bob Nevin, Dick Duff, and Arnie Brown from Toronto for Andy Bathgate and Don McKenney. In 12 seasons with the Blueshirts, Seiling scored 50 goals and added 198 assists. He also accumulated 423 penalty minutes, but his most impressive statistic was the +248 defensive rating he racked up over those 12 seasons. Except for his final abbreviated year in New York, he never finished with a negative rating.

The Rangers got off to a so-so start, compiling a 5–3–2 record during the month of October. But when they won only one of their first six games in November they needed something to turn the season around and a visit by the lowly California Golden Seals on November 17 proved to be just what the doctor ordered. Led by Rick Middleton, who became the first Rangers rookie to score four goals in a game (needing only four shots to accomplish the feat), the Rangers routed the Seals, 10–0, and went on a 7–3–3 run.

DEREK SANDERSON: "Middleton was as gifted a player as I have ever met. I met him in his rookie year. I was his centerman and I was stunned at how good he was with the puck and how good he was in the corners. And he went in those corners, he never went in to hit anybody, but he always came out with the puck. And that's the job isn't it? Not to run someone over. But Ricky had a deft pair of hands. We used to call him 'Silky.' He was such a nice kid and he had talent, he should have been Rookie of the Year."

A little more than a month later on December 19, the Rangers were on the wrong side of a blowout at the hands of the Bruins at the Boston Garden. Injuries and illness had hit the Rangers hard and Francis brought nine players up from Providence to fill in for regulars including goaltender Curt Ridley, who had a 13–3–4 record and a respectable 2.73 GAA at Providence. Ridley got his first NHL start that night and wound up sharing a Rangers record that still stands today. The rookie netminder surrendered four goals in the first period and two more in the first 43 seconds of the second period. But that wasn't the record! The Bruins scored a record five goals in 2:55 against Curt and Eddie Giacomin. First Boston's Bobby Schmautz scored at 19:13 of the first period. Then Ken Hodge scored 18 seconds into the second period followed by a goal by Phil Esposito 23 seconds later. Giacomin then came in to replace the beleaguered Ridley and promptly surrendered a goal to Don Marcotte 15 seconds later. Johnny Bucyk then scored at 2:08 to set the record.

CURT RIDLEY, *Goaltender, 1974*: "If I remember correctly and it's close to forty years, I think the flu bug was going around. Because quite a few of the Rangers were out, and I think Villemure had the flu. It was a great experience but to this day I still have nightmares. What was the score, ten-something? Eleven-something? The Cat pulled me after six and Giacomin went in and they pumped five by him so I didn't feel that bad."

The Bruins won the game, 11–3, outshooting the Rangers, 44–16.

Emile Francis later spoke to reporters about starting the rookie. "We've been thinking about playing Ridley a long time. There was no better place to play him than just forty-five minutes from Providence. It's important for a goalie to get used to a defense and he had four of his buddies from Providence with him. He was the Lone Ranger in the first period. I took him out like you would take a pitcher out in baseball. I told him he played real well."

CURT RIDLEY: "Emile was like a father figure to everybody. He just said, 'Man, it was a tough one. Keep your chin up and don't worry about it. Stuff happens.'"

But was it fair to throw a rookie playing his first game in the NHL into a situation like that?

CURT RIDLEY: "Not in that situation, no not really. Being limited with the Rangers players, their star players being out and Boston had a full blown out squad. I think Orr scored two on me and Espo scored two on me and Bobby Schmautz and Ken Hodge."

Ridley got another start ten days later and beat the Kansas City Scouts, 2–1, at the Garden.

CURT RIDLEY: "He gave me another shot and I should have had a shutout, should have! But I think it was Simon Nolet. He put one over, I think it was my right side high in the corner. I should have had it. That would have been great; I would have redeemed myself in my own mind."

Following the loss to the Bruins, the Rangers won eight of their next nine games and finished the first half of the season with a 21–11–8 record.

However, the second half of the season was not as kind to the Rangers, as they posted a 16–18–6 record due largely to a string of injuries to key players.

The Blueshirts had already lost Bobby Rousseau to a back injury earlier in the season. Rousseau underwent spinal fusion surgery but the injury ultimately ended his career.

Ron Harris suffered a broken pelvis on November 23 when he threw a hip check at Bobby Orr. Orr tried to avoid the check and his knees caught Harris in the hip, breaking his pelvic socket. It was first thought that Harris, who spent three weeks in the hospital, two of them in traction, was finished for the season. But he made a remarkable recovery and returned to the lineup in March. Dale Rolfe also injured his knee in the game. Then, the very next night, Walt Tkaczuk broke his right leg. Tkaczuk missed twenty-two games while Derek Sanderson centered for Fairbairn and Greg Polis, who had been shifted to the left-wing slot.

Originally expected to replace Vic Hadfield on the Ratelle line, Polis had trouble adapting to the line's slower style, resulting in a lot of icing calls and unsuccessful single man rushes. Steve Vickers was then promoted to the Ratelle line and Polis eventually settled in with Tkaczuk and Fairbairn and got hot in February and March, scoring four goals against Minnesota and a hat trick against the Penguins. He finished the season with 26 goals and 15 assists.

STEVE VICKERS: "I loved playing with Walter and Billy but Jean Ratelle was an incredible hockey player. He could pass whatever way he wanted—forehand, backhand, it was incredible. It was a good year, I got forty goals, but it had a pretty rotten ending."

Rick Middleton broke his leg in mid-January and missed two months. At the time of the injury Rick was leading all rookies in scoring with 18 goals and may have won the Calder Trophy if not for the injury.

Then in mid-February Brad Park fell victim to the notoriously bad Garden ice when his skate caught a rut, damaging ligaments in his knee. He missed five weeks, during which time the Rangers won only five of the fifteen games they played.

EMILE FRANCIS: "It was past the trading deadline and they had a track meet at the Garden the night before and we had an afternoon game the next day. The puck's shot into Brad Park's corner, he turns to go back, steps on the ice that hadn't frozen properly from the track meet, slid into the boards and tore up his knee.

"He came back and tried to play in the playoffs with a brace like Joe Namath's but he couldn't turn. It happened to him twice and he was our key guy on defense and on the power play. Two out of three years it happened to him."

But the most devastating injury occurred in early March when Dale Rolfe suffered a broken ankle, another injury that was due to the poor ice conditions at Madison Square Garden.

EMILE FRANCIS: "One night Dale Rolfe goes behind the net to pick up the puck. He goes down the left side of the rink, right across from the Rangers bench. All of a sudden, there's nobody near him and bingo—he goes right into the boards. He stepped on a piece of ice that had broken away. They put him on a stretcher and I'll tell you I was sick. His foot was turned backwards. He had a compound fracture and never played another hockey game.

"So now after the game I was so pissed off. This was the third time it happened. We lost Park twice and now Rolfe all on account of the ice. So, I go to the press room and I say I come from Saskatchewan and they've got better ice on the highways up there than we've got in Madison Square Garden.

"So the next day after practice I get a call from [Garden president] Irving Mitchell Felt. He says, 'I'm really disturbed with the statement you made.' I said, 'Oh really! Let me tell you something. I've lost Brad Park twice and I just lost Dale Rolfe because you people won't put down ice and leave it in there. If you don't think that I'm right, you go up to Saskatchewan in January, February, or March and you'll see what I'm talking about. You can skate down the highway, it's so cold, it's like 35 below.' And he hung up on me.

"We always had the worst ice in the league. [Knicks president] Ned Irish always said, 'I don't want my basketball people sitting on cold ice.' I said what the hell are you talking about. We put people on the moon for crissakes. They've got insulated floors. I told them call Chicago, call Boston. They've got insulated floors."

DALE ROLFE: "I looked down and tried to get up, but my ankle was angled to the right and there was blood coming out of my skate. That's Madison Square Garden ice, eh? It's that simple. It was quick and sudden and it went off just like a rifle bullet. Bang. I hit the boards and it was the end of a mediocre career. Doctor Nicholas said he had never seen one like it and he said you'll be lucky to walk. I can walk, but not well. I have to use a cane sometimes. And if you think back there were a lot of players who broke ankles and legs on the Garden ice. You had the circus in there with animals pissin' all over the place. There was bound to be bad ice."

DEREK SANDERSON: "MSG was a very powerful venue, Ice shows, the circus, everything and even when the Knicks played they would take the ice out. In Boston they don't. They cover the ice and put the parquet floor down. But in New York they didn't do that. They stripped the ice, melted it and took it out. So, we always played with new ice. And God is that hard. The worst ice in the league was in New York. The Rangers had an uncanny amount of back injuries and hard falls and blown knees and ankles. I remember Dale Rolfe, he went into the end boards, when the ice gave out on him. He was flying to get an icing call and he snapped his ankle, the bone was sticking right out of the boot. I told him Dale, I'm sorry. He said, 'Well, I'm collecting career ending insurance.' He got $750,000. I think he bought a hotel."

Rolfe went to training camp the following fall, but found skating difficult and retired. He finished out the rest of his contract doing scouting work for Francis.

Due to the many injuries, Francis was forced to shuffle thirty players in and out of the lineup including four netminders. The injuries did open up playing time for some promising rookies, however. Scrappy winger Bert Wilson held his own against the league's tough guys including Bobby Nystrom, Ted Harris, and Phil Russell. John Bednarski made his NHL debut and played well as did eighteen-year-old Dave Maloney. Nick Beverley, who didn't see much action early in the season, became a valuable asset in the second half with his steady and efficient defensive play.

The Rangers didn't clinch a playoff spot until the final week of the season, finishing with a 37–29–14 record for 88 points, only five points ahead of the last place Atlanta Flames. The 88 points represented their lowest total since the 1966–67 season. They tied for second place with the Islanders and won the tiebreaker because they had more victories than the Isles.

Offensively, the Blueshirts had a great year, scoring the most goals in franchise history up to that point (319) and setting records for power-play goals (84) and hat tricks (9). But defensively they surrendered 276 goals, the most in their division and the most of any Rangers team since the 1943–44 season when most of their better players were in the armed services.

Steve Vickers led the team with 41 goals and Rod Gilbert finished with 97 points (36–61), six ahead of linemate Jean Ratelle (36–55). Rookie Rick Middleton recorded 22 goals and 18 assists in 47 games. Fellow freshman Ron Greschner finished fifth in the voting for the Calder Trophy and led all rookie defensemen in scoring, finishing with 37 assists, one short of the Rangers' record and five shy of the NHL mark.

Meanwhile, Derek Sanderson had a stellar comeback season, scoring 25 goals with 25 assists in 75 games, leading the team with 106 penalty minutes and posting a +10 defensive rating. He also wasn't shy about saying what was on his mind.

DEREK SANDERSON: "I said something in the dressing room one day. I said no wonder we always fuckin' lose. Everybody goes in five different directions. In Boston if one guy went someplace, everybody went with him. That was Bobby Orr's two drink rule; everybody had to go out together after a game. You did so much traveling together in those days. Park, Tkaczuk, and Fairbairn got along very well and Gilbert was a bit of a playboy and Jean Ratelle was a solid, happily married guy. Ratty would never do anything untoward. Straightest guy I even met in hockey. Loved his wife, loved his family. Dedicated to them and that was really something to admire. Because all the stuff that was going on around him, Jean was always a class act. He never partook. He always stayed away. He was different, but a great guy.

"The Cat was great, he knew everybody and he was an honest man. The coaches in my day were honest. Harry Sinden said to me once, the most important thing is the players gotta believe you. Like in practice you tell them to do the board-to-board, once more and that's it. Don't lie to them."

The Blueshirts also set a franchise record with 1,049 penalty minutes due mostly to a pair of brawl-filled games, one against the St. Louis Blues and the other not surprisingly against the Flyers.

The game against the Blues, which occurred in mid-December, was a nasty affair from the start with a number of fights in the first two periods. But when Blues winger Claude Larose butt-ended Greg Polis in the face late in the third it set off a wild bench-clearing brawl in which even the goaltenders, Giacomin and the Blues' John Davidson got involved. Referee Dave Newell needed a pencil and paper to record all the penalties which totaled 32, setting a Ranger franchise record.

Then, in early February, the Rangers went into Philadelphia's Spectrum with something to prove.

DEREK SANDERSON: "We went into Philly one night when I was with the Rangers. We started kind of slowly coming out of camp and they had the Broad Street Bullies back then. They had all those big guys like Schultz, Dupont, Saleski, and Battleship Kelly, they had all of those nut cases. And they had a pretty good team because they had Bernie Parent. Anybody wins the Stanley Cup, look at their goalie.

"So the Cat got us in after warmups. And he says, 'I don't give a shit about the two points but you're gonna get their respect.' And he goes around the room, 'Gilles Marotte, Captain Crunch, you haven't crunched anybody.' He goes around the room he gets to me. 'Oh yeah, Sanderson, yeah, big shot shit disturber, you haven't disturbed anything. I got you guys because you're supposed to be tough, do something! I don't want that game getting into the double digits of seconds before the brawl starts.' And we went out that night and fought them toe-to-toe and I'll tell you what we had a good season against them. We played them hard and they played us hard. And there was never any cheap shots. They knew what was gonna happen."

Evidentially the Rangers got the message. Rookie John Bednarski battled Dave Schultz 13 seconds into the first period, which took more than an hour to complete. About a minute later Steve Vickers and Bobby Clarke fought and when Reggie Leach came to Clarke's rescue he was ejected for being the third man in. At around the six minute mark a major brawl broke out that involved Don Saleski, Sanderson, Park, Jerry Butler, and Vickers (who received a game misconduct). A few minutes after that, Irvine and Bob Kelly squared off and Schultz intervened and earned a game misconduct. In all, the Rangers were whistled for 49 minutes in penalties and the Flyers 45 in the first period alone. Then in the second period Bert Wilson won a clear decision over Ted Harris. In between fights, Billy Fairbairn, Brad Park, and Jerry Butler scored for the Rangers, who for once won the battle as well as the war, 3–1.

Goaltending, which had long been a strong point for the Rangers, was no better than average during the 1974–75 season. Giacomin was plagued by knee problems and played in just 37 games, winning only 13, the fewest games played and victories since his rookie season in 1965–66. His 3.48 GAA was also his highest since that rookie season. Conversely, Gilles Villemure played the most games in his NHL career appearing in 45 matches, winning 22 and posting a 3.16 GAA. Curt Ridley posted a 5.19 GAA in his two appearances. Francis also acquired journeyman Dunc Wilson on waivers from the Maple Leafs to provide more depth in goal. Wilson appeared in three games and posted a 4.33 GAA.

The Playoffs

Due to the new conference and division structure, the playoffs were expanded from eight to twelve teams with the top three clubs in each division qualifying for the postseason. The first-place teams earned an opening-round "bye" while the teams that finished second and third were seeded one through eight based on their regular-season record. These teams then paired off (with one playing eight, two playing seven, etc.) in a best two-of-three preliminary round with the winners advancing to the quarterfinals where they were reseeded along with the first place teams.

The short opening-round format was not popular among the players or coaches. "Nobody likes to play a best-two-out-of-three series," Rod Gilbert told reporters. "It's just too short. Anything can happen, a goalie can get hot for a couple of games and that's all a weaker team needs. How often has a club lost two games in a four-of-seven series yet come back and win? You can't do that this year. Somebody's going to be caught by surprise, mark my words." Those words would prove to be extremely prophetic.

The Rangers' first-round opponent were the Islanders, who had improved dramatically since their 30-point debut in 1972–73.

High draft picks and shrewd selections by GM Bill Torrey had brought the Islanders good young players such as Denis Potvin, Clark Gillies, and Bob Nystrom. And well-thought-out trades supplied hungry veterans such as J. P. Parise and Jude Drouin. With Al Arbour behind the bench the Isles improved to 56 points their second season and jumped to 88 points and a playoff spot in their third.

The Rangers won the season series, 3–2–1, but the Islanders had won the last two games between the clubs. The two teams had finished in a dead heat for second place in the Patrick Division, but the Rangers won the tie-breaker with four more victories. And although the Blueshirts scored 55 more goals than the Islanders, the Isles were much better defensively surrendering only 221 goals, 55 fewer than their Manhattan rivals and the third-lowest in the league behind the Flyers and Kings.

The series opened in Madison Square Garden where, after a scoreless first period, Park and Stemkowski gave the Rangers a 2–0 lead in the second. But then the Islanders fought back in the third period, first getting a power-play goal from Billy Harris at the five minute mark. Then Jean Potvin broke in alone on Giacomin, who stumbled on his way out to challenge him. Potvin skated around the fallen goaltender and scored into the empty net. Finally, Clark Gillies split the Rangers defense and scored what proved to be the game-winner. Giacomin, who usually never blamed his teammates for goals he allowed, wasn't too happy about the lack of support on Gillies's game-winner, telling reporters, "You're supposed to have help on a play like that."

Giacomin wasn't the only Blueshirt upset with the way they had let the game slip away from them. "We had them until we stopped hitting in the third period," said Ted Irvine. "We let up and they wouldn't quit. It was a mental thing on our part." Derek Sanderson took an optimistic view. "The Islanders are nervous now. If they don't win at home, they'll never beat us at the Garden." Young defenseman Ron Greschner was also very upset by the loss. "We'll stuff it down the Islanders' throats next game," he told reporters in the locker room.

And the Rangers did just that as the series moved to the Nassau Coliseum, blasting the Islanders, 8–3. Billy Fairbairn scored a pair of goals and Jean Ratelle and Steve Vickers each notched a goal and three assists. It started out as a chippy game that got nastier as the Islanders' frustration grew. Referee Ron Wicks called fifty penalties including five 10-minute misconducts and ten fighting majors. In all, Wicks handed out 170 minutes in penalties, 101 of those minutes against the Islanders.

With the series tied at a game apiece, the action moved back to the Garden where Gilles Villemure, who had started Game Two, once again got the nod. However, Gilles was not sharp, fanning on a 25-foot slapper from Clark Gillies, giving the Islanders a 1–0 lead at the end of the first period. Denis Potvin then scored twice in the second period to give the Islanders a seemingly insurmountable 3–0 lead. Francis pulled Villemure in favor of Giacomin following Potvin's second goal and the move seemed to bring the Rangers to life. Five minutes after he entered the game, Giacomin got into a shoving match with the Islanders' Garry Howatt in front of his net, hoping to give his team a spark and to get himself into the game. Giacomin received four minutes in penalties and Howatt two for the fracas and Pete Stemkowski was ejected for being the third man in.

Trailing 3–0 going into the third, the Rangers made a strong comeback, getting a pair of goals from Billy Fairbairn and the game-tying marker from Steve Vickers late in the period to send the game into overtime.

Unfortunately for the Blueshirts, the overtime didn't last very long. Following the opening faceoff at center ice the puck went into the corner to Giacomin's left where Vickers pursued it. Jude Drouin blocked Vickers's clearing attempt and shot towards the Rangers net where J. P. Parise deflected the puck past Giacomin just 11 seconds into the extra session. It was the quickest playoff overtime goal in league history.

Vickers called it the most embarrassing loss he ever suffered. But Giacomin was complementary to the upstart Islanders. "You've got to give them credit. They should have been demoralized by what we did to them the other night, but they forgot all about it."

BRAD PARK: "That was a surprise. It was a two out of three series and that year we got knocked out and the Bruins got knocked out. We went into the third period down three to nothing and we tied it up and we hit a couple posts and we were all over them. Then we end up making a turnover in the first ten seconds into the overtime and we're out of it. That's what they call sudden defeat."

BILL FAIRBAIRN: "That was kind of a heartbreaker. I still remember that because Parise scored that goal and it was very, very disappointing to lose right in the Garden like that. That was the start of their rein, their dynasty. They had good hockey players too. I think Nystrom was underrated. So that kind of started things off for them to go on a roll and it was very upsetting, really."

STEVE VICKERS: "Nick Beverley and I got crossed up with our signals in the corner. I think Nick took the blame but it was my fault, I admit it. It's just the way it happened. I should have been more cautious behind my net but I put it right on Jude Drouin's stick. Brad was all over top of Parise but he got a stick on it. What are you gonna do—go to the showers. But that was life-and-death that two out of three series."

EMILE FRANCIS: "How the hell we went to a two out of three series. Nobody wanted it but it was pushed through by the owners. I don't know who the hell sold them on that idea. You play eighty-something games to get into the playoffs then you play a two-out-of-three series. And they came into New York and beat us in the first game and Eddie didn't have a good night that night. I thought it was one of the toughest nights he ever had. Then we went out to the Island and I put Villemure in and we beat them bad. So then we came back to play the third game and they had us down 3–0 and I put Eddie in and that turned it around for us. We tied it up. They couldn't get out of their own end for most of the third period but we couldn't score to save our souls. And we go into overtime and bang, bang the game's over! It was an awful ending. The Bruins were also knocked out early that year."

For the record, the Kings, who had their best season since their inception with 105 points, were eliminated by the Maple Leafs and the Bruins were ousted by the Black Hawks.

Parise's goal proved to be the beginning of the most successful run in Islanders history. They continued to improve each season and five years later won the first of four consecutive Stanley Cups.

For the Rangers, however, the loss was perhaps the most humiliating defeat in their forty-nine-year history. It was the first time they had failed to win a playoff game at home since 1969 when they were swept by Montreal who had also beat them four straight in 1967. But this was not the fabled Flying Frenchmen. This was the three-year-old Islanders who were appearing in their first-ever playoff series. The Islanders, whom the Rangers had beaten fourteen of their first fifteen meetings and initially had to pay a $4 million indemnification fee for the right to set up shop in the Blueshirts' territory. The loss proved to be the beginning of the end of the Francis era, and for many it would be their last playoff game as Rangers.

Giacomin's Gracious Gesture

Following their Game Three victory, the Islanders were sitting in their team bus in the bowels of the Garden waiting for stragglers. There was a knock on the door and the bus driver opened it expecting to see a player or maybe one of the fans. Instead he was surprised to see Ed Giacomin standing at the door. "Congratulations, guys!" Eddie told the Islanders while boarding the bus. "You deserved to win the way you played. Good luck in Pittsburgh. I'll be rooting for you to go all the way and win it."

"Every guy on that bus was deeply moved by what Eddie did and said to us," coach Al Arbour recalled. "It was a good example for all our young players to see what a man like Eddie is really like."

NHLPHA's First Good Guy Award

In the spring of 1975, the New York Rangers chapter of the Professional Hockey Writers Association which dated back to the late 1920s initiated its Good Guy Award that was meant to honor the Ranger who was the most cooperative with the press. Players could win the award only once.

Ted Irvine was the first recipient of the Good Guy award. Irvine had won the Player's Player award the previous season and was also well known for his charitable work, especially with disabled children.

TED IRVINE: "When you get away from the game and look back at some of the things you've done and when I look at the fact that it was the first year that the writers set up that award and I remember Denis Potvin won it for the Islanders. It was a tremendous honor and the Player's Player award with the Rangers, it's the same because when your teammates vote you a valuable guy on the team, that was special. Those years in New York, I was so lucky because I won the Charlie Conacher Humanitarian Award (1974–75) for my work with the Special Olympics and that led me to start the Manitoba Special Olympics years later.

"So many good things happened to me in New York and I got some wonderful letters from the writers when I retired. Hugh Delano sent me a wonderful letter about my role with the Rangers. The sportswriters were very good to me. The only guy who didn't care for me was Stan Fischler. He said I was a mediocre hockey player who never reached mediocrity (laughs). But I respected the guys for their work and it was an honor to win that award."

14

1975–76

The End of an Era

FOLLOWING THEIR EMBARRASSING first-round loss to the Islanders in the 1975 playoffs, it was clear that changes were on the horizon as the Rangers entered their fiftieth anniversary season.

The core group of Blueshirts had been together for nearly a decade with little playoff success to show for it and Emile Francis knew that changes had to be made both on the ice and behind the bench. One of the first items on Emile's summer agenda was to find a new coach for the Rangers. Francis had served as both general manager and coach for most of his tenure with the club, but with expansion and the WHA invasion there were now many more teams and players to keep tabs on. He knew that he couldn't continue to do both jobs and it was time to find a coach he could rely on. It has also been said that the hiring of a new coach was a mandate set down by the Garden's hierarchy. So as Emile began his search for a coach the first person he thought of was former Montreal Canadiens tough guy John Ferguson.

EMILE FRANCIS: "We were at war with the WHA and I was at the point where I couldn't do everything. I was the general manager and coach so I figured that I had to bring someone in here to replace myself as the coach. I hadn't had a lot of success doing that because I had brought in Larry Popein and that didn't work out and I brought in Boomer Geoffrion and that didn't work out. So, I figured Ferguson would be the logical candidate. So I called him and arranged to interview him in Montreal.

"I always respected John Ferguson as a player, not only with Montreal but in Cleveland before that. I had played in Cleveland, so I had gotten to know him real well and I thought he was a very important guy to the Montreal Canadiens organization when they brought him in there. He changed the complexion of that team completely.

"John Ferguson came from British Columbia and one of the big things out there is lacrosse and he was a real good lacrosse player. Now in Canada they had just started a professional lacrosse league and John had the franchise in Montreal and he was the president, owner, and coach. So when I talked to him about coming to New York, he said, 'Well, we're in our first year in the league and I really can't tell you that I'm that interested right now. I own this team and I want to look after my investment.' And I told him that I understood how he felt. That's where it stopped. So then I hired Ron Stewart, who had played for me and had an excellent resume as far as coaching in the minors. He had won a championship in Springfield and went out to the West Coast and did very well. So that's why I hired Ron Stewart. Because I knew I couldn't continue to do both jobs."

Harry Howell's name also came up as a possible candidate, but many thought that he would have been too easy on the players.

Ron Stewart played for six different teams during his 21-year NHL career, winning three Stanley Cups with Toronto. Used primarily as a defensive specialist, Stewart scored 44 goals including eight short-handers and a dozen game-winners and added 37 assists in 306 games over six seasons with the Blueshirts.

Following his retirement at the end of the 1972–73 season, Stewart became the coach of the Portland Buckaroos of the Western Hockey League, a position that Francis had recommended him for. He took

Portland to the WHL finals where they lost to the Phoenix Roadrunners. The next season he moved to Springfield of the AHL, leading the Indians to the Calder Cup championship. Although he only had two years of minor league coaching experience, Stewart had a reputation of being a no-nonsense disciplinarian. Francis signed him to a two-year contract.

There were also changes in the executive suite at the Garden that didn't bode well for the Rangers. Alan Cohen had been named President and Chief Executive Officer of Madison Square Garden. Cohen had a reputation as a "bottom-liner" and he came armed with a mandate to trim payroll and get rid of any dead wood as he saw fit.

EMILE FRANCIS: "Alan Cohen came out of nowhere and he didn't know a puck from a Sputnik. The first time I met him was at a Frank Sinatra concert at Madison Square Garden. Sinatra was making a comeback and I was there with my wife and Dennis Ball who was my assistant general manager and his wife. All of a sudden Alan Cohen came wandering over with his two daughters who were about eighteen, nineteen years old. So these girls start asking me, 'How come you dealt this guy, how come you dealt that guy?' So I'm trying to be as nice as I can, but I tell Alan that those girls had no business talking about this stuff here. It was in front of a group of people and he stood there like a nothin'.

"So the next day I had to go back in the office and I call in Dennis Ball. And I said 'Dennis, you and I have been together a long time and that could end very shortly, because that guy you met last night, Alan Cohen, the new chairman and president of Madison Square Garden, he and I could tangle. I can't tell you when but it's gonna happen. But when that happens, I'll be gone because he's the guy who will make the ultimate decision and they'll bring in somebody new and you could be gone too. So in the next few months I'm gonna look for a place for you because you've been a loyal, hardworking guy and I'm gonna find a place for you other than here with the New York Rangers. So he says, 'No they couldn't do that.' I said, believe me, they can do anything they want. I'm gonna find you a job and I got him a job with the St. Louis Blues as assistant general manager.

"I was also worried about Frank Paice who had been a trainer for the Rangers for thirty years and he didn't even have a pension with Madison

Square Garden. He had a pension with the Rangers but it was small and of course he had Social Security. So I called him in July and told him, Frank, I want to talk to you and your wife, come out this weekend to Long Beach. So I got the two of them together and said, Frank you don't have a pension with Madison Square Garden, the only way I can get you a pension is by you agreeing with me saying you're gonna retire. I'll approach Bill Jennings and tell him you're been here thirty years and you should have a pension. So he says I don't want to retire. I said, Frank listen to me, I'm not gonna be around here too long. I'm gonna tangle with that guy they just brought in and when that happens, they could bring in somebody new and you could be wiped right out. I'm trying to look after you and your wife, so tell me that you'll retire and I'll get you a pension, because Bill Jennings and I are very close and I can make it happen. So he says, if that's what you want. I said, I don't want it; I just want to make sure that you and your wife are looked after. So I talked to Jennings and I got him a pension. It wasn't a big one but it was something. It was more than he had."

Francis was also busy on the trading front, attempting to rebuild the Rangers in the same manner he did years before: from the goal out.

With both Giacomin and Villemure in their mid-thirties and showing signs of aging, Emile went out and acquired John Davidson from the St. Louis Blues. Davidson was considered by many to be the best young netminder in the league. The deal also brought veteran winger Bill Collins back to the Rangers in exchange for three of the toughest Rangers: Ted Irvine, Jerry Butler, and Bert Wilson.

TED IRVINE: "The trade was pretty devastating. We had lost to the Islanders in overtime the previous year and you could see the dismantling of the team coming. But when Jerry Butler, Bert Wilson, and I got traded it hurt. Dennis Ball was the GM in St. Louis and they had high hopes for us. But we got to St. Louis and it was a good bunch of guys but it wasn't such a together team as we had in New York. So you realized how good you had it in New York.

"We'd go back to play the Rangers and there was a real emptiness. It was pretty much the end of my career because it just wasn't the same comradeship or emotion when you went into other teams' buildings. So that was the downfall of my career, I just didn't have a spark after that. Because in New York I had a role and the guys respected me for it and I respected them and to this day we talk about not winning that Stanley Cup and how close we were. And then Eddie Giacomin getting traded that hurt him and all the guys said, boy, I sure wish we could have won it together. You think you're gonna get back to it but you just don't.

"And I'll tell you about contract negotiations. People ask if we had lawyers in those days. No, we didn't need them because we dealt with Emile Francis. I was making $15,000 when I came to New York and Emile said, 'You can't live on that,' so he gave me a two-year contract for $19,000. That first year I got twenty goals and went to see him in training camp in Kitchener.

I said, 'Emile I had a pretty good year and I'd like to renegotiate.'

"He said, 'Teddy, you've got another year on your contract. What are you gonna do if I don't sign you?'

"I said there's an investment company in Canada that said if I don't play hockey they'd take me on right away. He asked me the name of the company, I told him and he reached across the table shook my hand and said good luck, they're a good company! So I looked at him and said uh-oh. So he started to laugh. He said, we think you had a good year too, what do you think you're worth?

"I said $25,000.

"He said that's a lot of money.

"I said, I know.

"[He said] 'Well, we've been thinking about it and we're gonna give you $27,500 for each of the next two years.'

"So I walked out of the room and said, 'I think there's something wrong here. I think I was supposed to ask for $30,000.'

"But we had a lot of fun and great, great memories. I still remember the fans in New York, 'Hey Irvine, ya bum!' I loved it. I absolutely loved it."

John Davidson had been the Blues' first pick in the 1973 amateur draft following four strong seasons with Calgary of the WCJHL, taking home the MVP award in his final season in 1972–73. The son of a Canadian

Mounted Policeman, Davidson went directly from juniors to the NHL and was one of the leading candidates for the NHL's Rookie of the Year award. Unfortunately, he was hampered by a knee injury late in the season and the award eventually went to Denis Potvin of the Islanders.

At 6-foot-3, 200 pounds, the twenty-two-year-old Davidson took up a lot of net. But he was also extremely agile for a big man. Davidson showed great promise in his two years in St. Louis, posting a 3.37 GAA in 79 games for the offensive-minded Blues. But during the offseason the Blues had acquired Gilles Gratton, a young netminder playing for the Toronto Toros of the WHA and also signed their top draft choice, goaltender Ed Staniowski, making Davidson expendable.

Francis also signed winger Pat Hickey and center Wayne Dillon, who were both previous Rangers draft selections but had decided to play for Toronto of the WHA instead. Hickey, twenty-two, was selected in the second round of the 1973 amateur draft after the Blueshirts had taken Rick Middleton. In two seasons with the Toros, the tough, speedy winger scored 61 goals with 63 assists along with 102 penalty minutes. To help sweeten the pot for Hickey, the Rangers also selected his younger brother Greg in the 1975 draft and signed him to a contract.

Wayne Dillon, twenty, was the Rangers' top choice in the 1975 draft. Following an outstanding 1972–73 season with the Toronto Marlboros of the OHA in which he scored 47 goals and added 60 assists, Dillon decided to forego his final two seasons of junior hockey to play in the WHA. In two seasons with the Toros, Wayne recorded 59 goals and 101 assists.

The acquisitions of Davidson, Hickey, and Dillon along with the continued development of younger players like Rick Middleton, Steve Vickers, and Ron Greschner was indicative of the turnover the Blueshirts had experienced during the last few seasons. Only eight players remained from the team that lost to Boston in the 1972 Stanley Cup Finals: Stemkowski, Tkaczuk, Fairbairn, Giacomin, Villemure, Park, Ratelle, and Gilbert, and even that would change very shortly.

The Rangers got off to a dismal start, going 4–5–1 through the month of October. And following three consecutive lopsided losses to Buffalo (9–1), the Islanders (7–1), and Philadelphia (7–2), Francis was livid and laced into the team, telling them that he was putting them all on 72-hour recallable waivers. What followed was perhaps the most chaotic ten-day stretch in Rangers history, a period in which Emile Francis deconstructed the team he had painstakingly built over the past ten years.

Surprisingly, the first player to go was Gilles Villemure, who was sent to Chicago for veteran defenseman Doug Jarrett on October 28. Villemure hadn't been playing, had recently gone through a divorce, and told Francis that if he could get anything for him he should trade him. Villemure, who was thirty-five years old, had spent his entire career in the Rangers organization, making brief appearances for the Blueshirts in the mid-1960s before earning a spot as Giacomin's partner in 1970–71. In 184 games as a Ranger, Gilles posted an impressive 98–53–23 record with 13 shutouts and a 2.62 GAA. In 14 playoff appearances, the steady little netminder posted a 5–5 record with a 2.93 GAA. Meanwhile, Jarrett, who had not played for Chicago due to a knee injury, not surprisingly reinjured his knee in his first game with the Blueshirts and sat out the next two weeks.

GILLES VILLEMURE: "I was having problems at home and I said to Emile, if you want to trade me go ahead and the next day I was gone. There was a big turnover there. I don't know why or who was behind it. You hear different stories. But everybody was being moved."

Two days later, Derek Sanderson was sent to St. Louis for a first-round pick in the 1977 draft. Sanderson was coming off an outstanding comeback season, scoring 25 goals with 25 assists and finished with a +10 defensive rating. Unfortunately, he and Stewart had a run-in when Sanderson was a rookie with the Bruins and now ten years later, the new Rangers coach didn't want him around. Sanderson then scored five goals in his first six games in St. Louis, including a last-minute goal in a 5–3 victory over the Rangers.

DEREK SANDERSON: "The Cat told Stewart you've got five centermen, you've got Ratelle, Stemkowski, Tkaczuk, Dillon, and Sanderson, which one goes. Ron Stewart and I had a fight in my rookie year with

Boston and Stewart said get rid of Sanderson. Emile said, 'He was a plus 10, he had 25 goals and 25 assists, I don't really want to lose him. Think that over.' And Stewart said no, I don't want him on my team. So that was it.

"I had a good year. I liked it in New York. I lived on 59th and First Avenue in one of those high rise buildings looking over the Queensboro Bridge. Gilbert and I were the only two that lived in the city. We used to get off the bus from the airport and we were home. The rest of the guys parked their cars at the rink and had to drive home from there. And then Greschner and Middleton used to get off the bus with me and stay over because we used to go out and party. It was great. New York was great. I've never been in a town where you go to bed at four o'clock, sleep to eight or nine and then get up and go to dinner. It was crazy and it was open all night. It was a tough spot for me but it was a lot of fun. Great bunch of guys, great city. Everybody was nice."

The next day happened to be Halloween and following practice the Rangers were getting ready for a flight to Montreal for a game the following night. At about 4 p.m. Ed Giacomin received a phone call from Emile Francis asking him to meet him at the Rangers practice rink in Long Beach at 6:30. When Giacomin reminded Francis that he'd miss the flight to Montreal, the GM responded, "You're not going to Montreal."

When Giacomin arrived at the Long Beach site Francis told him that Detroit had claimed him on waivers and that he was no longer a New York Ranger.

ED GIACOMIN: "It was a Friday night, after the team had left for Montreal. I got a call from Emile to come down to Long Beach where we practiced. It was an eerie night, with the wind coming off the bay and not a car in the parking lot, and then he tells me that he put me on waivers and that I was picked up by Detroit. They didn't even get a player in return, but supposedly they got $30,000. I look back to 1975 even today and I still don't completely understand what happened. I was thirty-six years old at the time and after ten years with the Rangers, I honestly believe I was one of the most down to earth, honest individuals to ever wear a Rangers sweater. Because I did everything I could for the game and the community and at no time did the almighty dollar enter my mind.

"When I became a Ranger they traded four players for me [Marcel Paille, Jim Mikol, Aldo Guidolin, and Sandy McGregor] and I made the lowest salary a goalie could ever make. If you were the number one draft choice you made a million dollars and I was comparable to a first-round pick in those days and I made $9,500. I wanted to play professional hockey and I was fortunate enough to be a New York Ranger.

"I made the NHL when there were six teams and I was one of only six goalies playing in the league so the salary didn't mean anything to me. I just wanted to be in the NHL. Luckily I was rewarded as time went on thanks to Emile Francis who understood the game and backed the goaltender."

News of the deal filtered out slowly and even Giacomin's teammates didn't know that he was no longer a Ranger. During the 6 o'clock news, WNBC TV's Marv Albert reported that the Rangers had made a deal but that the player involved had not yet been notified and details were not available. That night at 11 p.m. WNBC's anchorman, Chuck Scarborough, ran down the three top stories as a lead-in for the broadcast. The first two items have long been forgotten but he finished by saying "... and the Rangers ice Ed Giacomin."

Walt MacPeek of the *Newark Star-Ledger* called Jean Ratelle in his Montreal hotel room to get his reaction to the trade. Ratelle thought MacPeek was referring to the Sanderson deal and was shocked to learn that Giacomin was now a Red Wing. "It can't be true," the stunned Ratelle replied. "We knew Eddie wasn't on the plane but we thought he was coming up the next day. I'm shocked that they got rid of Eddie. It wasn't his fault. Maybe I'm next to go," he said prophetically.

Francis later explained that he wanted to develop the twenty-two-year-old Davidson as the next Rangers starter but knew he couldn't play him in the Garden where every goal he surrendered would bring chants of "Eddie . . . Eddie." It wasn't fair to the young netminder. Giacomin had started four games thus far that season, going 0-3-1 and allowing 19 goals. Francis had been trying to make a deal for Eddie over the summer. However, at thirty-six with a bad knee and a $175,000 salary he found no takers for him, so he had to put him on waivers. "It was one of the toughest decisions I ever had to make," Francis told the assembled media. "But I've got to put the interests of the New York Rangers ahead of my personal feelings. We're not pinpointing Eddie. In no way was this a shove at him. I have the greatest respect for Ed Giacomin. He gave us outstanding service for many years. There's no finer competitor in the game. But we've got to rebuild the team."

At the time of the deal it wasn't clear whether Giacomin would actually report to the Red Wings or retire. And ironically, the Red Wings' next game would be in New York against the Rangers on Sunday night. The afternoon of the game Giacomin and his longtime friend and accountant Paul Levine met with Red Wings GM Alex Delvecchio at the Statler-Hilton hotel across from the Garden. After talking with Delvecchio about his future with Detroit, Eddie agreed to play for the Wings that night.

Giacomin then walked to the hotel where the Rangers were staying and chatted with some of his former teammates in the coffee shop. A few hours later he stepped out on to the Garden ice for warm ups wearing a Red Wings uniform with number 31 on the back.

Eddie had always played with a lot of emotion and the fans returned that emotion tenfold that evening. The Blueshirts became the visiting team in their own building as the noise level and electricity in the Garden that night were greater than at any time in recent memory. The soldout crowd chanted "Eddie . . . Eddie" throughout warmups and the National Anthem, delaying the start of the game as Giacomin's former teammates at the other end of the ice tapped their sticks to the rhythm of the crowd. Eddie wiped the tears away and stopped 42 shots to beat the Rangers 6–4 as the crowd cheered every save made by Giacomin and booed every Ranger goal. Some of the Rangers apologized to Giacomin for scoring on him that night.

BRAD PARK: "In the summer I was surprised because we traded Teddy Irvine, Bert Wilson, and Jerry Butler to St. Louis for Billy Collins who was thirty-two years old and John Davidson who was a promising goal-tender. So I knew we had three goaltenders and that was going to create a logjam. Then when Eddie went that was a total surprise. Eddie was a fixture with the Rangers and Madison Square Garden and when he came back to play we actually threw the game. There's no doubt about it. It was the only game I'd ever thrown in my life. But that was the amount of respect we had for Eddie."

ED GIACOMIN: "There's no doubt in my mind, the best memory of my career was November 2, 1975. I don't think any athlete has been treated that way. Every other athlete has had a planned evening, but this was not planned. And I think it happened because, since I spent ten years with the Rangers, I also spent ten years with their fans. Everything I went through, they went through. Every goal, every win or loss, every fight. They went through it with me. And I think the feeling was, 'How could you do that to one of us?' And I firmly believe that because of what the New York fans did for me that night I made the Hall of Fame. Because there are certain criteria for making the Hall of Fame. You have to have records, but most have been on Stanley Cup winners, I wasn't. I had something rare. I was so popular because of the New York fans. And I said it then and I'll say it now, the New York fans, who I enjoyed playing for so much, put me in the Hall of Fame."

EMILE FRANCIS: "The crowd was chanting 'Eddie . . . Eddie' for the first fifty-five minutes and 'Kill the Cat' for the last five. I remember the chief of security came running down and said, 'Emile, we gotta protect you.' I said, 'Listen, I walked in here by myself, I'll walk out of here by myself. Somebody may get me but I'll take a couple with me, believe me.'"

Following the game, many of Giacomin's former teammates who would have normally gone out to eat and drink in the city, gathered at Eddie's home in Manhasset instead. They came by to pay their respects and give Eddie a proper sendoff, talking and drinking until the wee hours of the morning.

But Giacomin was not the last to go. Less than a week later on November 7, in a deal that shocked the hockey world, Jean Ratelle, Brad Park, and minor league defenseman Joe Zanussi were sent to Boston for Phil Esposito and Carol Vadnais. Francis and Boston's GM Harry Sinden had been talking about a trade for more than a month. The deal originally included Espo and defenseman Dallas Smith, but Francis didn't want Smith and insisting on Vadnais instead.

EMILE FRANCIS: "We were both playing like horseshit. And I had brought in Ron Stewart to coach, because I was at the point that I couldn't do both jobs and remember we were in a war with the WHA back then too. So, we both got off to a bad start. And we would have never made a deal with Boston or Montreal or Philadelphia. But Harry Sinden and I were at a meeting and I said, 'Harry, we're both going bad. Have you ever thought of making a trade?' He said really? But I said there's no sense talking about the deuces and the treys, in other words the seventeenth or eighteenth players. If we're going to make a trade let's talk about some key players. So, he said let's talk in a couple of days and we talked for about a month. We were probably both really hoping that the teams would straighten out and start playing better. But it didn't happen. So I remember saying to him, 'Harry, we'd be willing to talk about trading a couple of key guys Ratelle and Park if you put in Esposito and Orr.'

"'Oh, no way' he said, 'I'd never trade Bobby Orr.'

"So I said, 'Let's keep talking,' and eventually neither team got straightened out and we had to do something so we did. We kept talking and eventually we made the trade. I sure as hell didn't want to trade Park and Ratelle and he didn't want to trade Esposito and he sure as hell wouldn't trade Orr but the thing was neither team was getting any better so we had to try to do something to straighten things out.

"I knew we had our shot at winning the Cup and didn't make it so now we had to do something. That's why you're the general manager you've got to make those decisions.

"Same as when you win, you've got to know when to move people because if you stay with the same team eventually it's gonna catch up to you and then you've got nothing. You've gotta keep rebuilding. That's what happened with the Islanders, they won four in a row but then they all got old and hurt and they were done."

The Rangers were in Oakland that morning and Park knew something was up when he got a call from Stewart at 7 a.m. asking him to come to his room. He knew they weren't going to be talking about strategy. He knocked on the coach's door and when Stewart opened it, Park asked, "Where am I going?" "Boston," replied Stewart.

Park's main concern was his family and his twenty-two-month-old son Robbie who had cerebral palsy and was getting special care in New York. Now he would have to find a hospital in Boston that could also care for his son.

BRAD PARK: "We were on a West Coast swing. I was the captain and somewhat of a big name on the team and probably the highest paid guy at that time. So I felt somewhat secure that I was a major part of the organization so that when it happened it was a major shock. My first reaction was that I didn't want to go but then I sat down and I contemplated and I said this is my job and that's part of the job. So if it's a bad situation I'll go and make the best of it. If it's a good situation, I'll move forward. Did I have a bad taste for the Rangers for doing it—yeah. I was very upset with them."

The trade also meant that Park would be playing in Boston where he was once public enemy number one because of the comments he made in his book, *Play the Man*.

BRAD PARK: "Most of the guys I had conflicts with were gone. Bobby Orr and I got along terrific. Another guy I might've had a conflict with was Wayne Cashman and he turned out to be a terrific guy and Terry O'Reilly was wonderful. When we got there the team was in last place and they started to do much better. Unfortunately, after ten games Bobby's knee went out on him again and he never played for the Bruins again."

At the time of the trade many fans and members of the media thought Park was overweight and out of shape. But in reality Brad was suffering from "the gunk" which was a nasty rash that many players had at the time. The puffiness that made Brad look overweight was actually a reaction to the steroids he was taking to ease the itching that was caused by the rash.

HOWIE ROSE: "Something wasn't right with Park that the Bruins were able to straighten out. I think Brad said it had to do with his medication, because he had 'the gunk,' an allergy to the equipment. And he was gaining weight, not because he was overeating, but because the medication they were giving him was a steroid apparently and it made him balloon to some extent. But it wasn't poor conditioning or anything else that had Park playing below his standards it was just the wrong medications. Well, he got to Boston and they changed all that and he was an All-Star for many years to come. Jean Ratelle was always going to be a favorite, but they were getting Phil Esposito and there's something to be said for that."

BRAD PARK: "I had 'the gunk' and I went to a dermatologist out in Cedarhurst, Long Island, and she looked at it and took samples of it. She said, 'I don't know what this is, I don't think I can cure it but I can give you steroids that will stop you from scratching.' I said okay because that's a big part of it. What happened was with the steroids my weight stayed the same but my jowls swelled up and my head turned curly so I didn't look like I was in shape but my weight was exactly the same. Once I got traded to Boston the trainers started washing my hockey underwear every day which they hadn't done in New York so basically once I got there they started washing my underwear every day and cleaning it and the gunk went away and I wasn't taking any more steroids. The trainers in New York a lot of times it was easier just to hang the underwear up and let it dry, I mean they might have washed it once a week but in Boston John Forrestal was the trainer and he washed it every day."

Up the coast in Vancouver, Bruins coach Don Cherry was breaking the news of the trade to Esposito. Phil had heard rumors about being dealt and knew that it was a part of a player's life. When Cherry and Bobby Orr knocked on his hotel room door that morning he knew they weren't there to shoot the breeze. When Cherry began to tell him about the trade, Espo stopped him in his tracks. "Grapes, if you tell me it's New York I'll jump out that window." Cherry responded, "Bobby, get away from the window."

Espo's linemate, Wayne Cashman, wasn't too happy about the trade either. Upon hearing the news, he trashed his hotel room, and threw the television through the window into the parking lot below.

Rangers PR Director John Halligan and his assistant, who happened to be his wife Janet, had forty-eight hours' notice of the deal and were told that there were to be no leaks to anybody. So that morning, they had to call every Rangers beat reporter at 8:30 a.m. telling them that there would be an 11 a.m. press conference. When one of the scribes asked Janet if it was "big," she replied, "Would I be calling you if it wasn't?"

Park and Ratelle stopped by the Rangers locker room to pick up their equipment and say goodbye to their suddenly former teammates. They then flew to Vancouver where they each had an assist in Boston's 4–2 loss to the Canucks the next night.

EMILE FRANCIS: "Believe me, trading Jean Ratelle was just as hard as putting Ed Giacomin on waivers. You have to remember that Ratty and I had been together for fifteen years. We started out in juniors. But before he left for Boston, he and his wife came over and he said I can't thank you enough for all the years I've been with you, starting in juniors. He was such a classy guy. Usually you trade a guy and he says 'Screw you.' But not him. That was just the way he was and just a real good player. In fact three, four months after we made the trade I ran into Harry Sinden and he said, 'You know something, we never realized how good a hockey player Jean Ratelle was until we got him.'

"The thing I feel sorry for Jean as well as Rod Gilbert and Brad Park, they never won a Stanley Cup. I never coached a team to the Stanley Cup. We always seemed to have the bad luck of getting the wrong players hurt at the wrong time. We did everything but win. We had some good teams but to win the Stanley Cup you gotta be good and you gotta be lucky. And you gotta stay away from injuries."

WALT TKACZUK: "The trade broke my heart. I think because we hadn't won for all those years with some good teams, probably upper management above Emile Francis, they told him, 'Listen, you gotta do something.' And they tried to make trades to make the team better. They gave away some pretty good players in that process. They got rid of Rick Middleton for Kenny Hodge who didn't play too long for the Rangers and Middleton played the next ten years for the Bruins and probably scored twenty-five to thirty-five goals a number of times for the Bruins. So they made some decisions that weren't as well thought out as they should have been.

"They traded Park, Ratelle, they got rid of Eddie Giacomin, later they traded Billy Fairbairn, the whole team was changing. They never got rid of me, I think I was under contract, maybe nobody wanted me. I don't know what their reason was but it didn't feel real comfortable being there. It took the heart right out of me.

"For the first few years I just didn't feel real good about being there. Then after a while I started getting my mind back in shape and that's so important, to be mentally ready to play. But it took the heart out of some of the players that were there in the early seventies. And then they brought in some good players like Anders Hedberg and Ulf Nilsson and John Davidson came in and he was a fantastic goaltender. John brought us to the finals and we had a good team then. He basically stood on his head. Johnny had a bad knee and a bad back but he was stopping everything they were throwing at him."

Esposito had won five scoring titles, two MVP awards, and a pair of Stanley Cups in Boston. He was acquired for his scoring ability and because the Rangers needed a vocal leader and Espo certainly was vocal. He was named captain right away but wasn't happy about it. In his 2003 autobiography, *Thunder and Lightning,* written with Peter Golenbock, Espo explained that when he reported to the Rangers in Oakland, not only was he given Larry Sacharuk's number 5 jersey, even though Sacharuk was with the team but not playing, it also had a "C" on it signifying that Phil would be replacing Park as Ranger captain. "I can't be captain of this team, I just got here," Espo told trainer Frank Paice.

"What the fuck is going on here? I couldn't believe how stupid they were. Rod Gilbert should have been the team captain, or Walt Tkaczuk. Years later I asked Emile Francis why and he said, 'I wouldn't have made Rod Gilbert captain if he was the only player on the team.' The Cat said Rod wasn't the captain type. I disagreed with him totally."

WALT TKACZUK: "I don't know if guys make a big deal out of that whether you're captain or assistant captain they just play the game. The captains and assistant captains are communicators; they're supposed to be leaders and communicate the thoughts of the players to the coaching staff. And Phil was a good communicator and a good player so I don't think there were any issues there. Not that I was aware of anyway."

Esposito scored two goals and added an assist in his Ranger debut, a 7–5 loss to the Seals in Oakland on the night of the trade. Vadnais didn't report to the Rangers until nearly a week later due to a complication in his contract—a "no-trade" clause that nobody seemed to notice. "I was shocked by the trade," Vadnais told reporters. "How could I be traded when my contract said I couldn't be? I had asked for the clause because it's aggravating to be uprooted in the middle of the season, moving a family out of one house into another. I told them trade me in the summer but not during the season. But they did anyhow and so what else can you do? You ask them to make it up in dollars."

HOWIE ROSE: "The era ended on November 7, 1975, when Emile made the trade with the Bruins. They ceased to be Emile Francis's Rangers after that. And that didn't necessarily have to be a bad thing if Emile would have been given the time to rework it. But it just reeked of desperation. It worked out okay, they didn't get fleeced, but as far as the era of Emile Francis—it ended the day he shook hands with Harry Sinden."

If there was one person who was happy with the events of the previous two weeks it was Alan "Bottom Line" Cohen, the new president and

CEO of the Garden, the guy who was rumored to have ordered Francis to trim the payroll. Despite having to lay out more cash to keep Vadnais happy, it was estimated that the four deals saved the Rangers about $250,000 in salaries.

Unfortunately, Cohen was not happy that all the changes in personnel did little to help the Blueshirts get over the .500 mark. At the time of the trade with Boston, the Rangers had a 5–7–1 record. Six weeks later on December 23, they were 15–17–4 and going nowhere. The Rangers had an eight-day break in their schedule that year to accommodate "Super Series '76" in which two teams from the Soviet Union played an eight-game exhibition series against NHL teams. The Soviets won five of the eight games (5–2–1) including a 7–3 victory over the Rangers. However the break in the schedule gave Cohen the opportunity to access the performance of Coach Ron Stewart as well as Francis.

EMILE FRANCIS: "We had five rookies on that team. It takes at least three months when you're breaking in rookies. It was Christmas Eve and my phone rings. Now in all the years I ran that team, Irving Mitchell Felt [former MSG chairman and president] would meet with Bill Jennings and I in the beginning of the season and at the end of the season and that was it. He never called me, never interfered, nothing. So this guy Cohen calls me on Christmas Eve, and he told me. 'I want you to fire the guy you brought in here, Stewart, and you go back in and coach yourself.' So I said to him, 'Let me tell you something. I've run this team for twelve years and I didn't need any help and I don't need any now.' And I hung up the phone.

"I was so pissed off. I knew he and I were gonna tangle. So at that time I was chairman of the general managers committee and we had a meeting scheduled in Montreal that weekend. So I had to go to Montreal and after the meeting I went back to the hotel and was sitting there with Steve Brklacich, one of my top scouts and the phone rings. It's Bill Jennings. He says 'How are you?'

"'Fine.'

"'How'd your meeting go?'

"'Good.'

"He said, 'Where are you going from here?'

"I said 'the Rangers are playing in St Louis on Tuesday, so I'm planning to fly out there tomorrow.'

"So he says, 'Evidentially, Alan Cohen spoke to you over the last week.'

"So I said, 'Yes, Christmas Eve.'

"So he says, 'Mr. Cohen would like to meet with you tomorrow at 2 p.m. in room 200 at the Garden.'

"I said, 'Okay I'll be there.'

"He said he'll be there.

"I said fine.

"I hung up the phone and said to Steve, 'Well, this is something I anticipated and this is it.' He said, 'What do you mean?' I told him, 'I gotta meet Alan Cohen tomorrow at the Garden at 2 p.m. This is it!'

"Anyway, I got back to New York about 11 a.m. and went to my office and started getting my things together. So my secretary for many years, Rita White, comes in and says 'What are you doing, Mr. Francis?' I said, 'Rita, I gotta meet Mr. Cohen at 2 p.m. and this is it.' She said, 'Are you kidding?' I said, 'No I'm not. I'm an old Boy Scout, always be prepared.'

"So I go up to room 200 and ring the doorbell and Bill Jennings opens the door and he's got a glass in his hand and he tells me to come in and sit down. So I go in and ask Bill, where's Mr. Cohen? 'Oh, he said he had a very urgent meeting and wouldn't be able to be here. I've got to speak to you on his behalf.' So I said go ahead.

"He says, 'These are your choices. You can quit or you can be fired.'

"So I said to him, Bill you've been with me now for twelve years, have you ever seen me quit on anything? I took over you guys when you had one playoff in nine years, I've never quit on anything in my life. You go ahead, you wanna fire me, go ahead.

"He said 'You're fired!' And then he said 'It will take about twenty minutes for us to get a press release together to announce what happened.'

"I said, 'I'll tell you what you can do with your press release, stick it up your ass. And I grabbed my briefcase, said 'See ya later' and I left.

"I got home and I remember my wife saying, 'Don't you feel bad?' I said not a bit. I never look behind, I'm looking ahead. I'm not worried about this. If that's the way they want to operate, it's their decision. I'm not worried about getting another job in the National Hockey League. I had several job offers within twenty-four hours, believe me. But I held out until I got the deal that I wanted. I said that if I ever ran another team I want to own part of that team. And any interview I had, and I had about four, I'd say, okay I'd be interested in coming here, but I want 10 percent of the team. And they'd say no, and I'd say, fine there's nothing more to talk about and I'd get up and leave."

In the meantime, Bill Jennings knew that Francis had spoken to John Ferguson during the summer and called the former Canadiens enforcer asking him to come to New York immediately. Fergie was on a business trip at the time but took the next flight out. When the pair met at the Garden, Jennings offered him the general manager's position. "I don't want to take the Cat's job," Ferguson told Jennings. "We've got to make a change," replied Jennings. "I'll talk to Emile. He'll be moved up to vice president." Ferguson signed a four-year deal that would pay him $100,000 annually. Francis had previously offered him only a one-year deal to coach the team when the two had met during the summer.

Francis was replaced as GM by Ferguson on January 7. Fergie also replaced Stewart behind the bench, giving the former coach a job in the scouting department. Ferguson was the first GM or coach in the Rangers' fifty-year history who was hired from outside of the organization and at thirty-seven became the youngest general manager in the NHL. He gained exposure while serving as assistant coach and assistant GM for Team Canada in 1972. Ferguson impressed many with his upbeat attitude even when the Russians dominated early in the eight-game series. He had been offered coaching positions by the Bruins, Blues, Kings, Canucks, and the Toronto Toros of the WHA. But he held out until offered a general manager's position, so he could have more control over his own destiny and bring in the type of players he wanted.

Emile still had two years left on his contract and retained his position as vice president of the Rangers, limiting himself to administrative duties with nothing to do with the day-to-day operations of the team.

BRAD PARK: "They had basically dispersed the team, you know the trade over the summer with St. Louis, myself, Eddie Giacomin, Gilles Villemure, Derek Sanderson went. They had ruptured the nucleus of the hockey club so it really was not a surprise when Emile was let go. I thought about it and I don't think Emile wanted to do all those deals. I think that it came from upstairs but it was the wrong decision, I mean he was the best general manager they had in thirty years.

"We were a family with all those guys. There wasn't an ego on the team that would cause a problem. We all got along; there were no rivalries, no dislikes for anybody. On the road after a game we would all go to the same restaurant, after practice we would all go to the same place for lunch. It was just a great group to be together."

BILL FAIRBAIRN: "That was pretty sad. We still had a good team and why it was broken up I'll never know. You can't just take the top players and bring in other top players from other teams and make it work because you're taking two players and putting them with fifteen other players. Yeah, that was kind of the decline of the team and when that happened with the Cat it kind of demoralized a lot of the players that played for him back then. You try to put out but it was different, a lot different."

WALT TKACZUK: "What I liked about Emile was that he made everybody feel that they were important on the team. Whether they were the goal scorers, the checkers or the third and fourth liners he had a role for everybody to play and every role was important to win hockey games and he made you and your role important so that you wanted to play for him."

Once Ferguson got to see the Rangers up close he immediately pronounced them overpaid and out of shape. His goal was to restore their pride and self-respect.

When Fergie took over, the Blueshirts had a 15–20–4 record. They won their first two games with their new boss behind the bench but then went winless in their next seven games. They also went through a nine-game winless streak from February 20 to March 11 and finished the season in last place in the Patrick Division with a 29–42–9 record and missed the playoffs for the first time in nine years, scoring only 262 goals and surrendering 333, the most in franchise history.

Injuries limited Davidson's playing time and the Rangers, who had started the season with Giacomin and Villemure—once the best one-two goaltending combo in the league—were forced to rely on Dunc Wilson and rookie Doug Soetaert in net. Rod Gilbert scored 36 goals along with 50 assists to lead the team in scoring with 86 points. Steve Vickers finished right behind him with 30-53-83 and Esposito scored 29 goals and added 38 assists for 67 points. Carol Vadnais scored 20 goals and added 30 assists.

The Bruins, on the other hand, were able to turn their season around, finishing first in the Adams Division with 113 points. Jean Ratelle scored 31 goals with 59 assists in 67 games with Boston and added eight goals in the playoffs, the most of his NHL career, and added eight assists. Brad Park scored 16 goals with 37 assists in 43 games and added three goals and eight assists in the playoffs.

Ed Giacomin appeared in 29 games for Detroit, posting a 12–14–3 record with a 3.45 GAA and two shutouts. Gilles Villemure saw action in 15 games with the Black Hawks, going 2–7–5 with a 4.29 GAA. Derek Sanderson registered 24 goals and 43 assists for the Blues in 65 games and added another goal in the playoffs.

In his twelve years as general manager, Emile Francis took a team that hadn't gotten into the playoffs in four seasons and built it into a perennial contender that made it to the postseason for nine consecutive years.

Francis still holds the Rangers record for most games coached, 654 (342–209–103), most coaching victories, winning percentage (.602), most playoff games coached 75 (34–41), and most playoff victories.

EMILE FRANCIS: "Bill Jennings was a partner in Simpson Thacher and Bartlett, one of the biggest law firms in New York. And one of their biggest clients was Madison Square Garden. So that's why he was in no position to stand up for me when this guy [Alan Cohen] came on the scene. I swore that I'd never talk to Bill Jennings again. When I went to St. Louis, he'd call me and my wife would answer the phone and I'd tell her, 'I'm not here.' But then he got sick with cancer and his wife Betsy called and said, 'Bill always said that you were the best friend he ever had. He's dying and I'd really appreciate it if you came to see him. He'd really like to see you.' I told her I'd be there and went the next day. It was lucky that I went because he died three days later. But we had been together for so long.

"Then when Bill died, his wife called and said, 'Bill would like you to do his eulogy, would you agree to do that?' I said I certainly would. So we went and the minister says, 'And now to deliver the eulogy,' and I start to stand up, 'is the Secretary of State Cyrus Vance.' Bill and Vance had gone to Princeton and Yale together and he spoke and was as dry as dry could be. So he finishes and the minister asks me to speak. I went up there and I had them crying and laughing within ten minutes because I knew Bill better than anybody. And I said for you people in here no doubt he'd talk to you and have lunch with you. But it took me awhile to figure out that all he was doing having lunch with me was figuring out what we were gonna talk about at ten o'clock that night! I finally had to tell him, Bill, I get up at six in the morning. I can't get on the phone at ten at night and talk for an hour or two. You wanna talk to me, talk to me when we're having lunch. I had them laughing."

Gone But Never Forgotten

Ed Giacomin, Jean Ratelle, and Brad Park each left their mark on the Rangers record book as well as their fans.

In 538 games with the Rangers, Giacomin posted a 266–172–89 record with 49 shutouts and an overall 2.73 GAA. In 65 playoff games, Eddie was less successful, going 29–35 with one shutout and a 2.81 GAA.

Giacomin shared the Vezina Trophy with Gilles Villemure in 1970–71 and was voted the team's MVP three times and won the Frank Boucher Trophy as the most popular Ranger. He played in six All-Star games and was selected to the First All-Star team twice and the Second team three times.

Giacomin held the team record for most shutouts (49) until surpassed in 2013–14 by Henrik Lundqvist. He was the league leader in games and minutes played four times and led in wins and shutouts three times. He also led the league in games and minutes played and victories in the 1972 playoffs.

Giacomin played two more seasons with Detroit before retiring after the 1977–78 season. Overall he posted a 289–209–96 record with 54 shutouts and a 2.82 GAA in 609 regular-season games.

Giacomin was supposedly offered the Rangers coaching job by John Ferguson in the summer of 1978, but when Fergie was replaced by Freddie Shero, that offer went by the wayside. Giacomin then became the color analyst for Islanders television broadcasts for one season.

Eddie was inducted into the Hockey Hall of Fame in 1987 and returned to the Rangers as a goaltending coach and special assignment scout when Phil Esposito took over the operation in 1986. In March of 1989, Giacomin had his number 1 jersey retired and raised to the rafters alongside Rod Gilbert's number 7.

"Gentleman Jean" Ratelle was perhaps the classiest player to ever wear a Rangers jersey. His skill and elegance reminded many of Jean Beliveau, the almost regal center for the Montreal Canadiens. In 862 games Ratty registered 336 goals with 481 assists for 817 points and only 192 penalty minutes. In 65 playoff games he registered nine goals and 33 assists.

He led the Rangers in points four times, goals three times, and assists once. Ratelle also led the team in playoff assists three times and tied for the lead in playoff points twice. At the time of his departure Ratelle held the team record for 30-goal seasons with six. He was voted team MVP and Most Popular Player twice and won the Player's Player award five times. He made four All-Star appearances and played in the 1972 Summit Series against the USSR.

Jean played five additional seasons with the Bruins before retiring in 1981. He reached the 40-goal plateau twice, both times with the Rangers. He never accumulated more than 28 penalty minutes in a season and won two Lady Byng Trophies. Overall, Ratelle averaged nearly a point a game, recording 491 goals and 776 assists for 1,267 points in 1,281 regular season games. In 123 playoff matches, Jean scored 32 goals with 66 assists for 98 points.

Ratelle was given the Bill Masterton Trophy for perseverance, sportsmanship, and dedication to hockey in 1971 and the Lester B. Pearson Award as the most outstanding player in the NHL as voted by fellow members of the National Hockey League Players' Association in 1972. Ratelle was inducted into the Hockey Hall of Fame in 1985.

Brad Park played 465 games for the Rangers over eight seasons, scoring 95 goals and 283 assists and 738 penalty minutes. In 64 playoff games he scored 12 goals with 32 assists. As a Ranger he made the league's First All-Star team three times and the second team twice. He was also named the Rangers MVP and won the Frank Boucher award in 1973–74.

Park led the Rangers in points, assists, and penalty minutes in 1973–74 as well as sharing the lead in points (with Stemkowski) and assists (with Rolfe) in the 1974 playoffs. He appeared in six All-Star games while with the Rangers and played in the 1972 Summit Series against the USSR.

Brad Park produced some of his best offensive totals as a Bruin, actually playing in more games (501) and accumulating more points (100-317-417) than he did as a Ranger. He helped Boston get to the Stanley Cup finals in two consecutive seasons and finished second to Denis Potvin in the voting for the Norris Trophy twice. He also made three more All-Star game appearances while with the Bruins. In 1983 he signed with Detroit as a free agent and played two more seasons in the Motor City before retiring as a player in 1985 at the age of thirty-seven. He then coached the Red Wings for 45 games during the 1985–86 season. Park was given the Bill Masterton trophy in 1984 and inducted into the Hockey Hall of Fame in 1988.

Overall in 1,112 games Park scored 213 goals and added 683 assists for 896 points along with 1,429 penalty minutes. In 161 playoff games, Park registered 35 goals and 90 assists for 125 points with 217 penalty minutes.

15

Aftermath and Analysis

THE BLUESHIRTS OPENED the 1976–77 season wearing vastly redesigned uniforms featuring the Rangers crest on the front and wide stripes down the shoulders and sleeves. Designed by Edd Griles, the new uniforms were supposed to make the players look bigger. John Ferguson also began the process of bringing in new players to fill those uniforms.

In his first draft as an NHL general manager, Fergie didn't do too badly, but he could have done better. He selected Don Murdoch with the sixth pick in the first round, but the St. Louis Blues chose Bernie Federko at number seven. Then in the second round he picked Dave Farrish at number 24, but later Toronto drafted Randy Carlyle at number 30. Ferguson later selected Mike McEwen in the third round.

However, in May of 1976, Ferguson made perhaps the worst trade in Rangers history, sending young winger Rick Middleton to the Bruins for thirty-one-year-old Ken Hodge.

According to Ferguson, the trade was made for a number of reasons. First, Phil Esposito was nagging him to trade for his old Bruins linemate. Secondly, the Rangers needed size and Hodge was 6-foot-2, 210 pounds, and third, the Blueshirts needed scoring and Hodge had scored a lot of goals with Esposito as his centerman. Hodge also won two Stanley Cups with the Bruins so he had the kind of experience Fergie wanted in the Rangers locker room.

Bruins GM Harry Sinden originally wanted Steve Vickers in return for Hodge, but Sarge had been the NHL's Rookie of the Year a few years earlier and Fergie didn't want to trade him. But Rick Middleton was another story. He was a young player with a knack for scoring, but he had also fallen under the influence of Derek Sanderson when the Turk was at his worst. Even after Sanderson was traded, Middleton continued to burn the candle at both ends. So Ferguson offered Middleton, and Sinden gladly accepted.

The party line at the time was that the trade was made to save Middleton's career, which led one beat reporter to wonder aloud, "I guess they don't have any bars in Boston?" The rest, as they say, is history. "Ricky McNifty" cleaned up his act and had a great career in Boston, scoring over 400 goals and recording almost 900 points in 12 seasons with the Bruins. Hodge, on the other hand, scored only 23 goals in 96 games over two seasons. He retired at the end of the 1977–78 season but played 37 games with the Binghamton Dusters of the AHL in 1979–80.

During his first year behind the Rangers bench, Ferguson had seen the Rangers get pushed around and he knew they needed more toughness, so in June he acquired Staten Island native Nicholas Evlampios Fotiu who was under contract with Hartford of the WHA at the time. To gain Fotiu's release Ferguson had to promise the Whalers that the Blueshirts would play a preseason game in Hartford the next year with the Whalers keeping all of the gate receipts. It turned out to be money well spent as Nicky stood up for his teammates and led the Rangers with 174 penalty minutes. In addition, his charity work and pregame ritual of throwing pucks into the upper reaches of the Garden made him a fan favorite.

Fergie also signed goaltender Gilles Gratton that summer to back up John Davidson. Gratton who would become known as "Grattoony the Loony" believed that he had lived many previous lives including one as a sailor in the twelfth century, a Spanish priest, and a British surgeon among other things. He was known for "streaking" before practice, playing piano in the nude, doing upside down pushups in the shower, and his goaltender mask which was painted to resemble a lion. Unfortunately, he was not as well known for stopping pucks and posted an 11–18–7 record with a 4.22 GAA in his one season on Broadway.

Ferguson then tried to add scoring punch to the lineup by sending Billy Fairbairn and Nick Beverley to Minnesota in exchange for Bill Goldsworthy. The thirty-two-year-old right wing, who had posted 30 and 40 goal seasons with Minnesota, managed only 10 goals and 12 assists in 61 games with the Rangers that season.

Ferguson had benched Fairbairn earlier in the season, ending the winger's 394-game ironman streak and finally traded him in mid-November.

BILL FAIRBAIRN: "When Ferguson came in he didn't like the style that me and Walter played. He didn't like that at all. He was kind of on us all the time about different things, even in practice he would get kind of ticked off at us because they would be working on the power play and we'd be the penalty killers and we wouldn't give them the puck. He got kind of fed up with that and he wouldn't let us kill penalties in practice. It was a different attitude in the dressing room with the players and everything else. It took Wally a while to get used to it but then I got traded and I was out of the mess."

Bill Fairbairn played in 536 regular-season games for the Rangers, scoring 138 goals with 224 assists for a total of 362 points with 102 penalty minutes. Included in those goals were 25 power play goals, 12 short-handers, and 25 game-winners. In 52 playoff games he scored 13 goals with 21 assists. In all, he played in 658 NHL games scoring 162 goals with 261 assists.

BILL FAIRBAIRN: "For me it was like going from a broken family to a team where the players didn't hang around together. There were a lot of college players on the North Stars when I went there and it was hard to fit in. There weren't many players who had played in the league long. Tom Reid was there for a long time, Dennis O'Brien, Gary Smith, and Ernie Hicke, so I kind of hung around with those guys and enjoyed their company like it was in New York in the early days. But it wasn't the same, not nearly the same. Hockey wasn't as much fun when I got traded there and my back was giving me problems then, too, so I missed a lot of games because of it.

"After I went from Minnesota to St. Louis nobody hung around together. You went to the rink and practiced and then you wouldn't see them until the game. It wasn't a team that looked out for each other, but that's the way a lot of the teams were. I guess playing in New York for so long I had no idea. I would think that Boston was like New York with the players that they had in their heyday. It's a lot better when you know that everyone is your friend and they've got your back.

"The funny thing is that I started and finished my career with the Cat. The reason I quit was my back was bad. I'd go down and I couldn't get up. I had to stay on my feet because if I got knocked over, I couldn't get up. You know if you can't help the team or play up to your potential then you shouldn't be playing. So that was my main reason for quitting. I talked it over with my wife and she said you know you can't play because you can't skate, so that's what happened. And it was very fitting to start off with the Cat and end with him.

"I still love New York and I love the team I played with. It was very disappointing all the years I was there that we were contenders but we just couldn't come up with the Cup. That was the only bad part about being there. But my life wouldn't be as it is now if I hadn't gone to New York and played with the players that I was with. I couldn't have played for a better coach than Emile Francis. I can't say enough about him. I made a lot of friends and still have a lot of friends from the game. I love New York and still love the Rangers. They are my only team."

As for Tkaczuk, Walt suffered an eye injury in 1981 which forced him to retire.

WALT TKACZUK: "It was a freak accident. We were playing in the Garden and the puck came up and got me square in the eye. I grabbed onto the boards, and the guys helped me up. My legs were getting a little faint and they brought me into the dressing room and were looking at my eye. They stitched up the cut and the doctors looked at the eye and said to stay here and relax, you're not going back in the game tonight. So, I'm sitting in the back room looking at the game on TV and it was blurry. And I said what the heck's the matter with that TV? So, I closed the eye that got hit with the puck and everything came back into focus. And then I opened it up and I said, Oh shit, there's something wrong here. So, I went to Lenox Hill hospital that night and there was the main doctor and about four or five interns there and he looked at me first and then he said okay, I want you all to look at the eye and tell me what you see. So the puck had pushed the eyeball to the back and there was swelling and scar tissue and I lost my central vision.

"So, they gave me pills to get rid of the swelling as quickly as possible and it took about a month of taking those pills and then going off of them slowly and by the end of the month they looked at the eye again and said you won't be able to play again. They said they couldn't operate on that part of the eye; there are not that many people with that type of an injury. They said maybe in another ten or fifteen years if you want to go see if there have been any new developments. So I came back to Canada and about ten years later I went to the eye clinic in London, Ontario, and the doctor looked at my eye and told me that there's probably nothing we can do with your eye. So I'm living with it. You adjust, everything's fine. The only thing is you don't want to lose your other one.

"I got hit in February of 1981 and I was still under contract and Craig Patrick was the coach and I was standing between the benches and Craig asked if I wanted to do some pre-scouting. So I said yeah I'll try that. So he sent me to Toronto and they put you up so high that I couldn't see the players. I could tell who they were by the way they skated, I could see their breakouts but I couldn't really see the players.

"So I told Craig I can't see, it was too high for me. The press boxes were generally really high. So, he said okay that's fine, why don't you come behind the bench and just talk to the players. If you see anything that you can help them with, just talk to them individually. So I did that for a little while and then Craig says to me why don't you change the defense and I'll change the forwards. I said okay that's good. Because when I was a centerman the first thing I looked at when I went on the ice wasn't the line I was playing against, but the defense I was playing against to see where the weakness was. So, I made sure that when I changed the defense I had certain defense pairs against certain forwards, because I knew how I felt as a player. I did that for a little while and then Craig said, why don't you change the forwards and I'll change the defense. So, I did that until the end of the year.

"And then Patrick hired Herb Brooks. He said I'm hiring Herb Brooks and I can't keep you as an assistant because Herb has to hire his own assistants, but if you wanna talk to him that's fine. So I talked to Herb and he then told Craig that he'd be happy to have me working with him. So then I worked for the next two years with Herb as an assistant, Wayne Thomas and myself. I really enjoyed it but around 1985 my children were getting to the point where they were finishing public school and going to high school and I decided to head back to Canada. And I'm happy I did."

Fergie's many changes didn't bring the desired results and the Rangers finished in last place in the Patrick Division with a 29–37–14 record for 72 points a slight improvement over their dismal 29–42–9 record of the previous year.

The next year, Ferguson promoted Jean Guy Talbot, a former teammate with the Canadiens to the head coaching spot. Talbot is remembered more for the warm-up suit he wore behind the bench than for any coaching expertise he may have imparted on the young Rangers. Talbot enjoyed being with the players and telling stories about the glory days of the Canadiens. However, many players complained that Talbot didn't communicate with them and never told them what they were doing wrong.

Once again, Ferguson did well enough at the amateur draft but he could have done much better. Armed with two picks in the first round thanks to a trade Emile Francis made in 1974 when he sent Gene Carr to the LA Kings, Ferguson selected Lucien DeBlois at number eight and Ron Duguay at number thirteen. Solid picks indeed, but at the time Mike Bossy was still on the board waiting to be selected by the Islanders at number fifteen. In the second round, Fergie selected Mike Keating at number twenty-six, but seven picks later the Isles grabbed John Tonelli.

When asked years later why he didn't pick Bossy when he had the chance, Ferguson blamed scout Tommy Savage who complained that Bossy wasn't tough enough to play in the NHL. Savage told Fergie of a game in which Bossy sat on the bench while the rest of his teammates were brawling on the ice. Bossy may not have been a fighter, but he wound up scoring 573 goals in a ten-year career that included a Calder Trophy, a Conn Smythe Trophy, three Lady Byng Awards, and four Stanley Cups.

In mid-November with the team playing at a sub .500 level and sinking fast, Fergie sent Goldsworthy and Hodge, both thirty-three-year-old highly paid right wingers to New Haven of the AHL. Then on Thanksgiving eve, he released longtime Ranger Rod Gilbert. The thirty-six-year-old right winger had scored only two goals in the Rangers' first nineteen games and Ferguson sensed that Rod's best days were behind him. Fergie also didn't care for Gilbert's attitude. He feared that Rod's lackadaisical demeanor would rub off on the younger players. Gilbert was also the leader of a clubhouse clique that was constantly at odds with Phil Esposito, and Fergie didn't consider him to be a team player.

Gilbert had been rebuffed by Ferguson and Bill Jennings the previous summer when he tried to get the Rangers to pick up a two-year option on his contract. Sensing that he was being phased out, Gilbert staged a ten-day walkout during training camp in an effort to get some assurances but returned to camp after getting none from Ferguson. But those ten days away from camp hurt him and he started the season slowly. He had been put on waivers twice, but none of the other teams were interested, especially considering that the additional two-year option would automatically kick in if he was moved to another team.

Gilbert was paid the remainder of his contract and signed a consulting contract with the Rangers.

Gilbert played in 1,065 games over 18 seasons with the Blueshirts and still leads the franchise in goals (406) and points (1,021). In 79 playoff games Rod registered 34 goals and 33 assists. He still holds the team record for shots on goal in a single game (16 at Montreal on February 24, 1968). He also shares a record of five assists in a single game which he achieved three times, with three other Rangers. He was named the Rangers MVP three times, appeared in eight All-Star games, and was given the Frank Boucher Award as the most popular Ranger four times including the last two full seasons of his career. Rod became the first Ranger to have his number retired in October of 1979 and was inducted into the Hockey Hall of Fame in 1982 along with Emile Francis and received the Lester Patrick Award for service to hockey in the United States in 1991.

Later in the season with the financially strapped Cleveland Barons on the verge of folding, Alan Cohen gave Ferguson $1 million to buy the contracts of goaltender Gilles Meloche and forwards Dennis Maruk and Charlie Simmer. Unfortunately, the league froze the Barons assets before Ferguson could make the deal. But then John discovered that Ulf Nilsson and Anders Hedberg of the WHA's Winnipeg Jets would be free agents at the end of the season. So he shifted gears and spent the money on the two Swedes instead of Meloche, Maruk, and Simmer.

The Blueshirts finished the season with a 30–37–13 record and qualified for the playoffs but lost to Buffalo in a three-game series. However, the Blueshirts had lowered their goals against by 30 goals and with the Swedes on their way, it seemed as though things were looking up for Ferguson and the Blueshirts.

However, Cohen was fired as Garden president early in 1978 and replaced by sports impresario Sonny Werblin. Gilbert quickly caught Werblin's ear and waged a campaign to have Ferguson fired and recommended the hiring of either Fred Shero or Scotty Bowman. When it was determined that Bowman wasn't available, Werblin started talking to Fred Shero's agent even though "Freddie the Fog" was still under contract with Philadelphia. Flyers owner Ed Snider got wind of Werblin's actions and filed tampering charges against the Rangers with the NHL. The irony of the episode was that the Flyers wanted to get rid of Shero anyway, but now they could at least get something of value from the Rangers for his services. In the end the Rangers wound up giving the Flyers a first-round draft pick and $200,000 for the right to hire Shero as coach and general manager.

Later that summer, the Garden laid down a sheet of ice for an elaborate press conference to introduce Nilsson and Hedberg to the media.

Fred Shero was pictured on the ice with the duo but not a word was said about the fact that it was Ferguson who signed them.

Sixteen years, three general managers, nine coaches, and countless players later, the Rangers finally won their first Stanley Cup since 1940 in June of 1994.

Analysis

In 1964, Emile Francis took over virtually every aspect of a hapless Rangers franchise that had not made the playoffs in four years and proceeded to rebuild it from the ground up. He reorganized the minor-league system and acquired players that had the skill and size to bring the team back to respectability. He restored pride in the franchise and worked tirelessly to promote the game of hockey in New York and beginning in 1966–67 the Rangers reached the postseason for nine consecutive seasons.

Emile's regular-season coaching record of 342–209–103 is impressive. And yet he never won a Stanley Cup, posting a 34–41 mark with a mediocre .453 winning percentage in the playoffs. Under Francis, the Rangers advanced to the Stanley Cup finals only once in nine attempts, while suffering five first-round losses and three second-round eliminations.

Why? Were the players too small or not tough enough? Did Emile put too much pressure on them to win during the regular season? Of course, there were injuries to key players, but every team suffers injuries. They could certainly score during the regular season but fifteen of their forty-one playoff losses during that time were by a single goal.

It's also been said Emile may have been too loyal to some of his older players, keeping them past their prime. And perhaps one of Emile's greatest failures was not finding a coach as good as himself to run the team, thus giving him more time to devote to his duties as general manager.

HOWIE ROSE: "The unfortunate reality is that as much as we love that team is that they did not have the level of star to compete with or to outshine or outplay Hull or Mikita in Chicago and Orr and Esposito with the Bruins when it came to beating the Black Hawks or the Bruins, although they did eventually beat them both. They just seemed to be a little short.

"I had Rod Gilbert tell me many years ago that he and a couple of other guys had gone to Emile and begged him to get a little tougher to give these guys a little more protection. But Emile said no we're not playing the game that way. Because by then the Flyers had really established themselves and I've always felt the Bruins' toughest teams had more guys that could play at a higher level than the Flyers' toughest teams did. And I always thought it wasn't so much the Rangers being intimidated by the Bruins although I think at times they probably were, they just didn't match up. The Bruins' best players were better than the Rangers' best players and that was enough, especially when one of them was Bobby Orr.

"If Emile had a fault, it's that he never hired a strong coach. He was so involved that he would never disassociate himself enough and hand the reigns over to a strong coach and let him do his thing. I don't know if it would have been any different if Freddie Shero had taken the job. Maybe it would have been different. Who knows? But by the time Freddie got here, although it worked out great that first year, after that he was in a downward spiral in his life. And maybe Emile sensed that.

"You could make the argument that it was time for Emile to go and John Ferguson presented a whole different persona because the image of the Rangers by the time Emile left was that they weren't tough. They were a team that got pushed around and they didn't win because they were intimidated. You could argue with that emotionally, but intellectually and objectively it's kind of hard to disagree with it. So I think the idea of what John Ferguson represented to a lot of fans was refreshing at that time and I'm not sure what might have happened if they kept him around longer but everything changed when Sonny Werblin came in. Werblin wanted stars and that's how he always operated. And Fergie went on to have some success in Winnipeg of the WHA. So to some extent it worked out for him. I just remember thinking that it was time because the Rangers weren't going to turn it around any time soon. Given that so many of them had grown old together and yet it was only a few years after they let Emile go they were in the Stanley Cup finals.

"The Islanders and the Devils can thank Emile Francis in part for their existence in this market because of everything that Emile did, not only to build the Rangers but to contribute to the Met League to everything he did to raise hockey awareness in New York. But he was a tireless promoter for the Rangers and it wasn't an easy thing to get hockey on the back pages back then."

GERRY ESKENAZI: "In the forty-something years I covered sports for the *New York Times* the two most fascinating characters I've met were Emile Francis at the beginning of my career and Bill Parcells when I was covering the Jets towards the end of my career. Both guys transformed crappy franchises, really almost by the force of their will. Emile was really so smart and he had his hand in everything, in every part of the operation and of course he helped bring hockey to New York not only with the Rangers but he helped form junior hockey leagues and that kind of thing. He was also extremely manipulative and very suspicious, but in retrospect I really loved the guy.

"He was great to the press also, he would always give us his time. One of the first books I wrote about hockey before I wrote *A Year on Ice* was a book just simply called *Hockey*. It was the first really sophisticated picture playbook written about hockey and he actually came over to my house and stayed with me for over an hour diagramming plays and the basics of hockey. He was just great that way and to think that the guy was general manager of the team as well as a coach and I suspect that at some level he was also the equipment manager and the trainer.

"I think being general manager and coach eventually hurt the team because you can't be in the position as a coach telling a guy how good he is or how well he's doing and then negotiating with him for a contract and you saying, 'Hey wait a second, your plus-minus wasn't that great.' You can't do it both ways. Once money is involved then everything becomes a little suspicious as far as players are concerned. But in the old six-team league when I started writing about hockey, it wasn't uncommon to be the coach and the general manager. I think in some cases some of the guys might've been the president of the team as well.

"You could say that Emile may have been too loyal but then he goes and trades Eddie Giacomin when he still had a number of years left. But

I think he probably was maybe a little too loyal but I don't know if that was a failing. There were so many other things going on with the Rangers and Emile. The thing is he never had the dominant players so the whole key to his success was putting together the best lines and having a system of hockey and staying with it and keeping them focused. But I'm not sure that staying with players too long was a fair criticism of Emile.

"In trying to analyze why Emile had this Hall of Fame regular-season record and was under .500 in the playoffs I think there were two factors involved. One, he had the ability to have his team extremely disciplined and playing at a fairly high level over the course of seventy games or so. That's enough very often to give you a winning record over clubs that would have a down night or something like that. His practices were very instructional. They were always geared to the team that they were playing as well as trying to figure out what his own problems were so he was really very good in that way.

"Another reason why his regular-season record may have been better than his Stanley Cup record was that he got the most out of players who weren't as good as other teams because of his style of coaching. But then when it got down to the playoffs, because it was such a short series there is also luck involved but there is also the talent factor and the talent factor of great stars.

"So you can look at it both ways with Emile Francis—either he was able to get the most out of his players and they failed in the playoffs because they weren't as good as the other teams, they weren't an elite team, or because they did not have the star or because he did not permit a guy like Rod Gilbert to go off on his own. I guess of all the players, Gilbert would have been the one to have lifted the team, although he wasn't really a big guy. But Francis didn't allow his players the freedom to become great stars and that could have been a reason why they didn't win in the playoffs because everything was a team concept.

"What often happens in the playoffs sometimes you need one guy to carry you and the Rangers didn't have that guy, whether they didn't have that because the actual players weren't on the superstar level or Emile's style kept them down. I often wonder what Bobby Orr would have done under Emile Francis. But he did have Brad Park, but even Brad was restricted somewhat.

"So you could look at it two ways, either he was good enough to make them better than they really were in the regular season but then who they really were ultimately showed up in the playoffs against the elite teams.

"The Rangers had sort of stagnated by the time Emile was let go. I wasn't surprised. I thought he got them about as far as he could. Now just because you don't win a championship should you be fired? If your only standard is winning a championship then yeah, but there's lots of other clubs that didn't win championships either and he immediately went to St. Louis and revived that franchise. I think he had his run in New York and given the changes that were going on at the Garden he wasn't going to be successful in New York at that point in time.

"When Sonny Werblin took over one of the first things Sonny wanted was to get the Rangers out of Long Beach. He was a theatrical guy. He had started a company called MCA [Music Corporation of America]. He had been the agent for Johnny Carson and Elizabeth Taylor. He was a real Hollywood-Broadway guy. I know this sounds crazy but he said he wanted the Rangers drinking in New York bars. He wanted them to be part of the New York scene and so when he took over the Garden that was part of his standard and that was why he didn't want Bill Jennings around.

"I remember Sonny once told me why he wanted to get rid of Bill Jennings. I was very friendly with Sonny from when I was covering the Jets. Remember Sonny was the guy who made Joe Namath sort of a Broadway institution with the Jets. And I remember he once said about Joe that when he walks into a room he lights it up. But what he said about Bill Jennings was that when Jennings walks into a room he depresses it. So that was Sonny's standard. His standard was whether you were theatrical or not. He wanted guys that were dramatic.

"It seemed to me that throughout their history whatever the Rangers were doing it wasn't good enough, they had to be something else. Emile Francis took over a club that didn't have any history of winning so he brought in veterans. They were too small so he brought in big guys. Until they finally won the Cup, whatever they were doing wasn't good enough.

"And I think it also points out something about sports and that is that fans do not accept the fact that they may have a good team but it just isn't good enough to win the championship and then it's a disappointment but if that's the case the Rangers were disappointment for fifty-four years and they weren't but that is the perception."

Author's note: *I grew up watching these guys so I may be a little biased, but Emile Francis took a failing franchise and rebuilt it into one of the best teams of his era, there's no disputing that. You really have to wonder where the Rangers would have been if Tommy Ivan would have moved a little faster in 1960 and hired Emile for Chicago instead of dragging his heels and allowing him to come to New York.*

Yes, there were a few disappointing seasons when we thought that is was going to be our year, but overall those teams provided fans with entertaining hockey and enough memories to fill this book and several more.

Emile helped put hockey back on the map in the New York area and paved the way for both the Islanders and the Devils. He started a youth league and probably did more to promote the sport in this area than anyone who came before or after. He restored a fan base that was dwindling. The majority of the fans who can now "Die in peace" after the Blueshirts finally won the Stanley Cup in 1994, grew up watching Emile's Rangers.

Emile was indeed loyal to his players, but if a deal was there to be made, he made it. He almost had Johnny Bucyk and he was willing to part with at least four roster players for Bernie Parent, even though he had found and nurtured Eddie Giacomin. And I guarantee that there were quite a few other near misses along the way that haven't been mentioned.

Emile can be faulted for not hiring better coaches, but I'm not sure he really wanted to relinquish that kind of control to someone else, at least not right away. I once asked him what he liked better, being general manager or coaching. He told me that it was about equal. He liked certain aspects of both jobs. And it's interesting to note that he had a number of assistant GMs during his tenure, most notably Jackie Gordon, but after Harry Howell and Donnie Marshall, who he had made assistant coaches, were traded, he never designated anyone to replace them.

I think when he hired Geoffrion as coach there may have been a handshake deal with Boomer to get him to agree to play for the Rangers. Sort of "play a couple of years, help me with the young players and then you can move behind the bench." After all, the reason Boomer came out of retirement in the first place was because Montreal reneged on their promise to make him their coach, so there would be an incentive there. Larry Popein was a mistake, but at that time it was important to Emile to work with someone he knew, someone from within the organization. Popein had been in the organization for a long time. He knew the systems and the players; he just didn't know how to handle them. As for Ron Stewart, he was never really given a chance.

As far as team toughness is concerned, unlike the Flyers who brought the sport down to a minor-league Slap Shot *level, Emile respected the game of hockey and refused to "goon it up." He wanted guys who were tough but skilled—guys who could play the game but wouldn't be pushed around.*

But by the mid-1970s, considering the volatile nature of the Garden's executive suite, it was time for Emile to move on. He certainly would have tangled with Sonny Werblin and his departure would have been inevitable. At that point the Rangers needed another rebuild, and Emile would not have been around long enough to see it to fruition.

Emile Francis ended his sixteen-year association with the Rangers in April of 1976, resigning from his position as team vice president with two years remaining on his contract. The very next day, the Cat took over the St. Louis Blues, becoming executive vice president, general manager, and coach. He was also named to the team's board of directors as well as becoming a 10 percent shareholder. "I've joined the Blues for three reasons," Francis said at the press conference in St. Louis. "I've always had a great deal of respect for the Salomon family, I'm impressed with the enthusiasm of the fans in St. Louis and I've always wanted to be a shareholder. I'm fooling around not only with someone else's money but also with my own."

The Blues were once the most successful of the first six expansion teams both on and off the ice. They sported a veteran roster and made the playoffs in each of their first six seasons, including three trips to the finals. They also led the league in attendance for five consecutive seasons from 1970–71 through 1974–75. But in 1977 after three disappointing seasons they were close to bankruptcy with a $7.5 million mortgage on their arena, a slew of hefty contracts, and a lot of empty seats. It got so bad that Francis had to pay stick companies out of his own pocket. The league was set to disband the Blues when the Ralston-Purina Company stepped in to take over the team, under the condition that Francis stick around to run the franchise. Unfortunately, Ralston-Purina insisted on owning 100 percent of the team's stock so both Francis and senior vice president Lynn Patrick had to sell their shares back to the new owners. "They gave me a lifetime supply of dog and cat food," Emile later told reporters, "and my dog doesn't even like Ralston-Purina food."

After Emile's contract with the Blues ended in 1983 he moved east to become general manager of the Hartford Whalers. Under Emile's guidance the Whalers made the playoffs for the first time in six seasons in 1985–86. The next season Hartford finished in first place in the Adams Division and qualified for the postseason for the next six years.

For his efforts Francis was named NHL Executive of the Year by both the *Hockey News* and the *Sporting News,* and in 1989 he was named team president.

Finally, in 1993 after a forty-seven-year career, Emile retired. His overall record including the games he coached in St. Louis is 388–273–117 and 39–50 in the playoffs.

Emile was awarded the Lester Patrick Trophy for his contributions to hockey in the United States in 1982 and inducted into the Hockey Hall of Fame that same year.

EMILE FRANCIS: "I've been very fortunate; I'm now in six Halls of Fame for hockey and baseball. I'm in the Hall of Fame in Saskatchewan for baseball and hockey, I'm in the New York Hall of Fame, I'm in the National Hockey League Hall of Fame and it was like a dream really because I never thought about the Hall of Fame. My dream always was to play in the NHL but I never thought about getting into the Hall of Fame. It was a real honor and thank God that my mother and my brother who have since passed away were there. Em's mother and her three sisters all died since but they were all there. They were all healthy and they all came to Toronto and it was very enjoyable.

"To me it's like when you win. It's always nice to win when you have teammates with you or players that you coach, you're together like a family. And that's why it was so nice because you don't think so much of yourself going in, you think that it's going to give enjoyment to your family. That to me is more important than what it meant to me. It meant so much to my family.

"My dad died when I was eight years old, so I never had a dad, and my uncle who was my mother's brother was really the one who got me playing hockey and baseball because he made his living playing both. And he was the guy who put me against the garage and threw baseballs at me. Same thing in hockey, he coached me from the time I was eight years old. The last thing my mother said to me was that we never would have made it without your two uncles. She had three brothers and two of them were very involved with me because we came from the same area and they really looked after me, because it was during the depression and things were tough. Both had steady jobs on the railroad and they never told me and she never told me but there's not a doubt in my mind that they helped her financially. That's what families are all about.

"So it was a real nice evening. I went in with Rod Gilbert, [Henri] Pocket Rocket Richard, and Normie Ullman and I was up and down like a toilet seat because not only was I inducted but Rod also asked me to speak.

"The thing that I was most proud of was the Ranger teams I had, they worked. They had the fundamentals of the game down pat, they had the system that I put in down pat and they never strayed from that system. We always competed. We were in every game. They never threw the towel in. We may have gotten beat 5–1 or 6–1 the odd time but we didn't quit. We were just having a bad night and when you play eighty-two games you're gonna have the odd bad night and there's nothing you can do about it.

"The beauty of the whole thing was that two years after I left New York they fired Alan Cohen and called me and asked if I was interested in coming back to run the Rangers. I said are you kidding? I loved New York, it was the best time of my life, but I'd never go back there. Ironically I ended up in Hartford, and after Cohen got fired he put a group together to buy the Boston Celtics. So a sportswriter calls from Boston and asks me what I think of Alan Cohen, the guy who bought the Celtics. I said I'd like to see that son of a bitch in the middle of the road and I'd be driving a car and I'd run right over him. So Cohen called the insurance company that owned the Whalers at the time to tell them to shut that guy up. And I would have too because he took all the twelve years of eighteen-hour days and ran them right down the drain. And when I tell you I worked eighteen hours a day, I'd get home at seven o'clock at night and be up past midnight making deals. But I enjoyed it, and if you enjoy what you do you're very fortunate and very lucky and I was lucky.

"New York was the best years of my life; I'll never forget them. I could walk down the street and cab drivers would yell to me, 'Hey Cat!' The fans were great!"

ACKNOWLEDGMENTS

WRITING THIS BOOK has been one of the most challenging, yet reward-ing, projects I have ever attempted and there are many people that I want to thank for their help and support along the way.

I'd like to first take a step back and mention how grateful I am to my parents, Grace and George Grimm, for instilling in me the joy of reading and the value of books. I'm also very grateful to Dr. Alexander Palacios who has helped me battle glaucoma and saved my vision a number of times over the last forty-odd years.

I want to thank my wife, Theresa, for her patience, support, under-standing, and editing skills. Many times I had to chase her out of our "office" because I needed the room to do an interview, but she always gave me the time and space I needed.

I'd also like to thank my good friend Steve Carroll for his longtime support and encouragement.

I owe a huge debt of gratitude to Dylan Wade and the NHL Alumni Association who helped me obtain contact information for the players that I interviewed. This book could never have been completed without their help.

I'm extremely grateful to George Kalinsky for allowing me to use his photograph of Emile on the cover of this book. That picture has always been one of my favorites and perfectly captures the way many fans and players remember Emile during games. Thanks also to Jay Moran, author of *The Rangers, The Bruins, and the End of an Era* who very generously gave me permission to use most of the photographs in this book. I also wish to thank Michael Rappaport of the New York Rangers PR Department and Tony Accordino for helping me obtain additional photographs.

My thanks also to fellow authors Matthew DiBiase, Brad Kurtzberg, and Kevin Shea for their support and advice. I'm also grateful to Kevin Greenstein of Insidehockey.com for posting my *Retro Rangers* stories on his site, many of which became the foundation for this book. Thanks also to hockey columnist Rick Carpiniello for his encouragement and support. I also need to thank Rick Resnick, former publisher of the *Blueshirt Bulletin* for including my *Blue Seat Point of View* articles in his newspaper for many years.

Of course, I never would have ever dreamed of writing this book if it hadn't been for the encouragement of the late John Halligan who took the time to give me feedback about my newsletter SportStat . . . The Ranger Report in the 1980s. I would also like to thank former Rangers PR Director Barry Watkins who gave me a press pass when I was writing SportStat, introduced me to the working relationship between the Rangers and the media, and gave me one of the best pieces of advice I've ever received: "It never hurts to ask."

I also want to thank the people at Skyhorse Publishing, Editorial Director Jay Cassell and my editor Ken Samelson as well as his staff for steering this novice through the publishing process.

Lastly, but probably most importantly, I want to thank Emile Francis for his overwhelming generosity and abundant patience. I love the man and could listen to his stories for hours. Once again, this book could not have been written without his cooperation.

I'm also extremely grateful to the many players who agreed to be interviewed for this book as well as Michael Cosby, writers Gerry Eskenazi and Stu Hackel, and broadcasters Sal Messina, Bob Wolff, Jiggs McDonald, and Howie Rose. They all made time for me, answered every one of my questions and best of all, made me feel like an old friend.

BIBLIOGRAPHY

Books

Albert, Marv. *Ranger Fever*. New York: Dell Books, 1973.

Albert, Marv. *I'd Love to but I Have a Game*. New York: Doubleday, 1993.

Boucher, Frank. *When the Rangers Were Young*. New York: Dodd, Mead, 1973.

Brewitt, Ross. *Clear the Track, The Eddie Shack Story*. Toronto: Stoddart, 1998.

Chadwick, Bill. *The Big Whistle*. New York: Hawthorn Books, 1974.

Diamond, Dan. *The Official National Hockey League Stanley Cup Centennial Book*. Montreal: Tormont, 1993.

——— *The Official National Hockey League 75th Anniversary Commemoratative Book*. Buffalo, NY: Firefly Books, 1994.

——— *Hockey: Twenty Years*. Toronto: Doubleday Canada, 1987.

Delano, Hugh. *Eddie: A Goalie's Story*. New York: Atheneum, 1976.

Denault, Todd. *Jacques Plante: The Man Who Changed the Face of Hockey*. Toronto: McClelland & Stewart, 2009.

Eskenazi, Gerald. *A Year on Ice*. New York: Coward-McCann, 1970.

——— *A Sportswriter's Life*. Columbia, MO: University of Missouri, 2004.

——— *Hockey*. Chicago: Follett, 1969.

——— *The Fastest Sport*. Chicago: Follett, 1974.

Ferguson, John and Stan and Shirley Fischler. *Thunder and Lightning*. Scarborough, ON: Prentice-Hall Canada, 1989.

Fischler, Stan. *Fischler's Hockey Encyclopedia*. New York: Crowell, 1975.

———— *Slap Shot!* New York: Grosset & Dunlap, 1973.

Fischler, Stan and Brad Park. *Play the Man*. New York: Dodd, Mead, 1971.

Fischler, Stan and Tom Sarro. *Metro Ice*. Flushing, NY: H & M Productions, 1999.

Halberstam, David. *Sports on New York Radio*. New York: McGraw-Hill, 1999.

Halligan, John. *New York Rangers: Seventy Five Years*. New York: Barnes & Noble, 2000.

Halligan, John and John Kreiser. *The Game of My Life: New York Rangers*. Champaign, IL: Sports Publishing, 2006.

Halligan, John, Russ Cohen and Adam Raider, *100 Ranger Greats*. Toronto: Wiley, 2009.

Hunt, Jim. *The Men in the Nets*. Chicago: Follett, 1967.

Irvin, Dick. *In the Crease: Goaltenders Look at Life in the NHL*. Toronto: McClelland & Stewart, 1996.

———— *Behind the Bench*. Toronto: McClelland & Stewart, 1993.

Kendall, Brian. *Shutout: The Terry Sawchuk Story*. Toronto: Penguin Books Canada, 1996.

Kiczek, Gene. *Forgotten Glory: The Story of Cleveland Barons Hockey*. Euclid, OH: Blue Line Publications, 1994.

Kreiser, John and Lou Friedman. *The New York Rangers: Broadway's Longest Running Hit*. Champaign, IL: Sagamore, 1997.

McFarlane, Brian. *The Rangers: Brian McFarlane's Original Six*. Toronto: Stoddart, 1997.

Moran, Jay. *The Rangers, The Bruins, and the End of an Era*. Bloomington, IN: Author House, 2009.

Sears, Thom. *Straight Shooter: The Brad Park Story*. Mississauga, ON: Wiley, 2012.

Shea, Kevin. *Derek Sanderson: Crossing the Line*. Chicago: Triumph Books, 2012.

Villemure, Gilles and Mike Shalin. *Tales from the Rangers Locker Room*. Champaign, IL: Sports Publishing, 2002.

Whitehead, Eric. *The Patricks: Hockey's Royal Family*. Toronto: Doubleday Canada, 1980.

Articles

Mark Mulvoy, "Dashing Through the Dough," *Sports Illustrated*, February 11, 1974. p. 74

Gary Ronberg, "Flashing Blades for a Mini-Mastermind," *Sports Illustrated*, March 2, 1970, pp. 21–23

Publications

New York Rangers Blue Books 1965–1976
New York Times, 1965–1976.
SportStat . . . The Ranger Report (1988–1993)